PATERNOSTER THEOLOGICAL MONOGRAPHS

Fixing the Indemnity

The Life and Work of Sir George Adam Smith (1856-1942)

PATERNOSTER THEOLOGICAL MONOGRAPHS

A full listing of titles in both Paternoster
Biblical and Theological Monographs
will be found at the close of this book

Cover photo: George Adam Smith with his wife Lilian in Quebec, 1896

PATERNOSTER THEOLOGICAL MONOGRAPHS

Fixing the Indemnity

The Life and Work of Sir George Adam Smith (1856-1942)

Iain D. Campbell

PUBLISHERS
Eugene, Oregon

Wipf and Stock Publishers
199 W 8th Ave, Suite 3
Eugene, OR 97401

Fixing the Indemnity
The Life and Work of Sir George Adam Smith (1856–1942)
By Campbell, Iain D.
Copyright©2004 Paternoster
ISBN 13: 978-1-59752-741-5
ISBN: 1-59752-741-6
Publication date 6/7/2006
Previously published by Paternoster, 2004

This Edition Published by Wipf and Stock Publishers
by arrangement with Paternoster

Paternoster
9 Holdom Avenue
Bletchley
Milton Keyes, MK1 1QR
Great Britain

PATERNOSTER THEOLOGICAL MONOGRAPHS

Series Preface

In the West the churches may be declining, but theology—serious, academic (mostly doctoral level) and mainstream orthodox in evaluative commitment—shows no sign of withering on the vine. This series of *Paternoster Theological Monographs* extends the expertise of the Press especially to first-time authors whose work stands broadly within the parameters created by fidelity to Scripture and has satisfied the critical scrutiny of respected assessors in the academy. Such theology may come in several distinct intellectual disciplines—historical, dogmatic, pastoral, apologetic, missional, aesthetic and no doubt others also. The series will be particularly hospitable to promising constructive theology within an evangelical frame, for it is of this that the church's need seems to be greatest. Quality writing will be published across the confessions—Anabaptist, Episcopalian, Reformed, Arminian and Orthodox—across the ages—patristic, medieval, reformation, modern and counter-modern—and across the continents. The aim of the series is theology written in the twofold conviction that the church needs theology and theology needs the church—which in reality means theology done for the glory of God.

Series Editors

David F. Wright, Emeritus Professor of Patristic and Reformed Christianity, University of Edinburgh, Scotland, UK

Trevor A. Hart, Head of School and Principal of St Mary's College School of Divinity, University of St Andrews, Scotland, UK

Anthony N.S. Lane, Professor of Historical Theology and Director of Research, London School of Theology, UK

Anthony C. Thiselton, Emeritus Professor of Christian Theology, University of Nottingham, Research Professor in Christian Theology, University College Chester, and Canon Theologian of Leicester Cathedral and Southwell Minster, UK

Kevin J. Vanhoozer, Research Professor of Systematic Theology, Trinity Evangelical Divinity School, Deerfield, Illinois, USA

For Anne

Commendations

Sir George Adam Smith was the longest-lived of those amazing 'Princes of the Church' who arose in Scotland in the latter half of the 19th century. With the perspective of history, how do we explain the mysterious, just-in-time appearance of such winsome men, whose intellects were as high as their devotion was deep, and who encircled each other in friendship, Smith among them, as well as Drummond, Ross, Watson, Stalker, Barbour, Ewing? Iain Campbell's compelling study assess the life and contributions of the remarkable George Adam Smith who, in one handsome countenance, united the warm heart of a village vicar, the razor sharp mind of a world-class critical scholar, the interpersonal skill and grace of a diplomat, the zeal of an evangelist. Preacher, master of Holy Land geography who yet worried about the poor, facile in Hebrew and steeped in then-new Biblical criticism, he urged, 'The pulpit is to preach the Gospel, not for criticism' through careers as minister, professor and university principal. Reading this story, one is moved to pray for another cycle of such 'Princes of the Church' to arise in our own day!
President Thomas E. Corts, Samford University

Dr. Campbell's intellectual biography of George Adam Smith is a most welcome addition both to the study of nineteenth and twentieth century Scottish theology and church life, and to the history of Old Testament scholarship. Approaching his subject in a manner which is at once critical yet also sympathetic and sensitive to the context, the author paints a picture of a very human scholar struggling to make Christianity relevant to the great concerns of his day. In so doing, Dr. Campbell sheds light on a number of issues: the often complex relationship between scholarship and ecclesiastical commitment; the subtle nature of the negotiation between higher criticism and confessionalism in church life; the response of the church to the social and culture upheavals of the late nineteenth and early twentieth centuries; and the perennially vexatious question of the relationship between heartfelt piety and hard-headed theological work. This excellent book deserves a wide readership in academic and ecclesiastical circles and will more than repay careful study.
Professor Carl R. Trueman, Westminster Theological Seminary

Contents

Foreword	xiii
Acknowledgements	xvii
Abbreviations	xix
Introduction	**1**
Setting the Scene	4
George Adam Smith: The Need for a Biographical Study	8
Chapter 1	
The Making of a Biblical Scholar (1856-1882)	**11**
Life in Scotland	16
Moody and Sankey	19
Life in New College	26
Home Mission Work	33
Egypt and Palestine	34
Assistant at Brechin	40
Hebrew Tutor	42
Conclusion	44
Chapter 2	
The Pastor: The Early Aberdeen Years (1882-1892)	**45**
Consolidating the Ministry	48
The Prophecy of Isaiah	62
Personal	70
Conclusion	76

Chapter 3
Traveller and Geographer: The Appeal of Palestine — 77
Scholarly Interest in Palestine — 78
Jerusalem — 91
Cartography — 99
Smith's Contribution to Historical Geography — 101

Chapter 4
The Professor: The Glasgow Years (1892-1910) — 105
The Life of Henry Drummond — 113
Smith on the Twelve Prophets — 115
Social Work in Glasgow — 126
The United Free Church and Controversy — 128
Personal — 139
Conclusion — 143

Chapter 5
Representative of Church and State: The War Years: — 145
Effects of the War — 146
Honour and Preferment — 153
Allied Ambassador to the United States — 166
Conclusion — 173

Chapter 6
The Principal: The Later Aberdeen Years (1910-1935) — 174
The University of Aberdeen 1910-1935 — 176
Smith's Contribution to University Life — 180
Smith's Scholarship 1910-1935 — 185
    The Schweich Lectures — 185
    Deuteronomy — 189
    Jeremiah — 193
    The Kirk in Scotland — 198
Conclusion — 202

Chapter 7
George Adam Smith: Retirement and Retrospect   206
In Retrospect   212
Evangelical Critic?   225

Bibliography   229

Person Index   248

Subject Index   253

Foreword

It is a real privilege for me to be able to welcome the publication of this fine piece of work by Dr Iain D Campbell.

Let me begin by commending to you the importance of the subject.

We have long needed an intellectual biography of George Adam Smith, a hugely influential figure in church and academy from the 1880s to the 1930s. In this revision of Dr Campbell's PhD thesis, a vital part of the history of biblical scholarship in Scotland has at last been told.

Smith's life is a fascinating story. Here you will meet the brilliant young student in Edinburgh and Germany, imbibing the new scholarship in an age of intellectual ferment. You will travel to Aberdeen, where the youthful minister of Queen's Cross Free Church quickly gains a reputation as an eloquent preacher, and where he begins to write his famed commentaries on the prophets. You will visit Palestine and watch him noting everything he sees and hears in meticulous detail, laying the foundation for his classic works on historical geography. You will move to Glasgow, as he takes up the Chair of Hebrew and Old Testament Exegesis in the Free Church College, inspiring students with vivid lectures in his characteristically descriptive prose. And then it's back to Aberdeen, as Principal of the University, to serve the longest tenure of any Principal in the University's modern history, and to continue producing works of biblical scholarship.

I have said nothing about India, or D. L. Moody, or social concern fuelled by the prophets, or a near-trial for heresy, or the Great War, or travels to the United States, or the spanning of three denominations, or mountaineering, or poetry, or a hundred and one other things which you will find in these pages. It really is an amazingly energetic and colourful life. His significance can be illustrated by the privileges bestowed in 1916, when he was not only elected as a Fellow of the British Academy, and as a member of the Athenaeum Club, and as Moderator of the General Assembly of the United Free Church, but was also knighted by the King, a very unusual honour for a clergyman. Dr Campbell tells the story well, with full use of the primary and secondary sources, and among the former his study of Smith's papers in the National Library of Scotland has been especially important in providing fresh insight.

Of course, Dr Campbell doesn't merely tell the story. The narrative unfolds with analysis of Smith's intellectual development and with discussion of a whole range of issues raised by his life and times. Of most interest to me were the questions posed by Smith's espousal of both evangelical faith and radical criticism. I remember some years ago, when engaged in research on William Robertson Smith, reading some of his sermon manuscripts and being amazed to find them impeccably orthodox and warmly evangelistic, not at all what I expected from the critic I was studying. We find the same phenomenon in Smith. According to their own profession these men were not liberals denying the gospel, but evangelicals who insisted that new views of Scripture and the conclusions of critical scholarship were perfectly consonant with evangelical belief, and indeed were essential to the integrity of contemporary gospel preaching. My own view is that they could live with this tension because they had the gospel before the criticism, and so were always drawing on the capital of their evangelical heritage. But the trajectory of their critical work would lead subsequent generations to draw very different theological conclusions from fragmented texts and dubious histories.

While I may not defer to Smith's reordering of Scripture, that should not be taken as disparaging biblical and theological scholarship in his or in any age. My attitude is the precise opposite, namely that we always need more and better scholarship, but scholarship that remembers the church. Smith recognised this last point, and in his own way he lived for it. He stands in the Scottish presbyterian tradition of the scholar-preacher. We must never forget that he was a parish minister for a decade before he was a professor, years when he combined biblical research with the demands of a large congregation. When he took up the Chair, his inaugural address made clear that his academic work should serve the preaching of the church. He continued to preach, and indeed that voice was always unmistakable in the cadences of his scholarly writings. With today's demands for sub-specialisations and for career academics, it is difficult to envisage pastors journeying towards professorships, as used to happen in the Scottish divinity faculties until fairly recently. But there remains a tremendous need for scholarship to remember the pulpit and for scholars to nourish the mission and ministries of the church.

So, let me turn now to commend the author to you.

Dr Campbell is the leading scholar-preacher in the pastoral ministry of the Free Church of Scotland. Trained at the Free Church College in Edinburgh, he also holds first-class degrees from the Universities of Glasgow and London, in biblical languages and in theology. He has served successive bilingual pastorates in the Hebrides, while continuing to research and write in a variety of theological disciplines and produce popular books for the Christian mind and heart. He is a marvellous preacher, combining exegetical insight and theological depth with devotional warmth and evangelistic passion. I know, because my mother is a member of his privileged congregation, and I hear much about what they enjoy on the island of my boyhood summers.

Iain completed this dissertation while minister of one of our largest congregations, and though his studies were interrupted by a period of disabling illness and spinal surgery he still submitted the thesis ahead of time. I sometimes wonder if there are two Iains. One is a married man with a family, based on the Isle of Lewis, who preaches several times a week, writes a weekly column in the island newspaper, undertakes all the varied duties of a busy parish and is fully immersed in the joys and sorrows of the local community. The other Iain lives on the Scottish mainland. Without family commitments he is free to attend committee and board meetings, preach in churches, speak at conferences, visit libraries, earn degrees and write books. (I have a similar theory about the Alister McGrath triplets).

During the time I have been rereading this thesis, I have been able to sit in on a fascinating series of seminars in "Scripture and Theology" at St Mary's College. Over recent years there has been a refreshing trend in biblical scholarship, frustrated by the fragmenting of the text in the past, to look at each book in its final canonical form. Along with that, many scholars now want to read the Old Testament theologically in the light of the whole canon, coming to it as professedly trinitarian believers who read it all as Christian Scripture. As Smith was a man of his times, maybe Iain will be a man for these specific times, contributing his own reformed, covenantal and christological perspectives to the contemporary theological reading of the Old Testament.

Perhaps a century from now, a young scholar will produce an intellectual biography of Iain D Campbell! May the Lord who has so richly gifted Iain, grace him over the coming years to produce a body of work that will demand such a tribute.

Alasdair I Macleod
Free Church of Scotland
St Andrews

Acknowledgements

This book is a slightly revised version of a doctoral thesis presented to the University of Edinburgh in 2001. My first duty, therefore, is to record my gratitude to my research supervisors, Professor Stewart J. Brown, Professor of Ecclesiastical History and Dean of New College, and Professor A. Graeme Auld, Professor of Hebrew Bible at New College. Their constant willingness to assist in many different ways was a source of real inspiration in completing this thesis. In particular, I should like to thank Professor Brown for suggesting the topic of the thesis, and for his enthusiasm for the project.

My studies could not have been prosecuted without the financial help received from the Church of Scotland Bursary, the Miss Elizabeth Drummond Trust, the Whitefield Institute, and the Ross and Cromarty Bursary from the Western Isles Council. I am indebted to the trustees of these scholarships for their help.

I should also like to thank members of George Adam Smith's family who met with me and gave me assistance. These included his late daughters, Janet Carleton and Margaret Clarke, whom I mention in the introduction, Lady Mary Corsar, who granted me an interview, and Professor Andrew Roberts, who offered many invaluable corrections and suggestions for the improvement of the script.

I should like to thank Dr Thomas E. Corts, President of Samford University, Alabama, and enthusiastic student of Henry Drummond and his circle, for corresponding with me by e-mail on aspects of this thesis, and for hosting me at his home University during a visit to America in November 2000. His enthusiasm for this study of George Adam Smith and the Free Church intellectuals of late Victorian Scotland has been an inspiration.

I am also grateful to Rev Alasdair I. Macleod of St Andrews for contributing the foreword. It was a chance remark of his, while he was Professor of Apologetics and Practical Theology at the Free Church College, Edinburgh, which first planted in my mind the possibility of research in this area. He has been an enthusiastic supporter throughout, and his foreword is characteristically over-generous. No-one exemplifies the ideal of the scholar-preacher more than he does himself.

Thanks are also due to Jeremy Mudditt and Anthony Cross of Paternoster Publishing for accepting my work for publication, and for their invaluable advice and help during the publishing process.

Finally, I would like to express my thanks to the many friends who have supported me during this project, showing enthusiasm for it and periodically asking about its progress. Not least, my wife and family have been an invaluable source of encouragement and inspiration. Their love, to use the title of Henry Drummond's famous sermon on 1 Corinthians 13, is to me "the greatest thing in the world".

Iain D. Campbell
March 2004

Abbreviations

AUR	*Aberdeen University Review*
GAS	George Adam Smith
HGHL	*Historical Geography of the Holy Land*
LAS	Lilian Adam Smith
MCPOT	*Modern Criticism and the Preaching of the Old Testament*
NIDOTTE	*New International Dictionary of Old Testament Theology and Exegesis*
NLS	National Library of Scotland
PDGAFCS	Proceedings and Debates of the General Assembly of the Free Church of Scotland
PDGAUFCS	Proceedings and Debates of the General Assembly of the United Free Church of Scotland
RGAUFCS	Reports to the General Assembly of the United Free Church of Scotland

INTRODUCTION

George Adam Smith was a man of many parts. The consummate biblical scholar, he loved mountaineering. He moved with ease among the slum-dwellers of Glasgow's Broomielaw, and he was entertained by American President Woodrow Wilson in the White House. He was arraigned before the General Assembly of the United Free Church of Scotland on a charge of heresy, and presided over it as Moderator a decade and a half later. He contributed zeal and passion to the evangelistic campaigns of Dwight L. Moody, yet championed the cause of liberal biblical criticism. The scourge of some theologians, he earned the respect of many conservative Old Testament scholars. His pen moved with equal ease over the pages of *The Expositor*, the *Palestine Exploration Fund Quarterly Statement* and the *Scottish Journal of Agriculture*. He strode like a colossus over the study of the topography and literature of Palestine, yet, as Principal of a burgeoning Scottish University, he familiarised himself with the demands and needs of subjects as diverse as medicine and botany. The consummate ecclesiastic, fiercely loyal to the ideal of a national Scottish Church, he was nonetheless respected across a wide range of professions and professional interests. The New York paper, *The Outlook*, was not exaggerating when it said in 1896 that Smith was "perhaps the foremost Old Testament scholar in the Free Church of Scotland" who had "published ... works of eminent and enduring value".[1] Yet a century later, even within Scottish church tradition, Smith is an all but forgotten figure.

This is reflected in the evident paucity of research and scholarly work done on George Adam Smith. Following his death in 1942, his wife, Lilian Adam Smith, produced an intimate and detailed memoir.[2] It was full, but hardly critical. Based largely upon personal diaries, and aimed at supplying future

---

[1] *The Outlook*, 4 July 1896, press cutting taken from pp74-75 of album of presscuttings, NLS Acc 9446 No 412. Smith's papers are referred to under the abbreviations NLS (National Library of Scotland) and 'Acc 9446' the Accession Number of the file.

[2] Referred to in the footnotes under the abbreviation LAS. This memoir, entitled *George Adam Smith: A Personal Memoir and Family Chronicle* (London, 1943), is an indispensable source of information. Of the other memoirs written by Smith's contemporaries which appeared following his death, the fullest is that of S.A. Cook, "George Adam Smith 1856-1942" in *Proceedings of the British Academy 1942* (London, 1942), pp324-46.

generations of Smith descendants with full biographical information on their famous patriarch, the memoir is a useful guide to a fruitful life. But it reads more like a companionable fireside reminiscence than a critical biography, and was more a cairn on Smith's memory than a critique of his work. That Smith's widow was able to produce so detailed an account in so short a time, however, is testimony to a lifetime of meticulous diary-keeping, and no intellectual biography of Smith can ignore her work.

Beyond it, however, little has been written on Smith. Even typing his name into an Internet search engine will yield few websites with information on George Adam Smith – invariably they will point to sites on Adam Smith, the more famous eighteenth century Scottish economist, to whom George Adam Smith was not related.

There have been few exceptions to this lack of interest. The most notable has probably been the work of Dr. Richard A. Riesen, whose thesis (1981) and subsequent book on the development of Scottish Old Testament scholarship under George Adam Smith, William Robertson Smith and Andrew Bruce Davidson helped to kindle fresh interest in the contribution of George Adam Smith to biblical scholarship. Dr Barbara MacHaffie's earlier doctoral work on the popularisation of biblical criticism in the nineteenth century – which resulted in a two-volume, wide-ranging thesis (1977) – paid attention to Smith's contribution to the development of Old Testament criticism, although only 12 pages of the 660-page thesis were specifically devoted to George Adam Smith himself. Dr William G. Enright, in his 1968 thesis on the changing nature of the evangelical sermon in the late nineteenth century, had referred often to the preaching of George Adam Smith as an example of an emerging genre, but its contribution to Smith studies was minimal.

Even in these studies, however, Smith was never centre stage – he always shared the spotlight, either with his predecessors in biblical scholarship, or his contemporaries on the late Victorian Scottish church scene. And while that ecclesiastical scene has spawned some important and exciting works of late,[3] the literature lacks an intellectual biography of George Adam Smith.

It is, of course, one thing to explain that there is a lacuna; it is quite another to explain why that should be. After all, Smith cuts a large figure in the period from 1880, when he emerged from his studies at New College, to the 1930s, when he retired as the last ordained Principal of a Scottish University. The three distinct phases of his career – pastoral ministry, Old Testament scholarship, and University administrator – have much in common, and show Smith to be an important and influential figure in Scottish religious and cultural life. As the first pastor of the new Queen's Cross Free Church in Aberdeen,

---

[3] Such as Douglas Ansdell's *The People of the Great Faith: The Highland Church 1690-1900* (Stornoway, 1998), T.E. Corts (ed.), *Henry Drummond: A Perpetual Benediction* (Edinburgh, 1999) and James L. Macleod, *The Second Disruption: the Free Church in Victorian Scotland and the Origins of the Free Presbyterian Church* (Edinburgh, 2000).

Smith consolidated his liberal evangelical pulpit and demonstrated how biblical criticism could – and should – be accommodated to the kerygmatic task of the church. These formative years also gave birth to his liberal commentaries on Isaiah and the minor prophets in Hodder and Stoughton's new publishing venture *The Expositor's Bible* commentary series. There were already emerging during the decade of his pastoral ministry the themes which would be later developed and for which he would gain recognition – the emphasis on geography as an important element of literary context, the emphasis on a synthetic and cohesive approach to history which was not confined to literary texts alone, the emphasis on the social gospel as a vital component of biblical Christianity, and the recognition of harmony between the burgeoning Darwinism of the nineteenth century and the record of the biblical text.

Smith's reputation as a critical scholar was consolidated and developed during his tenure of the Chair of Old Testament Language and Literature at Glasgow's Free Church College from 1892 to 1910. During that period Smith continued to publish on the results of his Old Testament research, all the time conscious that he was pouring new wine into old wineskins. The conservatism of the Scottish church struggled to contain the new learning, and Smith's near trial for heresy in 1902 is one of the most interesting and important aspects of his career, not least because of the light it sheds on the relationship between evangelicalism and critical scholarship of the Bible. This episode has been highlighted by Robert Davidson in an important article in *The Expository Times* for 1978-9, and demands further and up-to-date study. Smith spoke as a triumphalist – the new criticism, he declared in the lectures which had occasioned the trial, had overcome outdated theories of biblical inspiration and inerrancy. Yet for all his assurance, a large majority in the church did not agree with him. The resultant tension between the credal commitment of the Church Smith served and the conclusions of the critical scholarship in which he engaged make him a pivotal figure for our understanding of the Scottish church at the dawn of the twentieth century.

From 1910 to 1935 Smith was Principal of the University of Aberdeen. Returning to his former city was a pleasant experience, and there is every indication that he found his new post equally agreeable. It was, to all intents and purposes, like taking charge of a congregation all over again, although without the credal and confessional commitment of a pastorate. More than one contemporary of Smith's made that very point, and during the quarter century of his Principalship, Smith's University career and his Church work ran along parallel lines. But for all his churchmanship, or perhaps because of it, he was given near ambassadorial status in North America as the Great War progressed, and his 1918 tour of America, during which he drummed up support for the allied cause, is another important, but neglected, facet of his life and work which illustrates, among other things, the way the Church approached the War, and the way the War changed the attitudes of the Churches. There is a poignancy to the picture of the University Principal, whose two sons were included in the Roll of Honour of fallen alumni which he read in King's Cross Chapel, steeling himself to draw the sons of another continent into the same conflict. Smith invites sympathy; yet he does not seek it. Instead, the bitter pill of loss only serves to justify in his mind the cause for which his sons fell.

Smith's ideological stance in the War, as representative of both Church and State, invites analysis. So too do his efforts at consolidation afterwards, as the Church sought to come to terms with the disillusionment which followed the conflict. It was God's war while it lasted, and in the minds of churchmen like Smith it gave promise of spiritual revival and renewal. Instead, it threw up other issues, such as the increasing role of women in the Church and the State and the liberalising of education provision. Smith devoted his latter energies to the administrative matters of Aberdeen University; whether or not that was to the detriment of biblical scholarship is a subject requiring consideration.

It is difficult to find one adjective to describe Smith. He is a multiform character in a world – and in a Church – gradually shedding their uniformity. At the very least, the breadth of his interests and the colourfulness of his life and work make his life an interesting study. But his significance lies in the fact that at a time of transition in the Scottish nation, not least in the Church, and particularly in the place and study of the Bible in the Church, Smith stands as a symbol of change and of accommodation. For that reason alone, his life demands to be revisited.

Setting the Scene

Smith's life and work are to be understood against the changing world of nineteenth century Scotland. Intellectually, that world built on the Enlightenment of the preceding century, and witnessed profound changes in scientific theory and study. Economically, it was a world which would be transformed forever by the Industrial Revolution, with its far-reaching consequences for industry and society. Socially, it was a world which witnessed the rapid development of the city, with population growth accompanying dramatic urbanisation and associated problems of squalor and poverty in Scotland's cities. This, in turn, was paralleled by changes in political activity as the nineteenth century progressed, with the gradual erosion of the earlier Liberal hegemony, the development of the socialist movement, and the later rise of the Labour party.

These were issues which served to shape Smith's ideas and which determined his approach to ministry and to study. But the most profound developments of the century – and those most influential on his thinking – took place within the Church itself. Two quotations will serve to illustrate these changes. Historian T.C. Smout says that "at the start of the nineteenth century, the established Church of Scotland was in a position of substantial numerical superiority"[4]. Although there were several smaller, non-established Churches in

---

[4] T.C. Smout, *A Century of the Scottish People 1830-1950* (London, 1987) p184.

Scotland – the legacy of various divisions, separations and unions since the establishment of Presbyterianism in 1690 – and although there were evident tensions within the Church of Scotland itself, the century opened with one denomination dominating Scotland's religious landscape. By the end of the century, that denomination itself had split, and various aspects of its worship, such as the role of the Bible, the use of musical instruments and hymns, and the role of the Westminster Confession of Faith, were increasingly questioned, and traditional positions increasingly debated. Writing about the Church at the *end* of the century, A.C. Cheyne says that "the old exclusiveness – and possibly the old precision and consistency – of Reformed theology was relegated to the past; suspicion of 'dogmatism' and the elevation of life over doctrine were in the ascendant".[5]

Building on the concept of the nineteenth century as a revolutionary age, A.C. Cheyne describes the changes in the Scottish Church during the period as "Victorian Scotland's Religious Revolution".[6] It was a revolution, he suggests, which affected society in general, but profoundly altered the shape of the Church in particular. No study of Smith's life can ignore the witness of the nineteenth century to the changing position of the Scottish Church of the period in her relation to her creed, to the state, to society and social welfare, and, supremely, to the Bible. Nor can any study of the Scottish ecclesiastical scene ignore the profound effects of the Disruption and the consequent formation of the Free Church of Scotland in 1843. The new denomination was thirteen years old when Smith was born, and his life is a telling commentary on the first century after the Disruption, a religious century whose rich history still invites and requires further research.

The credal issue was concerned with the relationship of the Scottish church to the Westminster Confession of Faith, her 'subordinate' standard (so-called to distinguish it from her 'supreme' standard, the Bible). The deposition in 1831 of John McLeod Campbell, the brilliant, if eccentric, minister of Rhu in Dumbartonshire, showed that the winds of change were blowing through the Church and her relation to the Westminster standards. His proclamation of a more liberal and 'loving' Gospel led him to the conclusion that "the Assembly was right: our doctrine and the Confession are incompatible".[7] By 1866 the Moderator of the Free Church General Assembly noted that

> it is open to the Church at any time to say 'We have obtained clearer light over one or other or all of the propositions contained in this Confession, we must review it' ... if this freedom does not belong to us, then indeed we are

---

[5] A. C. Cheyne "The Religious World of Henry Drummond" in T.E. Corts, *Henry Drummond*, p5. This essay is also published in the collection of Cheyne's articles *Studies in Scottish Church History* (Edinburgh, 1999) pp185-198.
[6] The sub-title of A.C. Cheyne's *The Transforming of the Kirk* (Edinburgh, 1983).
[7] Quoted in Cheyne, *The Transforming of the Kirk*, p62.

in bondage to our Confession, and renounce the liberty wherewith Christ has made us free.[8]

The following year A. Taylor Innes, a prominent Free Church lawyer, published his magisterial work *The Law of Creeds in Scotland*, and observed: "that old creed is sure to trouble the modern church with a doubtful uneasiness – perhaps to burden it with weight, certainly to vex it with constraint".[9] The twilight of the century saw the Free Church leaders, such as Principal Robert Rainy of New College, pressing forward the adoption of a Declaratory Act, partly to facilitate Union with the United Presbyterian Church which had adopted a similar measure in 1879, but mainly because Westminster's predestinarian theology was "growingly felt foreign and even alien by, not the rationalistic, but, on the contrary, the evangelical and missionary sentiment of the Church".[10] The growing unease with the position of the Westminster Confession of Faith was an important factor in the background to Smith's life and work as a Scottish Churchman.

Secondly, the nineteenth century also witnessed a change in the Church's relation to the State. The evangelical leaders who left the Church of Scotland in 1843 regarded their 'Disruption' not as a disruption of the Church *per se*, but of the relationship between the Church of Scotland and the State which had legislated for her establishment. The 'Free' in her denominator was adopted to reflect the new denomination's freedom from State control. It was her argument that Establishment of the Church was the legitimate duty of the State, but controlling her was not. Even without State support, the Free Church of Scotland maintained the Establishment Principle. When the Patronage Act of 1874 dealt with the vexing question of ministers receiving patronage – the abuse of which had been one of the immediate causes of the Disruption – the debate shifted slightly. Could the continuation of the Free Church of Scotland be justified? The emergence of the disestablishment campaign further taxed the thinking of Churchmen, many of whom argued that only by being *dis*established could the Church be truly free. By 1870, prominent Free Churchmen like George Smeaton were saying that "Politics has much to do with it – I fear much more than religion".[11] Smith found himself along with many colleagues in the middle of this debate, the resolution of which was necessary in the move to wider Union in 1900 and the re-union of the Scottish Churches in 1929. It was rather ironic that after a Disruption and two unions the Established Church of 1830 had been replaced by at least four denominations in

---

[8] Quoted in Cheyne, *The Transforming of the Kirk*, p69.
[9] A.T. Innes, *The Law of Creeds in Scotland* (Edinburgh, 1867) p155.
[10] P. Carnegie Simpson, *The Life of Principal Rainy*, Vol 2 (London, 1909) p120.
[11] Quoted in G.N.M. Collins, *Heritage of our Fathers* (Edinburgh, 1974) p71.

1930 claiming to be its successor.[12] That Smith's career witnessed his transformation from being a pastor in the Free Church of Scotland to being a Professor in the United Free Church of Scotland and retiring as University Principal and a minister of the Church of Scotland is itself an interesting phenomenon; the issue of whether in fact he took into his retirement the constitutive principles of the Church of his birth is altogether more complex. But it is an important question to explore, not least because in the divided landscape of modern Presbyterian Scotland, the same questions are still being asked.

Thirdly, the attitude of the Church to social work and social welfare was transformed by events of the nineteenth century. As an agrarian way of life increasingly gave way to the demands of industrialisation, and rich and poor became increasingly distanced, so the problems associated with the growth of Scotland's cities called for the attention of the Churches. As early as the 1840s, Thomas Chalmers was engaged in schemes for poor relief, and although his parochial system was an attempt to tackle new problems with old solutions, the attempt nonetheless was there. It was mirrored, if not improved on, by the later attempts of James Begg, whose pastoral work in Newington led to his setting up the Scottish Social Reform Association in the 1850s. From the middle of the century onwards, the Free Church consolidated her vision of genuine social concern, and by George Adam Smith's student days, involvement by divinity students in 'home mission' schemes among the poor of Scotland's cities was symptomatic of increasing social concern and social work. Also contributing to this recovery of social engagement was the critical approach to the Old Testament prophets. Smith would base his prophetic call for Church involvement in social work on his Old Testament exegesis; it was not the case, as some alleged, that a theological vacuum created the need for social involvement. On the contrary, such involvement was of a piece with the new theology developing within the Church itself.

Which brings us, fourthly, to what is arguably the most important element of the changing Church scene in nineteenth century Scotland: the issue of the place of the Bible in the Church. When the Disruption took place, one of the Free Church's elder statesmen, Thomas McCrie, declared that "we have not separated from the Word of God, which we regard as the only infallible rule of faith and manners ... but we have separated from the civil power – separated because, while connected with it, we could no longer maintain our position except at the expense of trampling under foot what we regard as the immutable principles of truth".[13] Commitment to an infallible and immutable Bible was the hallmark of Calvinist confessionalism, and for that reason it also characterised

---

[12] These were the re-united Church of Scotland, the post-1900 Free Church of Scotland, the post-1929 United Free Church of Scotland and the Free Presbyterian Church of Scotland, which had seceded from the Free Church of Scotland in 1892.

[13] Quoted in Collins, *Heritage of our Fathers*, p60.

the Free Church of Scotland when she was born in 1843. It is therefore surprising to learn that within thirty years of the Disruption, the Free Church was thrown into controversy over the issue of biblical authority. When the brilliant professor of Old Testament at Aberdeen's Free Church College, William Robertson Smith, published an article on the "Bible" in the 1875 edition of the *Encyclopaedia Britannica*, asserting that the Bible had to be read and studied like any other book, and that the Old Testament had evolved alongside the Semitic religion which had produced it, the result was explosive. Robertson Smith's position may have become the orthodoxy of a later day, but in his own it was revolutionary. Church leaders found it near-impossible "to avoid an outright condemnation of biblical criticism and at the same time to maintain the unity of the Free Church",[14] yet men like Robert Rainy and George Adam Smith attempted to do just that. Having complemented their divinity studies in Scotland with theological study in Germany, many of the later nineteenth-century Scottish ministers were accommodating a new approach to the Bible into a Church committed to a particular view of it. It was inevitable that the disturbing of the traditional view of the Bible would disturb the Church too; Smith's role in that disturbance is one of the most important elements in a study of his life. That he was a master of modern, critical Old Testament studies is beyond dispute; his attempts to harmonise the evangelicalism of his Church to the conclusions of his scholarship is perhaps the central issue in a study of his career. His detractors accused him of worshipping scholarship; he himself claimed that his scholarship helped him the more to worship Christ. It is too simplistic to see the battle as one between the liberals and the conservatives in the Church; the issues are more complex. The battle was between those who said that the new criticism was what alone could produce a contemporary evangelicalism, and those who said that it could not be evangelical at all. In other words, if justification is needed for the publication of a life of Smith, it is that scholarly explorations still require to be made of the efforts to integrate critical views of the Bible with the prevailing evangelical ethos within which these developed – most notably the nineteenth century Free Church of Scotland.

George Adam Smith: The Need for a Biographical Study
Against this changing background, therefore, the following study takes a look at Smith's life and its importance for our understanding of the development of the Scottish Church of the period. The story is told from Smith's birth in India in 1856, to his death in Edinburgh in 1942. This intellectual biography treats Smith's life in chronological order, dealing with his years of training and preparation for ministry, his years as pastor in Aberdeen, his Glasgow years as Old Testament Professor, and his later Aberdeen years as University Principal.

---

[14] A.L. Drummond and J. Bulloch, *The Church in Late Victorian Scotland 1874-1900* (Edinburgh, 1978) p78.

In addition, because of the importance of these subjects, there are separate chapters on Smith's role as geographer of the Holy Land and his attitude to the Great War. I have also attempted to make a comprehensive bibliographical listing of Smith's publications, the first time this has been done in a scholarly work.

The following study is based primarily upon Smith's published works. Most of his books were published by Hodder and Stoughton, and his articles appeared in a wide variety of journals. But it is also based upon an original and extensive use of Smith's papers, deposited in the National Library of Scotland. These were inventoried by Smith's daughter, Janet, and officially presented to the Library in 1987. This biography has made detailed use of these papers, as well as incidental manuscripts in the Special Collections of New College Library, Edinburgh, the Public Record Office, London, and the Departments of Special Collections and Archives at Glasgow and Aberdeen Universities. I was also privileged to be able to interview two surviving members of George Adam Smith's immediate family at the outset of my studies: Mrs Margaret Clarke, Aberdeen, and Mrs Janet Carleton (Janet Adam Smith), London. Sadly, Mrs Carleton passed away in September 1999, and Mrs Clarke in August 2002, before this study was completed. The interview with these daughters provided an invaluable personal link to the subject of this study, and both ladies were very enthusiastic about the project.

Finally, I consider it necessary to insert a disclaimer at this point. Many of Smith's conclusions regarding the development and formation of the Old Testament text are not conclusions I share. As I demonstrate in the study, they are conclusions which are still being widely debated and discussed among scholars, both liberal and evangelical. But many of them still defer to a view of the Old Testament as a pre-Christian (or even sub-Christian) development of primitive ideas about God, in which the real makers of Israel's religion are the prophets, whose ethical and spiritual insights forged the faith out of which the pentateuchal legislation and literature developed. My approach to the Old Testament is rather different: it is that the Old Testament is a record of covenantal, redemptive revelation, in which God intervenes in the history of the world expressly to prepare for the coming Christ. As O. Palmer Robertson puts it, "God's initiatives in the establishment of covenantal relationships structure redemptive history. His sovereign interventions provide the essential framework for understanding the great biblical epochs".[15] Walter Kaiser makes the same point when he says:

> When God called Abraham and announced a promise that was to be given to him whereby the whole human race was to be blessed, it was a promise that would unfold in the history of Israel. This promise was renewed with David,

---

[15] O. Palmer Robertson, *The Christ of the Covenants* (New Jersey, 1980), p201.

preached by all the prophets, and began to be fulfilled from the very beginning of its announcement to its final fulfilment.[16]

There is, however a difference between studying the Old Testament as progressive revelation from God, and studying it as primitive religious evolution. Part of the struggle of the nineteenth century Scottish church was that while the creed came down on the side of the former of these positions, the scholars were coming down on the latter. To the extent that Smith described the relation between the two views as a 'war', he was right; but I doubt whether it was over in his lifetime, or is over yet. The indemnity – the price to be paid for securing the victory – is far from being fixed.

None of this means, however, that Smith's work is of no value to those who take a different approach to the Old Testament Scriptures. If for no reason other than that his life raises the issue of the relationship between biblical scholarship and evangelical faith, it is important to study his work. I can only hope that such a comprehensive overview of Smith's life as I have been able to offer here will fill at least part of the gap in modern studies of the intellectual life of Scotland in the post-Disruption period.

---

[16] Walter J. Kaiser III, *The Old Testament Documents: Are they Reliable and Relevant?* (Downers Grove, Illinois, 2001), p222.

CHAPTER 1

The Making of a Biblical Scholar (1856-1882)

The story of Smith's development from infant to biblical scholar takes us from mid-nineteenth century India to the Edinburgh of the 1870s, from the Free Church mission fields of the Orient to the Free Church divinity halls in Scotland. George Adam Smith was born in Calcutta on 19 October 1856, the son of George Smith and Janet Colquhoun Adam. George Smith was from Restalrig, near Leith; and, following an Arts course at Edinburgh University, he left for India in 1853 to begin a career which brought him into close contact with the Indian missionary work of the Free Church of Scotland.

George Smith did not go to India as a missionary - he was to describe himself some fifty years later as "a layman engaged in other duties, but having a personal interest in the missionaries of the Free Church of Scotland".[1] These other duties included the teaching of classics and philosophy at Doveton College.[2] This school had been established as a "Parental Academic Institution" in 1823 in Calcutta, and was given financial stability through the legacy of Captain John Doveton, a Baptist, in 1844.[3] When George Smith became Principal (at the young age of 20), there were 52 boarders at the school and 215 day boys.[4] Among Smith's achievements was to have the College affiliated to

---

[1] George Smith, "Half a Century's Growth of Protestant Missions in India", *The Missionary Record of the United Free Church of Scotland*, No. 25 (January 1903), p8.

[2] Although Professor S.A. Cook describes George Smith as "*master* of the Doveton College" in "George Adam Smith 1856-1942", *Proceedings of the British Academy,* 1942, p325, Smith described himself as "Professor of Classical language and philosophy" (George Smith to GAS from Edinburgh 21 July 1910, NLS Acc 9446 No 403). He became Principal in March 1854, following the death of the Rev Andrew Morgan.

[3] See the 42nd Annual Report of the Parental Academic Institution in Doveton College printed as "Reports on Colleges and Schools in India" in *The Calcutta Review*, Vol XLII (1866) pp 64-65.

[4] "Supplementary notes made from George Smith's letters to his father 1853-60", NLS Acc 9446 No 403. The growth in influence of the School can be seen in the fact that by 1864 the number of boys attending classes there was 380 (*The Calcutta Review,* Vol XLII, 1866, p65).

Calcutta University; as a result of this the College by 1855 had become "the largest school for Christian boys in Calcutta".[5]

George Smith arrived in Calcutta at a time of expansion and change, a time of increased opportunities for the Church's mission work, with progressive attitudes towards education undergirding his own vocation. In a personal reference, Smith acknowledged that in the "inexperience of youth forty years ago" he had not been "friendly to the educational method of missions",[6] but had come to regard such work as "the most powerful method for the conversion of India", and the educational workers in India as among "the ablest and most hard-working missionaries in the East".[7]

George Smith's childhood sweetheart, Janet Colquhoun Adam, came to Calcutta in 1855, "chaperoned by Mrs. Alexander Duff".[8] Janet Adam, according to Lilian Adam Smith, "with her deep blue eyes and dark hair, gave an impression of quiet happiness to all who knew her".[9] Her daughter was to describe her as having "a strong faith in God ... fearless, courageous, honest, of a sane judgement and as full of love as possible, especially for George Smith, her love of early days...".[10] They married soon after her arrival in India. Janet Adam and George Smith were to have eleven children, seven of whom were born in India. Of these, a daughter (born in 1868) survived only two days. George Adam Smith was the eldest.

Little is known of the domestic lifestyle of the Smith home into which George Adam Smith was born. According to the notes of Isabel Ross, the fourth child and first daughter (born in India in 1862) of George and Janet, George Smith had as Principal of Doveton College a salary of £480 and a house; he was also able to pursue academic studies with a view to the ministry.[11] The Smiths enjoyed a fair measure of comfort in their marital home in Calcutta, and with the birth of her first child, Janet could write of feelings of fulfilment and contentment: "Baby is a dear little man ... We think ourselves very rich ... He slept right through the christening ... I think myself as rich as

---

[5] "Reports on Colleges and Schools in India", p65. This has to be balanced, however, by the fact that in the mid-nineteenth century, "The Calcutta-Howrah region was fast becoming the main focus of population concentration in Bengal. The population of Calcutta was growing steadily as in the case of the other port cities in Asia" (R.Basu, "Urban Society in Bengal, 1850-72, with special reference to Calcutta", PhD, University of London, School of Oriental and African Studies, 1974, pp15-16).

[6] G. Smith, *The Conversion of India: From Pantaenus to the Present Time, AD 193-1893* (London, 1893) p192.

[7] Ibid., p193.

[8] Isabel Ross, Our Mother Janet Colquhoun Adam, NLS Acc 9446 No 403.

[9] LAS, p10.

[10] Ross, Our Mother

[11] Ibid. George Smith was later ordained an elder, but was not ordained to the ministry.

any queen and much happier for I have the dearest husband and dearest child in India".[12]

According to Geoffrey Moorhouse's history of Calcutta, this was a society which held attractions for foreign females. As a result, there were "more women in Calcutta than in any other British settlement".[13] Amongst the enticements which drew single females to Calcutta, Moorhouse says that

> if she got someone in the growing civil service ... it meant an assured income of £300 and a pension when he died; and she wouldn't need to wet nurse any babies, for the climate was an excellent excuse to farm an infant to an ayah.[14]

Janet Adam came to Calcutta not to find a husband, but certainly to marry. And, if her daughter's account is accurate, George Smith's income exceeded, as we have seen, even the figure Moorhouse quotes for the civil service. That she secured the services of an *ayah* - a wet nurse - is confirmed from Janet Smith's journal.[15] In the middle of an often hazardous voyage to Scotland in 1858, she writes: "when I remember how good our ayah used to be I often wish for her".[16] Such provision gave Janet Smith, who was not in the best of health following the birth of each of her children, respite from the recurring duties of the nursery. It also indicates the standard of living enjoyed by the Smiths in Calcutta.

The Smith home in Calcutta was happy, but it was not to be totally carefree. The Indian Mutiny of 1857 may have been "limited in scale and confused in meaning",[17] and the centre of the so-called Sepoy War in Delhi some 750 miles away, but it cast a long shadow. The initial act of violence reputed to have occasioned the Mutiny took place at Barrackpore, near Calcutta.

The sepoys were Indian soldiers, and in 1857 they outnumbered the European soldiers almost eight to one.[18] Their disillusionment with British control over the Indian army brought to a head the conflict between Indian traditions and Victorian imperial expansion. According to Lawrence James, the grievances of the sepoys extended to "the meddling arrogance of the

---

[12] Notes from letters of Janet Smith to her sisters-in-law, Mary and Hannah, in Leith, November 1856 (in Ross, Our Mother).
[13] G. Moorhouse, *Calcutta: The City Revealed* (London, 1986) p61.
[14] Ibid.
[15] The journal is an extensive account of the voyage of Janet Smith from India to Scotland in 1858-9 with her two sons, George and Dunlop. Lilian Adam Smith, interestingly, informs us that the transcribing of the journal occupied George Adam Smith in his retirement years (LAS, pp247-8).
[16] Janet Colquhoun Smith, "Notes from Journal", p15, NLS Acc 9446 No 1.
[17] James Morris, *Heaven's Command: an Imperial Progress* (London 1973) p222.
[18] Ibid, p223, where James Morris states that "The British were ludicrously thin on the Indian ground - in 1857 there were 34,000 European soldiers to 257,000 Indians".

missionaries whose schools taught young Indians to scoff at their parents' creeds".[19] The eighteen months of fighting which followed were bloody and gruesome, and "life in the war zone seemed to have collapsed into incomprehensible nightmare".[20] The war zone was in central northern India; Calcutta remained immune from the fighting, but felt the terror none the less. Moorhouse says that "nothing but British panic happened in Calcutta",[21] but the agitation was very real.

In the Smith household, the sense of terror was heightened by the illness of father and son, who were suffering from sickness and dysentery. Their physician would not allow them to leave their home, and Isabel Ross, George Adam Smith's sister, goes so far as to say that "for days the balance hung between life and death for these two dear ones".[22] To equip herself for the protection of her family, Janet attended revolver practice for women,[23] and kept her gun by her side.

She may have had more reason than most to worry. Ranu Basu, in his doctoral thesis on Bengali society in the mid-nineteenth century, argues that

> the aspect of Western influence which was disliked most by the urban Bengalis, both conservatives and progressives, was the extreme Westernization of some of the urbanites, especially the youth which sometimes culminated in their conversion to Christianity ... Cases of conversion to Christianity ... were reported and almost universally condemned by the urban Bengali press mainly on religious grounds.[24]

The native Bengali community often criticised conversion in terms of motive, arguing that many "became Christians for reasons which had very little to do with their religious convictions, for example, desire for money, desire to marry white/European women and the wish to hurt one's family".[25] Basu also argues that much of the Bengali opposition to Christianity had focused on the schools. Perhaps, therefore, what fuelled Janet Smith's concerns was not merely the political aspect of the Indian Mutiny, but the fear that if the native opposition to Mission Schools was so great, the Mutiny might become a pretext for concentrated action and violence towards them. Lilian Smith's romantic picture of the Calcutta home where quiet happiness pervaded[26] may not adequately reflect the sense of native hostility all around them.

---

[19] L. James, *Raj: The Making and UnMaking of British India* (London, 1987) p237.
[20] Morris, *Heaven's Command*, p229.
[21] Moorhouse, *Calcutta,* p76.
[22] Ross, Our Mother.
[23] Ibid.
[24] Basu, "Urban Society", pp161-2.
[25] Ibid., p163.
[26] LAS, p10.

The Making of a Biblical Scholar

The end of the mutiny coupled with the recovery of husband and child came as a great relief to the young mother.[27] Following the birth of their second child, James Dunlop Smith,[28] in August 1858, Janet Smith herself was not well, and was ordered home to Scotland to rest. She and her two sons left India on the *Clarence* in November 1858. In that same year, George Smith resigned from Doveton and took up the editorship of the *Calcutta Review*.

The faith and devotion which sustained Janet during the Mutiny also aided her on several occasions during the four-month crossing to London. This is evident from her journal, kept faithfully during the voyage, and written, for the most part, more as an extended letter to her husband than as a personal diary. She writes at the beginning of the voyage:

> our Saviour who sympathises in all our griefs will intercede for us and pardon our frail hearts. Meanwhile we must pray for each other and submit cheerfully to His will who hath ordered this domestic trial;[29]

and at the end

> I feel assured God meant to show his love for me in saving me alive so that through this I might be brought to the Saviour; this truth did not appear to me till lately in so strong a light as it now does and I now pray to Him that the lesson may not be lost on my soul, but that I may be purified by this trial and render thanks to God for having afflicted me...[30]

Despite the privations of life aboard the ship, young George Adam enjoyed some basic schooling; reference is made throughout the journal to the improvement in young Smith's spoken English. Of no small importance were the religious services on board ship; "here we are," Janet writes, "a small company of professing, and we hope real Christians, worshipping the only true God".[31] She herself was under constant medication to help with her illness; she

---

[27] That is not to say that Bengali attitudes were transformed overnight; nationalistic feeling still ran high. In 1861, for example, a Society for the Promotion of National Feeling among the Educated Natives of Bengal was inaugurated (see Moorhouse, *Calcutta*, pp80ff).

[28] Dunlop was himself to have a distinguished career in India, becoming Private Secretary to the Lieutenant Governor of the Punjab 1883-87, Settlement Officer, Sialkot 1887-1896, Commissioner, Hissar, 1896-7, Famine Commissioner, Rajputana, 1899-1900; Political Agent, Pulkhian States, 1901-4; Private Secretary to the Viceroy, 1905-1910. He was knighted in 1910, political ADC to the Secretary of State for India from 1910 to 1919. He died in 1921. For a record of Dunlop Smith's career in the service of the Viceroy, see Martin Gilbert, *Servant of India* (London, 1966).

[29] Janet Smith, *Journal*, NLS Acc 9446 No 311, p2.

[30] Ibid., p25.

[31] Ibid., p10.

writes, "I do still feel weak and sometimes faint but am the only lady who has not suffered from sea sickness".[32] Evenings were often spent in the company of other passengers, over a glass of wine and often playing games to pass the time. The long and arduous voyage was over at the end of March 1859 when the *Clarence* finally arrived in London. There, Janet's mother met them, before they journeyed north to Leith.

Life in Scotland

Their destination was Fillyside Cottage in Restalrig, Leith, home of "Aunts" Mary and Hannah. Mary Smith was George Smith's older sister, and Hannah Anderson was a cousin, the daughter of George Anderson and Matilda Taylor. Following the deaths of Mary's mother and Hannah's father, Adam Smith (George Smith's father) and Matilda Taylor married, so Mary and Hannah became stepsisters. Isabel Ross describes them as "our dearest friends" in childhood:

> The Aunts as we called them were devoted to each other and to us. They each took their own department in the household of children. Aunt Hannah attended to all matters domestic... Aunt Mary knitted stockings ... and looked after lessons. She studied Latin in order to be able to help the boys when they went to the High School of Edinburgh.[33]

Lilian Adam Smith further describes the two sisters as "young women of great character - Mary, the elder, was full of quick sympathy and imagination, a born storyteller; Hannah was more practical and had a keen, caustic wit".[34] Their influence on George Adam Smith must have been considerable; and his volumes on Jerusalem (first published in 1908) were dedicated "To the memory of M.S.", his aunt Mary in Leith. When Janet returned to India in 1860, Mary and Hannah began to bear the responsibility for the welfare of George Adam Smith; this would continue until his parents returned home in 1875, by which time his brother, Dunlop, William and Hunter, and his sisters Isabel, Minnie and Janetta, had all joined him.

George Adam Smith received his early schooling at Leith, and also at the Royal High School in Edinburgh, walking there and back each day, a distance of three miles each way. Although he was many miles away in India, George Smith maintained contact with his sons, giving them every encouragement in their studies. From Serampore he wrote in July 1865, as his elder son was preparing to attend Leith High School:

---

[32] Ibid., p12.
[33] Isabel Ross, "Our Friends", NLS Acc 9446 No 403.
[34] LAS, p12.

The Making of a Biblical Scholar 17

> Tell me the names of all the class-books you will get when you go back to the Leith School and ... what books of your own you have been reading lately and what sort of books you like best to read.[35]

Such letters, no doubt, were an encouragement to further study, and also stimulated an interest in correspondence to India; Isabel Smith mentions that every Sunday part of the routine was to write to their parents.[36] George Smith evidently enjoyed receiving such correspondence, and in his letters he encouraged his son both to continue his studies in earnest, and to maintain a sound Christian profession:

> This letter is all to yourself because your recent letters have pleased me much. When you are older you will probably join some society where essays are read and debates are held and that will help you both in composition and fluency of speech ... you are old enough to understand me when I ask you if you feel that you love Jesus Christ, and strive to do what you know to be right to resist temptations ... Prayer will be your great help - not only formal prayers with your brothers and sisters and dear Aunts, but prayer by yourself...[37]

By 1864 the household had expanded with the arrival of two more Smith children born in Serampore: William Townsend, born in January 1861, and Isabel Martha, born in June 1862. Isabel reminisces:

> These were the four of us left to be cared for by our dear aunts Mary and Hannah. George Adam like quicksilver took the lead in everything ... We walked across the Links to the South Free Church on Sundays. We loved old Dr Thorburn with his kind refined face and white hair.[38]

When the house in Leith became too small for the purpose of accommodating four children and two aunts, another house was obtained near the Meadows in Edinburgh, which became the Smith home for several years, before the aunts moved to another home near Inverkeithing. Correspondence with India continued, and George Adam Smith was constantly reminded of the need to work hard and to work well. So he is encouraged to "Cultivate accuracy about all things" and he is told "Do not be discouraged at the Greek verb. It seems difficult, but if you know Latin well and attend to your teacher, you will learn the beautifully scientific plan on which it is constructed and love Greek

---

[35] George Smith to GAS, 8 July 1865, NLS Acc 9446 No 2.
[36] Isabel Ross, NLS Acc 9446 No 4.
[37] George Smith to GAS, 6 January 1866, NLS Acc 9446 No.2.
[38] Isabel Ross, "Our Friends". Adam Smith had been an elder in South Leith Free Church during the ministry of the Rev David Thorburn.

more than Latin".³⁹ Communication by letter between parents and children was hardly ideal; but the habit of letter-writing remained, and when Smith studied abroad, his letters home to his parents and aunts were very full, very descriptive and very frequent. Later, when he was to experience life in foreign lands, the habit continued, and into his letters he poured descriptions of places, people and experiences; these detailed items of correspondence formed the basis for his subsequent writing of historical geography and his markedly descriptive prose.

When George and Janet eventually returned from India, their children hardly knew them. Isabel Ross, for example, would later write that she had no recollection of her mother until she came home in 1871 with three more children, Minnie, Hunter and Janetta. The absence of his father - who between 1860 and 1870 had gone on to become co-proprietor and co-editor of the *Friend of India* weekly newspaper as well as being India correspondent of *The Times* - seems to have had no detrimental effect on his son, who, as we have seen, was quick to take a lead as the oldest male in the household. It may, however, explain his extraordinarily close relationship with his own children in later years.⁴⁰

George and Janet Smith eventually joined their family in Edinburgh in 1870, when George became editor of *The Edinburgh Daily Review*. A property was purchased in Merchiston, Edinburgh, which was named Serampore House. As Lilian Smith reminds us,

> the whole family was for the first time all together. But not for long, for Dunlop, the brother with whom, until then, all George's life and interests had been shared, had to leave for Sandhurst, in preparation for the Indian army.⁴¹

Smith's was, therefore, a somewhat unconventional, but by no means unhappy childhood. Indeed, he could say that "There was nothing but love in Fillyside".⁴²

From High School Smith went to the University of Edinburgh, where he followed an Arts course, graduating MA in 1875. Although Henry Drummond, who was to be a colleague in Trinity College Glasgow later, and whose

---

³⁹ George Smith to GAS, July 1869, NLS Acc 9446 No 2.
⁴⁰ Cf. for example the following quotation from George Adam Smith's daughter, Mrs Margaret Clarke: "...my father loved children, and he couldn't resist it - he would pick me up and walk with me and carry me round the garden much to my mother's annoyance; she had just succeeded in getting me to sleep..." (*Transcript of interview with Mrs Margaret Clarke, daughter of George Adam Smith, Aberdeen, 20 March 1998;* the original tape recording is housed in the oral history collection, New College, Edinburgh).
⁴¹ LAS, p15.
⁴² Ibid.

biography George Adam Smith would eventually write, had commenced his Arts course earlier than Smith, Smith's description of Drummond's Edinburgh University sets the scene for his own University Arts course:

> In the first year of Arts at Edinburgh University in those days there was much on which one looks back now with considerable amusement. The students were either boys or bearded men fresh from the plough and the workshop.[43] In classics and mathematics the junior classes were below the standard of the senior forms in the High Schools. They worked through several Latin and Greek authors, not the most difficult, did a heap of prose exercises, and learned several books of Euclid with a little algebra...[44]

Classics formed the basis for an Arts course in the early 1870s, and Smith had no difficulty securing a place. His University career was not strikingly outstanding, but it did form the basis of subsequent interests. For example, in his resume of Smith's life, Prof. S.A. Cook wrote:

> ...he added to his studies political economy under Professor W.B. Hodgson: it was a subject in which he had an abiding interest, and it was to prove of practical value when he began to take an active part in civic and social affairs, and to write on the economic factors in ancient Palestine and the neighbouring lands.[45]

Moody and Sankey

There was, however, one singularly important event which shaped Smith's thinking during his undergraduate years. In 1873-4, Dwight L. Moody and Ira D. Sankey held their famous Gospel crusade in Britain. Although the mission receives only an incidental reference in Lilian Adam Smith's memoir, it was clearly a major influence in Smith's life and outlook subsequently, and it is important to look at the extent to which much of Smith's later theological and spiritual outlook was moulded by it.[46]

---

[43] On this, cf. the statement that "In the early 1860s [the universities] received no fewer than 23 per cent of their Arts Faculty intake from children of manual workers, many coming straight from parochial schools at the age of thirteen or fourteen" (T.C. Smout, *A Century of the Scottish People 1830-1950* [London, 1986] p217).

[44] *The Life of Henry Drummond*, pp28-9.

[45] Cook, *George Adam Smith*, p326.

[46] The Moody and Sankey campaigns have received concentrated study in the work of Janice E. Holmes, "Religious Revivalism and Popular Evangelicalism in Britain and Ireland 1859-1905", PhD, Queen's University Belfast, 1995, and Mark J. Toone "Evangelicalism in Transition: A comparative analysis of the work and theology of D.L. Moody and his proteges, Henry Drummond and R.A. Torrey", PhD, St Andrew's University, 1988. George Adam Smith devotes a chapter (Chapter IV) to "The Great Mission" in his *The Life of Henry Drummond*.

In spite of the vast amount of Christian work done in Scotland's growing urban areas during the course of the nineteenth century, "the death of hell, the rise of class, and the spread of other entertainment"[47] contributed to a steady decline of churchgoing. Old certainties were vanishing and alternatives to church attendance were multiplying. In this changing world, the evangelistic, revivalistic campaigns of the 1870s were for many a breath of fresh air.

Dwight Lyman Moody was born in Massachusetts in 1837. His father died when he was four years old, and in 1854 he moved to Boston, representative, according to one biographer, "of those who had come to Boston seeking their fortunes and a newer, more exciting manner of life".[48] Two years later, however, he moved to Chicago where he became an itinerant preacher who could "relate to the man in the street and to those in the top ranks of Chicago's social class".[49] At a YMCA convention in Indianapolis in 1870, Moody heard Ira Sankey sing, and an association began which led to the two names being forever linked in the story of American revivalism.

The links made through the YMCA in America and England, and the promise of financial assistance from prominent evangelicals in England, lay behind the decision of Moody and Sankey to minister in Britain. Despite Smith's description of Moody as "an unknown man" who came to Britain to preach "virtually without invitation or advertisement",[50] that was not the whole story. Moody was known and supported by some prominent publishers, particularly R.C. Morgan, whose paper *The Christian* served as a public platform and advertising agency for the evangelist.

The invitation to the evangelists originated with the Free Church of Scotland, though it is not clear which individual was responsible for it.[51] Few ministers in the Established Church (Archibald H. Charteris, later Professor of biblical criticism in Edinburgh University, was a notable exception) supported

---

[47] Smout, *Century*, p208.

[48] James F. Findlay, *Dwight L. Moody: American Evangelist 1837-1899* (Chicago, 1969) p45.

[49] This quotation may be more hagiographical than biographical; it is taken from "The Story of Dwight L. Moody" (http://www.moodychurch.org) downloaded from the internet on 21/11/98. Findlay is probably nearer the mark when he says that "Moody quickly accepted as his own this evangelical interest in the individual" (*Dwight L. Moody*, p67).

[50] G.A. Smith, "A Personal Tribute", introductory essay in H. Drummond, *Dwight L. Moody: Impressions and Facts* (New York, 1900) p5.

[51] Findlay states that "A minister of the Scottish Free Church in Leith [John Kelman]... was the first to advocate publicly extending an invitation to Moody and Sankey to come northward" (p153), while A.L. Drummond and J. Bulloch say that "James Hood Wilson, a Free Church minister of evangelical outlook who... had conducted a parish ministry during his years in Fountainbridge was largely responsible for the coming of Moody and Sankey" in *The Church in Late Victorian Scotland 1874-1900* (Edinburgh, 1978) p9.

the mission; it was largely the Free Church which endorsed it.⁵² The evangelicalism of the Free Church was fertile ground for the activities of the evangelists, who focussed on the "simple essentials" rather than the "complicated inessentials"⁵³ of the Gospel message. Smith suggests in *The Life of Henry Drummond* that the main result and benefit of the Moody and Sankey campaign was "to pour fresh power into the routine of Christian work".⁵⁴ What was needed was not necessarily new doctrines, but new power. Smith's assessment of Moody was that "he re-awakened in Scotland not a few echoes of Chalmers; and to read him again is to be filled with surprise that in the country of Chalmers so few of Moody's followers should have sustained the more liberal keynotes which he struck for them!"⁵⁵

Moody's appeal, however, was as large as his heart. With no theological education and no interest in church divisions, heir of the American revivalist tradition, he seemed like a breath of fresh air in a Scotland often torn by ecclesiastical strife and doctrinal controversy. In addition, as Mark Toone points out:

> The usually non-denominational aspect of these meetings also set a precedent for inter-denominational cooperation in the campaigns, a conspicuous element in Moody's missions and one that he took great pains to groom and promote.⁵⁶

For George Adam Smith, Moody's appeal lay in the fact that he spoke to the hearts and needs of his listeners. He acknowledged that Moody sometimes spoke rashly, and at other times crudely. The former of these he attributes, somewhat ungraciously, to the fact that Moody was a foreigner, the second to the fact that he was uneducated.⁵⁷ In spite of these traits, however – or perhaps

---

⁵² This fact seems to have been lost on the official writers of Free Church History, such as Alexander Stewart and J. Kennedy Cameron who in their post-Union apologetic for the Free Church wrote that "There can be no doubt that the teaching and methods of the American evangelists had a lasting influence upon the religious life of Scotland, and especially of the Free Church... there is reason to fear that in several directions their influence was the reverse of salutary" (*The Free Church of Scotland 1843-1910*, p52). The reader would not guess from this account that the reason for their visit lay with the Free Church itself.
⁵³ The phrase is taken from A.C. Cheyne, *The Transforming of the Kirk* (Edinburgh, 1983) p82.
⁵⁴ *The Life of Henry Drummond*, p56.
⁵⁵ Ibid., p57. Thomas Chalmers (1780-1847) was the leader of the Free Church of Scotland in 1843.
⁵⁶ Toone, "Evangelicalism in Transition", p93.
⁵⁷ So Smith: "They made mistakes. Mr Moody said some rash things, as a foreigner could not help doing, and many crude ones, as an uneducated man must ... But these faults soon sank from sight in the deep impression of a true zeal to win men for a better

because of them – Moody's novel style and practical message appealed to George Adam Smith. Moody's theology, Smith said, was "thoroughly experimental and busied with the actual life of men".[58] It was, to use David Bebbington's phrase, "homely divinity, spiritual yet practical".[59]

Smith also praised the movement for its practical results, as well as Moody for his practical preaching. He says that

> Mr Moody, who had the true imagination of the city, and the power to bring up before others the vision of its wants, inspired the Christians of Glasgow to attempt missions to the criminal classes and the relief of the friendless. The lodging-houses were visited, and every haunt of vagrants about the brick-kilns upon the South Side and elsewhere. Temperance work was organised, and although there were, as always in that work, very many disappointments, a considerable number of poor drunkards were befriended and reformed.[60]

To Smith, this was of paramount importance, and underlined his growing conviction that the churches must be involved in social mission and social improvement. Smith himself legitimised the social work of the Church as a valid end in itself, and not simply as a means towards spiritual advantage. In the thinking of Smith, this represented the "manliness" of Christianity.[61] Janice Holmes draws attention to this also when she comments that "Moody, and other evangelists, particularly in the late Victorian period, were at great pains to promote a masculine image of Christianity, with a muscular and robust faith, that would appeal to men",[62] and that would in consequence translate belief into action.

---

life..." (*The Life of Henry Drummond*, p56). cf. also Holmes: "British denominations believed that public worship ought to maintain certain standards of decorum and propriety and that conversion was a solemn event with doctrinal implications. This caused them to view Moody's efforts - with his poor grammar, American accent, sentimental stories and simplistic conception of conversion - as not only vulgar and uncouth but also in opposition to the right means of propagating the gospel" (p100).

[58] Ibid., p58.
[59] D.W. Bebbington, *Evangelicalism in Modern Britain: A History from the 1730s to the 1980s* (London, 1994) p163.
[60] *The Life of Henry Drummond*, p61.
[61] In particular, Smith draws attention to the impetus given the Young Men's Christian Association movement through the work of the Mission. The young men who became part of this movement were looked after spiritually, and were to be engaged in work of social improvement. Smith regrets that "the manly and liberal views of the evangelist" were not carried out "by *all* the institutions which he did so much to invigorate" (*The Life of Henry Drummond*, p62).
[62] Holmes, "Religious Revivalism", p119.

But what of the theological aspect of the mission? Is there any evidence to suggest that Moody's theology was influential in the thinking of Smith? From one point of view it is difficult to answer this question, if only because Smith's theological outlook in the mid-1870s eludes us. It was by no means certain that when Smith embarked on an Arts course in Edinburgh he would enter the ministry, although Lilian Adam Smith says that when he graduated in Arts "his boyish dream of being a minister had ... grown into resolve".[63] She comments on the earnestness of Smith's character and his determination for work, his loving nature, his sense of humour and his tolerance for other views;[64] but of his own theological convictions at the close of his University career we know virtually nothing. There is a sense, therefore, in which what Smith has to say about Moody's theology and the message of the Mission, casts valuable light for us on his own outlook and convictions at this important stage of his life.

Of Moody's theology and influence, Smith speaks both positively and negatively. He says, for example, that

> the prejudices of those who for years had resisted every attempt to introduce instrumental music into public worship were overcome, and they lustily sang with Mr Sankey and his organ.[65]

The introduction of instrumental music into public worship was a feature that led increasingly to changes in the worship of the Church. But more than the form of the worship influenced Smith. The content of Moody's gospel was also profoundly influential: "His gospel, which had its centre in the atonement, was the gospel of an Incarnate Saviour".[66] Or, to put it otherwise,

> Mr Moody spoke of the peril of life, of the ghastly hunger of the soul without God, of conscience and of guilt; then, with passion and with tenderness, of God's love and of the Saviour Christ, who is among us today as surely as on the shores of Galilee or by the Pool of Bethesda.[67]

Smith elucidates and enumerates the primary emphases of Moody's preaching with reference to its influence on the preaching of Drummond; the latter of which, Smith reckoned to be an echo of the former:

> [Drummond's] preaching ... ranged over all the great doctrines and facts of Christianity: Sin and Salvation, Penitence, the Atonement, Regeneration, Conversion, Sanctification, the power of the Spirit, Christ's teaching about

---

[63] LAS, p15.
[64] Ibid., p16.
[65] *The Life of Henry Drummond*, pp55-56.
[66] Ibid., p57.
[67] Ibid., p59.

Himself and about a Future life ... He stuck close to the Bible. He used the incidents of the Old Testament to enforce the teaching of the New, just as older evangelists did. His theology was practically that of the leaders of the movement ...[68]

It is clear that these doctrines and tenets of Christianity were embraced by Smith and were brought home to him particularly as he listened to Moody preach. To them he could easily, and gladly, give his consent.

Not that Smith was an uncritical observer of the Mission. His biography of Drummond was written some twenty years after the first stages of the Great Mission, and the criticisms of it there may reflect his considered and mature thought rather than summarise defects apparent to him at the time. Nevertheless, the faults were evident, not merely, as we have seen, in what Smith regarded as Moody's uncouthness, but also in the movement as a whole, of which he says that "so vast and rapid a movement was bound to suffer the defects of its qualities".[69] Among these he notes that many of the converts lapsed into worldliness (especially drunkenness); many also regarded the excitement and enthusiasm of the meetings to be normative (of these Smith says that "their excitement and the habits which it has formed have not been beneficial to Christianity"[70]); and the idealism of the whole Mission movement "conspired with the general excitement to destroy in a certain class of minds all sense for facts".[71]

Smith was careful to distance Moody himself from the excesses of some of his followers. "In the leaders", he says, "there was no want of the healthy discrimination and genial charity without which our religious zeal so fatally develops into Pharisaism".[72] Indeed, Smith owed Moody a great deal, and retained contact with him afterwards.

One result of the evangelistic campaigns was the formation of the so-called Gaiety Club, set up through the influence particularly of Henry Drummond, in order to foster and continue the kind of practical Christian work which Smith saw as a positive aspect of the Mission. Smith himself was to join the Gaiety Club in 1883. This was some ten years after Moody's first visit to Scotland, and Smith's late entry into the Club may reflect the somewhat unsettled nature of his post-theological training. Only after his ordination may he have felt that his life had settled somewhat, and he could devote himself to the meetings at which his former student friends met.

The Club was called after the Gaiety Music Hall in Edinburgh where it held its first meetings (although the title was also probably intended to reflect the joy

---

[68] Ibid., p94.
[69] Ibid., p91.
[70] Ibid.
[71] Ibid.
[72] Ibid., p90.

of faith in the experience of this young, rising generation of evangelists). The first members of the group were mostly ministers and New College students. Among the latter were D.M. Ross (later Smith's brother-in-law) and Robert Barbour, whose acquaintance was important to Smith himself in subsequent years. Smith appraises the group thus: "I do not think that there can be anywhere a group of friends who have more constantly shared each other's aspirations, or who have more benefitted by each other's criticisms".[73] Lilian Smith's memoir suggests that the club became an annual gathering of former New College students determined "to meet, once a year for friendly intercourse and discussion".[74] Indeed, in later years the club was to discuss such matters as Irish Home Rule and other political issues.[75] Smith also supported Drummond's evangelistic meetings. These were patterned on the Moody style of mass gathering, with Drummond himself assuming the lead role of evangelist; "when he spoke," says Smith, "the hall was full, and at the after-meetings there were groups of inquirers".[76]

There was, however, one point on which Smith differed notably from Moody and from the traditional Free Church orthodoxy. Moody, Smith alleged, had "a narrow and unscriptural theory of inspiration".[77] It is difficult to know at what point Smith developed this view; was he aware of it as he listened to Moody preach, or is it a later development? It is given expression in the biography of Drummond, written almost a generation later, and arguably, it is this new view of inspiration that informs Smith's critical studies at the turn of the century.

Kenneth Ross, in his study of the origins of the Free Church case 1900-1904, links Smith's developing reformulation of the idea of biblical inspiration directly to the Moody campaign. Ross quotes from Smith's *The Modern Preaching of the Old Testament* (1902) and then says:

> Parts, at least, of the old orthodoxy were regarded by the New Evangelists as hostile and alien elements which they were called to uproot ... Christ himself they claimed as the first great Critic and they felt it was no coincidence that their movement had originated around the time of the remarkable work of the Holy Spirit which followed the Moody and Sankey mission of 1873-5. When they turned their guns on the old orthodoxy, it was holy warfare in which they were engaged.[78]

---

[73] Ibid., p108.
[74] LAS, p45.
[75] *The Life of Henry Drummond*, p264.
[76] Ibid., p107.
[77] *The Life of Henry Drummond*, p92.
[78] K.R. Ross, *Church and Creed in Scotland: The Free Church Case 1900-1904 and its origins* (Edinburgh, 1988) pp169-170.

This is perhaps to overstate the case. Smith and others did not set out consciously to engage in a wholesale overturning of traditional orthodoxy. But it is true that new views of the Bible which were current, coupled with the novel aspects of the American evangelism, gave rise to views of the inspiration of the Scriptures which could not be readily harmonised with traditional Free Church doctrine. The irony was that as far as biblical inspiration was concerned, Moody was nearer to that traditional doctrine than Smith himself.

If he was aware of this fact, Moody himself had no interest in making anything of it. Mark Toone concludes that "though Moody had little use for the products of more liberal scholarship, he handled these problems as he did so many other potential areas of tension. He ignored them".[79] Or, if he did not ignore them he at least played them down. Many years later, when Smith visited Yale in 1899, he and Moody shared the same platform. Moody, apparently, was asked how he could share the platform with Smith when they differed so radically in their beliefs in inspiration. "Perhaps," he answered, "in God's sight we are not so far apart as we appear to be to man".[80]

The Moody and Sankey campaign occurred at a formative period of Smith's development, as he was pursuing his undergraduate Arts course. It was a movement with which, for the most part, he could identify; and along with others in the Free Church, he saw no variance between Moody's preaching and that of the Church to which he belonged. There were elements common to both which formed the core of the Evangel. Yet there was a whole new mood and ethos for change. Smith emerged from the experience of American evangelism keen to enter the Divinity Hall, where he would have his views of inspiration finely honed.

Life in New College

Smith graduated from the University of Edinburgh with an Arts degree in 1875, having studied, among other things, Greek, Latin, English Literature, Philosophy and Political Economy. His Divinity training then took him to New College, where he spent the next four years preparing for the ministry.

New College was built between 1846 and 1850 as the Divinity Hall of the new Free Church of Scotland. Its first faculty included Thomas Chalmers, whose vision for New College was that it would be "a free university for Scotland, championing the principles of spiritual independence, evangelical religion and the democratic intellect".[81] The faculty in Smith's day included George Smeaton as Professor of New Testament Exegesis, Robert Rainy as

---

[79] Toone, "Evangelicalism in Transition", p117.
[80] Recounted in *Two Centuries of Christian Activity at Yale*, eds. J.B. Reynolds, S.H. Fisher, H.B. Wright (New York, 1901) p111, footnote 1.
[81] S.J. Brown "The Disruption and the Dream: The Making of New College 1843-1861" in D.F. Wright and G.D. Badcock (eds.), *Disruption to Diversity: Edinburgh Divinity 1846-1996* (Edinburgh, 1996) p36.

The Making of a Biblical Scholar 27

Professor of Ecclesiastical History, James MacGregor as Professor of Divinity and Alexander Duff as Professor of Missions. The man who made the greatest mark on George Adam Smith was undoubtedly Andrew Bruce Davidson, who taught Hebrew at New College for over forty years, from 1858 to1902.

A.B. Davidson (1831-1902) was a native of Ellon, Aberdeenshire. His early teaching career was in the Free Church School there, where he taught from 1849 to 1852 after graduating from the University of Aberdeen. He was a student at New College between 1852 and 1856; thereafter a two-year probationary year was spent without charge and after it Davidson embarked on his life's work as a teacher of Old Testament.

Davidson himself owed a great deal to the German critic Heinrich G.A. Ewald, with whom he studied in Göttingen. In his centenary appraisal, T. Witton Davies said of Ewald that

> his interest [lay] not so much in questions of introduction, authorship, date, and the like, as in the subject-matter to be expounded: the times, the prophetic message, what it meant, and what it means... in the class Ewald applied the teaching of the ancient prophets to his own time.[82]

This may have been due as much to Ewald's interest in German politics as to his acumen in the study of Hebrew, and on at least one point (the dating of the law) Ewald rejected the theories of de Wette and Wellhausen, and was regarded by the latter as a "bar to progress".[83] Nevertheless, according to Davidson's biographer, "Göttingen left an indelible stamp on Davidson's mind".[84] In Germany, Davidson was exposed first hand to the insights and advances of Higher Criticism, and these he disseminated cautiously but effectively in his New College classroom.

Smith regarded Davidson as a pioneer in Scotland in the teaching of Higher Critical views of the Bible. Presenting a portrait of Davidson (by Sir George Reid, President of the Royal Scottish Academy, painted when its subject was 66, in 1897), Smith commented that

---

[82] T. Witton Davies, *Heinrich Ewald: Orientalist and Theologian 1803-1903: A Centenary Appreciation* (London, 1903) p73. Interestingly, Davies goes on to compare George Adam Smith's commentaries on Isaiah with Ewald's work on the prophets, and says that Smith too brought the message of the prophets alive for his own times.

[83] This was Wellhausen's view of Ewald who rejected the idea that the Pentateuch was a late collection of documents, dating from the Babylonian exile. For citation and discussion see J.C. O'Neill, *The Bible's Authority: A Portrait Gallery of Thinkers from Lessing to Bultmann* (Edinburgh, 1991), pp144-145.

[84] J. Strahan, *Andrew Bruce Davidson, DD, LLD, DLitt* (London, 1917) p67. Strahan says that "I have the idea that if there were any two men who influenced Davidson they were Ewald abroad and Candlish at home" (p68).

it was to Professor Davidson more than to any other individual that we owed the revival of Semitic studies which has distinguished our generation, and which has been so fruitful in results, not only in the department of the Old Testament, but in the whole temper and tendency of theology in our day.[85]

When Smith enrolled in New College in 1875, Davidson was at the zenith of his career, having published a Commentary on Job, and the first edition of his Hebrew grammar, the 27th edition of which is now in print. Smith has left us a first-hand account of what it was like to sit under Davidson as a teacher. He reckoned that by 1870, Davidson's reputation was at its peak,[86] and that "The Church owned, in him, her greatest teacher".[87] To enter Davidson's classroom was, Smith reckoned, "to feel oneself on a floor of absolute security ... We were in the care not only of a very keen intellect, but of one which was thoroughly master of its subject".[88]

In the teaching of exegesis and theology, Smith describes Davidson as "one man against an ancient and an honoured system",[89] who, by the sheer force of his intellect and charm of his personality carried his students beyond entrenched and dogmatic views of prophecy into the new regions mapped out by critical thinking. Smith acknowledges a difficulty in stating categorically the extent to which Davidson embraced all the new theories of the time; it is possible that the teaching of Robertson Smith, his most famous student, overtook Davidson and forced him to come to an opinion on questions of criticism in which he had little interest himself. "What is doubtful," says Smith, "is the date of Davidson's approach to the new views, as well as the extent of his adherence to them, and the degree to which he was drawn towards such

---

[85] Quoted in Strahan, p169. It is, perhaps, worth noting that Higher Critical views of Scripture had already appeared in Britain during the ferment of the nineteenth century, such as in the works of William Van Mildert in 1814 and Frederic William Farrar in 1855. The publication of *Essays and Reviews* in 1860, by a group of Anglican scholars, is generally seen "as firing the opening salvo in the final assault upon the traditional concept of Scripture" (Nigel M. de S. Cameron, *Biblical Higher Criticism and the Defense of Infallibilism in Nineteenth Century Britain* [New York, 1987] p57). As far as Scottish biblical criticism is concerned, Davidson is correctly assessed as one who "introduced advances in higher criticism to his New College students...." under whose influence "New College increasingly opened up to continental and English scholarship, embracing new theological perspectives while at the same time preserving the distinctively Scottish biblical emphasis and common-sense tradition" (Brown, "The Disruption and the Dream", p50).

[86] Smith's assessment of Davidson's work and career, containing much of a personal and reminiscent character, is preserved in three successive articles contributed to *The Union Magazine* during the three months of March-May 1902.

[87] G.A. Smith, "Professor A.B. Davidson - I", *The Union Magazine* (March 1902) p111.

[88] Ibid., p162.

[89] Ibid., p205.

The Making of a Biblical Scholar 29

adherence by the swifter convictions of his pupil".[90] Smith himself believed that for Davidson, the study of the Old Testament is centred on the record of religious experience:

> ...it was the religious experience of the individual, and, especially in doubt and in failure, the assertion of the personal consciousness, whether against dogma, or fate, or deity, which most attracted Davidson and excited his powers to their highest pitch.[91]

This led to an emphasis upon the reading of the prophets in their own time and historical context. The older, uncritical view of prophecy in the Church was that the prophetic utterances were vaguely connected with the "illimitable futures"[92] into which the prophets spoke. Davidson, however, "created the prophet's world out of the prophet's soul".[93] Smith recalls a moment of magic in Davidson's classroom:

> The next item ... we got from our Master was the gift of historical vision. The prophets whom we studied with him had been to us all but figures speaking in vacancy ... He changed all that. He waved his wand, and their world rose about them. He waved his wand - I use the words of choice. It was a magical change. By no purple painting did he kindle our imagination. One morning - I at least date from that day my awakening to the reality of the prophets - he said: "The prophet always spoke first to his own time". They had "times" then![94]

There were clear traces of Ewald here, in Davidson's contemporisation of biblical prophecy. But as Smith noted, "... even from Ewald we always came back to our master".[95]

Smith's respect for Davidson was obviously reciprocated. Davidson considered Smith one of his most distinguished students, and perhaps this contributed to consideration of Smith as a temporary replacement for Robertson Smith in Aberdeen. When asked to supply a reference for George Adam Smith, for the purposes of Smith's applying for a Hibbert Scholarship in 1878 to allow him to study and travel abroad, Davidson wrote:

> Mr George Adam Smith is the son of a gentleman who has distinguished himself in literature both in India and at home. He himself has clearly shown

---

[90] "Davidson – II", p161.
[91] "Davidson – I", p110. There are many echoes of this point in Smith himself.
[92] "Davidson – II", p162.
[93] Ibid.
[94] Ibid.
[95] Ibid.

literary abilities of a decided kind. He has had a successful career as a student both at the University and the New College, Edinburgh. At the latter he has devoted himself with great zeal and much success to the study of Hebrew and the Religion of the Old Testament.[96]

Under Davidson, therefore, Smith developed a strong interest in the study of the Old Testament from a critical (that is, an ethical and religious) point of view. Encouraged by his mentor and tutor, Smith studied abroad for two summers; these trips were of immense significance in shaping his attitudes to the Old Testament; in the summer of 1876 he went to Tübingen, and in the summer of 1878 to Leipzig.[97]

Smith studied in Tübingen from 21 April to 6 August 1876, and he maintained regular contact with home by letter. On the way out he stopped at Brussels. There he experienced a Roman Catholic service for the first time:

> I tumbled into one of the cathedrals where I saw services and a grand procession, but the incense sickened me ... It was the first Roman Catholic service I had ever seen, and I was astonished, yes perfectly astonished, to see so many people rich and poor, old and young, paying such devout attention to such mummeries. The procession was one to the tomb (imagined) of Christ and there were above a hundred intelligent looking men ... Then some more priests - looking if possible more stupid and idiotic than their predecessors and displaying if possible even less interest than these did on what was going on.[98]

The ritual was heightened on account of it being Good Friday, and clearly the high ceremony of the cathedral did not appeal much to him. Perhaps the fault lay less in the ritual and more in the apathy Smith detected in the clergy, as a subsequent visit to a church service shows:

> I saw ... the communion administered - but all was ... nonsense - bowing and crossing oneself and kneeling and opening and shutting little doors and folding and unfolding and refolding of cloths - and all the while yawning; I wonder what the priests think they are doing when they go out so.[99]

---

[96] "Testimonial from A.B. Davidson", NLS Acc 9446 No 12. The application was unsuccesful.

[97] There is a discrepancy over the chronology of these visits in the published memoirs. Prof. S. A. Cook says that "Summer semesters were spent at Tübingen (1876) and Leipzig (1878)" (p327), while Lilian Smith says that "the first course was at Leipzig and the following year he went to Tübingen" (p16). Smith's correspondence confirms Cook's dating, which Lilian Smith does homologate later in her biography (p195).

[98] GAS to George Smith, 14 April 1876, NLS Acc 9446 No 13.

[99] GAS to George Smith, 16 April 1876, NLS Acc 9446 No 13.

The Making of a Biblical Scholar 31

At Tübingen Smith came in contact with other British students with whom he found lodgings. One of these was W.R. Sorley, who was later to become his brother-in-law. By May he was settled into the way of German lecturing and German classes. He studied Genesis with Professor Diestel, "a clear and vigorous speaker ... he seems very orthodox".[100] While listening to Diestel helped improve his German vocabulary, Smith found it frustrating that "I cannot make out what his theory of the authorship is; he has only given us as yet a history of the different opinions...".[101] Under Professor Roth he studied the History of Religions, a subject for the study of which Tübingen enjoyed an international reputation. This approach to Christianity viewed the development of Christian ideas in the general context of religious development in antiquity, quite apart from a distinctive Christian theology. Smith commended to his father Roth's view, expressed in his lectures on Buddhism, that "the only hope for India ... was to be found in Christianity".[102] This was confirmation of views which had inspired George Smith in his work in India.

The conduct of the students he found oppressively quiet - "no applause, no hissing, no scraping of any kind".[103] On the whole, however, he could write about his time in Tübingen

> I like the life here, except that I am parted from you all. However when I feel lonely which I generally do ... I have recourse to my Bible and the Album which drives if not the homesickness at least the loneliness away. But I enjoy the rest of the time pretty well. One thing for which I prefer it to Edinburgh is the total absence of all meetings and engagements of any sort. One's time is entirely one's own.[104]

Smith partly financed his studies in Germany by teaching English to a Bavarian lad. The opportunity for research under some of the finest continental theologians was greatly appreciated by Smith, who in turn commended it to others. The following year, for example, Donald Matheson, a fellow student, could write to Smith and to "all you old Tübingers for sounding the praises of Alma stepmater so loudly and long as to induce me to come here...."[105]

When the opportunity for a further continental study trip presented itself two years later, Smith seized the moment and sailed for Leipzig in the summer of 1878. Despite being plagued with a boil on his hip, Smith quickly settled down

---

[100] GAS to Janet Smith, 26 May 1876, NLS Acc 9446 No 13.
[101] GAS to George Smith, 29 May 1876, NLS Acc 9446 No 13.
[102] GAS to George Smith, no date, NLS Acc 9446 No 13.
[103] GAS to George Smith, 29 May 1876, NLS Acc 9446 No 13.
[104] Ibid.
[105] Donald Matheson to GAS, 15 May 1877, NLS Acc 9446 No 14.

to study in a place which he described as "the capital of Lutheranism and the centre of all that is best in German theology".[106]

Despite some hints in his correspondence that he preferred Tübingen to Leipzig,[107], he heard a variety of distinguished scholars during this second continental study trip. Among these was Friedrich Delitzsch, "one of the lions of the University".[108] Smith would engage with the views of Delitzsch later, in his commentary on Isaiah. Delitzsch appealed to Smith not least because of his willingness to meet socially with English-speaking students, usually in a hotel or restaurant, for discussion of various aspects of Old Testament exegesis. Smith learned much from such interaction. Some of his highest praise, however, was reserved for Adolf Harnack:

> I consider I have made a discovery, at least as far as foreigners are concerned, in the youngest professor the theological faculty contains, a man on the student's side of thirty and yet of enormous learning ... a splendid *nous* for understanding and explaining history, which I never met with so fully developed in any of my professors before except Rainy and Davidson. Harnack, for that is his name, has been lecturing this summer on symbolism and I have learnt whole volumes of church history...[109]

Smith was singularly fortunate in the experience, for this was Harnack's final year at Leipzig (he was appointed to a full chair in the University of Giessen the following year). More a historian of theology than an exegete, Harnack emphasised a developmental theory of religion, in which "whatever happened in history is relative ... critical biblical study has to sort out all that is less than rational, less than human, less than divine".[110] Smith describes him as "the coming man here - note his name".[111]

Smith's debt to German teachers and German theology was acknowledged often, perhaps most poignantly many years later in his lectures in America during the First World War. In speaking of the German threat during the Great War, he said with a hint of sadness, "not a few of us had grateful memories of German schools and teachers".[112] In his work on the German critical scholars, Professor J.C. O'Neill summarises the continental approach to the Bible thus:

---

[106] GAS to [Alexander] Whyte, no date (probably July 1878), NLS Acc 9446 No 15.

[107] For example, he writes to his aunts: "I frankly say I do not enjoy this as much as Tübingen..." (no date, NLS Acc 9446 No 13), and to Alexander Whyte "I have not enjoyed myself so much as I did at Tübingen, for here University life is not so exclusively German...." (no date, NLS Acc 9446 No 13).

[108] To Alexander Whyte, ibid.

[109] Ibid.

[110] H.M. Rumscheidt "Adolf von Harnack" in D.K. McKim (ed.) *Historical Handbook of Major Biblical Interpreters* (Leicester, 1998) p492.

[111] To Alexander Whyte, ibid.

[112] G.A. Smith, *Our Common Conscience* (London, 1918) p126.

The Making of a Biblical Scholar 33

"The Bible, instead of being a book giving information about God and containing his promises, was seen as the record of how humanity came to understand itself and history".[113] This is precisely how Smith was to express his concept of the Old Testament, showing the influence of the German schools on his thinking; in his view, the Old Testament is

> not a set of dogmas, nor a philosophy, nor a vision; but a history, the record of a providence, the testimony of experience, the utterances called forth by historical occasions from a life conscious of the purpose for which God has called it and set it apart through the ages.[114]

The corollary of this is that the Old Testament required to be approached critically, in order that the historical impulse could be traced. Although Smith regards the Old Testament as containing and reflecting a history, his position echoes the German assumption that "the Old Testament was unreliable as history, and could be used only if it was radically reinterpreted".[115] While Smith acknowledged that such criticism, when conducted "in a purely empirical spirit and without loyalty to Christ", had "shaken the belief of some in the fundamentals of religion, distracted others from the zealous service of God, and benumbed the preaching of Christ's Gospel,"[116] it was equally true that the use of historical and textual criticism (as practised by Christ himself) was "not merely scholastic or historical, but thoroughly evangelical".[117] That was a point hotly to be contested in succeeding years. One correspondent, writing to Smith in Germany, enquired of him towards the close of his study there: "Do you expect to be orthodox enough for the Free Church when you come home?"[118] That, in a sense, was the theological nub of the issues which faced the Free Church of Scotland increasingly in subsequent years, and in which Smith would play an important role.

Home Mission Work

But Smith's time in New College also kindled other interests, not least as a result of the opportunities afforded there for practical Christian work. Lilian Smith tantalises her readers with the briefest glimpse of this, stating that "during his course at the New College, George had been active in Home Mission work, from which he had gained valuable experience".[119] She goes on

---

[113] O'Neill, *The Bible's Authority,* p8.
[114] *Our Common Conscience,* p325.
[115] G. Bray, *Biblical Interpretation Past and Present* (Leicester, 1996) p298.
[116] G.A. Smith, *Modern Criticism and the Preaching of the Old Testament* (London, 1902) p24.
[117] Ibid., p28.
[118] Sophie Bryant to GAS, July 14 1878, NLS Acc 9446 No 12.
[119] LAS, p17.

to recount that on one occasion Smith doffed his hat by a close on Edinburgh's High Street, because, as he put it, "It's there I did my first mission work and met some of the poorest but the bravest people I have known, and learned more from them than they could have learned from me".[120]

Edinburgh in the 1870s had its share of the problems caused by nineteenth-century urbanisation. Not only were there social problems associated with the rapid growth of cities, such as squalor, sickness and widespread poverty; it was also evident that "such laws as mid-Victorian Westminster did make to help solve problems of urban squalor were often framed in a manner inappropriate for Scotland".[121] If an English-dominated Parliament, however, was slow to address problems in urban Scotland, the Free Church was not. As part of this engagement, the 1874 Free Church Assembly provided for students to be employed in home mission work attached to city congregations. Smith's period of home mission work was based at the New North Free Church in Edinburgh over the winter of 1878. The minister, Robert G. Balfour, had written to Smith in October 1878, while Smith was studying at Leipzig, informing him that the congregation's Mission Committee was "unanimous in wishing you rather than any other".[122]

Smith's diaries (of which few survive) give a flavour of the student missionary's activities. In December 1878 he visited a Miss Hogg, who "Half-promised to come to meeting. But I could not get what I wanted from her".[123] The following day he visited Miss Campbell, and records that he "Talked with her, read a chapter and prayed".[124] Not that it was all easy. He records on 31 December, while distributing leaflets, that he "met with a rebuff in top flat of 35 Bristo Street. Offered them a bill. He said there was no occasion for it there and gave me it back. I foolishly let it fall, so he crumpled it up and shied [?] it in my face, saying something about impertinence...."[125]

Smith's later interest in social wellbeing and the social gospel grew largely out of his firsthand experience of meeting people in their homes and developing a relationship with them. These lessons he was to carry with him into his Aberdeen ministry, and into his Glasgow Professoriate. The seeds of a genuine social concern were thus sown in these New College days.

Egypt and Palestine

At the conclusion of his New College studies, Smith received an invitation from a friend of his father, Dr Lansing, a missionary with the United Presbyterian Church of America, to accompany him on a trip to Cairo. The

---

[120] Ibid.
[121] Smout, *Century*, p42.
[122] Robert G. Balfour to George Adam Smith, NLS Acc 9446 No 312.
[123] "Ancient Days" - Visiting book of George Adam Smith, NLS Acc 9446 No 314.
[124] Ibid.
[125] Ibid

The Making of a Biblical Scholar

purpose of the trip was to help him with some mission work there over the winter of 1879-1880. A difficult sea-journey in December 1879 took him to Lisbon and Algiers before arriving at Cairo at the end of the month. For Smith, every stop was both an adventure and an education, and again his letters home are filled with lengthy descriptive prose which brought the images of these cities to life for his family. Of Algiers he wrote:

> What a strange sight ... The squares are filled with palms, and among the crowd of strolling Frenchmen, who have brought over a sober edition of Paris life, move any number of tall broad-shouldered Arabs in their long white robes ... How like ghosts they look in the shade of the palms. I suppose Algiers is what Cairo will turn out to be when I see it - a meeting place of East and West.[126]

One of the most significant - and little known - events of this trip occurred with the arrival of the ship, the SS Canara, at Port Said. Smith recounts the events to his mother:

> What was my surprise to see Robertson Smith step on board the *Canara* and take possession of the bunk I had just vacated. He was on his way to Jedda, and thence to Aden to go to the interior of Arabia ... I had time to have a chat with him ...[127]

This chance meeting between George Adam Smith and the famous Old Testament scholar William Robertson Smith may well have been the first time the two met for any length of time. The significance of the meeting, far away from ecclesiastical and theological controversies in Scotland, cannot be overlooked, for it offered a unique opportunity to discuss events in which their lives were both involved. Robertson Smith was drawing near the close of his professorial career in Aberdeen, and George Adam Smith had only recently graduated from New College in Edinburgh. The likelihood of their having met personally before this point is extremely remote.

William Robertson Smith (1846-1894) had been appointed, at the age of 23, to the Chair of Hebrew at the Free Church College in Aberdeen. Influenced both by A.B. Davidson and by German theologians, Robertson Smith soon after his appointment to Aberdeen became a propagator of German critical views of Scripture. These came to public notice in 1875, with the publication of his article "Bible". This article led to a five-year campaign against him for unorthodox views, which eventually led to his dismissal from his post in 1881.

---

[126] GAS to parents, Algiers December 1879, NLS Acc 9446 No 16.
[127] GAS to mother, Cairo, 21 December 1879, NLS Acc 9446 No 16.

His subsequent career was spent at Cambridge as Professor of Arabic. W.R. Smith died tragically young at the age of 47.[128]

Lilian Adam Smith's memoir gives the impression that the first meeting between the two Smiths of Old Testament scholarship took place when George Adam Smith moved to Aberdeen to conduct Robertson Smith's classes. The meeting in Port Said is little known. Yet it must have been significant. George Adam Smith wrote home:

> He spoke freely of his case, but I had better not repeat all he said. He seems to anticipate deposition in May - at least he feels certain he won't stand another delay in the case. He was wild at Rainy (don't tell any one) as a leader, and seemed to think our Kirk in a bad way. He says he banishes all thoughts of his case as it would kill him. He seemed anxious for news, but I could tell him nothing. He said it would be a great mistake for anyone who ... believed as he does ... to leave the church if he is deposed. I agree with him.[129]

In the event, the deposition came about a year later, in 1881. However, Smith's correspondence shows the increasing alienation which Robertson Smith was feeling towards leaders of the Church like Robert Rainy, from whom he might have expected support. One cannot help feeling that George Adam Smith's correspondence rings true. Robertson Smith was ploughing a lonely furrow, and the Free Church leadership was increasingly distanced from him. Robertson Smith's desire that those who sympathised with him (George Adam Smith describes them as "we of the right-minded sort at home"[130]) should remain in the Church, probably did more to secure the right for critical scholarship within the Free Church Colleges than anyone realised.

William Robertson Smith's deposition is almost universally portrayed by modern authors as a thoroughly distasteful episode in late nineteenth century church history. Criticism of the Church's action is evident in Alec Cheyne, who bemoans the fact that "despite all his learning and his forensic brilliance, Smith was removed from his Chair as unworthy to be trusted with the training of

---

[128] Recent studies of William Robertson Smith include R.Riesen, "Faith and Criticism in Post-Disruption Scotland, with particular reference to A.B. Davidson, W.R. Smith and G.A. Smith", PhD, Edinburgh 1981 (particularly chapter 3); A.L. Drummond and J. Bulloch, *The Church in Late Victorian Scotland 1874-1900* (Edinburgh, 1979) chapter 2; W. Johnstone (ed), *William Robertson Smith: Essays in Reassessment* (Sheffield, 1995); J. Rogerson, *The Bible and Criticism in Victorian Britain: Profiles of F.D. Maurice and William Robertson Smith*, (Sheffield, 1995); and J.A. Dearman's entry on Smith in McKim (ed), *Historical Handbook* pp359-363. The standard biography remains that of J.S. Black and G. Crystal, *The Life of William Robertson Smith* (London, 1912).

[129] GAS to mother from Cairo, 21 December 1879, NLS Acc 9446 No 16.

[130] Ibid.

The Making of a Biblical Scholar 37

candidates for the Free Church ministry.[131] It is present in Robert Carroll, who speaks of Robertson Smith's "crucifixion".[132] It is also present in Michael Fry, who speaks of Robertson Smith's prosecution as being "forced by a Highland critique of fanatical Calvinists, who if anything aroused distaste among Scots at large".[133] Fry goes on to state that Robertson Smith's experience did not limit his influence.

Such caricatures are born out of prejudice, not of historical research. There is evidence that Robertson Smith's abrupt manner and fiery temper may have had as much to do with his treatment as anything. But there is also the unmistakeable fact that that his views were at variance with the doctrinal position to which his Church was committed. And there is not the inconsiderable fact that a professorship at Cambridge was hardly evidence of crucifixion or academic exile. The Church simply had no option, if she were to remain to her constitution, but to move towards deposition; as a consequence, the recalcitrant Professor rather landed on his feet. It was left to a subsequent generation of scholars to demonstrate how the new learning might be incorporated into the life of the Church.

As George Adam Smith recollected, looking back on the encounter with Robertson Smith in Egypt, "He seemed buried under his pith-helmet...but I wish my hat enclosed what that helmet does".[134] His respect for the Professor was great, and his meeting with him was one of the most important experiences of his own life, confirming in his mind the necessity of remaining in the Free Church in order to continue the work of critical scholarship.

George Adam Smith continued his visit to Egypt, remaining there for most of the Spring. Part of the time was used to learn Arabic, under the tutorship of Socrates Spiro. Smith found his first exposure to Oriental life and culture fascinating. He wrote to his aunts:

> To live in Cairo is to live in a chop sea between two cross tides. The West and East meet here with no little confusion ... People told me I should be disappointed with the East. I wasn't, only because I came here with not a single imagination about it. I had read nothing - or next to nothing, and Oriental life has always lain outside my conceptions.[135]

---

[131] A.C. Cheyne, *Studies in Scottish Church History* (Edinburgh 1999), p133.
[132] Writing in *William Robertson Smith: Essays in Reassessment*, p148 n.1.
[133] M. Fry, *The Scottish Empire* (Edinburgh 2001), p247. Virtually the same language appears in S. Lamont *When Scotland Ruled the World: The Story of the Golden Age of Genius, Creativity and Exploration* (London 2001), p160, with the additional suggestion that "History has vindicated him against his accusers."
[134] Ibid.
[135] GAS to aunts from Cairo, 30 December 1879, NLS Acc 9446 No 16.

The sights of Egypt - broken down buildings left in a heap of rubble in the streets, large and silent mosques, the howling of a crowd of people forming a funeral cortege, the sun setting behind the pyramids (with a transformation of landscape in glorious colour which, Smith says, "I have only seen equalled on our islands off Ross-shire and in Skye"[136]) - all these Smith carefully noted and encapsulated in the evocative prose style which characterises his letters. The Muslims he pitied; sensing in the silence of the mosques the Muslim apprehension of God, Smith concluded that "they cannot pray except they look to Mecca, and they look to Mecca not because they find God there, but a sinful man like themselves".[137]

Although in April 1880 Smith could write to his parents of leaving Cairo with very great regret at parting not only from the place but also from "all the kind friends there, both natives and Americans",[138] the greater prize lay ahead. From Egypt Smith made his first visit to Palestine. It was a journey Smith was initially reluctant to make, for reasons which he does not express fully; a short postcard sent to his father in February 1880 says:

> do you know I have a feeling against visiting Palestine?...Whatever I finally resolve upon, you will agree with me that it is foolish to cut short opportunities that I may never have again.[139]

Thankfully Smith did not succumb to his feelings, and in Palestine he met with and spoke to many natives, and gained a deep understanding of Palestinian life and culture. The land, according to his wife's memoir

> unfolded itself to him in all its many aspects. His eyes were opened to see the reasons and the meanings of words and events which, until then, he had only partly understood, and there is no doubt that the idea of writing a book upon the country was born in his mind from that first solitary journey.[140]

Whether or not the idea of a publication was conceived at this time, Smith was to state in the preface to the first edition of the *Historical Geography of the Holy Land*, that "personal acquaintance with the land" was a necessary feature of the study of geographical and historical context.

The intrusion of foreign and non-Oriental nationals into Palestine filled Smith with loathing, however. The bazaars he described as "horrible places,

---

[136] Ibid.
[137] Ibid.
[138] GAS to mother from Middle East, 11 April 1880, New College Library Special Collections, MSS.SMI 1.4.1.
[139] GAS's postcard to his father from Thebes, 16th February 1880, NLS Acc 9446 No 16.
[140] LAS, p18.

full of filthy flea-infested crowds. They are not Oriental. German watchmakers and carpenters, Polish shoe-makers, Spanish merchants ... Russian tea-sellers ... Americans in all sorts of dresses..."[141] He would also inform his readership that

> In the Spring of 1880 I made a journey through Judea, Samaria, Esdraelon and Galilee; that was before the great changes which have been produced on many of the most sacred landscapes by European colonists, and by the rivalry in building between the Greek and Latin churches.[142]

A sense of disquiet pervades Smith's correspondence for the trip. Of the environs of Jerusalem and the supposed site of the crucifixion, where guides sought to point out the hole in which Christ's cross was placed, he writes:

> it is all saddening - the work done for mankind was so great, and the results are so very much the other way from that which the Maker intended.[143]

There were, however, memorable moments, such as bathing in the Dead Sea ("my arms were aching from the intense efforts required to move through such dense water"[144]) and witnessing the sun rise over Jerusalem:

> I rose yesterday morning at half past four and rushed up the Mount of Olives in the soft warm dawn to see the sun rise over the mountains of Moab on the other side of the Jordan valley ... I enjoyed the sight of the city waking up exceedingly.[145]

George Adam Smith had woken up too, alive now to the fascination of the Holy Land and the various aspects of its life and character. As a student of Biblical theology and a traveller in the Orient he was poised to make a detailed descriptive study of the Holy Land, meeting the three-fold criterion he laid down for such a study:

> personal acquaintance with the land; a study of the exploration, discoveries and decipherments especially of the last twenty years; and the employment of the results of Biblical criticism during the same period.[146]

---

[141] Ibid.
[142] G.A.Smith, *Historical Geography of the Holy Land* (HGHL), preface to the first edition (1894), reprinted in the twenty-second edition, pxi.
[143] GAS to parents, New College Library Special Collections, SMI 1.4.1.
[144] GAS to parents, Monday 19th April, ibid.
[145] Ibid.
[146] HGHL, px.

Assistant at Brechin

For all Smith's enjoyment of the relatively carefree months of 1880, it was a time of personal searching and evaluation as he weighed up various possibilities for his future ministry. He found in his father at this time a confidant and friend with whom he could discuss the work which lay before him. The American mission in Egypt had rekindled in him an interest in foreign missionary work. "Foreign missions", he wrote to his father in March, "have a great attraction for me, an attraction that has grown the more I have seen of missions here".[147] His mother considered it a major obstacle to foreign missions that he disliked teaching; and although the evidence for this evaluation is unclear, he partly agreed.[148] He did not close the door on this possibility, stating to his father "I am willing and indeed must leave the question open to prayer till I return".[149]

A second possibility was that he would return home to minister in a home congregation. In March he was of the opinion that "if I am to be at home I should like to be where there is some work to be done among our home heathen. I hate the prospect of returning to a big congregation".[150] By the following month, however, he had dismissed this option, saying "I hesitate more and more to take full charge anywhere - at home or abroad for a little time yet".[151] The reason for this hesitancy was to be found, strangely perhaps, in his high regard for the ministry, in which, he reckoned, more than in any other profession, delay at the beginning "helps a man immensely in the end".[152]

A third possibility was occasioned by the absence of William Robertson Smith from the Aberdeen College. Smith had discussed the possibility of his working there with John Duns, the Professor of Natural Science at New College, who, he says, "spoke so openly to me of it".[153] That he was not merely interested but wished to work at Aberdeen is clear from his correspondence, which becomes increasingly agitated on the subject. In March, after requesting money from his father for the trip to Palestine, Smith asks: "Do you hear anything about the plans for Smith's Chair next winter? I hope Duns won't forget me. Has he ever spoken of it?"[154] Three weeks later Smith is still absorbed with this matter, and the question to his father becomes rather more direct: "...of course this is strictly private, there is the chance of Robertson Smith's Chair being vacant next winter again and of my appointment to it.

---

[147] GAS to father from Cairo, 15th March 1880, NLS Acc 9446 No 17.
[148] Ibid.
[149] Ibid. But he confides to his mother: "Of course, I would go to no place but India if I went at all" (to mother 17th March 1880, ibid).
[150] Ibid.
[151] GAS to father from Cairo, 7th April 1880, ibid.
[152] Ibid.
[153] Ibid.
[154] GAS to father from Cairo, 20th March 1880, ibid.

The Making of a Biblical Scholar 41

Have you any chance of sounding Duns or Davidson upon the matter without appearing to be pushing me?"[155] Exegetical courses had been conducted in the Free Church College in Aberdeen by Professor Salmond, Professor of Systematic Theology there since 1876 (and Robertson Smith's closest rival for the Chair in 1870), and later Principal. Clearly George Adam Smith had an interest in serving the Church in this capacity; perhaps his travels in the Orient helped to kindle his passion for tutoring in Hebrew language at home.

A fourth possibility, and one which he eventually decided upon, was to take up an assistantship in a congregation on returning home, while still entertaining the hope that he might serve in the Aberdeen College. Two options for ministry in Scottish towns lay before him. The Rev John Laird of Cupar Free Church, had written to Smith's father in January. The congregation had hoped to elect a colleague and successor to Laird, but the election had failed, and they had decided upon an assistant "who may be colleague, if he succeeds well with us. Your Son has been recommended to me... Do you think he would be willing to come here on his return?"[156] This was attractive to Smith, who told his father "I have known several of Mr Laird's assistants and they all declare the desirability of Cupar for a young fellow".[157]

Cupar remained a strong possibility for Smith until he received a letter from the Rev John Fraser of Brechin West Free Church in April (following an informal letter the previous month), "offering me the assistantship if I can begin by the first of June".[158] Smith was swayed both by a letter he received from the Rev Henderson, who had just left the Brechin assistantship to become minister at Insch, and who warmly commended the post; and, more importantly, by the opinion of Robertson Smith who advised him to accept the Brechin assistantship. So it was that the Rev James Fraser reported to his Kirk Session on 13th May that "they had engaged the Rev G.A. Smith for six months, and that he was to enter on his duties on Sabbath the 6th June".[159] Little detail survives of the six-month assistantship in Brechin. That he ministered favourably, however, is demonstrated by the following tribute engrossed in the Kirk Session minutes at the end of his term, which was cut short by the decision of the Commission of Assembly appointing him tutor in Aberdeen:

> The Kirk-Session cannot part with Mr Smith without expressing as they hereby do express, the sense they have and which they know the

---

[155] GAS to father from Cairo, 7th April 1880, ibid.
[156] Rev John Laird to George Smith, 30th January 1880, ibid.
[157] GAS to father from Cairo, 20th March 1880, ibid.
[158] GAS to father from Cairo, 7th April 1880, ibid.
[159] Minutes of the Kirk-Session of Brechin West Free Church 13th May 1880, Scottish Records Office, CH3/623, Volume 1, p518. Unfortunately, Professor S.A. Cook in *Proceedings of the British Academy*, 1942, dates his assistantship wrongly, settling him in Brechin in October 1880 rather than in June of that year.

congregation also have of the very high value of his services during all the time he has been assistant in the congregation. Mr Smith has made himself in the highest degree acceptable both in the pulpit and in his visitation of the sick and aged and it is with very great regret that the Kirk-Session are obliged to accept his resignation in consequence of the important duties that the College Committee have called him to discharge in the Free Church College Aberdeen during the current session.[160]

Even the local newspaper, *The Brechin Advertiser*, saw fit to report Smith's farewell sermon, calling it "an eloquent and impressive discourse", at the close of which

Mr Smith made a short but feeling reference to the circumstance and thanked the congregation, both office-bearers and members, for the kindness he had received during his stay in Brechin.[161]

The Daily Review stated that "Though so short a time in Brechin Mr. Smith has taken a distinguished place there as an able preacher and an accomplished scholar".[162] Short as the assistantship was, it helped carve out the niche Smith was making for himself as a preacher and scholar of note.

Hebrew Tutor

Following the General Assembly of 1877, Robertson Smith had, in the words of his biographers, an "enforced relief from College work".[163] His classes were taken by others from 1877 onwards. The Aberdeen College had been training candidates for the ministry of the Free Church of Scotland since the Disruption; some 70 students had passed through it before a permanent building was opened to house the College in 1850. The first Professor of Hebrew was Marcus Sachs who died in 1869. Robertson Smith had succeeded him the following year, while still a Probationer, and largely on the testimonials of German theologians as well as Scottish teachers. Robertson Smith has rightly been described as the College's "most distinguished scholar" in biblical studies.[164] Whether the entrenched dogmatic Calvinism of the Free Church is the whole reason for his removal is still debatable; it is interesting that the official history of the College comments that "many have felt that by a more

---

[160] Minutes of the Kirk-Session of Brechin West Free Church 28th November 1880, Scottish Records Office, CH3/623, Volume 1, p533. Smith was succeeded as assistant by the Rev R. Barbour.
[161] *The Brechin Advertiser*, 30th November 1880, NLS Acc 9446 No 10.
[162] *The Daily Review*, 6th November 1880, ibid.
[163] Black and Chrystal, *Life of Robertson Smith*, p240.
[164] H.R. Sefton, "Christ's College, Aberdeen", in *Dictionary of Scottish Church History and Theology* (Edinburgh, 1993) p169.

considerate and conciliatory manner he might have gone far to diminish the opposition to his views".[165]

There is an echo of this in Lilian Adam Smith's memoir of her husband, who called on Robertson Smith before taking up tutoring the Hebrew language class. There, Robertson Smith is described as "the fiery little man",[166] who was none too pleased to see the "newly-appointed substitute". Robertson Smith is reputed to have asked, "What would you do if I should refuse to obtemper the decision of the Assembly and insist on taking the class myself?" To which George Adam Smith replied, "Then, I would be proud to go and sit among your students".[167]

As Lilian Smith pointed out, many of the students under Smith's tutelage at this time were not much younger than himself. The duties placed upon him were in Hebrew language, and the number of students was not large. Doubtless Smith used the opportunity to widen his reading and consolidate his studies. The College Committee's Report to the General Assembly of 1881 reflects his dedicated commitment to the work of the College:

> The Committee having to provide for the teaching of Professor Smith's Hebrew classes, appointed for that purpose the Rev George Smith MA, a distinguished student of the New College. He has discharged the duties assigned to him to the entire satisfaction of the Senatus.[168]

Smith remained at the Free Church College in Aberdeen tutoring in Hebrew language for two sessions until the newly formed Queen's Cross Church in Aberdeen sought him as their first pastor. That he had shown his ability to teach Old Testament language and literature is proved from the following quotation taken from the testimonials by his former students to his fitness on being considered for the Hebrew Chair in Glasgow in 1892:

> We found in Mr Smith an enthusiastic teacher, distinguished for wide and intimate knowledge of his subject ... Our early experience of him as a linguist and exegete raised in us expectations of his success which are being abundantly fulfilled in his unique contributions to the expositions of the Old Testament.[169]

---

[165] R.G. Philip, "Chapters from its History: 1855 to 1900" in *The Church College in Aberdeen: Free Church College 1843-1900; United Free Church College 1900-1929* (Aberdeen, 1936) p16.
[166] LAS, p19.
[167] Ibid.
[168] Report of College Committee (Report V) to the Free Church General Assembly of 1881, p3.
[169] "Testimonial from Students at Aberdeen Free Church College, 1880-82 to the Rev George Adam Smith MA", in *The Glasgow Hebrew Chair: Testimonials in favour of the Rev George Adam Smith, M.A., Aberdeen*, NLS, Acc 9446, No 322, p7.

The question arises as to Smith's - and, indeed, the Church's - interests at this point. Why did Smith not wish to remain in an academic post? Conversely, why did the Church not appoint him to the post following Robertson Smith's suspension?

One might surmise that the Free Church had had enough of appointing probationers to College Chairs. As soon as the death of Professor Sachs had been announced, Davidson had given Robertson Smith some Hebrew language classes at New College[170] clearly priming him and paving the way for him to succeed Sachs. Indeed, it was George Adam Smith's assessment that "apart from Davidson's influence and the possibilities which Davidson's teaching unfolded in Hebrew, Smith might have been lost to theology".[171]

The Church did not want, however, to be placed in a similar situation again. Perhaps, therefore, in order to avoid a second Robertson Smith case, the Church's subsequent policy was to appoint to professorial chairs men who had had at least some pastoral experience. This may well be one reason why Smith did not pursue an academic career immediately.

In George Adam Smith's own experience, the hesitancy he had known in Egypt gave way to clarity of vision and certainty of spirit. He had wished to serve as assistant and also to conduct Robertson Smith's classes. But before the General Assembly of 1882 appointed George Cameron of St. John's, Glasgow, an experienced pastor, to fill the now vacant Chair in Aberdeen, George Adam Smith had already decided to take full charge of a congregation in Scotland.

Conclusion

The formative period of George Adam Smith's life laid the foundations for a life of service to the Church in Scotland. Born at a remove from the places where his life work would be prosecuted, Smith grew up within the ethos of the late Victorian Free Church of Scotland, at a time of transition, of new ideas and of new horizons for biblical scholarship. He retained an interest in the East and in travel generally, with an underlying imperialist philosophy. A student in Germany and a traveller to Palestine, with many interests besides his immediate theological ones, Smith was a wanderer and an explorer of the world and its ideas. When, in later years, he would come to make his own contribution to biblical scholarship and theological enquiry it would be on the basis of these formative interests. Through a sequence of formative personal relationships, such as with his father, with Henry Drummond and with William Robertson Smith, as well as in the wider church context in which he worshipped and studied, Smith was preparing for church service, with interest both in pastoral ministry and theological education. It is to his early Aberdeen years as minister-scholar that we now turn.

---

[170] Black and Chrystal, *Life of Robertson Smith*, p115.

[171] G.A. Smith "Professor A.B. Davidson I", *The Union Magazine*, March 1902, p111.

CHAPTER 2

The Pastor: The Early Aberdeen Years (1882-1892)

The need for a new congregation in the west end of Aberdeen, as a response to the mushrooming of the city, had come under consideration by the Presbytery's Church Extension Committee in 1872, but it was five years later, in 1877, that practical steps were taken to this end. In his account of churches in Aberdeen, Alexander Gammie outlines the way matters progressed:

> In the early part of 1877 the Church Extension Committee of the Presbytery had the matter under consideration, and invited an expression of opinion on the part of members of the Free Church resident in the western suburb. In course of time it was reported that a number of gentlemen belonging to the west-end, wishing to take a public spirited interest in the Church's prosperity and progress, had met with the committee and certain well-known friends of the Church. The result, after conferring on the whole situation, was a complete unanimity of opinion that the time had arrived for taking active steps towards the formation of a congregation.[1]

The Disruption of 1843 had seen all fifteen ministers in Aberdeen join the Free Church of Scotland. Callum Brown, in his sociological study of Scottish religion in the nineteenth century, suggests that we must take the secession among the clergy "as a measure of lay secession for which no accurate statistics exist".[2] Clearly, therefore, Aberdeen was characterised by widespread support of the Free Church.

In Aberdeen itself, the shape of the emergent Free Church was to a large extent determined by the kind of men who left the Establishment in 1843. Callum Brown includes among the elders who adhered to the Free Church of Scotland

> an aspiring and socially dynamic breed of commission agents and merchants ... [who] displayed their entrepreneurial vigour and recently acquired wealth

---

[1] A. Gammie, *The Churches of Aberdeen: Historical and Descriptive* (Aberdeen, 1909) p168.
[2] C. Brown, *The Social History of Religion in Scotland* (London, 1987) p39. See also I.R. MacDonald, *Aberdeen and the Highland Church 1785-1900* (Edinburgh, 2000), especially chapter 22, for a discussion on the effects of the Disruption in Aberdeen.

by changing house and business very rapidly, moving westward within the city to new developments at some distance from the older and more staid middle-class streets.³

The corollary of this, as Brown goes on to demonstrate, was that church membership among the working class was low; but the net effect of such "upward mobility"⁴ was that the construction of new places of worship was of practical necessity and also became a realistic possibility.

The Convener of the Presbytery's Church Extension Committee was Professor Stewart D.F. Salmond, who had taught Systematic Theology in the Free Church College in Aberdeen since 1876, and would become its Principal in 1898. Professor Salmond reported to the Presbytery in December 1877 regarding the interest in a new church, and was a leading negotiator in the enterprise. He would also become interim-moderator for the new congregation. The proposal received the backing of the Rev John Laidlaw, who was minister of the Free West Church⁵ and who recognised, according to Gammie, "it would mean that several of the older and larger churches, such as his own, would have to part with a number of their members".⁶ The General Assembly of 1880 sanctioned the application to have a new charge set up in Queen's Cross, provided the congregation would be able to send at least £160 to the Sustentation Fund annually towards supporting a ministry. The Assembly added:

This is a proposed new charge in a west-end suburb of Aberdeen. A church is in course of erection. The population is large and increasing, and there

---

³ Ibid., p151. See also A.A. MacLaren, *Religion and Social Class: The Disruption Years in Aberdeen* (London, 1974).

⁴ Brown uses this phrase in dealing with the social composition of Free Church congregations, which, he argues, tended to rise into the later nineteenth century (Ibid., p152).

⁵ Callum Brown quotes a local comment from Aberdeen at the turn of the century to the effect that "the height of a merchant's ambition in Aberdeen was a house in Crown Street and a seat in the Free West Church" (p151). John Laidlaw was to become Professor of Systematic Theology in New College, Edinburgh, that same year, 1881. Interestingly, in proposing him, Dr Adam of Glasgow ventured the opinion that had the church in previous years appointed men of pastoral experience to their Colleges, "possibly ... they have been rid of a great many of their recent troubles" (PDGAFCS, 25 May 1881, p145), a clear reference to the fact that William Robertson Smith had been appointed Professor with no ministerial experience. Perhaps this explains why George Adam Smith did not continue his academic career without first entering into the ministry.

⁶ Gammie, *Churches of Aberdeen*, p167.

seems no reason to doubt that a large and self-supporting congregation will soon be formed.[7]

The area chosen was "the triangular piece of ground lying west of Albyn Terrace, and forming the junction at Queen's Cross of Albyn Place and Carden Place",[8] while the design of the building was won in an open competition by John Bridgeford Pirie. Pirie was a young man of 26, who provided "for a handsome edifice in granite at a cost of about £6000, exclusive of £3000 for site and extras".[9] By the late nineteenth century, Aberdeen's granite industry had become world-famous. Historian Heather Lyall suggests that "the reconstruction of Marischal College (1891-1904) was probably the zenith of the granite industry's achievements";[10] which would imply that the construction of Queen's Cross Free Church occurred at a point close to the peak of the construction industry's achievements in the city. The same mason who worked on Marischal College, John Morgan, was also contracted to build the new Church; when the congregation was consolidated he became a founder member. The new building was opened for public worship on 18 April 1881.

Later that year the congregation held meetings with a view to calling their first minister. Professor Salmond reported to the Presbytery on 6 December 1881 that

> The congregation had elected by 67 to 3 Mr George Adam Smith, MA, Preacher of the Gospel, and at present Hebrew Tutor in the Free Church College Aberdeen as their Pastor, and requesting the Presbytery to take the necessary steps for moderating in a Call to Mr Smith with all convenient speed...[11]

The Call, which was eventually signed by 107 members and 92 adherents,[12] was placed in Smith's hands by the Presbytery on 10 January 1882, and was accepted. Alexander Gammie's account of Queen's Cross confirms that Smith had preached there several times as a probationer,[13] and one wonders to what extent Professor Salmond, as a common link between the College where Smith was engaged as temporary tutor and the congregation which was eventually to

---

[7] PDGAFCS, 1 June 1880, p304.
[8] Ibid.
[9] Ibid.
[10] H.R. Lyall, *Vanishing Aberdeen* (Aberdeen, 1989) p73.
[11] Record of the Free Presbytery of Aberdeen, 6 December 1881, Scottish Record Office CH3/2, Volume 4, p119.
[12] In the Scottish Presbyterian tradition, it is the right of the communicant members (i.e. baptised members who also receive communion) of a congregation to call a minister. But those who belong to the congregation without being communicant members – adherents – concur in the call of the members.
[13] Gammie, *Churches of Aberdeen*, p168.

call him, was the catalyst which brought the two together. After Smith had accepted the call, the Presbytery then prescribed ordination trials – a final examination prior to ordination. These included a homily on the miracles of Elijah and Elisha, a lecture on Psalm 91, a popular sermon on Ephesians 1:7 and a thesis "on the points of difference between the Lutheran and Reformed doctrines of the Person of Christ".[14] Smith's ordination trials were sustained by the Presbytery on 7 February 1882, and he was ordained to the ministry on 20 April that year. The Rev R.G. Balfour introduced him to the congregation the following Sunday (23 April), and Smith preached his first sermon as the new minister that evening. "That," his wife was to write some sixty years later, "was the beginning of a ten years' ministry that is spoken of with admiration and gratitude even to this day".[15]

Consolidating the Ministry

As the first minister of a new charge, Smith had an important role to play as leader of the fledgling community of believers in Queen's Cross. In a sermon preached in 1931 at the jubilee of the opening of the Church, Smith recalled some of the difficulties, as well as the encouragements, of these first few years of ministry. In this sermon, Smith considered that "under divine blessing", the success of the new congregation was in no small part due to "the devotion and foresight of the Presbytery's Committee in planning and erecting a new Church just here. For this part of the City was then rapidly extending".[16] Smith continued:

> We were not what we were called – a wholly west end people. Both west and south of Queen's Cross were still numbers of workers in the Bleachfield and the Rubislaw Quarries with not a few gardeners, crofters and farmers, of whom we had our share. It was a happily and a usefully mixed congregation. I never more reluctantly gave away disjunction lines[17] than to the considerable number of families .. I think about twenty, who emigrated to work in the granite districts of Vermont.[18]

Smith refers in this sermon to the territorial districts of the congregation. These were revised at a meeting of the Presbytery in November 1882 with a view to aiding the work of pastoral visitation.

---

[14] Record of the Free Presbytery of Aberdeen, 10 January 1882, Scottish Record Office CH3/2, Volume 4, p124.

[15] LAS, p20.

[16] "Sermon preached for the fiftieth anniversary of the opening of Queen's Cross Church: April 12 1931", NLS Acc 9446 No 321.

[17] The term used for the certificate of membership granted to church members when they leave one congregation to join another.

[18] Sermon, NLS Acc 9446 No 321.

The Pastor: The Early Aberdeen Years 49

In his jubilee sermon Smith also recalled the many contributors to the work of the congregation in its Sunday Schools, Bible Classes and literary society. Smith pays tribute to this "number of young men who joined us and gave their energies to our work".[19] He also refers to the fact that the sacrificial devotion of the congregation to the material needs of the Church allowed the work to prosper in its early stages. There were heavy financial implications for the infant congregation. Smith reckoned that "the Church and Organ Chamber cost together nearly £10,500".[20] But, Smith said,

> Besides meeting the ordinary annual expenses of an unendowed congregation contributing well to the Sustentation, foreign mission and other funds of the Free Church of Scotland, the people with the help of some outside friends and a grant of £1000 from central extension funds paid off that debt in twelve years. Of the £10,500 required, more than £7,700 came from the members themselves.[21]

To which Smith adds the telling comment that "we used to congratulate ourselves on starting with a large debt instead of ... hampering traditions".[22]

Smith also pays tribute to the ministerial assistants who helped him during these early days, and also in subsequent years at Queen's Cross. The first of these was Charles Anderson Scott, who became a close colleague, and who accompanied the Smiths on their visit to Palestine in 1891. He would subsequently minister in London and pursue an academic career.[23] John Kelman was Smith's next assistant. Son of a Free Church minister, who, like Smith, was raised in Leith, he later ministered in Aberdeenshire, Edinburgh and in the United States of America as minister of the historic Fifth Avenue Presbyterian Church of New York. It was Kelman who looked after the congregation while the Smiths travelled to Palestine in 1891, and he would also accompany Smith on his third visit there in 1901. A brilliant theologian, Kelman was to receive honorary Doctorates of Divinity from Edinburgh, Princeton and Yale, and was noted for "the fine manliness of his spirituality".[24] A third assistant was Edward Roxburgh, who followed Kelman in 1891 and who also joined the party which accompanied Smith to Palestine in 1901. Of these assistants Smith says that

---

[19] Ibid.
[20] Ibid.
[21] Ibid.
[22] Ibid.
[23] Lilian Adam Smith designates him Professor on page 205 of her memoir.
[24] This was the assessment of theologian John Baillie, as recounted in A.C. Cheyne, *Studies in Scottish Church History* (Edinburgh, 1998) p208.

not only in teaching Bible Classes but by their wide knowledge of literature and their sound tastes, instituting circles for general reading they were most helpful in enlisting the sympathy and loyalty of the youth of our people.[25]

In an age when church life was dominated by the centrality of the pulpit, the single most important factor which contributed to the settling and consolidating of a strong and settled congregation was Smith's own preaching. Perhaps the greatest evidence of this is to be found in the letters written to Lilian Adam Smith after the death of her husband in 1942. One correspondent wrote:

> The greatest event in my life is my contact with your dear husband, admiring his genius, listening to his incomparable preaching and thrilled by it.[26]

Another spoke of the "erudite and eloquent young minister" who had come to Queen's Cross in 1882.[27] And the Kirk Session of Queen's Cross in 1942 penned the following tribute in their minutes:

> Almost immediately he caught the ear of the city and a great congregation gathered to hear this new and arresting voice. His fame spread far and wide ... There was a prophetic note in his preaching which matched the need of that day...[28]

Smith preferred to preach systematically and consecutively through themes and through whole books of the Bible, and would write out his sermons in full. Over the course of his first year in the new charge he preached a series of sermons on Elijah and Elisha. He made it known at the outset that he had not only an exegetical but also a practical interest in doing so: "I wish," he said in his first sermon on "Why Elijah had to come" (4 September 1881) to take up as our subject for the next few Sabbath evenings the prophet Elijah – what he was and did, and what his life and the lives of the men and women around him teach us to be and to do – and what to shun...".[29] Smith's sermons were characterised by a warm devotional and practical concern. His aim was to encourage a vital and virile Christianity, such as he had experienced in the Moody and Sankey campaign. In a sermon on Psalm 36 he was to say that

---

[25] LAS, p205.
[26] William Ross to LAS, 5 March 1942, NLS Acc 9446 No 74.
[27] Theodore Watt to LAS, 9 March 1942, NLS Acc 9446 No 74.
[28] Excerpt from the Minute of the Kirk Session of Queen's Cross Church, 8 March 1942, NLS Acc 9446 No 74.
[29] Sermons on Elijah and Elisha from the first year at Queen's Cross: Sermon 1 – "Why Elijah had to come" (on 1 Kings 16), NLS Acc 9446 No 320.

the fault of many Christians is that they turn to some theological definition or to some mystical refinement of it, and their hearts are starved. We must seek the loving-kindness of God in all the breadth and open-air of common life.[30]

Smith thus ranks among those who made this a great era of preaching in Scotland, part of a great tradition, deservedly noted as "a man of brilliant scholarship and outstanding preaching gifts".[31]

For Smith, the Bible was to be handled not as a text-book for theological formulations, but as "a Revelation of the living God – of His Person, His Character and His Will".[32] That revelation, Smith argues in his exposition of Acts 8, culminates in Jesus Christ, where God

has made our greatest suffering and shame His own problem and endeavour; He is anxious for us just where conscience tells us we need to be most anxious; He is helpful to us just where our helplessness is most felt.[33]

In this way Smith sought to demonstrate that the Bible's revelation of God is as a God who has entered in to the very needs and concerns of modern man. To quote from his own lecture on *The Preaching of the Old Testament to the Age*, Smith's was

Preaching for today .. preaching to the exact conditions and temptations of our own life. You have minute introspection and analysis of character; you have abundant emphasis of the value of the individual soul to God; you have the soul wakening to feel its solitary relation to God, and rejoicing in the purely spiritual character of religion.[34]

It was preaching also with which Smith was at home, and which he could handle with comfort and ease to the extent that he could describe the Queen's Cross pulpit as one "which I loved and found freedom in".[35]

Smith took care not simply to educate his congregation through Bible-based preaching, but also through addressing some of the pressing issues of the

---

[30] G.A. Smith, *Four Psalms* (London, 1896) p65.
[31] J. Philip, "Preachers" in *Dictionary of Scottish Church History and Theology* (Edinburgh, 1993) p667. Philip names Smith among a galaxy of preachers during what he calls the "transition period" of Scottish church life (the late nineteenth century), alongside A.B. Davidson, A.B. Bruce, James Stalker, Henry Drummond, James Denney, Alexander Whyte, John Kelman and Hugh Black.
[32] G.A. Smith, "The Ethiopian and the Old Testament: Acts 8:26-40", *The Expository Times*, Vol 1, No. 10 (July 1890), p235.
[33] Ibid., pp237-8.
[34] G.A. Smith, *The Preaching of the Old Testament to the Age* (London, 1893) pp55-56.
[35] Ibid., pp9-10.

Church. These he addressed particularly to the younger members of his congregation. An example is his 1884 sermon based on Deuteronomy 6:20-23, subsequently printed under the title *A Few Plain Words to the Young Members of my Congregation on the Differences between Presbyterianism and Episcopacy and the Alleged Possibility of a Union*. The sermon was a response to the "Episcopal Commemoration", a gathering of Anglican bishops and clergymen from Scotland, England and America. Episcopalianism had enjoyed a sudden revival in the years after the Disruption,[36] and Smith was concerned to ground his congregation well in the principles of Presbyterianism. Lest any should think that there was legitimacy in the concept of apostolic succession, and therefore in a possible union of Presbyterianism and Episcopalianism, Smith preached on the issue of the differences between the two. The sermon begins by underlining the facts of biblical revelation. "Our religion", Smith states, "is neither a philosophy nor a sentiment, nor only the aggregate of individual beliefs. Christianity is a History; that History began with the Incarnation...".[37] Nevertheless, Smith concedes, there are controversies internal to Christianity; in this sermon he seeks to address the question "What is the exact issue between the Presbyterian Church and the Episcopal?"[38] Smith argues that the point of difference is neither liturgical – the adoption of set forms in the one and not in the other – nor episcopal – the office of bishop in one as opposed to the other. To Smith part of the problem was a social one – in Scotland, he argued, episcopacy "is identified almost exclusively with the upper classes".[39] He cannot identify this with Scotland's democratic character, so he attempts to show that the introduction of episcopacy to Scotland was itself an outrage, a despotic act by a despotic Archbishop (James Sharp). The witness of history, therefore, Smith contends, favours Presbyterianism over Episcopacy; but more important is the witness of faith. The concept of apostolic succession he finds abhorrent and unChristian:

> [the Presbyterian's] faith in the one High Priest, Jesus Christ, and in the Priesthood of all believers through Christ, repels with horror the notion of a special priestly caste in the church.[40]

---

[36] See, for example, A.C. Cheyne *The Transforming of the Kirk* (Edinburgh, 1983) p90 and the article on "Episcopalianism" by H.R. Sefton in *Dictionary of Scottish Church History and Theology*, pp296-8.
[37] G.A. Smith, *A Few Plain Words to the younger members of my congregation on the differences between Presbyterianism and Episcopacy and the alleged possibility of a union*, Aberdeen, 1884, p3.
[38] Ibid., p5.
[39] Ibid., p9.
[40] Ibid., p14.

Smith urges his young members to "imitate the large charity of their mother" (that is, their mother church), and to rejoice in the Church's comprehensiveness and breadth.

The sermon is a clear statement of Smith's convictions regarding the nature of Scottish Presbyterianism. Yet at the same time as he is charging Episcopalianism with being class-orientated, his own congregation has been established among the rising middle class of west Aberdeen. It is doubtful whether the Presbyterianism Smith advances could escape some of the charges he levels against the Episcopalians. There is also a hint of intellectual snobbery in Smith's approach, as he describes the "intelligent Presbyterian" as the one who is prevented by the prelatic orders of Episcopalianism from "going over to an organization which maintains and vindicates its schism from the Church of his country".[41] Some might argue that this was a bit much coming from a Presbyterian, whose tradition was renowned for its schisms.

Perhaps, however, one of the benefits of this sermon is its clear statement of what Smith regarded as "catholic truth":

> It is the Fatherhood of God: it is the Divinity of our blessed Saviour; it is the Atoning virtue of his death; it is his resurrection; it is the giving of the Holy Ghost; it is the existence in this world of a Catholic and imperishable Church of Christ; it is the hope of Christ's second advent to judge the world, and the certainty of Eternal life for believers through Him.[42]

Richard Riesen quotes this passage to demonstrate that although "the absence of theology is conspicuous in Smith's writings",[43] the essential elements of evangelical orthodoxy are nonetheless to be found there. It is precisely at this point, however, that a tension begins to emerge between Smith's anti-dogmatism and his concern for evangelical orthodoxy. The emphasis in Smith's preaching falls upon a *factual* rather than a *dogmatic* basis for Christianity in the incarnation and its ongoing relevance for human life. For Smith it was axiomatic that the history of Christianity "was to be conterminate with the progress of humanity",[44] with the Christian church itself making the history by continually keeping before its view "[Christ's] own Personal Ideal".[45] "God", he says, "speaks to us in facts, not forms".[46] In a letter to his brother-in-law, David Ross, he urges him to say that

---

[41] Ibid., p15. Smith did, however, establish and maintain many friendly relations with episcopalians and representatives of other church orders.
[42] Ibid., p13.
[43] R. Riesen, "Faith and Criticism in post-Disruption Scotland with particular reference to A.B. Davidson, W.R Smith and G.A. Smith", PhD, Edinburgh, 1981, p20.
[44] Smith, *A Few Plain Words*, p4.
[45] Ibid.
[46] G.A. Smith, *Isaiah*, Vol 1, p216.

the Atonement was a fact. It really took place – this sacrifice for sins, if we are to believe the Bible .. Thunder it out in big letters – "not a dogma, but a FACT".[47]

Similarly in describing the early life of Henry Drummond, Smith says that he came to reject "Evangelical Christianity of a doctrinal form",[48] and Smith himself was concerned to foster an evangelicalism that was less dogmatic and obscurantist, and one which "distinguished between complicated inessentials and simple essentials".[49]

The difficulty is that Smith himself is being dogmatic when he sets down the nature of catholic truth. If his statements reflect his understanding of the substance of evangelical faith, then he is setting up a standard by which such faith can be measured. While opening much traditional orthodoxy to discussion and debate, Smith wished to retain a non-negotiable core of doctrine for preaching. So while it was true that "the outcome of the concessive approach of the New Evangelism was, at the least, equivocation regarding the most fundamental Christian belief",[50] it was also the case that the new approach required to build upon a core of Christian doctrine. To that extent, despite his assertions to the contrary, Smith has to be dogmatic as well as factual in his presentation of the Gospel. This tension between the dogmatic and the factual is what Smith sought to clarify through his subsequent biblical scholarship.

Smith was a sincere and earnest preacher; and the rise of membership in the congregation from 169 in 1882 to 713 in 1900[51] is itself a tribute to the drawing power of his ministry. In an age of great preachers, it was no mean achievement.

As well as being actively involved in ministry, Smith pursued other interests. He frequently met with other ministerial colleagues in different manses around Aberdeen for friendship and for discussion. The discussions at such meetings ranged over a wide range of subjects. The following piece of doggerel, scribbled on the train in a letter to David Ross following one such meeting, reveals not only Smith's penchant for verse (it is hardly poetry!), but also highlights some of the issues on the young ministers' agenda:

Oh if I were a Professor
With nine months of vacation,

---

[47] GAS to David M. Ross, 1883 (no date), NLS Acc 9446 No 6.
[48] G.A. Smith, *The Life of Henry Drummond*, (London, 1899) p26.
[49] Cheyne, *Transforming of the Kirk*, p82.
[50] K.R. Ross, *Church and Creed in Scotland: the Free Church Case 1900-1904 and its Origins* (Edinburgh, 1988) p220.
[51] Figures taken from W. Ewing, *Annals of the Free Church of Scotland 1843-1900*, Vol 2 (Edinburgh 1914) p174.

I'd balance my disturbed digestion
And tackle every social question
And put to rights the nation.
I'd clear my brains
And write great books,
And take men off the tenterhooks
Of doubt and hesitation.
I'd throw up Drummond's *Natural Law*
And quickly point out any flaw
In that hallucination.
The Soudanese I'd pacify
And righten all the wrongs of Skye
Without procrastination.
A liquor Bill I'd quickly draft
To sweep the country fore and aft
Of that abomination.
I'd purify all drains and sinks
Invent some good teetotal drinks
And serve my generation.
I'd settle disestablishment
To our own funds bring increment,
Surplus and sustentation.
The Equal Dividend would rise
In leaps before your very eyes
Beneath my cultivation.
Each Sunday I would generously
Unto some brother give supply
Who needed recreation.
But Saturday I'd keep myself
And spend it – oh too happy elf! –
In joy and jubilation.
All this I'd do – and a great deal more
If I were but a Professor
With six months of vacation.[52]

The poem is amusing to read, and, if it does not exactly demonstrate Smith's literary skill, at the very least it furnishes evidence of an artistic streak. At a deeper level, however, it gives an insight into his personal interests and concerns, and presumably it highlights some of the topics under discussion at the theological club. It confirms Lilian Smith's record of Saturdays spent mostly in preparation for Sunday, and also casts light on Henry Drummond's *Natural Law*. Smith's mature opinion of this book, newly published in 1883,

---

[52] GAS to David Ross, 1885 (no date), NLS Acc 9446 No 6.

and regarded as Drummond's main work, is to be found in the biography of Drummond which was published in 1899. *Natural Law in the Spiritual World* was an attempt to reconcile science and religion by arguing that the laws that are operative in nature also operate in the same way and to the same extent in religion. According to Smith "It was not his greatest work";[53] Smith regarded it as based on unprovable assumptions. "It does not necessarily, nor even probably follow," wrote Smith, "that because laws have a certain continuity throughout the physical universe they must also prevail in the spiritual experience of man".[54] But the verse reveals something of the influence of Drummond's work among contemporary theologians.

Clearly too, current issues, national and international, were much on the mind of the young minister, issues as diverse as the Sudan campaigns and the Skye Land Riots. But there are two subjects raised in the poem which deserve closer analysis. The first is the issue of disestablishment, which Smith says he would settle if he could. The disestablishment question was to dominate many of the Free Church's discussions in the latter part of the nineteenth century, with the roots of the question going back into the Disruption itself. The Free Church of Scotland at the Disruption regarded herself as the Church of Scotland in every respect, as the heir of the Scottish Reformed heritage. One clear difference between the two denominations, however, was that the Church of Scotland was established by law, and recognised by the civil authority as the Presbyterian Church in Scotland. Although the new denomination was separating from this establishment, the principle of establishment was clearly embodied in her foundational and constitutional documents.

The reason that the evangelical party had separated from the established Church was the abuse of patronage. This was a system whereby landowners provided both the properties and the stipends for parish ministers; the power of the landowners was such that they could in effect force a minister upon a congregation irrespective of their wishes. The Veto Act of 1834 – passed in an Evangelical-dominated Assembly – was a compromise between those who were pro-patronage and those who were all too aware of its abuses, and who wished the mind of a Christian congregation to be a factor in the settlement of a minister over them. Such "non-intrusionists" were the main power group in the Free Church in the years leading up to the Disruption. And when their philosophy of non-intrusion carried the day, it was on the clear understanding that Establishment as a principle remained constitutional and fundamental.

In 1874 the Patronage Act was passed, and a new question arose. That was whether the situation that now obtained was sufficient to deal with the root cause of the Disruption, and allow a re-union of the great Scottish churches. Some of those who campaigned strenuously for the abolition of patronage – such as Archibald C. Charteris (a leading Church of Scotland clergyman and

---

[53] Smith, *Drummond*, p136.
[54] Ibid., p142.

founder of the *Life and Work* magazine) and Norman Macleod (minister of the Barony Church, Glasgow) – professed that the reunification of the Scottish churches was their ultimate goal. It was a pity, however, that other churches were not consulted, and there were deep divisions and suspicions within the Free Church over the effect and consequences of the Act. James Begg considered it "a most marvellous Act", but Rainy and others viewed it otherwise. "If a boy breaks a window with a stone," said Rainy to the 1874 Assembly, "and afterwards removed the stone, it would not by any means mend the pane of glass".[55] Thus the abolition of patronage by itself was insufficient to repair the damage. The window of spiritual independence still remained broken, although the stone of patronage had been removed.

By 1885, leading figures of the Free Church - including George Adam Smith - were demanding immediate disestablishment.[56] Smith himself had concrete ideas for the course of the Church in the future. He makes it clear – following Rainy and the majority in the Church – that he wished to see an eventual re-alignment and re-union of the Scotttish churches, and in his view establishment was a stumbling-block:

> ... as soon as the panic in the Auld Kirk dies down and the inevitable reaction begins, we disestablishers ought to strike in with extremely generous proposals; for instance, we ought to leave all buildings to the Church and reiterate our willingness to leave them also all endowments but the teinds[57] ... I wish the Established Church to be as generously treated as possible, because my chief aim is the reconstruction of the Church of Scotland and if we give them as much of endowment and of building they will bring it with them into the common church in which I hope some day to sit down with them...[58]

---

[55] Quoted in P. Carnegie Simpson, *The Life of Principal Rainy*, Vol 2 (London, 1909) p272.

[56] Cf for example the comment in Augustus Muir *John White* (London, 1958) p95: "Nearly fifteen hundred ministers who called themselves 'the Liberal Clergy of Scotland' sent a petition to Mr Gladstone asking him to take steps to put an end to Establishment, which they called 'this religious scandal and political injustice' ... there were some who, when they dipped the pen and signed with such youthful zeal, would have marvelled greatly if they could have foreseen that they would one day proudly officiate in scarlet cassock as chaplains to the sovereign: for among the signatories on the petition were those of George Adam Smith, Alexander Martin and R.J. Drummond...".

[57] Teinds, a Scottish word for "tithes" or "tenths", were a system of ministerial revenue which went back into the Middle Ages. A system for paying ministers' stipends based on the teinds was in place in the Church of Scotland until the passing of the Church of Scotland Properties and Endowments Act in 1925.

[58] GAS to David M. Ross, (no date – probably 1886), NLS Acc 9446 No 6.

A manifesto for disestablishment bearing the signatures of 1475 Scottish ministers was forwarded to Gladstone. Agitation in Ireland, however, and the defeat of the first Home Rule Bill in 1886 dominated Gladstone's Parliamentary interests at this time. Following the fall of his government, the disestablishment campaign was marginalised in Parliament.

A second issue highlighted in Smith's verse which deserves some comment is the question of the church's role in social improvement. Since the days of Thomas Chalmers, the Free Church leader, the Free Church of Scotland had shown an interest in social needs and conditions. In the mid-nineteenth century, however, the concern of the Church was more to preach a Gospel of humble submission than to tackle the root causes of the social problems which men faced. There was, to use Donald C.Smith's phrase, a philosophy of "official passivity"[59] offered to the working poor, the teaching "not only that the existing pyramidical social structure was socially and politically desirable, but that it was rooted in the divinely ordained structure of the universe".[60] Chalmers, for example, commended the lot of "a Christian among the poor ... fixed for life to the ignoble drudgery of a workman, and yet he is on the full march to a blissful immortality ... in the filth and raggedness of a hovel, that is to be found on which all the worth of heaven, as well as all the endurance of heaven, can be imprinted..."[61]

Signs of a change are discernible in James Begg's pastoral work in Newington. Decried by his opponents because of his unyielding stand on various theological issues, he was instrumental in setting up the Scottish Social Reform Association in the 1850s, campaigning for better homes for the poor, reform of land laws and parliamentary justice for Scotland. Begg's was an important influence in the recovery of a genuine social concern in the Scottish Church.

George Adam Smith represents a growing interest and awareness within the Church of the importance of social concern. One sign of this interest is to be found in the series of lectures held in both Queen's Cross, Aberdeen, and Free St. John's, Dundee, in 1885 and subsequently published under the title *Christianity and Social Life*. Contributors included Professor A.B. Bruce who, in his lecture on "The Kingdom of God" argued that every minister needs to have "a love of men, not merely of church members",[62] and David Ross, who

---

[59] D.C. Smith *Passive Obedience and Prophetic Protest: Social Criticism in the Scottish Church 1830-1945* (New York, 1981) p47.

[60] Ibid., p54.

[61] T. Chalmers, "Sermon on the advantages of Christian knowledge to the lower orders of society" in *Sermons preached in St John's Church, Glasgow* (Glasgow, 1823) pp374-5.

[62] Quoted in D.C. Smith, *Passive Obedience*, p270.

posited that the work of Christianity "is not merely to save individuals but to regenerate society".[63]

Smith's basic philosophy of religion and evangelicalism included this social emphasis. Congregational agencies, he would later urge in the General Assembly of 1895, were "one of the most unique and blessed instruments of social welfare that God entrusted to His servants";[64] and again in the Assembly of 1898 he would argue that Scotland's cities required ministers "who would plead with them and intercede for them, not only in God's ears, but in the ears of their fellowmen and the civic authorities, winning for them their proper claims of light and air, and the other blessings that civilisation brought".[65] His own contribution to the lectures on *Christianity and Social Life* was on "Christianity and Labour" in which he addresses the charge that Christianity has nothing to do with labour and work. Although he concedes that "a large number of working men are in the interests of Labour hostile to Christianity, that they regard it as a religion identified with the classes immediately above them, and with the dominant economy of society under which they believe they have never had fair play",[66] nonetheless it is his contention that biblical Christianity – however individual Christians may have behaved in the past – has been a force for good in the lives of men. He deals with the issue of slavery in the first five hundred years after Christ. Slavery was regarded both as a historical fact and a natural principle. Not even with the conversion of Constantine was this social scandal criticised. But gradually, Smith argues, "Christianity changed the slave from a tool into a brother-workman".[67] Christianity thus changed the condition and status of slaves, and "wiped the curse" off the work which slaves were called to perform. It was, he argued "belief in the Incarnation which possessed men's souls for the first time with the dignity of Labour",[68] and brought society in this way under the influence of Jesus Christ.

Smith then brings this paradigm to bear on the nineteenth century, where, in the early years, Smith argues that "the rage for wealth"[69] led to women and children being treated as less than human, and sees that a change in attitude to labour came at one level from Thomas Carlyle in his attack upon the evils of capitalism. Carlyle's heart, says Smith, "overflowed in righteous indignation at the sight of it all".[70] Interestingly, Smith describes Carlyle as a "prophet", but says that, unlike the Hebrew prophets, he had no constructive and concrete

---

[63] Ibid., p271.
[64] PDGAFCS, 28 May 1895, Record, p81.
[65] PDGAFCS, 23 May 1898, Record, p82.
[66] GAS, *Christianity and Social Life: A Course of Lectures* (Edinburgh, 1885) p52.
[67] Ibid., p58.
[68] Ibid., p63.
[69] Ibid., p65.
[70] Ibid., p66.

suggestions for the improvement of society.[71] Smith argues that the vacuum in Carlyle's outlook was filled by the forerunners of the critical movement in Britain, from men such as F.D. Maurice, whose biblical criticism gave rise to a view of Christianity as a powerful force for social good and social change. Smith summarises:

> The result of this century's experience may be summed up in the utter disenchantment of society from belief in any merely economic or material system, and the renewed faith of mankind in moral force as being the only real social reformers.[72]

Smith was not happy with his lecture. The delivery of it had been delayed by the singing of an inordinate number of hymns; he felt that "the preliminary services were too long", and he confided to his brother-in-law that "in my nervousness I started at too rapid a rate and with my voice on too high a pitch".[73]

But more than the mechanics of delivery disappointed him. He felt that the substance of his lecture did not do justice to its theme. In his letter Smith summarises his principle that Christianity gave society a spiritual freedom which ennobled work and brought an end to injustice. But in his application of this to contemporary society he regarded his lecture as weak, and intended to rewrite it.[74]

The lecture hinges on the attempt to show parallels between slavery in early Christian society and the social abuses of the nineteenth century. Smith's argument is that Christianity modified the principle of work in both cases, although there is an asymmetry as Smith concedes that Christianity did not try to free the slaves. There is a "movement in the progress of the working classes"[75] which Smith recognises, but which is the fundamental difference between the two societies which he is representing in his lecture. However, the main theme is on the pervasive influence of Christianity in its power to transform and to change the relationship between men, and, consequently the economic and political direction of nations. This is the essence of Smith's social concern, and underlines the fact that "among more progressive churchmen a remarkable social awakening was taking place".[76]

---

[71] Ibid. Compare also the statement in J. Gardiner and N. Wenborn (eds.), *The History Today Companion to British History* (London, 1995) p132 that Carlyle was "more critical than constructive".
[72] *Christianity and Social Life*, p70.
[73] GAS to David Ross, 1885 (n.d.), NLS Acc 9446 No 6.
[74] Ibid.
[75] Ibid.
[76] D.C. Smith, *Passive Obedience*, p273.

The historian T.C. Smout has advanced the view that the churches "were spurred to their new sensitivity towards social questions by fear of agnostic socialism: and they found respite from their own theological uncertainties in a gospel of action".[77] Increasingly, in Smout's view, social action grew out of the lack of theological certainty.

But it would be difficult to argue this from the sermons of men like George Adam Smith, for whom the Gospel had a profound social interest and bias. His underlying principle was that "the service of humanity is the service of Christ".[78] In a sermon dedicated to the young people of Aberdeen and their particular interests, he said:

> I do not think that we evangelicals, who count all our salvation by faith in Christ, and all our duty in living to Him, have yet wakened up to the fact that He counted service for Himself and service for his little ones as equivalent".[79]

This was a clear call to evangelicalism to become rooted and grounded in the warp and woof of life, engaging with contemporary thought and with the needs of contemporary society. In urging parents to set a good example before their children, he was underlying his conviction that the roots of social evil are found "in our churches, in our homes, in our hearts".[80] By analogy, the remedy is found there also; and particularly in homes and hearts permeated by the gospel.

To be sure, Smith was concerned to draw a distinction between altruism and evangelicalism. He warned that while "the service of the race is blessed... each man should establish his relation to God before determining his relation to his fellows".[81] But, growing out of that relationship, Smith argued that "life is governed by faith; that the truths we profess are the things that make history".[82] In other words, the Gospel contained, in Smith's view, the very dynamism of a genuine social concern which "brings out a new sacredness upon common life".[83] Far, therefore, from turning to social issues because he had no Gospel to preach, Smith found himself reaching out into society with the message of Jesus Christ precisely *because* of his understanding of the nature of faith. The social aspect of Smith's Gospel was not *in spite* of his evangelicalism, but was

---

[77] T.C. Smout, *A Century of the Scottish People, 1830-1950* (London, 1987) p205.
[78] G.A. Smith, *The Children more sinned against than sinning: A Sermon on the Manners and Morals of Young Aberdeen*, (Aberdeen, 1888) p5.
[79] Ibid.
[80] Ibid., p3.
[81] Summary of "a powerful and impressive exposition by the pastor [of Queen's Cross], the Rev George A. Smith, M.A., of the scope and teaching of the Parable of the Ten Virgins" in *The British Weekly*, 6 May 1887.
[82] GAS, *Isaiah*, Vol 1 (London, 1888) p374.
[83] Ibid.

an expression of it. Far from turning to social action as an alternative to a faltering Christian orthodoxy, Smith and his contemporaries gave the Church a social concern which grew out of the Bible itself, laying less stress on the primacy of individual piety, and more on the imperatives of a Christian social conscience.

The Prophecy of Isaiah

Smith's social concerns grew in part out of his detailed study of the Old Testament prophets, his commentaries on Isaiah being an important and abiding legacy of his ministry at Queen's Cross. Around 1887, Smith began lecturing on the Book of Isaiah.[84] Several who listened to these sermons later testified to their influence. One person who heard them was William Robertson Nicoll, who was Free Church minister of Dufftown, Banffshire (1874-7), and Kelso, Roxburghshire (1877-85), before becoming editor of *The British Weekly*. During a visit to the manse at Kelso in 1884, T.W. Stoughton, of the publishing firm Hodder and Stoughton, discussed with Nicoll the possibility of publishing a series of commentaries under the title *The Expositor's Bible*; this series developed under Nicoll's editorship with contributions from some of the leading Scottish preachers and teachers of the day.

Smith contributed two volumes on Isaiah to the series. Smith's starting-point in his exposition is that the *canonical* arrangement of the chapters has to be revised in order to recover the *chronological* order of the prophecies: as he puts it during the course of Volume 1, in commenting on Isaiah 24, "a consecutive reading of the Authorised Version is an impossibility".[85] Coupled with this is Smith's views of authorship; given that "no claim is made by the Book of Isaiah itself for the Isaian authorship of chapters 40-66",[86] he assumes that the unity of Isaiah is editorial rather than authorial. Ascription of passages to someone other than the prophet does not trouble him unduly if "it touches no dogma of the Christian faith".[87]

Smith argues that a chronological re-setting of the chapters is necessary in order to fix the historical situation. It "presupposes the exposition of them in relation to the history which gave them birth".[88] Smith consistently seeks to contextualise the oracles which have been grouped together under Isaiah's name. This is essential, in Smith's view, not only to an exposition of the book, but to an understanding of the theology itself: God, he urges, is "concerned

---

[84] Early work on Isaiah included "The Messiah in Isaiah i-xxxix", published in *The Theological Review and Free Church Quarterly*, Vol 1 (1886?), pp322-38. This article gave an indication of the direction in which his commentaries would go.
[85] GAS, *Isaiah*, Vol 1, p416.
[86] GAS, *Isaiah*, Vol 2, (London, 1890) p6.
[87] GAS, *Isaiah,* Vol 1, p402.
[88] Ibid., px.

with every detail of their politics and social behaviour".[89] Isaiah himself, Smith says, was both an idealist and a realist, who was interested in Jerusalem as "his immediate and ultimate regard".[90] Smith draws attention to what he calls Isaiah's *penetrativeness*,

> the keenness of a man who will not be deceived by an outward show that he delights to hold up to our scorn, but who has a conscience for the inner worth of things and for their future consequences.[91]

This is the quintessential prophet, the man who can see as God sees, and then perceive intuitively how God will act.

The insistence on fixing the prophetic oracles in actual historical circumstances is in the main what leads Smith to the conclusion that the Cyrus oracles found in Chapters 41-48 cannot be regarded as of Isaianic authorship. He argues that "unless Cyrus and his conquests were already historically present, the argument in [chapters] 41-48 is unintelligible".[92] In the light of this principle, he concludes that

> Second Isaiah is not a unity, in so far as it consists of a number of pieces by different men, whom God raised up at various times before, during and after the Exile, to comfort and exhort amid the shifting circumstances and tempers of His people; but ... it is a unity in so far as these pieces have been gathered together by an editor very soon after the Return".[93]

In Volume 1 of his commentary, Smith divides Chapters 1-39 into five Books. The first of these he dates from 740BC (the date of Isaiah's divine call and commissioning) to 727BC (the death of King Ahaz), the period Smith defines as Isaiah's apprenticeship. The second book he dates from the accession of King Hezekiah in 727BC to the death of Sargon (king of Assyria) in 705BC. Book 3 he subtitles as "Orations on Intrigues with Egypt and Oracles on Foreign Nations", setting these in the troubled politics of the ancient near east following the death of Sargon (705-702BC), and Book IV concentrates on Sennacherib of Assyria (701BC). In the fifth book Isaiah deals with prophecies which are attributable to no king or event in Isaiah's own lifetime. The distribution of chapters is as follows:

---

[89] Ibid., p9.
[90] Ibid., p22.
[91] Ibid., p24.
[92] GAS, *Isaiah*, Vol 2, p12.
[93] Ibid., p21.

BOOK	Chapters
1: 740-727BC	1-5; 9:8-10:4; 6-8, 9:1-8
2: 727-705BC	28; 10:5-34; 11-12; 20; 21:1-10, 38-9
3: 705-702BC	29-32; 14:24-32; 15-21; 23
4: 701BC	1; 22; 33;36-39
5: Undated	13-14; 24; 25-7

The undated and unattributed passages in the final Book Smith regards as of universal application, dealing with more abstract subjects, such as "the nature of God's poor [people]", "the material effects of sin" and "the resurrection". He regards criticism as affording "little help" in the attribution of these passages.[94]

Several themes emerge in the Commentary which anticipate some of Smith's later emphases and interests. He talks, for example, of "the geography of Israel's redemption",[95] a phrase which anticipates his later work on the geography of the holy land. The geographical context, coupled with Smith's artistic flair, is employed to great effect, such as in the following passage:

> ...surely there is no genial man, who has watched the varied forms of life that sport in the Southern sunshine, who will not sympathize with the prophet in his joyous vision. Upon a warm spring day in Palestine, to sit upon the grass, beside some old dyke or ruin with its face to the south, is indeed to obtain a rapturous view of the wealth of life, with which the bountiful God has blessed and made merry man's dwelling-place.[96]

As Professor W. Johnstone has observed, some of the most interesting passages are where Smith "presents the wider international historical context, or imaginatively recreates a dramatic scene ... or, shades of the *Historical Geography* to come, portrays how landscape has moulded event".[97]

Smith is also concerned to highlight the relationship between individual religion and socio-political action. "To Isaiah," he argues, "a nation's politics are not arbitrary; they are not dependent on the will of kings or the management of parties. They are the natural outcome of the nation's character. What the people are, that will their politics be. If you wish to reform the politics, you must first regenerate the people..."[98] In another passage he describes how

---

[94] GAS, *Isaiah*, Vol 1, p416. Cf. also the treatment of chapters 25-27, in which he says that "This bare statement of the allusions of the prophecy will give the ordinary reader some idea of the difficulties of Biblical criticism. What is to be made of a prophecy uttering the catch-words and breathing the experience of three distinct periods?" (p429).
[95] Ibid., p180.
[96] Ibid., p190.
[97] W. Johnstone, "They set us new paths: V. Six Commentaries on the Hebrew Bible 1888-1988", *The Expository Times*, Vol 100 (1988-1989), p164.
[98] GAS, *Isaiah*, Vol 1, pp224-5.

Isaiah's faith and his patriotism run free with the force of twin-tides in one channel, and we hear the fulness of their roar as they leap together upon the enemies of God and the fatherland.[99]

At the same time, Smith reminds us that Isaiah himself had passed through an intense individual and personal experience, and that he had the individual for his ideal, underlining his belief that "Personal influence is the spring of social progress, the shelter and fountain force of the community".[100] Smith sees the history of Israel shaped to a large extent by the individuals who strode across its stage, such as the great bible monarchs and prophets. This he saw as a major distinction between orient and occident:

> We moderns of the West place our reliance upon institutions; we go forward upon ideas. In the East it is personal influence that tells, persons who are expected, followed and fought for ... The history of the East is the annals of personalities...[101]

By reading the Bible history as a story of heroes, Smith could detect a Messianic strain in the Old Testament which he could say was Christ in the Old Testament. In this way he retained a traditional evangelical motif (of Christ in the Old Testament) while also absorbing the findings of higher criticism.

The structure of Volume 2 is similar to the first. In it, Smith covers chapters 40-66. These he regards as a separate prophecy, or collection of prophecies, which originated a century and a half later than Isaiah. Smith argues that the second part of Isaiah shows a people with no civic life, a people in exile who have few social responsibilities. He accepts that the order of chapters is largely chronological, and that the business of the author is to show "that the former things have come to pass, especially the Exile, the survival of a Remnant, the sending of a Deliverer, the doom of Babylon".[102] In commenting on 56:9, he concedes that there are pre-exilic elements in Second Isaiah[103], but he considers the question of authorship settled by the fact, among others, that Cyrus is named.[104] It is no defence of the divine inspiration of the book, he suggests, to say that Isaiah named Cyrus two centuries before he was born. Deutero-Isaiah

---

[99] Ibid., p325.
[100] Ibid., p393.
[101] Ibid., p392.
[102] GAS, *Isaiah*, Vol 2, p24.
[103] See ibid., p411.
[104] These other facts which determine for Smith that Isaiah was not the author of chapters 40-66 include: the fact that nowhere do they claim to have been written by Isaiah, the citations in the New Testament do not call the authorship into question, and no question of doctrine is threatened by the belief in a different author (ibid., pp5-7).

is thus *recording* the fulfilment of prediction (Isaiah had, after all, pinned the hopes of Israel on an individual) and not making one. Smith puts it thus:

> The question is not, Could a prophet have been so inspired? – to which question, were it put, our answer might only be, God is great! – but the question is, Was our prophet so inspired? Does he himself offer evidence of the fact? Or, on the contrary, in naming Cyrus does he give himself out as a contemporary of Cyrus, who already saw the great Persian above the horizon?[105]

Smith corroborates this view in his discussion on chapter 48:7. There, he argues God explicitly states that not all things are foretold. Indeed, there is, Smith argues, such a repeated emphasis in Second Isaiah on God's *new* deeds, that the place of Cyrus in the prophecy is explicable only in this way – as God's new work (providing salvation for the Jews from outwith themselves). The emphasis on this aspect of Cyrus' intervention settles for Smith the question not of who wrote Second Isaiah, but who did not write it.

Smith divides the second volume of his Commentary into four Books: Book 1, dealing with the Exile, Book 2 with the Lord's deliverance, Book 3 with the Servant of the Lord, and Book 4 with the Restoration of Israel. In dealing with the subject of the Servant by whom Jehovah is to restore his people, Smith concedes that the passage found its ultimate fulfilment in Jesus Christ, but is not necessarily written concerning any particular individual. Here Smith is conscious of the conservative views of messianic prophecy as being not only fulfilled in Christ, but as being intended to refer to Christ in the first instance. Smith states that he

> fails to understand, why critics should be regarded as unorthodox or at variance with New Testament teaching on the subject, who, while they acknowledge that only Christ fulfilled chapter 53, are yet unable to believe that the prophet looked upon the Servant as an individual, and who regard chapter 53 as simply a sublimer form of the prophet's previous pictures of the ideal people of God.[106]

In a useful summary of New Testament teaching on the Servant of Jehovah, Smith (Vol 2, pp278-89) shows how the prophetic note of Isaiah finds its denouement in the ministry and witness of Jesus Christ. His argument is that whomever the prophet regarded in the first instance as the Servant, Jesus is the real fulfilment of that promise of deliverance. Indeed, Smith goes as far as to say that "as we enter the Gospel history from the Old Testament, we feel at

---

[105] Ibid., p7.
[106] Ibid., p267.

once that Isaiah is in the air".[107] The relationship between the Servant in the Old Testament and Jesus the Servant in the New points to the continuity of God's work in history. It is because history is "one progressive and harmonious movement under the hand of God"[108] that the observations of the author of Second Isaiah find their fullest expression in the advent of Christ.

In both volumes, Smith emphasises the importance of biblical criticism. Smith's rearranging of the chapters, as well as his discussion of authorship and purpose, show him to be both a student and a proponent of critical views. Yet his position is not without difficulties. In both volumes, for example, he acknowledges the limitations of criticism. He concedes that "any chronological arrangement of Isaiah's prophecies must be largely provisional".[109] He also says regarding the purpose of chapter 24 that "criticism affords little help"[110]. Similarly, in volume 2, in dealing with linguistic peculiarities in chapters 40-66, he suggests that different forms and meanings are not necessarily evidence of differences of authorship. "But", he asks, "who is able to prove this?"[111]

Even his editor had difficulties with Smith's approach to the prophecy. In a letter to Marcus Dods, Robertson Nicoll confessed: "I am wrestling with George Adam Smith's *Isaiah*; he has chopped up the prophet terribly".[112] His former teacher, A.B. Davidson, reviewing the commentary in *The Theological Review and Free Church College Quarterly* acknowledged that "Mr Smith's book is not strictly a commentary, and readers may not find an answer to all difficulties connected with Isaiah in it".[113] He also questioned whether Smith, in his treatment of the unattributed chapter 24 "is quite consistent with himself here".[114] Both Nicoll and Davidson were expressing dissatisfaction with an apparently arbitrary treatment of the passages under consideration.

For all his criticism of the work, however, A.B. Davidson also praised Smith's commentary for its practical emphasis. He said

> Mr Smith's work corresponds far better to the idea of an exposition of Isaiah than any mere critical commentary could do; because it recognises the practical aim of the prophet in all that he said, and operates on precisely the same lines.[115]

---

[107] Ibid., p282.
[108] Ibid., p279.
[109] GAS, *Isaiah*, Vol 1, pxii.
[110] Ibid., p416.
[111] Ibid., p230.
[112] T.H. Darlow, *William Robertson Nicoll: Life and Letters* (New York, 1925) p87.
[113] A.B. Davidson, Review of G.A. Smith *The Book of Isaiah*, in *The Theological Review and Free Church College Quarterly*, Vol 3, n.d., p152.
[114] Ibid.
[115] Ibid.

The value of the commentary was not so much in terms of its contribution to scholarship – although the publication undoubtedly confirmed him as "one of the most learned and the best of the younger Scottish ministers"[116] – as in the emphasis on personal experience which Smith sought to draw out of Isaiah's work. The emphasis is constantly upon the effect of the evangel on day to day life – on the practical consequences of faith. "The test of godhead," he avers, "is plain deeds".[117] Smith demonstrated that a critical approach to the prophets – however arbitrary such an approach may appear – could stand the test of practical Christianity. As Barbara MacHaffie has put it in her work on the popularisation of biblical criticism in the nineteenth century:

> The theology advocated in the work was thoroughly evangelical in its character. True religion for Smith was based not on books or tradition but upon a personal experience of God as revealed in Christ. Here was no sterile dissection of a sacred book, but a method of approaching the Scriptures which could be of great service to the evangelical faith.[118]

At the same time, Smith raised questions regarding the meaning of passages which would concern subsequent expositors. Few, indeed, of the critical conclusions of the work would, even in Smith's lifetime, go unchallenged; in 1935 H. Wheeler Robinson, for example, would write:

> Naturally, the details of the exposition in these books have been affected by later works on the prophets. Present-day scholars have been forced to recognise smaller units in the prophecies and a greater margin of editorial work; for example, few would now venture to assign Isaiah xl to lxxi wholly to the exile.[119]

Still, Robinson conceded that "the books remain as the best of their kind, because of their living quality, because we can hear so plainly through them 'the sound of running history'".[120] And as such they proved to be of immense help to pastors and laymen. Peter Macdonald, for example, who had pastored large congregations in Stornoway and Edinburgh, wrote to Smith in 1907 acknowledging his debt to the Isaiah volumes. He had rediscovered in them

---

[116] S.A. Cook, "George Adam Smith 1856-1942", *Proceedings of the British Academy* (London, 1942) p328.
[117] GAS, *Isaiah*, Vol 2, p119.
[118] B. MacHaffie, "The People and the Book: A Study of the Popularisation of Biblical Criticism in Britain, 1860-1914", PhD, University of Edinburgh, 1977, p135.
[119] H. Wheeler-Robinson, "Sir George Adam Smith – The Sound of Running History", *The British Weekly*, 24 October 1935, p71. Lxxi (71) is obviously a misprint for lxvi (66).
[120] Ibid.

that God is a God "of principle, method, law ... I have proved the truth of this line of thought to which your words led me. Please even at this belated hour accept a fellow worker's gratitude".[121] It was no exaggeration to say that Smith "made the prophets of Israel, their lives and their message, absorbingly interesting and intensely real to countless thousands of people".[122]

G.T. Sheppard describes Smith as struggling impressively to show how "the modern perspective had reopened some of the most elementary questions for confessional Christian scholars".[123] At the same time, however, Smith's work is noticeably characterised by a paucity of critical engagement with other scholars. That may be a sign that he is truly a pioneer; it may also, however, reflect a desire to be less critical of contemporary scholarship in the interests of a more devotional approach. It is also important to note that *evangelical* scholarship on Isaiah has remained ambivalent on the question of the unity of the book. William Gentrup, for example, states that "the issue of authorial unity ... becomes moot when Isaiah is approached from the perspective of synchronic literary criticism. The book as it now exists has been designed to stand as a whole".[124]

On the other hand, Old Testament scholar O.T. Allis insisted that "biblical prophecy and the unity of Isaiah stand or fall together",[125] and his position ought to give us pause. While Smith would later go on to justify the task of biblical criticism on the basis of Christ's use of the Old Testament, he nowhere addresses the issue that is axiomatic for conservative evangelical scholarship, namely Christ's own endorsement of the authorial unity of Isaiah, which is, in the words of E.J. Young, "the unequivocal testimony of the New Testament".[126] Smith's endorsement of multiple authorship and mere *editorial* unity, the emerging consensus notwithstanding, can hardly claim the imprimatur of Christ and the apostles.

That Smith sought to remain abreast of contemporary scholarship, however, is clear from an article published in *The Expositor* in 1889, one of his earliest creative and scholarly publications. The article was on "Recent Literature on the Old Testament", and began by acknowledging the place of Julius Wellhausen in contemporary Old Testament studies. "The displacement he

---

[121] Peter Morrison to GAS, 22 June 1907, NLS Acc 9446 No 141.
[122] G.C. "Sir George Adam Smith", *Life and Work*, Vol XIII, 1942, p56.
[123] MacKim, *Historical Handbook*, p280.
[124] W.F. Gentrup, "Isaiah" in L. Ryken and T. Longman III (eds), *A Complete Literary Guide to the Bible* (Grand Rapids, 1993) p315.
[125] O.T. Allis, *The Unity of Isaiah: A Study in Prophecy*, (New Jersey, 1977) p122. Allis's position is an important contribution to the evangelical interpretation of Isaiah.
[126] E.J. Young, *An Introduction to the Old Testament*, (Grand Rapids, 1983, p211). See John 12:38-41, where quotations from 'first' and 'second' Isaiah are attributed to the same author.

caused was large", Smith wrote.[127] Smith goes on to review two German works on Old Testament theology, one of which (Baudissin's *Geschichte des Alttestamentlichen Priesterthums*) he commends for its *critique* of Wellhausen's ascription of P (the priestly code in the Levitical legislation) to Ezra (post-exilic). To Smith this argument was artificial, because "the murmur of running history is not in it".[128] Much ensuing discussion concerns the dating of P. Of particular interest are his comments on Von Orelli's *Isaiah*, in which Smith re-states his position regarding Cyrus in Second Isaiah. He wishes to argue that "The chapters are not prophecies of the certainty of Cyrus' coming; they are triumphant appeals to the fact that he has come".[129] In a discussion of a German pamphlet on Old Testament ethics, Smith makes a rare statement of the content of New Testament theology: "Christ's sinlessness, his self-sacrifice, His resurrection and gift of eternal life, and the fact that the men to whom He addressed the old law were themselves new creatures".[130] This article provides evidence that Smith was indeed a serious scholar of Old Testament contemporary scholarship, both in his own country and on the continent.

Personal

While the Isaiah volumes marked Smith's professional development as a scholar and expositor, he was also developing other interests. It was during his Aberdeen years that he took up mountaineering. A holiday in Lucerne, Switzerland, along with Isabel in 1883[131] gave Smith his first taste of mountain climbing in the Alps, and with it, a recreational interest was born. His wife remarks that "George now found the outlet which his mind and body needed. The great snow mountains drew him, and the endurance and skill required for climbing them gave him complete concentration away from his ordinary life".[132] The mountains provided him with illustrations for his preaching, as the following quotation from *Isaiah*, Volume 1, makes clear:

> Recall some day when, leaving your close room and the smoky city, you breasted the hills of God, and into opened lungs drew deep draughts of the

---

[127] G.A. Smith "Recent Literature on the Old Testament, *The Expositor*, Vol 3 No 10 (1889), p386.
[128] Ibid., p389; cf. n118 above.
[129] Ibid., p395.
[130] Ibid., p398.
[131] The date is from LAS, p25, but Janet Adam Smith dates the account a year later, in 1884 ("A Family Century in the Alpine Club", *The Alpine Journal*, 1982, p142). George and Isabel returned to Switzerland in 1884, and were involved in an accident in which both were thrown out of their carriage. They were singularly fortunate to have escaped with minor injuries, although Isabel seems to have been affected more than George (GAS to father from Grindelwald 20 August 1884, NLS Acc 9446 No 23).
[132] LAS, p25.

The Pastor: The Early Aberdeen Years 71

fresh air of heaven. What strength it gave your body, and with what a glow of happiness your mind was filled! What that is physically, Christ has made possible for us men morally. He has revealed stretches and eminences of life, where, following in His footsteps, we also shall draw for our breath the fear of God. This air is inspired up every steep hill of effort, and upon all summits of worship.[133]

Smith's climbing interests developed into membership of the Alpine Club, to which he was admitted in 1886. To his study of ancient texts he added now the study of ancient mountains. Climbing in the Swiss Alps gave Smith a release for body and mind that was necessary for one whose work at home required such intense intellectual and mental commitment. Writing to his sister after one of his climbs he said:

You wouldn't have known your reverend brother if you'd seen him racing down the rocks and grass, in knickerbockers and a shirt, with an ice-axe in his hand, and a knapsack on his back, and looking fiercely red as to his face.[134]

His geographical interest widened also through his membership of professional societies. He had been a member of the Scottish Geographical Society since coming to Aberdeen. He also became Secretary of the Geographical Section of the British Association for the Advancement of Science when it met in Aberdeen in 1885. His knowledge of both Palestine and Switzerland meant that he was often in demand for lectures on these subjects. Travel interests continued to fascinate him.

It was on a climbing visit to Switzerland in 1889 that Smith met Lilian Buchanan. Her father, George Buchanan, was Chief Medical Officer of the Local Government Board, well known both in London society and in government circles. Lilian herself had taught in London, and in 1889 was given the opportunity to travel to Switzerland with her uncle, Edward Seaton. Although she dedicates a chapter of the family memoir to her own pedigree and background, Lilian does not give the real reason for her willingness to travel so far from home in the company of her uncle. Earlier that year, in Spring 1889, while on a visit to Keswick she had become engaged to the Rev Arthur Heelis (whose brother, William Heelis, married Beatrix Potter). Only a few days into the engagement she thought better of the commitment she was making, and broke it off within a month. Naturally, she confessed privately, "I was very much upset and distressed for the pain I had had to give, and I was not in my

---

[133] GAS, *Isaiah*, Vol 1, p184.
[134] Quoted in Janet Adam Smith, "A Family Century", p145.

usual good health".[135] Her uncle, a young widower in his early forties whose company she enjoyed, was responding to the concerns of his sister, Lilian's mother, when he offered to take his niece to Europe. Lilian, her daughter was to write later, "was an excellent walker",[136] and was a member of a second party to arrive at the Riffel Alp (above Zermatt) in August 1889. George Adam Smith and his schoolmaster friend, Alick Tosswill, had already arrived. From all accounts, Lilian noticed Smith first, and enquired as to his identity. Dr Newman Hall, a Congregational Minister, told her that "The tall man is Tosswill, a master at Harrow, and the other is Isaiah Smith".[137] Lilian soon found out, to her great relief, that his name was not Isaiah! Their first meeting on 21 August was followed by mountain excursions and engagement four days later after the Sunday evening chapel service. Janet Adam Smith surmises that "It was through kind Alick Tosswill's contrivance that George and Lily were able to be together so much during these first days of their engagement".[138] "Men here rave about her," Smith wrote to his sister. "I know she might have had any of the rich handsome Englishmen but she has chosen the Free Church Minister and you can imagine how proud I feel".[139] To his father he said, "I have climbed my peak of peaks".[140]

Engagement was followed by a visit by Smith to London to meet the Buchanan family. He took the opportunity in London to see W. Robertson Nicoll, who impressed on Lilian that she was taking on a great responsibility. This prompted her to offer to break the engagement, but George assured her of his feelings for her. Their daughter Janet tells the story of the marriage:

George Adam Smith and Lilian Buchanan (after marriage she seldom used Lily) were married in Marylebone Parish Church on December 18 [1889], the date chosen so that GAS could attend the Alpine Club Dinner the night before. The service was conducted by Canon Rawnsley, with whom Lily had walked the Lakeland fells, and by Canon Wilson, with whom GAS had crossed the Col Durand. The bridesmaids – Florence and Helen Buchanan, Kate and Annie Smith, and two little girls to whom Lily taught music – carried edelweiss and were given presents of brooches shaped like ice-axes. There was a great turnout of Riffel Alp and Alpine Club friends, some of whom had combined to give a fine set of photographs of Zermatt and the peaks around. After a honeymoon in Paris (where the bride discovered that

---

[135] Lilian Adam Smith, *Recollections of a Grandmother*, privately circulated, 1977, p31, NLS Acc 9446 No 401.
[136] Janet Adam Smith, "Riffel Alp in 1889", p2, NLS Acc 9446 No 406.
[137] LAS, p32.
[138] Smith, "Riffel Alp in 1889", p5.
[139] Ibid., p4.
[140] GAS to Father from Zermatt, 29 August 1889, NLS Acc 9446 No 23.

wifely duties included proof-reading the second volume of Isaiah) they came back to the Queen's Cross Manse at 91 Fountainhall Road Aberdeen.[141]

"Greet the unseen with a cheer" was how Henry Drummond bade the new couple farewell after a stop in Brechin en route to Aberdeen,[142] and although Lilian was travelling into the unknown, she soon became an indispensable part of life in the manse. She acknowledges that "I had much to learn in those days",[143] but entered gladly into a work that required a full amount of entertainment, organisation and administration which were the inevitable effects of Smith's powerful ministry. She was also welcomed into the circle of Smith's ministerial colleagues, with Robert Barbour composing a poetic tribute to the "lily from an English lake" who had travelled north to Aberdeen as Mrs Lilian Adam Smith.[144]

Their first child, George Buchanan Smith, was born the following year, on 18th October 1890. His father was to write: "We used to say that he slid to us down a rainbow, one end of which I saw resting on the house as I came up the road a few minutes before his appearance".[145] A second son, Robert Dunlop Smith (Beppo) was born in October 1892. Both were born at 91 Fountainhall Road, and both were baptised in Queen's Cross Church. Both also would give their lives in the service of their country in the First World War.

Other congregations were aware of the power of Smith's ministry in Aberdeen, and several calls were addressed to him from other places. Largely

---

[141] Smith, "Riffel Alp in 1889", p6.
[142] LAS, p37.
[143] Ibid., p42.
[144] The lines are as follows:
Our head has fallen; fallen in the ample tree
Beneath whose generous shade this friendly band
First gathered. Brother clasped the outstretched hand
of brother; but who joined all hands was he.
Fallen is our head, and in our sorrow we
Stand orphaned. Bare to all the winds we stand
Trembling as if the next our face that fanned
Might be the chill breath of eternity.
Is this it? Or what is it? This soft breath
That blows from out the south, and with it blown
Something? – a lily from an English lake?
This is the breath of life and not of death!
Welcome already for our brother's sake
Henceforth and always welcome for thine own!
Composed by R.W. Barbour and written at the club meeting in Professor Drummond's, 14 January 1890, NLS Acc 9446 No 23.
[145] George Adam Smith, *George Buchanan Smith 1890-1915*, printed for private circulation (Glasgow, 1916) p1.

through Henry Drummond's influence in Australia, the congregation of Toorak, Melbourne, addressed a call to him. Drummond tried to convince Smith that while "the congregation is without doubt the St George's of Australia",[146] the preaching was generally poor. Another call came from Regent Square Presbyterian Church, London, an important city pulpit (which Smith himself described as "so great and useful a congregation"[147]), and one which people expected Smith to occupy, perhaps because of his wife's London connections. He declined both invitations.

A call from Free St George's, Edinburgh, to be colleague and successor to Alexander Whyte, was more taxing both for Smith and for his people. Whyte's was a prime Scottish pulpit, and a centre both of excellence and of influence. In a lengthy letter to his brother-in-law Smith discussed the implications of this call, and his response to it. Not only had Whyte sought to secure his services, but Principal Rainy himself had written to Smith saying that "a mind and influence like yours are grievously needed here among the younger Free Church people and among the younger people generally".[148] Smith was torn between his affection for Queen's Cross and the obvious need for a continued strong pulpit in the capital. He discussed the issue with Whyte, who had outlined a possible itinerary and plan of shared responsibility, but Smith was vexed that "he did not show any feeling for Queen's Cross in the matter".[149] A related issue was the vacancy in the Hebrew chair in Glasgow College, in which Smith, by 1891, was increasingly interested. He wrote:

> Of course, going to St Gs means closing the door to the Hebrew Chair in Glasgow; and that I feel. But I am conscious of purely selfish motives leading me to the Professor's Chair and so I have tried to shut it out of my mind altogether.[150]

At a meeting of the Presbytery on 27 January 1891, Commissioners from the Presbytery of Edinburgh presented their case, and Smith was asked to declare his mind on the matter, at which he reported that "having considered all the circumstances, the balance of his judgement pointed to declining the Call".[151] The Presbytery did not place the Call in his hands, but whatever relief Smith thought this would give him proved momentary as Rainy (for the Presbytery) and Simson (for the congregation of St George's) appealed against this decision to the Synod.

---

[146] Henry Drummond to GAS, 27 May 1890, NLS Acc 9446 No 24.
[147] Letter of GAS 5 Feb 1892 declining a call from Regent Square.
[148] GAS to David Ross, 1890? (n.d.), NLS Acc 9446 No 6.
[149] Ibid.
[150] Ibid.
[151] Records of the Free Presbytery of Aberdeen, 27 January 1891, Scottish Records Office, CH3/2 Vol 4, p527.

The newspapers carried full reports of speeches made at Presbytery and Synod, such was the public interest in the case. It was apparent also that a minority in Free St George's were not happy with Smith's theological position. *The North British Daily* reported that

> ...it soon became apparent that the volume on the first part of Isaiah which Mr Smith had written for The Expositor's Bible would form with certain influential and active members of the congregation the basis of an attack on Mr Smith himself as an advanced broad churchman and on the favourers of liberal theology in the Free Church.[152]

The same article also rounded on the minority who were attempting to block the Call for not doing the manly thing and accusing Smith with the specificity of a libel. *The Scotsman*, however, noted the requisition from the young men of Queen's Cross congregation who wrote to their minister at the beginning of 1891:

> You have given us strong intellectual and moral stimulus, human sympathy that has strengthened all our social bonds and conceptions, and religious ideals and insight that have deepened our spiritual life both in its activity and in its rest.[153]

An agitated crowd gathered at the Free Church College in Aberdeen to hear the subsequent debate at the Synod, which concluded the matter to the satisfaction of Queen's Cross, who heard that they were to retain the services of their minister a little longer. As a token of gratitude and esteem, the congregation offered him the opportunity to visit Palestine again for six months; the Presbytery granted him the necessary leave of absence on 3 March 1891. The story of this second trip to Palestine is told in the following chapter. That he was willing to indulge his love of Palestine in an extended term of travel, is perhaps a sign that he too was unsettled in Queen's Cross, possibly as a result of the various calls which had been addressed to him. Certainly he was thinking even at this stage of the academic chair in Glasgow.

---

[152] *North British Daily*, 15 December 1890, presscutting taken from NLS Acc 9446 No 23.
[153] *The Scotsman*, 15 January 1891, presscutting from NLS Acc 9446 No 23. *The Aberdeen Free Press* on 14th January 1891 also reported on the Aberdeen Temperance Society's decision "to send a memorial to Rev George A. Smith, Queen's Cross Free Church, expressing their great appreciation of his services in the city in behalf of the cause of temperance, and pressing upon him not to accept the call to Free St George's Edinburgh, but to continue his labours in the city", NLS Acc 9446 No 23.

Conclusion

The Aberdeen ministry came to an end in 1892, with Smith's transference to Glasgow and the commencement of the Professorship there. But the ministry in Aberdeen had established Smith as a preacher of rare eloquence, and a scholar of formidable proportions. He was also able to indulge his fondness for mountaineering and travel. The connections with London also linked him with the higher classes of British society. Smith's ministry helped lay a foundation for a new attitude which would harness the insights of modern criticism to the needs of the modern pulpit. In William Enright's discussion of nineteenth-century preaching he suggests (with reference to Smith) that as a rule "the preacher turned more frequently to history as a means of illuminating ancient customs and providing new insight into possible interpretations as the circumstances of the sermon text were explored".[154] This is what Enright calls "a new appropriation of the Bible in preaching",[155] which was a direct result of the marriage of higher criticism with pulpit ministry. Smith's view of the Bible determined his view of preaching. In the Isaiah Commentary, in dealing with Isaiah's call in chapter 6, he refers to what happens "when a preacher stands up with the Word of God in a great congregation".[156] Amid the powers that are operative in the event of preaching there is the power of the will, "and the result depends on our own will; it depends on our own will, and it is dreadfully determined by our habits".[157] By referring to the practical implications of Isaiah's prophetic message, Smith had sought to make preaching practical, leading to the development of Christian character and conduct. The dynamism of the Gospel he found not in some arid dogmatic view of biblical inspiration, but in the spirit of the living God revealed in the Word of God. His work as Professor would give him opportunity to develop his concept of believing criticism – that only when read through the eyes of modern criticism could the Bible be of practical value to men.

It is necessary first, however, to study Smith's interests in Palestine, for they undergird the creative period of his life and career on which Smith would embark after leaving Queen's Cross.

---

[154] W.G. Enright, "Preaching and Theology in Scotland in the Nineteenth Century: A Study of the Context and the Content of the Evangelical Sermon", PhD, University of Edinburgh, 1968, p341.
[155] Ibid., p340.
[156] GAS, *Isaiah*, Vol 1, p83.
[157] Ibid.

CHAPTER 3

Traveller and Geographer: The Appeal of Palestine

Smith's visit to Palestine in 1891 was the gift of a grateful congregation which had discovered that it was to retain the services of its minister. While his earlier visit in 1880 was somewhat solitary, this second was less so. Leaving their child in the care of a nurse with Lilian's parents in London, Smith and his wife were accompanied by Smith's former assistant, C.A. Scott, and P. Carnegie Simpson, future biographer of Principal Rainy. The expedition proper commenced in Egypt in March, with a visit to some of the famous sites there, following which the party explored Palestine. Thereafter they were zealous wanderers through biblical sites until they returned home in the autumn.

Lilian Smith's memoir of Smith is painstaking in the detailed description of this expedition, emphasising the relative importance of this particular visit. Smith is portrayed as studiously surveying every minute detail of landscape:

> While the rest of us were interested in the general aspect and scenery, he was making notes of the details of each place, and at the same time his imagination, backed by his historical knowledge, called to life the events of the past, and envisaged the possible developments of the country in the future. He would see in his mind's eye terraces of vineyards upon a certain limestone ridge, or fighting taking place on a hill like Gezer. Never a day passed without his careful readings of the temperature and barometric pressure, and never an evening, however long and tiring the day, without his minute recording of everything done, seen, and heard – places, people, views and contours, vegetation, soil, animals, rocks, water, trees and flowers.[1]

In Jerusalem the Smiths witnessed the religious celebrations of the Greek Orthodox Easter and explored the major biblical sites. These days in the city which Smith would describe as "the bride of Kings and the mother of Prophets"[2] were, in his wife's reckoning, "unforgettable".[3] The party climbed

---

[1] LAS, p49.
[2] GAS, *Jerusalem: The Topography, Economics and History from the earliest times to AD 70*, Vol 1 (New York, 1907) p4.
[3] LAS, p52.

Mount Hermon, snow-capped even in Spring, and then made their way to Damascus. There they stayed with friends who worked for the Edinburgh Medical Mission. It was part of Smith's intention during this trip to visit as many missionaries and mission stations as he could; the *Aberdeen Free Press* reported that he

> called at nearly all the mission stations in Palestine, especially those of the Free Church; and he also visited the Edinburgh medical Mission at Damascus, and Dr Carslaw's at Sweir. What struck him most, he informed our representative, was the number of young missionaries, of from five to eight years standing, who are at present in Palestine ... In Mr Smith's opinion, no mission should be formed in a country like Palestine without having a medical section...[4]

Soon thereafter their two companions left them, and Smith and his wife continued to travel throughout the area east of the Jordan. Ancient Greek and Roman temples were explored, and "George tired out all our men, whom he took with him in relays, to look for inscriptions".[5] In Moab, through the influence of the Rev Henry Sykes, a missionary, they were guests at a Bedouin feast in the desert.[6] At Beirut, on the way home, the Smiths were presented with a chameleon by an inn-keeper, which they looked after until the creature escaped and was lost to them in Lausanne, Switzerland. They were united again with their son in Arrochar; while they were in Palestine he had been brought north to George's parents. Shortly after their return in the autumn, Smith's assistant, John Kelman, who had looked after the congregation in Smith's absence, preached his farewell service from Queen's Cross and accepted a call to Peterculter.

Scholarly Interest in Palestine

Travel to Palestine was virtually unknown in the eighteenth century. From the end of the eighteenth century there was a rapid growth of European and American interest in the lands associated with the Bible. John Bartlett puts this in context:

---

[4] Presscutting from the *Aberdeen Free Press* [?] n.d. in journal of presscuttings about Smith in NLS Acc 9446 No 23.

[5] LAS, p56.

[6] In the preface to the first edition of the *Historical Geography of the Holy Land* (HGHL), Smith expresses regret that his second visit to Palestine was not as complete as he might have wished: "Unfortunately – in consequence of taking Druze servants, we were told – we were turned back by the authorities from Bosra and the Jebel Druz, so that I cannot write from personal acquaintance with those interesting localities, but we spent the more time in the villages of Hauran and at Gadara, Gerasa and Pella, where we were able to add to the number of discovered inscriptions" (pxi).

The nineteenth century saw the dramatic expansion of archaeological and biblical study. This expansion owed much to political and economic factors such as the quest for a land route from the eastern Mediterranean to India, the imperial designs of Napoleon (whose surveyors mapped Palestine), the arrival of the steam ship and the steam locomotive, the development of photography and of a cheaper printing technology, and the growth of education for all. In an era when the Protestant churches set a high premium on biblical knowledge and Sunday Schools flourished, there was increasing interest in biblical geography, biblical peoples and their customs, and a ready market for the hundreds of books, especially illustrated books, published on Palestinian travel.[7]

This led to the development of historical geography as a literary genre. In surveying this development, Robin Butlin distinguishes between historical geography and geographical history. The first he defines as

> the study of the geographies of past times, through the imaginative reconstruction of phenomena and processes central to our geographical understanding of the dynamism of human activities within a broadly conceived spatial context, such as change in the evaluation and uses of human and natural resources, in the form and functions of human settlements and built environments, in the advances in the amount and forms of geographical knowledge, and in the exercising of power and control over territories and people.[8]

Butlin defines geographical history as the "study of the history and geography of changes in the territorial possessions and boundaries of states, empires and royal houses and administrations".[9] He cites George Adam Smith as an example of the particularisation of the genre of historical geography in the area of biblical studies,[10] and describes the *Historical Geography of the Holy Land*

---

[7] J.R. Bartlett, "What has archaeology to do with the Bible – or vice versa?" in John R. Bartlett (ed.), *Archaeology and Biblical Interpretation* (London, 1997) pp3-4.
[8] R.A. Butlin, *Historical Geography: Through the Gates of Space and Time* (London, 1993) p1. Butlin's opening chapter is an interesting historical survey of the field of historical geography.
[9] Ibid., p12, although Butlin concedes that this field of study was also described in some places as historical geography.
[10] Butlin says: "In Europe the concept and practice of historical geography in the seventeenth and early eighteenth centuries, was closely associated with scriptural or biblical geographies of the Old and New Testaments. This them, as will be shown, continued to figure in historical geography throughout the nineteenth and the early twentieth centuries" (p2).

as "an important book whose intellectual context reflects wider currents of nineteenth- and early twentieth century thought".[11]

This intellectual context included the attempt to establish an approach to history that was not conditioned by literary texts alone. In his study of the *Annales* school of historical geography, pioneered by Lucien Febvre and Marc Bloch in the early twentieth century, Alan Baker has suggested that historical geography rose partly as a reaction against "positivist history – which believed that the 'hard facts' of historical reality were contained within documents".[12] The result of this reaction was a holistic and synthetic study of history which included not only the evidence of the texts, but evidence also from other disciplines. Baker notes that

> the inseparability of geography and history, their combination in the form of regional histories, is a fundamental tenet of the *Annales* school and directly reflects its search for synthesis, its trust in total history. Such an holistic conception of the study of history was inevitably associated with advocacy of an interdisciplinary approach which soon extended beyond collusion with geography to cooperation with the full spectrum of academic disciplines, all of which were considered as potential handmaidens to history.[13]

Smith, though writing earlier than the *Annales* school, nonetheless applies similar principles of synthesis to the biblical history. The development of the historical geography of ancient cultures, not least the Palestine of the Scripture history, grew out of a desire to relate the biblical source to external evidential sources, and thus produce a comprehensive view of the biblical world.[14]

For those who welcomed these new frontiers in biblical studies, the rediscovery of the Holy Land through a range of intellectual disciplines, would provide an objective, scientific, non-controversial and factual account of the Land of the Bible. An important development was the inauguration of the Palestine Exploration Fund (PEF) in 1865. The Archbishop of York, in his address at the inaugural meeting of the PEF, stated the principles on which the work of the Society would be conducted:

---

[11] Butlin, *Historical Geography*, p7.

[12] Alan R.H. Baker, "Reflections on the relations of historical geography and the *Annales* school of history" in A.R.H. Baker and D. Gregory (eds.), *Explorations in Historical Geography: Interpretative Essays* (Cambridge, 1984) p4.

[13] Ibid., p7.

[14] Cf. Walter C. Kaiser "The Current State of Old Testament Historiography" for a summary of some of the fallacies that have arisen out of this approach, such as that "History cannot include anything that does not have external documentation" (*A History of Israel from the Bronze Age to the Jewish Wars* [New York, 1998] p5). Kaiser is aware of the need for a holistic approach, but wishes to claim the biblical texts themselves as primary witnesses for Old Testament historiography.

1. That whatever was undertaken should be carried out on scientific principles.
2. That the Society should, as a body, abstain from controversy.
3. That it should not be started, nor should it be conducted, as a religious society.[15]

The intention to place on record only the facts discovered, and not an interpretation of them, proved extremely difficult. The Committee was resolved, however, "to provide accurate information as to facts, leaving it to others to utilize those facts in whatever way they may consider desirable".[16] The Fund's first major activities were based at Jerusalem. Although some of the conclusions of the Fund would remain open to debate, there is no doubt that the PEF did much to encourage a scientific study of the Old Testament. So Moorey:

> Debatable as some of the new biblical identifications would prove to be, and unsatisfactory as the archaeology might be without any means of dating sites, there has never been any doubt that in the long run this enterprise [the PEF] contributed more to the right understanding of the archaeology and ancient history of Palestine than any other single undertaking in the nineteenth century.[17]

George Adam Smith was to work closely with the PEF, both in his membership of its Council and in contributing to its Quarterly Statement. Indeed, as he looked back over the work of British excavations of Palestine, Smith could contrast it "with the work of the excavations of other nations, and he knew that in thoroughness especially, the British work far excelled".[18]

In her assessment of the archaeological work in Palestine in the nineteenth century, Naomi Shepherd says that the Palestine Exploration Fund "had been established at the height of the passion for the biblical geography of Palestine

---

[15] C.M. Watson, *Palestine Exploration Fund: Fifty Years' Work in the Holy Land; a Record and Summary 1865-1915* (London, 1915) p18. Although some looked on archaeology as championing the old orthodoxy, it was not primarily for that reason that the PEF was established. The primary interest of the emergent society was scientific, though undoubtedly in the interests of objective biblical scholarship.

[16] Ibid., p19.

[17] Roger Moorey, *A Century of Biblical Archaeology* (Cambridge, 1991) p19. This has to be balanced with the statement in P.G. Bahn (ed.), *Archaeology*, Cambridge Illustrated History (London, 1996) p163, that the Fund's attempt to investigate the topography of Jerusalem "were less auspicious".

[18] Report of address by GAS to the Glasgow branch of the Egyptian Research Students' Association, in *Glasgow Evening Citizen*, 26 October 1909.

which was already on the wane by the 1880s".[19] She suggests that the mood in the 1880s was different, as scientific methodology had advanced and the wider world picture was emerging. To concentrate on Palestine was to concentrate only on a small corner occupied by a vassal kingdom against the backdrop of a wider and more important world.

However, this was precisely what made Smith so passionate about the Holy Land, that in the light of the Old Testament, this small kingdom was superintended by "the ideal of a special covenant between God and the Hebrew nation".[20] To Smith the dominant religious ideology of the Scriptures was

> That the God of this little tribe should be the Sovereign of earth and heaven! ... Jerusalem asserted to be the centre of the whole earth, to which the Gentiles should bring their substance – Zion and Jordan exalted above all the hills and rivers of the world – Jews to be kings and priests to God, but the sons of the alien their plowmen and vinedressers![21]

For Smith the conjoining of Palestine's relative geographical isolation with its almost absurdly high profile in the Scriptures was the most attractive feature of his study. His was, consequently, not simply a Geography of the Holy Land, but a *Historical* Geography, from which the Scriptural and theological aspects could not be missed out. Smith could say of the prophets that

> Where others saw the conflicts of nations, aided by deities as doubtfully matched as themselves, they perceived all things working together by the will of one supreme God and serving His ends of righteousness.[22]

For Smith, too, the geographical study of Palestine was not a study in nationalism, but a study in Providence. It was not so much the study of the manners, customs and history of a people, as a study of the way in which that people had been covenanted in special relationship to God. This approach harnessed the testimony of the Old Testament writings and the witness of extra-biblical testimony to produce a theological naturalism[23] which sought to

---

[19] N. Shepherd, *The Zealous Intruders: The Western Rediscovery of Palestine* (London, 1987) p226.
[20] GAS, "The Ethiopian and the Old Testament: A Sermon on Acts 8:26-40" in *The Expository Times*, Vol 1, no. 10 (July 1890), p234.
[21] Ibid.
[22] GAS, *Isaiah*, Vol 1, 1888, p100.
[23] I have coined this phrase to describe the kind of enquiry Smith was conducting into the Palestinian history. The phrase should not be confused with natural theology, which is a specific branch of theological study. It is more akin to the philosophical naturalism which developed around the middle of the nineteenth century as an attempt to express an idealist view that a relationship can be discerned between "living things and the patters of distribution in space and time" (P.J. Bowler, *The Fontana History of the*

explore the relationship between the texts which spoke of God's election of Israel and the contexts in which this election manifested itself. For Smith, "details of the geographical and climatic elements are part of the language of revelation".[24]

By the time Smith visited Palestine in 1891, he had already shown a professional interest in geography by joining the Scottish Geographical Society and becoming its secretary in 1885. In his study of the Royal Geographical Society, T.W. Freeman has argued that the period from about 1885-1895 was a decade not simply of growing interest in geography and geographical education; it was also the case that "definition of the various aspects of geography was a natural preoccupation of the time along with the relation of geography to other subjects".[25] In her study of Scotland as a seed-bed of academic geography, Elspeth Lochhead identifies as a distinctive Scottish contribution to geographical studies a "holistic view of man and environment, which generally managed to avoid the pitfalls of extreme environmental determinism and related perspectives".[26] It is in this academic milieu that we find Smith developing his view of the geography of Palestine as a vital component of biblical studies, relating geography to historical theology and producing a *heilsgeographie* – a theological conception of geography. It was not sufficient, in Smith's view, to ask of the biblical narrative "what happened?"; it was necessary to ask "why did what happened just *then* also happen just *there*?".[27]

On his return home, Smith lectured on his visit to Palestine over the winter of 1891/2. These lectures he said were "descriptive of the Holy Land, the missions there, and the Christian churches in the East".[28] In December 1891 he delivered a lecture in Huntly Free Church to the Women's Bible Study Association on "The geography of Palestine in connection with the history of Revelation", in which he described Palestine as "a great bridge crossing between Egypt on the south and Assyria on the north, and enclosed on the one

---

Environmental Sciences [London, 1992] p249. See chapter 7, "The Philosophical Naturalists", for a discussion of this movement of thought).

[24] W.S. Lasor, D.A. Hubbard and F.W. Bush, *Old Testament Survey* (Grand Rapids, Michigan, 1994) p53.

[25] T.W. Freeman, "The Royal Geographical Society and the Development of Geography" in E.H. Brown (ed.) *Geography Yesterday and Tomorrow* (Oxford, 1980) p18.

[26] E.N. Lochhead, "Scotland as the Cradle of Modern Academic Geography in Britain", *Scottish Geographical Magazine,* 97 (1981), p108.

[27] T.W. Freeman, "Royal Geographical Society", p26.

[28] Presscutting from the *Aberdeen Free Press* [?] n.d. in journal of presscuttings about Smith in NLS Acc 9446 No 23.

side by the Eastern desert and on the other by the Mediterranean Sea".[29] Within the same week he addressed the Aberdeen Philosophical Society with a paper entitled "Notes of a recent journey through the Hauran and Gilead, with a number of inscriptions discovered during its progress".[30]

In addition, Smith began to publish the results of some of his findings. Articles such as "On Aphek in Sharon"[31] sought to identify an obscure Old Testament place reference in the light of his travels, and the paper read to the Aberdeen Philosophical Society was also published in the *Palestine Exploration Fund Quarterly Statement* (1901 pp 340-361). He also published, in 1891, a review of a guide-book to Palestine which he says he took with him on the visit to Palestine. This was Baedeker's *Palestine*, first published in 1876. Smith's review is significant not only for its evaluation of Baedeker's work, but also for Smith's description of what a "manual of sacred geography" should be: a book to help determine

> the distances and difficulties of biblical journeys, the lines of the ancient campaigns, and generally all the perspective of the Holy Land, as well as the latest results of biblical archaeology and geography.[32]

Lilian Smith also published her own accounts of the Palestine trip. In an 11-page booklet entitled *East of the Jordan*, she described her visit as "the most interesting tour I have ever made", and continued:

> The open-air life, the glorious sunshine, the varied scenery and the historic sites, have combined to make these three weeks joyous and memorable. I have learned and unlearned a great deal.[33]

She also wrote an article entitled "A Day in the Judæan Wilderness" for the journal *Onward and Upward*.[34]

---

[29] *The Huntly Express*, 12 December 1891, in journal of presscuttings about Smith in NLS Acc 9446 No 23. The metaphor of Syria as a bridge is explored by Smith in *The Historical Geography of the Holy Land*, London, 1894, p6.

[30] Page 15 of journal of presscuttings about Smith in NLS Acc 9446 No 23. The notice is of a meeting on 15 December 1891. The synopsis of the paper notes the inscriptions discovered by Smith: "Emperor Otho (69AD), King Agrippa II (81 AD), Roman legion etc., Sarcophagi, pre-Christian and Christian inscriptions".

[31] *Palestine Exploration Fund Quarterly Statement*, 1995, pp252-3.

[32] GAS, "The New Edition of Baedeker's *Palestine*", *The Expositor*, Vol IV, Fourth Series (1891), p467.

[33] LAS, *East of the Jordan*, n.d. The only copy of the journal is housed in a journal of presscuttings at NLS Acc 9446 No 412, between pages 84 and 85.

[34] LAS, "A Day in the Judæan Wilderness", *Onward and Upward*, December 1896, pp297-300.

Smith published his *Historical Geography of the Holy Land* (HGHL) in 1894.[35] By any standard, it was a remarkable piece of work, which included new maps and a comprehensive introduction to the geographical context of the biblical material. Smith's work is divided into three books; Book 1 deals generally with the land, in its relation to the history of the world, its form, climate and scenery, and also the questions of faith which relate to aspects of the geography of Palestine. Book 2 deals more particularly with Western Palestine, and Book 3 with Eastern Palestine. Five appendices deal with geographical passages and phrases in the Old Testament, the theory of Israel's invasion of Western Palestine, the wars against Sihon and Og, the bibliography of Eastern Palestine, and the subject of roads and vehicles in Syria.

Smith operates on the principle that, as a theological concept, geography may have a symbolic, or even a spiritual significance, so that "geographical categories are being employed, but their literal geographical reference has completely disappeared. The geographical has become the servant of the spiritual",[36] and becomes "God's testing ground of faith".[37] In such a context, Smith says, "the geography of Syria exhausts the influence of the material and the seen, and indicates the presence on the land of the unseen and the spiritual".[38] For the Christian, in Smith's view, "his Bible is [Palestine's] geography from Beersheba to Antioch".[39]

In Smith's view, geographical references are not incidental but integral to the manner in which the biblical world is portrayed. The preacher's art is employed here in the manner in which Smith dramatises the scenes of biblical narrative. To read the HGHL is to be drawn into the world of word-pictures: "Let us stand off the land altogether, and take its appearance from the sea";[40] "Having gone round about Judæa, and marked well her bulwarks, we may now draw some conclusions as to the exact measure of her strength – physical and moral";[41] "As you stand upon that last headland of Gilboa, 200 feet above the plain, your eye sweeps from the foot of Tabor to Jenin, from Tell el-Kasis to

---

[35] In his tribute to Smith's work, Yehoshua Ben-Arieh dates the HGHL wrongly, stating that it was written after the first visit in 1880 (he also gives a wrong date of 1899 for the second visit). Ben-Arieh includes the HGHL even although it falls outwith the time parameters of his study, since he regards Smith's name as "inseparably linked with the concept of the historical geography of the Holy Land" (*The Rediscovery of the Holy Land in the Nineteenth Century* [Jerusalem, 1983] p225).

[36] G.W. Grogan, "Heilsgeographie: Geography as a Theological Concept", *The Scottish Bulletin of Evangelical Theology*, Volume 6, Number 2 (Autumn 1988), p89.

[37] J.M. Monson, quoted in D. Sutherland "The Interface between Theology and Historical Geography", *The Scottish Bulletin of Evangelical Theology*, Volume 11, Number 1 (Summer 1993) p22.

[38] HGHL, p76.

[39] Smith, *Syria and the Holy Land* (London, 1918) p6.

[40] HGHL, p119.

[41] Ibid., p297.

Bethshan ..."[42] The sermonic style is evident throughout. In the words of Professor H. Wheeler Robinson, Smith's approach helped readers to "hear the sound of running history in the Old Testament".[43] Geographer Robin Butlin assesses the work as

> a pioneer book written by a powerful communicator and preacher, whose primary concern was to evoke and use an array of modern scientific and critical techniques for an essentially evangelical purpose, but whose intellectual milieu ... reflects wider currents of thought and ideas.[44]

Butlin explores the influences on Smith's thinking – the Bible as a primary source, the changing face of Palestine, and the development of the study of geographical context, as well as the intellectual connections which enabled Smith to produce his pioneer volume. He sets Smith's work in the context of "a watershed or divide in work on the historical geography of the Holy Land",[45] standing midway between works which relied for the most part on secondary sources, and later works which would incorporate a wide corpus of new scientific discoveries. At least one reviewer recognised this when he stated: "It is, of course far from completing its task; it is really only the first opening up of what will hereafter prove a fruitful field of study".[46]

In the words of one geographer, "The descriptions of Smith read like poetry";[47] another writer comments on Smith's "plastic and poetic gift of English expression".[48] To the criticism that the book is "*too* eloquent", A.B. Bruce offered the following response:

> If that be so the fault will be pardoned, in the first place as the defect of the author's qualities, in the next place as making the work readable, but chiefly because, on second thoughts, the fault is seen to be a virtue. For who could fitly handle the historical geography of Palestine that came to his task in a dry-as-dust spirit, devoid of imagination and poetry, prosaically describing

---

[42] Ibid., p381.

[43] H. Wheeler Robinson, "The Sound of Running History", *The British Weekly*, 24 October 1935, p71.

[44] R. Butlin, "George Adam Smith and the Historical Geography of the Holy Land: contents, contexts and connections", *Journal of Historical Geography*, 14.4 (1988), pp387-8.

[45] Ibid., p395.

[46] W.M. Ramsay, "Professor G.A. Smith's *Historical Geography of the Holy Land*", *The Expositor*, 5th series, Volume 1 (1895), p57.

[47] Gary L. Paxton *Eretz Israel*, Faith Brethren Publishing, n.d., Chapter Six, downloaded from the Internet at http://www.htcomp.net/fbp/ on 29 October 1998. Paxton's work draws heavily on the HGHL.

[48] W. Manson, "Sir George Adam Smith", *Dictionary of National Biography*, 1941-1950, p793.

the physical features without electric thrills communicated by the heroisms of which it was the theatre?[49]

In his illuminating preface to the first edition of the HGHL, Smith outlines the philosophy behind the work. He acknowledges the amount of work done in the exploration of Palestine in the previous twenty years, paying tribute both to the international character of this work, and the distinctive contribution of the Palestine Exploration Fund. The nature of these archaeological and historical studies is such, he argues, that a new summary is warranted. But he argues that "an equally strong reason for the appearance at this time of a Historical Geography of Palestine is the recent progress of Biblical Criticism".[50] He claims that his is the first historical geography to pay heed to the two-fold duty of serious students of Scripture: the duty, first, of "regulating the literary criticism of the Bible by the archaeology of Syria", and the converse duty of showing the "helpfulness of recent criticism" in writing the geography of the Holy Land.[51] This point Smith explores in his chapter on "The Land and Questions of Faith". His guiding principle is this: "That a story accurately reflects geography does not necessarily mean that it is a real transcript of history ... let us at once admit that, while we may have other reasons for the historical truth of the patriarchal narratives, we cannot prove this on the ground that their itineraries and place-names are correct".[52] On the other hand, he maintains that geographical descriptions authenticate biblical passages "as testimonies of the truth of the narratives in which they occur".[53]

This is all very well; but Smith's uncritical acceptance of the findings of higher criticism on the question of authorship of biblical texts rather begs the question. He admits that issues related to authorship must be decided on grounds other than geographical ones; yet he goes on to contrast the descriptions of Jerusalem in proto-Isaiah with those of deutero-Isaiah without offering evidence for the dual authorship. This rather assumes his point that "the evidence of geography mainly comes in support of a decision already settled by other proofs".[54] At the same time he states that even second Isaiah contains passages whose topography is as Palestinian as that of first Isaiah.[55] In

---

[49] A.B. Bruce, "The Rev George Adam Smith, DD, LLD", *The British Weekly*, 30 July 1896.
[50] HGHL, pxvi.
[51] Ibid.
[52] HGHL, p108.
[53] Ibid., p109.
[54] Ibid.
[55] GAS, "Isaiah", in J. Hastings (ed.), *A Dictionary of the Bible*, Vol 2 (Edinburgh, 1904), p494, where Smith says that 56-7 "is the passage which most clearly reflects the scenery of Palestine".

a similar way he argues that geographical reflection proves the composite authorship of the Pentateuch.[56]

Yet even in his Isaiah commentaries, Smith had made the point that Isaianic descriptions of Jerusalem, for example, vary according to the perspective from which the prophecies are uttered. In commenting on Isaiah 2-4, Smith suggests that the prophet offers a three-fold view of the city: an idealistic view, a realistic view, and a revelatory view.[57] He correctly surmises that "what characterises the bulk of these visions is penetrativeness, the keenness of a man who will not be deceived by an outward show ... but who has a conscience for the inner worth of things".[58] In volume 2, dealing with Second Isaiah (chapter 40), he rounds on the critics who insist that terms like "Jerusalem", "Sion", and "cities of Judah" reflect eye-witness and contemporaneous situations; "it is not," he argues, "the vision of a Jew at home that has determined the choice of these names, but the desire and dream of a Jew abroad".[59] In one part of the commentary he even suggests that it is necessary to approach the references to Jerusalem in Second Isaiah in the same way as one would approach the apocalyptic vision of Jerusalem in the Book of Revelation.[60]

Smith's view of the religion of Israel is similarly allied to his interest in Palestine's geography. In a sermon on Psalm 121, he regards the hills as "sacraments"[61] and consequently aids to faith in one sovereign God. Similarly, he suggests, "For our faith in the incarnation ... a study of the historical geography of Palestine is a necessary discipline".[62] By looking at the life of Christ in the light of Palestine's geography, he suggests, we will avoid an abstract Christology, and we will avoid treating Christ as though he is our contemporary. By thus using geography to set a historical context, Smith believes that we can get much closer to the facts of the biblical narrative than would otherwise be the case. In this sense Smith anticipates the development of form criticism in the study of biblical narrative, where "form is integral to meaning".[63] Where the biblical story is studded with geographical reference, there is not only physical description intended, but also spiritual significance.

---

[56] Ibid.

[57] Isaiah, Vol 1, pp25-34. Cf. T.L. Brensinger on "Jerusalem" in NIDOTTE, Volume 4 (Carlisle, 1997) pp773-4, where he argues that Jerusalem appears in the later prophets from a three-fold perspective: the city as representing the entire community, as a "corporate representative in speeches of salvation or deliverance", and as a symbol of "the ultimate consummation of Yawheh's glorious plan".

[58] Ibid., p24.

[59] GAS, *Isaiah*, Vol 2, p72.

[60] Ibid., p398.

[61] GAS, *Four Psalms* (London, 1896) p101.

[62] HGHL, p114.

[63] S. Greidanus, "The Value of a Literary Approach for Preaching" in L. Ryken and T. Longman III (eds) *A Complete Literary Guide to the Bible* (Grand Rapids, Michigan, 1993) p515.

Sometimes he may be understood as arguing that there is a more intimate relationship between faith and geography than between faith and history. At the same time, his argument that the geographical contours of Palestine were directly related to the moral power of Israel seems tenuous. There is no *a priori* reason to posit "the geography of the land forming barriers to Israel's growth, by surmounting which the moral force that is in her becomes conspicuous".[64]

For Smith, the geography of the Holy Land lays the foundation for a developmental view of Israel's religion. Although geographical study cannot fully answer all the questions that arise in connection with literary criticism of the Old Testament, he assures his readers that "when we rise to the higher matters of the religion of Israel, to the story of its origin and development, to the appearance of monotheism, and to the question of the supernatural ... the testimony of the historical geography of the Holy Land is high and clear".[65] Again, however, Smith assumes that Israelite religion was originally polytheistic. He replaces the view of the French critic Renan concerning Israel's primitive monotheism with the critical view that "in the Semitic religion, as in the Semitic world, monotheism had a great opportunity".[66] Later he argues that the fertility of the land invited polytheism, and made monotheism highly unlikely.[67]

The geography, therefore, has become a foil for the revelation; and the emergent monotheism has developed not because of, but in spite of, the geographical position of Israel. Neither assumption – either that the fertility of the land necessarily inclined to polytheism, or that the monotheistic religion of Israel was a late development – is evident on *a priori* grounds. Smith's argument in the HGHL is that the physical nature of Israel would have led to the Semitic nation being polytheistic were it not for the revelation which they received from God.[68] But this appears to be a highly circular argument. It is difficult to see how the geography illuminates Israel's *theology* by paying close attention to the contours of the land, while it is of use to our understanding of the *revelation* only if we take the land as a foil. His conclusion is:

> For myself, I can only say that all I have seen of the land, and read of its ancient history, drives me back to the belief that the monotheism which

---

[64] HGHL, p113.

[65] Ibid., p111.

[66] Ibid., p30. Smith also took issue with Renan's view, that the Semite was a born monotheist, at the Summer School of Theology in Oxford in 1894, when he lectured on "The Preparation for Prophecy". According to A.S. Peake's reporting of Smith's lecture in the *Methodist Times* for 9 August 1894, Smith demonstrated "not simply that the tendency to monotheism did not exist, but that even those causes which favoured such development were unable to produce it among the Semites. The monotheism of Israel was traced to the direct revealing activity of God".

[67] Ibid., p90.

[68] Ibid., p113.

appeared upon it was ultimately due to the revelation of a character and a power which carried with them the evidence of their uniqueness and divine sovereignty.[69]

The HGHL quickly became not only a popular reference work, but also a standard textbook on the subject. The *Oxford University Gazette*, for example, noted that it had been added as a textbook in the University.[70] While it is undoubtedly true that the book pioneered the study of the geography of Palestine in relation to the findings of biblical criticism, the main weakness of the HGHL was its lack of personal biblical references. The landscape, in and of itself, is only part of the story. The power of the biblical narrative rests, as Smith stated so powerfully in the Isaiah volumes, in the potential with which individual human life is endowed.[71] In this regard, *Jerusalem* was unquestionably superior, grounding the geographical study as it did in the personal narratives of the Old Testament. The HGHL, on the other hand, tends to be more detached from personal life, although containing many biblical allusions. Following its publication, Smith received many letters, including some which questioned one or two of his conclusions, such as from Stephen Lawley of Exeter, who both applauded Smith for not trying to identify precisely every biblical location, but who also said that "on p292 it is a little staggering to be told that Isaiah 10:28-32 relates to no 'actual facts'".[72] Whether Smith succeeded in making Palestine "a visible background to the Bible"[73] is questionable; to a large degree, issues of geography dominate, and remain in the foreground. That Smith was able to cover so much ground in one volume, however, deserved high praise, and the book was received to wide and justified acclamation.

It is fitting to note here the reference to the HGHL in the campaign of General Allenby during the First World War. After Allenby became commander of GHQ, Cairo, Lloyd George, the Prime Minister, expected him to take Jerusalem before Christmas (of 1917). Allenby's biographer takes up the story:

The Prime Minister then presented Allenby, with whom on this further acquaintance he had become more impressed, with *The Historical*

---

[69] Ibid.

[70] Presscutting from the *Oxford University Gazette* (n.d.) on p47 of Journal of presscuttings, NLS Acc 9446 No 412.

[71] Cf, for example, Smith's argument in *Isaiah*, Vol 1, p393, that "personal influence is the spring of social progress, the shelter and fountain force of the community".

[72] Stephen Lawley to GAS, October 31, 1894, NLS Acc 9446 No 137. Smith discusses Isaiah in the context of examining "The Borders and Bulwarks of Judea".

[73] H. Wheeler Robertson, "Sir George Adam Smith: The Sound of Running History", *The British Weekly*, 24 October 1935, p71.

Geography of the Holy Land by Sir George Adam Smith, which included a detailed geographical survey of the area. 'I was convinced that this work was a better guide to a military leader whose task was to reach Jerusalem than any survey to be found in pigeon-holes of the War Office'.[74]

Allenby's Palestine campaign was successful; he received Jerusalem's surrender on 9 December 1917 and walked into the city on the 11th "its first Christian master since the Crusades".[75] S.A. Cook's claim that Allenby "studied both the Bible and HGHL almost daily"[76] is confirmed by an incidental reference in a letter to Lilian Adam Smith from a cousin following Smith's death. In it, there is mention of a Colonel Rupert Humphries, who served with Allenby, and who reported to the writer of the letter that Smith's work had given Allenby suggestions for his final "attack on the Turk", and confirming that Allenby had studied the Bible and the HGHL on a regular basis.[77]

Jerusalem

The main lacuna in the HGHL was that there was no treatment of Jerusalem.[78] A series of articles on the city written by Smith appeared in *The Expositor*

---

[74] B. Gardner, *Allenby* (London, 1965) p114.

[75] A.J.P. Taylor, *The First World War* (London, 1963) p206.

[76] S.A. Cook, "George Adam Smith 1856-1942", *Proceedings of the British Academy*, 1942, p33.

[77] Letter to LAS from cousin Rosalind Leslie (wife of Brigadier Rupert Leslie) in Swindon, 4 March 1942, NLS Acc 9446 No 145. Cf. also the summary in G. Frederick Owen, *Abraham to Allenby* (Grand Rapids, Michigan, 1939) pp304-5: "Biblical scenes and events of bygone days crowded the minds of the British soldiers as they fought for and gained place after place of which they had heard from the lips of their parents, Sunday School teachers and ministers. It was not unusual for the officers to inform their men regarding the historical significance of the places before they were taken, and General Allenby often consulted the Bible, the Apocrypha, Josephus, and George Adam Smith's *Historical Geography of the Holy Land* as well as the annals of the Crusades. This he did because each of the works contained accounts of military successes and failures on these very hills and plains. No other sources offered such a store of exact information regarding Judean topography and military strategy". Cf. also Stanley A. Hunter "The Water of the Nile Flows into Palestine!", *The United Presbyterian*, 26 Dec 1918: "General Allenby is a great Bible scholar, and he is thoroughly familiar with the battles of the Old Testament. I spent an evening with him, going over Sir George Adam Smith's book on Palestine, and following the advance of the British through the old Bible places". See also Eric H. Cline "In Pharaoh's Footsteps: History Repeats itself in General Allenby's 1918 March on Megiddo" from *Archaeology Odyssey* (a website of the Biblical Archaeology Society), Spring 1998 (downloaded from the Internet at http://scholar.cc.emory.edu./scripts/BAS/cline.html on 23 September 1998).

[78] In the preface to *Jerusalem*, Vol 1, p vii, Smith states: "In the *Historical Geography of the Holy Land* it was not possible, for reasons of space, to include a topography of

between 1903 and 1906, and were later reprinted with additional material in two volumes entitled *Jerusalem: the Topography, Economics and History from the Earliest Times to AD 70*. The first volume appeared in 1907, the second in 1908. They were in a sense even more of a pioneering work than the HGHL, since "hitherto there had been no specific study of Jerusalem".[79]

While the principles governing *Jerusalem* were the same as those governing the HGHL, the focus of interest was much narrower, and it drew on two further visits to Palestine (in 1901 and 1904) during which Smith concentrated his studies on the holy city. Volume 1 divides into two books, Book I dealing with topographical subjects (sites and names), and Book 2 with the economic and political background to Jerusalem. Volume 2 contains Book 3, which is a historical study of Jerusalem (and which his wife, Lilian, assessed as "one of the best pieces of work George ever did"[80]).

The introductory essay in Volume 1, "The Essential City" is a summary of the place and significance of Jerusalem. A superb piece of writing, it introduces the reader to the main points of importance of the city who "knew herself chosen of God, a singular city in the world, with a mission to mankind".[81] Though inferior to other places in learning and philosophy, Jerusalem became "the home of the Faith, the goal of most distant pilgrimages, and the original of the heavenly City, which would one day descend from God among men".[82] In these introductory remarks, Smith recalls some of his travels around Jerusalem. These serve as a fitting introduction to his description of the holy city.

Unlike the HGHL, *Jerusalem* contained photographs as well as maps. Many of these were taken by Smith himself, and made the book more appealing. Quite apart, however, from their aesthetic value, the photographs were an important contribution to the academic study of the Holy Land. In her study of the role of photographs in disseminating geographical information, Joan Schwartz has argued that photographs had a wide appeal, particularly as European travel developed in the nineteenth century:

> Through travel photographs, in concert with other forms of representation, Victorian viewers who had never travelled came to share impressions of place. Not only as a pool of visual facts, but also as symbols of imperial expansion, colonial development, commercial enterprise, military might, and

---

Jerusalem, an appreciation of her material resources, or a full study of the historical significance of her site and surroundings."

[79] Cook, "George Adam Smith", p334.

[80] LAS, p106. Some 35 years later, Smith's friend and colleague, David S. Cairns, described the Jerusalem volumes as "indispensable to the serious professional student of the Bible" in "Sir George Adam Smith", *Religion in Life*, Vol XI Number 4 (Autumn 1942) p537.

[81] GAS, *Jerusalem*, Vol 1, p4.

[82] Ibid., p7.

scientific knowledge, these mutually-held visual images contributed to national identity, stimulated patriotic effort and reinforced one's sense of place in the world.[83]

Schwartz's view that "the camera, like the pen and the brush, when wielded by Western travellers, depicted the world in Western terms",[84] may not be entirely discordant with Smith's own view of Jerusalem. Recognising that "East and West hotly contended for her",[85] Smith argues that the physical location of Jerusalem suggests that "Providence had bound over the city to eastern interests and eastern sympathies".[86] His work may be seen as a liberating of the essential city from its eastern aspect, an attempt, as he puts it, to "bring the spell with him out of the history".[87]

The site of the city and the surrounding areas is the concern of Book 1, in which Smith seeks to identify some biblical and historical sites around the environs of Jerusalem. Smith devoted a chapter to Jerusalem's geology on the grounds that "in all departments of his work ... the historian is dependent on the geologist".[88] Here Smith is heavily dependent on secondary scientific sources;[89] although one reviewer did take care to highlight that Smith, while availing himself of these insights, "is not blindly dependent upon them. He has studied the problems on the spot".[90] An examination of the rock formation around the city, Smith suggests, gives important clues about the city's water supply and consequently its topography. This is further examined in his treatment of "earthquakes, springs and dragons", where he is again dependent on other scientific analyses, but finds it necessary "to consider the effect of earthquakes on ancient mythology"[91] as a precursor to biblical exegesis. For example, although he admits that his study of the waters of Jerusalem leave him "baffled by many of the answers of which we have been in search",[92] Smith nonetheless finds that without such careful analysis it is impossible to do justice to the many water illustrations in the Bible.[93] The geography is once again given symbolic and spiritual significance, and is invested with a moral quality that

---

[83] Joan M. Schwartz, "The Geography Lesson: photographs and the construction of imaginative geographies", *Journal of Historical Geography*, 22.1 (1996) p31.
[84] Ibid.
[85] *Jerusalem*, Vol 1, p7.
[86] Ibid., p11.
[87] Ibid., p22.
[88] Ibid., p50.
[89] Butlin, "George Adam Smith", p389, draws attention to the "great care taken to make use of the carefully evaluated and most recent scientific sources" in Volume 1.
[90] H. Mann, Review of *Jerusalem* in *The Daily News*, 25 May, 1908, NLS Acc 9446 No 142.
[91] *Jerusalem*, Vol 1, p70.
[92] Ibid., p132.
[93] Smith mentions Psalm 46:4, Ezekiel 47:1,5; Isaiah 33:21ff (Ibid., p133).

transcends the historicity of the biblical narrative, whose purpose is "not an accurate historical recital, but moral impressiveness".[94]

Book 2, on the economics and politics of Jerusalem, draws on an earlier article on "Trade and Commerce" written by Smith in 1903.[95] In this article Smith had emphasised the effects of eighth-century trade expansion on Jerusalem, raising Judah "to a pitch of wealth and luxury which the Hebrews had not before reached".[96] The classical prophets made their appearance at this time, decrying greed and urging sobriety and self-control in the use of wealth. In Book 2 of *Jerusalem*, Smith examines the growth of the capital at the expense of the provinces; Jerusalem evolved into the only legitimate place of sacrifice-worship and the place of pilgrimage for many of the faithful. Given its physical elevation, Smith asks, "how were her finances regulated, and whence did she draw provision both for so numerous a non-productive population and for the temporary but immense additions to it caused by the Temple festivals?"[97] There follows a detailed examination of Jerusalem's natural resources, and an examination of the commercial imports, temple revenues, royal trade, crafts and industries which, in a city most unfitted, in Smith's words, "to be the home of industries",[98] nonetheless acknowledged that all its resources it owed to the benevolence of God.[99] A discussion of the government and policing of the city and a note on the term "the multitude", the common people, who laid the foundation for the Christian church of the New Testament conclude this section.

Volume 2 provides a narrative history of Jerusalem from about 1400BC to the Gospel period. Smith is unwilling to admit the Genesis 14 passage, in which the mysterious Melchisedek, "king of Salem" meets Abraham, for consideration in this history, on the grounds of its ambiguity.[100] More recent commentators, while highlighting the difficulty of integrating the Melchisedek pericope into the wider narrative of Genesis, are nonetheless ready to concede that Salem is an ancient Sumerian name for Jerusalem, and that the Genesis 14 story does contribute to the history of Jerusalem.[101] While touching briefly on

---

[94] GAS, *Isaiah*, Vol 1, pp49-50.
[95] "Trade and Commerce" in *Encyclopedia Biblica*, T.K. Cheyne and J.S. Black (eds), Vol IV, (London, 1903) pp5145-5199. The article is a wide-ranging and extensive piece of scholarship.
[96] Ibid., p5174.
[97] *Jerusalem*, Vol 1, p276.
[98] Ibid., p372.
[99] Cf ibid., p374: "the good artificer is not despised in the Old Testament; on the contrary, his gifts are regarded equally with those of the husbandman as from God".
[100] *Jerusalem*, Vol 2, p4.
[101] See, for example, V.P. Hamilton *The Book of Genesis Chapters 1-17*, The New International Commentary on the Old Testament (Grand Rapids, Michigan, 1990) pp408-410. For further discussion see M.J. Paul, "The Order of Melchizedek (Psalm

ancient letters and documents relating to Jerusalem, for Smith the history proper begins with David's conquest, and with the religious impulse which inspired David to bring the Ark of the Covenant to the city. "The national unity", Smith says, "had never been maintained, or when lost had never been recovered, except by loyalty to the nation's one God and Lord. His Ark implied Himself. It was His Presence which sealed the new-formed union, and consecrated the capital".[102] Smith credits David with making Jerusalem the religious centre which she became, even if it was the prophetic word and the deuteronomic legislation which were the chief factors in her development: "The Man, whose individual will and policy seem essential to the career of every great city, Jerusalem found in David ... The drama of Jerusalem is never more vivid than while David is its hero".[103]

Subsequent kings, from Solomon through to Ahaz, governed in David's shadow, but made their own contribution to Jerusalem's development. In his description of the location and building of the Temple, Smith warns that the text of 1 Kings 5-7 has "suffered from the wear of tradition, from attempts at repair, and from insertions by a later age, to which the Temple was of more importance – the object at once of greater superstition and of more careful definition between the degrees of holiness ascribed to its various parts – than it was under Solomon itself".[104] Nonetheless he finds that the national annals of Judah furnish us with sufficient information to explain the Temple and its service; the editor of the Book of Kings, he suggests, edited the Temple passages from these annals.[105] The rapid growth of the Temple's importance he argues from the fact that it was the king's, that it had command over national life outside Jerusalem, and that its treasures accumulated from an early stage.[106] With Ahaz, Jerusalem comes under the domination of Assyria, and the stage is set for the appearance of Isaiah, "the greatest statesman who ever swayed her life".[107]

Smith discusses the place of Jerusalem in the major prophets, the statesmen who safeguarded the role of Jerusalem as the city chosen by God. Elsewhere Smith describes Jerusalem as the focus of Isaiah's great interest: "She is his immediate and ultimate regard, the centre and return of all his thoughts, the hinge of the history of his time, the one thing worth preserving amidst its disasters, the summit of those brilliant hopes with which he fills the future".[108]

110:4 and Hebrews 7:3), *Westminster Theological Journal*, Volume 49:1 (Spring 1987), pp195-211.
[102] *Jerusalem*, Vol 2, p38.
[103] Ibid., p47.
[104] Ibid., pp57-8.
[105] Ibid., pp109-110.
[106] Ibid., p111.
[107] Ibid., p131.
[108] GAS, *Isaiah,* Vol 1, p22.

In typical prose style, Smith says that "the fires which David and Solomon kindled in Jerusalem ... leap into high, bright flame at the powerful breath of Isaiah".[109] While other prophets spoke the divine word to the city, it was Isaiah's contribution that secured, amid the political upheavals through which she passed, a "mind to read her history and proclaim her destiny".[110]

In a chapter on "The Ideal City and the Real", Smith examines the biblical literature which represents Jerusalem as the ideal of religious life. The exilic poetry and narrative mourned the loss of the city and anticipated a return. However, the later prophets, he argues, turned their attention from king to priest as the pivotal figure in Jerusalem's life, so that the return after the exile was not of a kingdom, but of a colony.[111] In the Second Temple period, Smith finds in Israel on the one hand a lofty idealism that God had somehow returned to his place in Jerusalem, but on the other an increased superstition – "the contradiction of the idea that He dwelt only there";[112] from the sacredness of the Temple there developed "the dogma of its inviolableness",[113] and the consequent superstitious confidence that God would never leave it. Not until the coming of Jesus was this superstition dealt with definitively, for "the Messiah promised to the Temple supplanted the Temple".[114] And although Smith recognised that biblical criticism still had a long way to go before it could answer the questions thrown up by the facts of Jerusalem's history, nonetheless our assurance of the truth of the Gospel is not dependent on the definitive findings of criticism:

> About the broad results there is no question: the rise of a new religion from the heart and the home of the old one, the hesitating steps upon which at first it ventured, and its final break from the Jewish system in the faith that all which this had mediated was become more directly and surely possible through the Person and Work of Jesus. Even before Israel's Altar was for ever quenched, Jesus in the experience of His followers had taken the place of the Temple and of everything for which it stood".[115]

The crucifixion of Jesus represented the gross ignorance of Jerusalem of her religious position and heritage – it was the final confrontation of the City and

---

[109] *Jerusalem*, Vol 2, p147.
[110] Ibid.
[111] See also Smith's *Book of the Twelve Prophets*, Vol 2, p189: "Israel is no longer a kingdom, but a colony. The state is not independent: there is virtually no state. The community is poor and feeble ... We miss the civic atmosphere, the great spaces of public life, the large ethical issues. Instead we have tearful questions, raised by a grudging soil and bad seasons, with all the petty selfishness of hunger-bitten peasants".
[112] *Jerusalem*, Vol 2, p311.
[113] Ibid., p312.
[114] Ibid., p521.
[115] Ibid., p522.

the Man, Smith says;[116] nevertheless what was "a sunset to herself" was "the dawn of a new day to the world beyond".[117]

In Butlin's view, this analysis of Jerusalem's history is "a remarkable combination of scholarly erudition, intuition, historical imagination and depth of feeling".[118] Indeed, Smith's work on Jerusalem is cited in modern works on the same theme.[119] James Denney, the distinguished theologian and Smith's colleague at the Free Church College in Glasgow to whom Smith gifted a copy of the Jerusalem volumes, also drew attention to the admirable mix of qualities which fitted Smith eminently for the work of writing on Jerusalem:

> He has the eye of the geographer or the military engineer for the physical features of a situation, the vivid imagination by which the historian recognises great events, the enthusiasm and penetration of the prophet who discerns and interprets the spiritual crises in a nation's life. Without this combination of gifts and interests, which keeps his own mind alive at every point, so thorough a book must have become intolerably heavy; as it is, it can be read from beginning to end with no less delight than gain".[120]

For Denney, however, the main appeal of *Jerusalem* lay in what he considered the emancipation of Jesus from naturalistic criticism. Recent criticism, Denney believed, had attempted "to strip Jesus of the character in which He comes before us in the Gospels, and in which alone He can be the object of Christian faith".[121] By painting the picture of Jerusalem on a large canvas, as Smith had done, Denney believed that this naturalistic view of Jesus was undermined. In private correspondence with Smith, Denney congratulated Smith on putting his finger on the essential difference between the Old and the New Testaments: "...whereas before there were men who could say *I know*, now there was somebody who could say *I am*".[122] The Jesus of the Gospels, Denney insisted, had to be believed in terms of his own self-assessment; and in showing how Jesus had appropriated to himself all the prophetic strands in Jerusalem's history, Smith had come to the heart of the Gospel:

> The Christian religion depends on two things: first, that we take Christ at His own estimate; and second, that Christ's estimate of himself was what it

---

[116] Ibid., p578.
[117] Ibid., p579.
[118] Butlin, "George Adam Smith", p389.
[119] Such as G. Auld and M. Steiner, *Jerusalem I: From the Bronze Age to the Maccabees, Cities of the Biblical World* (Cambridge, 1996). Auld and Steiner describe Smith as "still after a century the undisputed doyen of biblical geography" (p2).
[120] J. Denney, "Jerusalem", *The British Weekly*, 28 May 1908, p177.
[121] Denney, p178.
[122] James Denney to GAS, 20 May 1908, NLS Acc 9446 No 142.

is represented in the Gospels to be. No one could have done a more timely service to the Christian argument, or done it with more convincing power, than Dr Smith in this chapter".[123]

Denney saw *Jerusalem* as serving not only a historical but an apologetic purpose in rendering Christ eminently suitable as an object of faith.

Perhaps, however, Denney proves too much. While Smith himself was willing to see a Messiah concept in the Old Testament which had its ultimate and consummate fulfilment in the coming of Jesus Christ, his interest lay less in the Christianising of the Old Testament and more in the Hebraising of the New. In this regard, Smith's approach to the Old Testament was different to that of William Robertson Smith. While Robertson Smith's treatment of the Old Testament contains a "Christian subtext" which R.P. Carroll regards as "a complete abandonment of his previously declared commitment to historical analysis of the prophets",[124] George Adam Smith's concern was to demonstrate that "Prophecy had ... associated the redemption of Israel with the virtue and even with the self-sacrifice of a single Personality".[125] The "Christian subtext" is missing from George Adam Smith's work, and to this extent he has moved beyond Robertson Smith in demonstrating that the Servant who will redeem mankind is "an Israel within Israel",[126] one who appeared on Jerusalem's stage, honouring her history in a manner that was "transforming and creative".[127] For Robertson Smith, Old Testament prophecy pointed towards an end which "swallowed up the Old Testament in the New";[128] while for George Adam Smith, the Jerusalem of the Gospels has simply developed from the portrayal of Jerusalem in the Old Testament: "just as in the former development it was the Person, Character and the Work of God which was everywhere the active Power, so here it is the Person, the Character and the Work of Jesus".[129]

Professor D.S. Margoliouth, in a review of *Jerusalem*, regarded Smith's view of the biblical history as "conservative".[130] This he took to be an advance on current scholarship, since Smith had taken the time "to watch the development of morality"[131] in the biblical history. Margoliouth felt, however, that Smith had given Isaiah too high a place as the one who "made" Jerusalem,

---

[123] Ibid.
[124] R.P. Carroll "The Biblical Prophets as Apologists" in W. Johnstone (ed.), *William Robertson Smith: Essays in Reassessment* (Sheffield, 1995) pp53-4.
[125] Jerusalem, Vol 2, p533.
[126] Ibid., p550.
[127] Ibid., p554.
[128] W.R. Smith, "On Prophecy", in J.S. Black and G. Chrystal, *Lectures and Essays of William Robertson Smith* (London, 1912) p348.
[129] *Jerusalem*, Volume 2, p554.
[130] D.S. Margoliouth, "Dr G.A. Smith on Jerusalem", *The Expositor*, 7th series, No. 6, (1908), p520.
[131] Ibid.

and argued that no doctrine of the first Isaiah "was preached by him for the first time".[132] On the other hand, he is willing to concede the importance of Isaiah's role in bringing to Jerusalem a religious conviction which made her "the praise of the earth".

Margoliouth notes Smith's reconstruction of the Ezra-Nehemiah history, which highlights the ways in which Smith's historiography defers to the conclusions of biblical criticism. The history at this point requires to be reconstructed, and Margoliouth is satisfied with Smith's effort to do so.[133] On this intriguing question on the post-exilic fortunes of the city, as well as the problems of the biblical record, Smith had intended to include an appendix to Volume 2, which space did not allow.[134] He discussed them in the second volume of his work on the Minor Prophets.[135]

One of the disappointing features of the Jerusalem volumes was that Smith was unable to extend the history to the limits of the title. He did not, in fact, bring the history up to AD70. This was pointed out in one review which said that "the natural conclusion would have been the siege and destruction of Jerusalem by Titus; and it was planned to end with this; but the concluding chapter together with an appendix have been crowded out by the size to which the second volume has grown".[136] This only demonstrates, however, the massive amount of work which Smith had done in bringing the study up to the early narrative of the Book of Acts. The volume of writing, presumably, also prevented fulfilment of W. Robertson Nicoll's wish of seeing Jerusalem and the HGHL published together in two volumes.[137] Desirable as this may have been, it is arguable that in their form and substance they are different; the Jerusalem volumes for example, are more Bible-oriented than the HGHL. It was probably better that they stand on their respective merits.

Cartography

The maps in the HGHL and *Jerusalem* were the work of John George Bartholomew (1860-1920), whose association with Smith was a major contribution to twentieth-century cartography and the development of the Bartholomew map-making business. In thanking Bartholomew for his help with the maps, Smith claims that they were the first orographical maps of Palestine,

---

[132] Ibid., p524.
[133] Ibid., p526.
[134] Cook, "George Adam Smith", p334, n.2.
[135] GAS, *The Book of the Twelve Prophets*, Volume 2 (London, ed. 1902) chapter xv.
[136] Review of *Jerusalem* in *The Times Literary Supplement*, 28 May 1908 (unattributed – collected in NLS Acc 9446 No 137).
[137] W. Robertson Nicoll to GAS: "I feel I must not lose a moment of time in congratulating you on your truly monumental and magnificent work. Do you not think the time has come for revising the HGHL and making such additions as you may think proper? What we wish is to issue it uniform with *Jerusalem* in two volumes" (29 April 1908; NLS Acc 9446 No 142).

that is, maps which showed the mountainous elevations by using different colours for different heights,[138] instead of simply using varieties of black and white shading for this purpose. Prefacing the Jerusalem volumes, Smith thanked Bartholomew "for all the trouble he has taken in their preparation, as well as for the clearness and impressiveness with which they have been achieved".[139]

If it was true that Bartholomew had "got his head screwed on the right way in the matter of maps",[140] then Smith had his head screwed on the right way by employing Bartholomew's services for the purposes of his geographical studies. Not only was John G. Bartholomew a man of foresight and wisdom, rightly dubbed the "Prince of Cartographers",[141] the firm he represented was a hive of industry. Towards the end of the nineteenth century, Bartholomew's was, in Elspeth Lochhead's words, "a real focus of activity, having strong links with the scientific community centred in Edinburgh".[142] Links and connections were important in Smith's works, as Butlin argues:

> The important connections are those which concern, for example, developments in the nature of historical geography and the scientific and artistic exploration of Palestine, but wider connections existed with other geographers and geographical and scientific societies, and [Smith's] work may also be viewed in the context of major debates on the critical appraisal of the Bible as historical evidence and on the compatibility of religion with Darwin's theory of evolution.[143]

The connection with Bartholomew was itself a door into an important scientific milieu which gave Smith an interest in, and a relevance to, a wide variety of disciplines.

Eventually Hodder and Stoughton would publish, in 1916, Smith's *Historical Atlas of the Holy Land*, planned by himself and Bartholomew as far back as 1894.[144] By 1910, Bartholomew wrote to Smith saying that "I have always been postponing the actual printing of the Bible Atlas until we would

---

[138] HGHL, pxviii.

[139] *Jerusalem*, Vol 1, pxiv.

[140] A comment made by Archibald Geikie of Edinburgh and recorded in the official history of the map-making firm in L Gardiner *Bartholomew: 150 years* (Edinburgh, 1976) p30.

[141] Ibid.

[142] E.N. Lochhead, "Scotland as the Cradle of Modern Academic Geography in Britain", *Scottish Geographical Magazine* 97 (1981) p99.

[143] Butlin, "George Adam Smith", p392.

[144] So Smith, in the preface to the first edition of the *Historical Atlas of the Holy Land*, 1916, pvii. The delay was due to "other literary works and the duties of my office". In 1935 he would produce a second edition along with John Bartholomew, the son of John G. Bartholomew.

get Eastern Palestine satisfactorily finished and that has proved most difficult as nothing seems to be completed".[145] Completion was still not in sight by the time war broke out in 1914. In August of that year, Bartholomew was hopeful that with the postponement of some other contracts, the Bible Atlas would finally see the light of day: "As most of our other atlases are cancelled, or postponed, awaiting developments, this is obviously the time to get on with such work as the Bible Atlas, which is beyond all modern changes".[146] The remainder of 1914 was spent in sending proofs back and fore between Bartholomew and Smith (who had by this time moved to Aberdeen), and the atlas finally appeared two years later.

Butlin calls into question the accuracy of one or two details in the atlas, suggesting that the length of time which elapsed between initial planning and final publication did not allow for modernisation of Smith's first maps.[147] Nonetheless, it was to be a major landmark in the Bartholomew tradition, praised by the Bartholomew historian as "an astonishing compendium of religious history",[148] which

> emerged unique, owing nothing to what had gone before, an excellent example of the selective thoroughness and artistic refinement which John George preached, and the accurate up-to-date treatment which had come to be associated with his name.[149]

Smith's Contribution to Historical Geography

S.A. Cook is probably going too far when he says that Smith's work in the field of historical geography was "revolutionising".[150] In a more sober assessment, A.B. Bruce recognised that there were other studies of aspects of Palestinian geography which would answer more detailed questions.[151] Nonetheless he was ready to admit that there was something distinctive in Smith's contribution:

> Not antiquarian investigation into the claims of particular spots to be sites of historic towns, not a running commentary on biblical texts, not photographic pictures of what can be seen from selected viewpoints ... but a comprehensive idea of Palestine as a whole, with careful description of its

---

[145] J.G. Bartholomew to GAS, 14 June 1910, New College Special Collections, MSS.SMI.1.4.4.
[146] J.G. Bartholomew to GAS, 27 August 1914, New College Special Collections, MSS.SMI 1.4.4.
[147] Butlin, "George Adam Smith", p391.
[148] Gardiner, *Bartholomew*, p52.
[149] Ibid., p53.
[150] Cook, "George Adam Smith", p334.
[151] A.B. Bruce "The Rev George Adam Smith DD, LLD", *The British Weekly*, 30 July 1896, where Bruce cites several works which took a detailed look at subjects related to the geography of Palestine.

separate parts in their organic relation to the whole, and in connection with the historic drama enacted on the soil.[152]

As a geographer, Smith was able to give a comprehensive and holistic view of matters relating to the physical aspects of the biblical history. His strength lies in his ability to bring together a wide range of academic interests and weave them into a whole. The passionate interest in geography, which grew out of his travels to the Holy Land, provided him not only with a frame of reference for biblical studies, and a background to the biblical literature, but also became a handmaid to his linguistic and theological interest in the Old Testament.

Modern writers are still ready to acknowledge the important role of Smith in the development of biblical geography. O. Palmer Robertson, for example, speaks of Smith's HGHL popularising a technical treatment of the subject,[153] while Max Miller writes in *Biblical Archaeologist* that the pioneers of the discipline

> made significant headway in clarifying the historical geography of Palestine. Edward Robinson's *Biblical Researches in Palestine and the Adjacent Regions* and George Adam Smith's *The Historical Geography of the Holy Land* are not just classics; they contain most of what we know today about Palestinian toponymy – including ancient place-names and the approximate or specific locations of biblical cities and villages. This sort of information is basic for any attempt to reconstruct the history of biblical times.[154]

On this view, Smith's work is foundational to subsequent treatments of the historical geography of Palestine, with writers such as Y. Ben-Arieh talking of the HGHL as a "classic" and demonstrating its "popularity and timelessness" from the number of subsequent editions.[155]

However George Adam Smith's approach has been subjected to recent criticism. Keith Whitelam, for example, while acknowledging the important work done by Smith, questions the imperialist and colonialist treatment of the Holy Land by his – and similar – studies. For Whitelam, Palestine, in Smith's treatment, "has no intrinsic meaning of its own, but provides the background and atmosphere for understanding the religious developments which are the foundation of Western civilization".[156] The HGHL Whitelam describes as "a

---

[152] Ibid.

[153] O. Palmer Robertson *Understanding the Land of the Bible: A Biblical-Theological Guide* (New Jersey, 1996) p1.

[154] Max Miller, "Old Testament History and Archaeology", *Biblical Archaeologist,* 50/1 (March 1987), p56.

[155] Ben-Arieh, *Rediscovery of the Holy Land*, p226.

[156] Keith W. Whitelam, *The Invention of Ancient Israel: the silencing of Palestinian history* (London, 1996) p41

classic Orientalist expression of Europe's Other",[157] in which there is no real or authentic "history", since the indigenous Palestinian history is silenced in the interests of "Israelite" history, and the history of Western monotheism.

This thesis is part of a larger discourse among scholars as to the extent to which "ancient Israel" is an authentic historical concept. For Philip R. Davies, for example, a major contributor to this discussion, "ancient Israel" is a scholarly construct, literary in form, and sometimes given a vague geographical and historical setting in the Palestinian world (of whose history we know almost nothing). Davies accuses such scholarship of "a retrojective imperialism, which displaces an otherwise unknown and uncared-for population in the interests of an ideological construct".[158] Both Davies and Whitelam take issue with Smith's reading of the biblical texts, and his citation of them as primary witnesses to the biblical history.

In spite of this position, it is still a valid argument that the biblical texts themselves ought to be integrated into reconstructing the history of Palestine. The observation of V. Philips Long is still pertinent:

The social sciences can be useful ... in pursuing questions that the text does not address, or does not address directly. But are we well advised to seek to escape the *constraints* of the text in matters that it *does* address?[159]

While it is true that Smith's approach may be viewed as part of imperialist discourse, the approach of Whitelam and Davies seems to call into question the legitimacy of Smith's attempt to reconstruct a *historical* geography of the Holy Land. It is by no means obvious that Smith's contribution to historical geography was informed merely by his Western imperialism. Smith's visits to Palestine were an attempt to feel the beat of the ancient civilisations. And to the extent that he wrote what he saw, and also marshalled the evidence of the contemporary biblical writings as he understood them through the tools of modern criticism, his was not an attempt to silence the Palestinian history in the interests of a merely academic construct of ancient Israel.

During the visit to Palestine in 1891, John Kelman, assistant at Queen's Cross Church, wrote to Lilian Adam Smith and said that "it is like dreaming to follow your description of the route through all the sacred places one loves so well, and makes them all so real. It must be very strange to you, as if the ancient days had sailed across time into your own life, and you were living both BC and AD together".[160] The geographical studies enabled Smith to live "both BC and AD together", forging a comprehensive view of the continued work of

---

[157] Ibid., p42.
[158] Philip R. Davies, *In Search of 'Ancient' Israel* (Sheffield, 1992) p31.
[159] V. Philips Long, "The Art of Biblical History" in M. Silva (ed), *Foundations of Contemporary Interpretation* (Leicester, 1997) p370.
[160] John Kelman to LAS, 21 May 1891, NLS Acc 9446 No 18.

God across the ages. This reflected his concern to make the prophets live for the present, to relate the Old Testament to contemporary life. It was a theme that Smith was to take with him into his new sphere of service as Professor of Old Testament in Glasgow, and one which would draw him into further controversy during his Glasgow years.

CHAPTER 4

The Professor: The Glasgow Years (1892-1910)

The Free Church General Assembly of 1892 was highly significant. Not only did it appoint Smith to the Chair of Hebrew and Old Testament Exegesis in its Glasgow College, it also passed the Declaratory Act, the purpose of which was to clarify the precise terms in which the Church related to her Confession.

The Scottish Church had traditionally secured its doctrinal orthodoxy by requiring of newly licensed and ordained ministers that they "subscribe their approbation of the [Westminster] Confession of Faith".[1] Subscription affirmed an unqualified acceptance of the statements of the Westminster Confession of Faith[2] (although the Free Church founding fathers entertained differences of opinion on credal subscription[3]). However, with a broader doctrinal atmosphere developing within the Free Church of Scotland, it is not surprising that the 1880s witnessed attempts at confessional change. The rise of the new biblical criticism, together with a new scientific worldview, meant that "many of the fundamental Christian doctrines – of God, of man, of sin and the fall, of providence and of Scripture – came under penetrating scrutiny".[4] But, as Kenneth Ross points out, it was not simply in the details of the Confession that the Free Churchmen of the 1880s found difficulties. He says:

> It was the essential Calvinistic system of theology which was their target. It was through their influence that the movement for Confessional revision gathered pace throughout the 1880s.[5]

Principal Rainy superintended the passage of the Act on the basis of his belief that the Church had a constitutional right so to define her confessional

---

[1] Act of Assembly of Church of Scotland, 1690, quoted in A. Innes, *The Law of Creeds in Scotland* (Edinburgh, 1867) p77.
[2] See I. Hamilton, "Subscription, Confessional" in N.M. de S. Cameron (ed.), *Dictionary of Scottish Church History and Theology* (Edinburgh, 1993) pp805-6.
[3] Kenneth R. Ross, *Church and Creed in Scotland: The Free Church Case 1900-1904 and its origins* (Edinburgh, 1988) pp195-6.
[4] A.C. Cheyne, *The Transforming of the Kirk* (Edinburgh, 1983) p77.
[5] Ross, *Church and Creed*, p198.

position.⁶ At the very least the Act meant that the Free Church of Scotland was "no longer bound with the former stringency to the utterances of Westminster".⁷ This was not lost on a minority of commissioners who dissented from its adoption, and later seceded to form the Free Presbyterian Church of Scotland.⁸

Smith's allegiance to the revisionist party led to a motion to delay an appointment to the Old Testament Chair in Glasgow. The Rev Murdoch Macaskill, Dingwall, argued that to appoint Smith "would intensify tenfold the feeling of alarm and suspicion that prevailed throughout the Church", and would "bring down upon their heads additional misery to that which had been brought down upon them by recent events".⁹ Such alarmist claims, however, failed to convince the majority of the Assembly, who agreed with Dr Ross Taylor that

> while [Smith] was a man who was open to receive light from whatever quarter, he stood firm upon this: that the Scriptures had been given by inspiration of God, and this he would teach to all who came under his instruction.¹⁰

Smith's status as a scholar was unrivalled, and his claims to the Chair on academic grounds unquestioned; it was additionally true, however, that the appointment of a leading evangelical scholar in the higher critical tradition further secured the progress of the New Evangelism within the Free Church of Scotland.

The Free Church College in Glasgow had opened in 1856 – the year Smith was born – under the Principalship of Patrick Fairbairn. While William Cunningham led a campaign to centralise theological education in Edinburgh, others, led by Robert Candlish, wished to see the new Free Church become truly national, with centres of theological excellence developing in different parts of the country. As historian Stewart J. Brown has written, "As a national Church, it was incumbent on the Free Church to respect the aspirations of the different regions, recognising that Aberdeen and Glasgow had long traditions of theological education".¹¹ This extensionist view won over Cunningham's

---

⁶ See P. Carnegie Simpson, *The Life of Principal Rainy*, Vol 2 (London, 1909) Chapter 19, esp. p130.

⁷ Cheyne, *Transforming of the Kirk*, p85.

⁸ See J.L. Macleod, *The Second Disruption: the Free Church in Victorian Scotland and the Origins of the Free Presbyterian Church of Scotland* (Edinburgh, 2000).

⁹ PDGAFCS, 1892, p81.

¹⁰ Ibid., p84.

¹¹ S.J. Brown, "The Disruption and the Dream: The Making of New College 1843-1861" in D.F. Wright and G.D. Badcock (eds) *Disruption to Diversity: Edinburgh Divinity 1846-1996* (Edinburgh, 1996) pp44-5.

so-called policy of limitarianism, although the controversy was protracted and bitter.

A centenary history of the Glasgow College opined that "George Adam Smith ... was one of the chief glories of the College in the days of its widest fame".[12] The reputation of the College was enhanced by other "glories", including James Stuart Candlish in Systematic Theology, Thomas Martin Lindsay in Church History, and Alexander Balmain Bruce in Apologetics and New Testament Exegesis. Henry Drummond occupied the Chair of Natural Science at the College. Drummond's great concern was to achieve an academically respectable synthesis of science and religion. In his *Natural Law in the Spiritual World*, Drummond expressed a strong dislike for propositional theology, and argued that science itself demonstrated the need for a theistic approach to matter.[13] The corollary of this was that the laws of science could also be applied to the doctrines of the Bible. Drummond used this to great effect in his talks with young people, on topics such as "The Geography, Arithmetic and Grammar of the Kingdom [of God]".[14]

This fusion of evangelicalism and scientific expertise made Drummond attractive to those who sought to develop a contemporary apologetic in the face of advancing Darwinian naturalism. But according to the Trinity College[15] centenary booklet, Drummond's classes were not popular among the students, some of whom "could not be persuaded that his subject was vital to the curriculum, however interesting he might make it".[16] Smith, however, believed that Drummond served the students well by drawing their attention to "the common facts of nature",[17] which theological subjects – if considered abstractly – might overlook.

---

[12] Stewart Mechie, *Trinity College Glasgow 1856-1956* (Glasgow, 1956) p34.

[13] Cf. Smith's comment in *The Life of Henry Drummond* that Drummond was "a teacher with a strong, fresh mind of his own; not only a subtle expert in religious experience, but one who enforced the principles of Christianity apart from ecclesiastical formulas" (p252).

[14] "First" by Henry Drummond: an address to the Boys' Brigade, Glasgow (n.d.), published as a tract by Stirling Tract Enterprise.

[15] The name Trinity was given to the Free Church College in 1929. When the United Free Church of Scotland was formed in 1900, the College became the United Free Church College. In 1929 the union of the Scottish Churches took place, and the College became identified with the University's Faculty of Divinity, and continued to teach theological subjects in its Lynedoch St buildings. These buildings were sold in 1973, and the Library was donated to the University. D.F. Wright comments that "Although now housed wholly in University premises, Trinity College lives on under its Principal and Senate" ("Trinity College, Glasgow", in *Dictionary of Scottish Church History and Theology*, p829).

[16] Mechie, *Trinity College*, p34.

[17] Smith, *Drummond*, p251.

Smith's inaugural lecture, delivered on 2 November 1892 and subsequently published as *The Preaching of the Old Testament to the Age*, showed that he regarded the modern critical view of the Old Testament as indispensable both for interpreting and contemporising the biblical message. Smith also made it clear what the end of theological scholarship ought to be:

> for myself I should like to say that if my call to this chair were a call away from practical work, I would not be here. I have not left a pulpit which I loved and found freedom in, for any other ultimate purpose than the one for which the Church sent me to it, or with any other confidence than that the free and full study of the Old Testament by teachers and scholars together has for its inevitable result the preaching of God's simple Word to the people.[18]

Smith deals with the difference criticism of the Old Testament has made to preaching. He disavows any connection between modern critical thought and rationalism, claiming that "nearly every leader in Old Testament criticism ... is a believer in evangelical Christianity".[19] Smith argues that criticism has not disturbed the evangelicalism of the Church; in fact, he suggests that large tracts of the Old Testament have remained unquestioned and uninterrupted by criticism:

> Unquestioned? I should rather say, fortified, explored, made habitable by modern men. There are the prophets ... No historical criticism can affect these fields; across them the preacher of today may move with all the confidence and undistracted boldness of his fathers – nay, with more freshness, more insight, more agility, for the text is clearer, the allusions better understood, and all the old life re-quickened out of which these books originally sprang.[20]

The variety of the Old Testament literature, Smith suggests, provides ample scope and material for preaching, and also motivates the preacher as he reads of the prophets, the situations in which they found themselves, and the styles of their ministries. The usage of this literature will result, he says, in "preaching for today ... preaching to the exact conditions and temptations of our own life".[21]

In the view of Old Testament scholar Professor Stanley A. Cook, the lecture was "a fair representation of [Smith's] general position in Old Testament

---

[18] G.A. Smith, *The Preaching of the Old Testament to the Age* (London, 1893) pp9-10.
[19] Ibid., p33.
[20] Ibid., pp37-8.
[21] Ibid., p55.

criticism".[22] At the time of its publication, *The Scottish Weekly* hailed the lecture as "a very fine one, wide in scope, keen in spiritual insight, beautiful in style and severely orthodox".[23] The emphasis on *preaching* is an important one, and reflects a desire on Smith's part to popularise and advance the higher critical movement within the Church. Smith was overtly stating his position that criticism was necessary to evangelicalism.[24] This meant that in the first instance it was the religious and ethical impulse of biblical religion that ought to furnish the materials for preaching, rather than the dogmatic assertions of the Westminster Confession of Faith. From the outset of his academic career, Smith made it clear that he, and his church, had nothing to fear (and much to gain) from the critical approach to Scripture, even if his position ran the risk of making Bible interpretation the preserve of a qualified few.

Smith exemplified this approach in his own handling of the biblical text. In a sermon on Psalm 19:9, for example, he highlights the fact that "in spite of the low levels from which the religion of Israel had to start, there was present in it from the first a moral purpose and energy which was not present in any of the other religions – the germ and potency of that perfect will of God which through it was ultimately revealed to man".[25] Both by precept and example, Smith showed that material for preaching was provided by a careful, critical analysis of the biblical text.

Smith had little tolerance for any other approach to preaching. In an interview with Smith, journalist Harold Anthony asked him whether he thought that Scottish preaching had been "cursed by the insistence upon creed at the expense of conduct", to which the following response was given:

"Yes," Dr Smith rejoined, "and that is still going on in the Highlands. The pseudo-Puritans had the same fault, but the real Puritans were strongly ethical in their preaching".[26]

This comment highlights another significant aspect of the debate over higher criticism within the Scottish church: the issue of a north/south divide. Historian James Macleod has explored this in his work on the origins of the Free Presbyterian Church of Scotland. He suggests that

---

[22] S.A. Cook, "George Adam Smith: 1856-1942", in *Proceedings of the British Academy* (London, 1942) p330. Cook qualifies this by saying that Smith's position on Old Testament criticism was "moderate, through with a definite trend towards the Right rather than to the Left" (ibid.).

[23] *The Scottish Weekly*, 10 October 1894, p1331, in NLS Acc 9446 No 412.

[24] See my "Fact not Dogma: George Adam Smith, Evangelicalism and Biblical Criticism" in *Scottish Bulletin of Evangelical Theology*, Vol 18 No 1, Spring 2000, pp3-20.

[25] G.A. Smith, *The Forgiveness of Sins and other Sermons* (New York, 1904) p35.

[26] Harold Anthony, writing on Professor George Adam Smith in *The New Age*, 3 January 1895, collected in presscuttings in NLS Acc 9446 No 23.

during the fifty years between 1843 and 1893 ... an increasingly obvious divide had come to exist in the Free Church between the Highland and Lowland congregations ... It was a divide which was ultimately to manifest itself at the close of the nineteenth century in the form of a bitterly divided Church ...[27]

Smith's inaugural lecture was a reflection of a Lowland, rather than a Highland, attitude towards biblical scholarship. Yet it must also be noted that there were some Highland figures who sided with Smith, a fact that ought to give us pause in evaluating the extent of the Highland/Lowland divide at the turn of the century.[28]

The Minutes of the Senatus of Trinity College record that Smith took his seat on the Senatus on 3 November 1892, the day following his induction.[29] The Report of the College Committee to the 1893 General Assembly stated that a total number of 95 students enrolled at the Glasgow College during Smith's

---

[27] J.L. Macleod, "The Influence of the Highland-Lowland Divide on the Free Presbyterian Disruption of 1893", *Records of the Scottish Church History Society* Vol XXV (1995), pp402-3. See also his *The Second Disruption*, Chapter 3, and Douglas Ansdell's comment in his *The People of the Great Faith: The Highland Church 1680-1900* (Stornoway, 1998) p167: "As the nineteenth century moved on, this division seemed to be increasingly represented by the Highlands and the Lowlands. Those who clung to Free Church origins were known as constitutionalists. They had little sympathy with the progressive plans of the predominantly Lowland Free Church majority".

[28] cf. for example the following letter, sent to GAS from the Rev D.J. Nicolson, South Uist, in 1902, in which Nicolson informs Smith of an article which had just been published in the post-1900 *Free Church Monthly Record*: "I take the liberty of sending you a translation I made from the Gaelic of an article in the (so called Free Church) Monthly Record for this month on the Bible. I cannot give you an adequate idea of the evil such writings – especially the Polychrome Bible – have done among our people in the Highlands. I wish I could assure them that you have nothing to do with it. I do not often see the anti-union Record or any of their other publications though some of my people get them. I can hardly make them believe that our Professors are not tampering with the Bible... I can by no reasoning or explanation get them to believe but the new critical views make the Bible of no value. They readily believe such articles and speeches as the enclosed...". Nicolson goes on to express his personal appreciation for the publication of *Modern Criticism and the Preaching of the Old Testament* (D.J. Nicolson to GAS, 18 June 1902, NLS Acc 9446 No 29).

[29] Scroll Minutes of Free Church College, Glasgow, 3 November 1892, University of Glasgow archives, DC84 1/2/1. In Scottish Presbyterianism, installation to a College Chair was deemed to be equivalent to induction to a pastoral charge. See Smith's description and discussion of Henry Drummond's installation, for example, in *The Life of Henry Drummond*, pp246-7.

first session there.[30] While it was true that "in those days the sessions of all the theological colleges took only half the year"[31], nonetheless Smith had a full timetable of writing and teaching. He also served as Clerk to the Senate from 1896 until 1907, when the Senate recorded that it was "under no ordinary obligation to him and assure him of the great service he has rendered the College by his self-denying labours".[32]

Reminiscences of Smith's style as a teacher are rare, but one or two have been preserved in his wife's biographical record. Lilian Smith records, for example, the memories of J.L. Morison, one of Smith's students at Glasgow. Morison recalled Smith's vivid preaching on public occasions, especially one particular sermon on Amos, delivered in the Bute Hall:

> It was such a sermon as only a man deeply learned in his Hebrew history and topography, and just as much at home in Scottish literature and history, could have conceived. The impression it made on a young student's mind abides today more vividly than that of any other sermon or lecture I have ever heard.[33]

As a Professor, Smith expected his students to do some original thinking and not simply repeat what he himself taught. His journal for 1908-9, for example, in which the names and grades of students were recorded, contain such comments as "a _very_ good essay ... not a little original thinking"; "a _very_ good essay ... much originality"; "a good essay, but not full enough"; " a good statement of the question ... but nothing original".[34] The exacting standards of his career notwithstanding, Smith remained accessible at all times:

> A student who has sought his help on some intellectual difficulty or some matter of personal decision, has felt always this sense of quiet helpfulness and strength, and has come away the better for having been with him.[35]

---

[30] Report of College Committee 1893 p4, PDGAFCS 1893. During the same session, there were 133 students at New College, and 31 at the Aberdeen College, a total of 259 in training for the ministry during the year 1892/3.

[31] A comment by D.S. Cairns in his review of LAS *George Adam Smith: A Personal Review and Family Chronicle*, *Aberdeen University Review*, No. 90 (1944) p243. It is corroborated by Lilian Smith herself in her memoir (p70).

[32] Scroll minutes of Free Church College, Glasgow, 11 March 1907, University of Glasgow archives, DC84 1/2/1.

[33] LAS, p113.

[34] GAS Journal for 1908-9, New College Library Special Collections, MSS.SMI 1.6.6.

[35] Reminiscences by a Glasgow student in "The New Principal", *Alma Mater: Aberdeen University Magazine*, Vol 27, No.2 (27 October 1909) p15.

In 1893, the University of Edinburgh awarded Smith an honorary Doctorate of Divinity. At the same graduation ceremony, his father-in-law, George Buchanan, was awarded an honorary LL.D.[36]

While in Glasgow, the Smith family resided, first, in Sardinia Terrace, and then at Westbourne Gardens. They enjoyed a comfortable lifestyle in Glasgow; one daughter later recalled that the Westbourne Gardens house was "a high house ... looking onto communal gardens which were a great feature of our lives ...".[37] While they resided in Glasgow, a further five children were born to them: Lilian Mary (Maisie), in 1894, Alick Drummond (later Lord Balerno) in 1898, Isobel Kathleen in 1900, and Janet in 1905.

The commencement of Smith's Professorship coincided with the Free Church Jubilee Assembly of 1893. Of the 474 ministers who had formed the Free Church of Scotland in 1843, only 34 were still alive in 1893, and of these only 12 were able to participate in the proceedings. George Adam Smith was not a member of the 1893 Assembly, but attended, and drew inspiration from it nonetheless. In an interview for *The British Weekly*, Smith insisted that the principles of the Disruption leaders should be viewed as the foundation for a future reunited national Scottish Church:

> The ideas of Dr Chalmers and of other Disruption leaders are to be the guiding ideas of the Church of the future. We talk of the enthusiasm of the Disruption and of its great impulses of liberality and power, but we often forget that these impulses are with us still as permanent habits. The voluntaryism of the Free Church has stood the wear and tear of fifty most changeful and trying years, and whatever forms the reconstructed Presbyterianism of Scotland may take, our system will have a large share in making it.[38]

Many of the young ministers of the late nineteenth-century Free Church were inspired by the vision of a national Church, and Smith believed that the Free Church could be a paradigm for such a church: "We Free Churchmen have the inspiring knowledge that our system will ere long become the necessary system of all Churches".[39]

The publication of Smith's *Four Psalms* in 1896 represented the first work in Old Testament exegesis to emerge from his pen as Professor at the Free Church College. This small work was published as part of a series of "Little

---

[36] Two years later the University of Aberdeen conferred this same degree on Smith himself.
[37] Janet Adam Smith writing in Colin Bell (ed.), *Scotland's Century: An Autobiography of the Nation* (Glasgow, 1999) p22.
[38] "Professor G.A. Smith on the Free Church Jubilee: An Interview", *The British Weekly*, 1 June 1893.
[39] Smith quoted in *The British Weekly*, 24 October 1935, p72.

Books on Religion" under the editorship of W. Robertson Nicoll. In it, Smith gives an exegesis of Psalms 23, 36, 52 and 121. This work was more devotional than critical. Smith commends the four psalms for their evocative poetic style, and for the simplicity of their meditative approach. Of Psalm 23, for example, Smith observes that "the Psalm is not only theology. It is personal religion".[40] To this degree, he argues that the moment we make "assent to a dogma"[41] the test of our surrender to God, we have sullied the nature of true religion. The use of criticism for rendering the Old Testament intelligible comes through in the treatment of Psalm 36, where the psalmist's analysis of sin, according to Smith, can only be "intelligible, profound and true to experience"[42] if a scholarly reading and emendation of the text is adopted. Again, the devotional element is dominant: "The fault of many Christians is that they turn to some theological definition, or to some mystical refinement of it, and their hearts are starved. We must seek the loving-kindness of God in all the breadth and open-air of common life".[43]

A warm, pastoral work, *Four Psalms* exhibits an implicit use of criticism, a critique of dogmatic and confessional orthodoxy, and an emphasis on personal and practical religion which would be further explicated in the work on the prophets. At the same time, the publication of this non-contentious work may have been designed to ease the concerns of the conservative element in the Free Church, since there was little in it with which any Free Churchman could disagree.

The Life of Henry Drummond

Smith's biography of Henry Drummond appeared in 1898. Drummond died on 11 March 1897, and his passing was a great personal loss for Smith. Smith was commissioned to write Drummond's biography, and said that doing so was like trying to describe a fragrance.[44] At the same time, Drummond remained a highly controversial figure in Scottish church life. His attempt to reconcile evangelicalism and science won the admiration of many in his day; but others viewed him as a threat to the Church's orthodoxy.

Smith treats Drummond's detractors with disdain. Some he lumps together as "a curious chapter in the history of human delusions",[45] other criticisms of Drummond's views he regards as plain "unreasonableness".[46] His most vehement criticism is of the "heresy hunters" who had forgotten Drummond's contribution to the work of the Gospel:

---

[40] G.A. Smith, *Four Psalms* (London, 1896) p22.
[41] Ibid., p25.
[42] Ibid., p40.
[43] Ibid., p65.
[44] So LAS, p79; cf Smith, *Drummond*, p12.
[45] Ibid., p219.
[46] Ibid., p220.

His services as an evangelist, his character and influence, the great amount of positive Christian doctrine that he taught, were all ignored by these hot hunters of a fancied heresy.[47]

The biography was less the telling of Drummond's story than a vindication of the new evangelicalism represented by both Drummond and Smith himself. The Moody and Sankey mission is represented as having overcome the "prejudices" of those who had resisted any liturgical innovation or revolution;[48] A.B. Davidson is vindicated as a teacher of Old Testament theology, who showed his students that this theology was not the dogma of a Church, but "the living experience of a great people and its greatest individuals";[49] Smith remarks that "Professor Robertson Smith was sacrificed",[50] and he bemoans – in Drummond's own words – "the suicidal policy of the majority in their recent determination to lynch Smith".[51] It was time to abandon old ideas, and according to Smith "Drummond was forced from them by his study of facts in the departments of natural science and of Biblical criticism and Biblical theology".[52]

Smith is correct to say that the strength of Drummond's position was his underlying assumption that "truth is indivisible whether it be of science or religion".[53] But for both Drummond and Smith this meant that only by a critical reconstruction of the Old Testament could the claims of both science and religion be reconciled. Smith, however, ignores the fact that in attempting that harmonisation, Drummond was too ready to ascribe to the scientific theories of his day the very infallibility he was unwilling to ascribe to the biblical writers.

In attempting to capture both the content and passion of Drummond's addresses to students, Smith vindicates Drummond's evangelicalism, and thereby gives expression to his own:

> Modern science has enabled him to view life as a whole, and to perceive, with an eye, which, as he tells you, he also owes partly to science, that in the universe Christianity is at once the most natural and the most sublime of facts ... In the Christianity which he presents as the crown of the life of the universe, the spring and cause is Jesus Christ. He is the Source of all life and light; the assurance of the forgiveness of sins; the daily nourishment of the

---

[47] Ibid., p223.
[48] Ibid., p55.
[49] Ibid., p105.
[50] Ibid., p131.
[51] Ibid., p130.
[52] Ibid., p243.
[53] Ibid., p249.

soul; the one power sufficient for a noble life; the solution of all problems; the motive and example of all service.[54]

And, according to Smith, to read these addresses is to see "how ignorant and irrelevant was the criticism from which their author suffered".[55]

For Drummond, a non-doctrinal evangelicalism with a practical emphasis was needed for a new world of thought.[56] It was a world in which he and Smith moved with consummate ease and satisfaction. In Drummond Smith found a kindred spirit, and the telling of Drummond's story gave Smith another opportunity to introduce, justify and clarify the new world of these late nineteenth-century intellectuals.

Smith on the Twelve Prophets

Smith made a further contribution to the Expositors' Bible series in 1896 and 1898 with his two-volume publication *The Book of the Twelve Prophets*. These were further to enhance his reputation both at home and abroad as a Professor of Old Testament and a scholar within the critical tradition.

In his *A Century of Old Testament Study*, R.E. Clements points out that by the end of the nineteenth century the prophets had come to be regarded as the true creative pioneers behind the faith of Israel.[57] Smith's studies on the prophets appeared at a time, therefore, when study of the prophets had generated much discussion both in Scotland (under Davidson and William Robertson Smith) and on the continent (in the works of men like Heinrich Ewald and Bernhard Duhm). Smith stated as his aim in the commentaries on the twelve so-called "minor" prophets "to assist the bettering"[58] of the current state of prophetic studies.

As a general principle, Smith regards all of the twelve as having been added to by subsequent writer-editors, and suggests that criticism is indispensable in restoring the original text. At the same time he acknowledges that some questions lie outwith the scope of criticism, and that some critical conclusions may be quite arbitrary.[59] He also insists on the recovery of the socio-historical

---

[54] Ibid., p326.
[55] Ibid., p327.
[56] Cf D. Bebbington, "Henry Drummond, evangelicalism and science" in T.E. Corts (ed), *Henry Drummond: A Perpetual Benediction* (Edinburgh, 1999) p36.
[57] See R.E. Clements *A Century of Old Testament Study* (Cambridge, 1976) especially Chapter 4, "Interpreting the Prophets".
[58] Quoted from the Preface of Volume 1 of *The Book of the Twelve*, 1896, pviii. See Appendix 1 for a summary of Smith's chronology of the Twelve.
[59] Smith himself uses this word of his critical approach in the preface; having summarised what he regards as defects in previous criticism, he says: "Probably my own criticism will reveal many more. In the beginnings of such analysis as we are engaged on, we must be prepared for not a little arbitrariness and want of proportion" (ibid., ppx-xi).

conditions in which the prophets ministered, if their message is to have any relevance for contemporary life. Smith insists that "the prostitution of the prophets[60] is their confinement to academic uses".[61]

On the unity of the corpus, Smith suggests that "the inseparableness of the books is a proof of the ancient date of their union",[62] although this rather evades the question of why they were put together in the first place. Smith's conjecture that Jonah may have been included simply to round up the number of works to twelve, and his supposition that placing them together was merely to guarantee that they would not be subsequently lost, are rather arbitrary suggestions. Recent scholarship has advanced on this, recognising a genuine literary unity based on themes and theology common to the larger prophetic literature, so that together, the books "provide as comprehensive a prophetic theology as any of the three previous prophetic books".[63]

Smith believed that originally God was worshipped through tribal ritual, and the will of God discerned through omens and portents, both "natural" and "artificial". The field, he believed, lay open for men with moral insight and character to highlight, among the Jewish people, the purpose of God in making them His own. In this sense, Smith could argue that although criticism can provide a greater insight to the prophetic ministry of the Old Testament, it also shows our ignorance of the prophets and what they did. Nonetheless, "under their God, they made Israel".[64] Smith believed that the prophets were characterised by the following features: their union with God, their union with natural life, their independence of religious ritual, their independence from state authority, their freedom from religious ecstasy and their concern to expound God's will.[65]

It was in the eighth century, according to Smith, that prophecy developed:

> It was in the peace and liberty of this day that Israel rose a step in civilisation; that prophecy, released from the defence, became the criticism, of the national life; and that the people, no longer absorbed in their own

---

[60] A charge which had been laid against his own *Isaiah*.
[61] Ibid., pxi.
[62] Ibid., p5.
[63] Paul R. House, *Old Testament Theology* (Downers Grove, Illinois, 1998) p347. For further extensive and contemporary treatment of the redactional issues involved, see J.W. Watts and P.R. House (eds), *Forming Prophetic Literature: Essays on Isaiah and the Twelve in Honor of John D.W. Watts*, JSOTSup 235 (Sheffield, 1996) and P.R. House, *The Unity of the Twelve* (Sheffield, 1990).
[64] *The Book of the Twelve*, Vol 1, p19.
[65] This summary is taken from an unpublished notebook entitled "Three Addresses to the Men's Meeting, St Mark's, Argyle St" (in fact, the notebook contains notes for four lectures). These Bible Classes were held on Sunday afternoons for the study of the Scriptures. The quotation is taken from the first lecture, delivered on 10 January 1909, p12, New College Special Collection MSS.SMI 1.7.6.

borders, looked out, and for the first time realised the great world, of which they were only a part.[66]

This period marked a further transition in the history of Israel; with the emergence in Canaan, Israel had moved from a nomadic to an agricultural lifestyle, and now, under the reigns of Jeroboam and Uzziah, "city-life was developed, and civilisation, in the proper sense of the word, appeared".[67] The concomitant perils of urban life – superstitious pilgrimages to religious shrines, pride in glory and achievement, "mendicant priests and hireling preachers"[68] – all contributed to a turning away from Yahweh. The prophets saw it as their task, particularly in view of the threat from Assyria, to remind Israel of her commitment to God and her need for devotion to Him alone. Smith reckons that the growth of Assyrian power had a direct bearing on prophecy in Israel (and he devotes a chapter to this theme). His thesis is that the appearance of Assyria threatened the native Semitic idea of tribal deities ("a god for every tribe, a tribe for every god"[69]) by overpowering individual rulers and tribes in "one almighty impulse". The threat of world domination by Assyria meant that in the minds of the prophets "there was a great chance ... for a god with a character. And the only God in all the Semitic world who had a character was Jehovah".[70]

In commenting on each of the prophetic books, Smith first summarises the general argument, then turns to consider the character and circumstances of each prophet. Drawing upon his own experience of the Holy Land, and facilitated by his evocative prose, Smith establishes a context for each book.

For Smith, Amos is a reformer, a "founder of the highest order of prophecy in Israel",[71] who took what he had learned in the desert as a shepherd and applied it to what he saw in the city:

...Amos passes from the facts of his own consciousness to the facts of his people's life. His day in Israel sweltered with optimism. The glare of wealth, the fulsome love of country, the rank incense of a religion that was without morality – these thickened all the air, and neither the people nor their rulers had any vision. But Amos carried with him his clear desert atmosphere and his desert eyes. He saw raw facts: the poverty, the cruel negligence of the rich, the injustice of the rulers, the immorality of the priests. The meaning of

---

[66] *The Book of the Twelve*, Vol 1, pp31-2. In actual fact, as far back as Abraham's day, there was a universalistic emphasis in the revelation of the covenant (cf. Genesis 12:3; 17:4-8).
[67] Ibid., p34.
[68] Ibid., p42.
[69] Ibid., p54.
[70] Ibid.
[71] Ibid., p77.

these things he questioned with as much persistence as he questioned every suspicious sound or sight upon those pastures of Tekoa. He had no illusions: he knew a mirage when he saw one.[72]

In a similar manner, Smith sees the prophecy of Hosea growing out of the prophet's personal experience of pain and betrayal, through his marriage to an unfaithful partner. Smith's view of Hosea is that his grief "became his gospel".[73] Hosea, according to Smith, "was led to feel that his sorrow was the sorrow of the whole nation" and that "he comprehended that it was of similar kind to the sorrow of God Himself".[74] God's pain, he argues, was suggested by the prophet's own pain, but God's grace was the precedent of the prophet's. Hosea forgave his unfaithful spouse only because God had forgiven Israel. There is, therefore, in Smith's evangelicalism, an emphasis upon the prevenience of grace, but the nature of prophetic revelation is firmly rooted in human experience and moral sensitivity. Although their situations and personal predilections were quite different, Amos and Hosea were both able to deliver a word from God to their people because of the circumstances in which they found themselves.

Amos is described by Smith as the prophet of Law, and Hosea as the prophet of Love. Indeed, he charges Amos with leaving Hosea a problem: the problem of domesticating divine love within the revelation of divine law; or, as Smith puts it: "The prophet of Conscience had to be followed by the prophet of Repentance".[75] In his unpublished lectures on these prophets, Smith suggests a parallel between Amos and Hosea as forerunners, respectively, of John the Baptist and Jesus.[76] In an interesting aside, Smith suggests that the church at the turn of the twentieth century was facing a similar crisis:

> The older Evangelical assurance, the older Evangelical ideals have to some extent been rendered impossible by the realism to which the sciences, both physical and historical, have most healthily recalled us, and by their wonderful revelation of Law working through nature and society without respect to our creeds and pious hopes. The question presses: Is it still possible to believe in repentance and conversion, still possible to preach the

---

[72] Ibid., pp84-5.
[73] Ibid., p240.
[74] Ibid.
[75] Ibid., p229.
[76] *Three Addresses to the Men's Meeting*, Address 3. Smith, in his commentary, makes a great deal of the parallel between Hosea and Jesus. The parallelism he sees as ranging from the etymology of their respective names (*The Book of the Twelve*, Vol 1, p230), to the substance of their message. Smith evocatively calls Hosea's work "The Parable of the Prodigal Wife". He also, however, compares Hosea to St John, in identifying knowledge of God as the key to spiritual life.

power of God to save, whether the individual or society, from the forces of heredity and of habit? We can at least learn how Hosea mastered the very similar problem which Amos left to him, and how, with a moral realism no less stern than his predecessor and a moral standard every whit as high, he proclaimed Love to be the ultimate element in religion ...[77]

The text of Micah, Smith says, contains numerous interpolations, and in its present form is out of proper order. Nonetheless Smith accepts, on the testimony, he says, of most critics, the genuineness of the work as a whole. Smith paints an evocative picture of Micah's place of origin: Moresheth in the Shephalah, where "bees murmur everywhere, larks are singing ... [with] shepherds and ploughmen calling to their flocks and to each other across the glens".[78] The importance of Moresheth, Smith says, is that it stands near a valley-mouth which "has always formed the south-western gateway of Judea",[79] through which many important embassies and passengers came. These were "days of great excitement"[80] in which Micah called the earth to heed the word of God. Although Micah was contemporaneous with Isaiah, their interests differed. While warning against over-stating the contrast between them,[81] Smith shows how Micah's interests focussed upon the south as offering a possible inroad for Assyrian aggression, while Isaiah concentrated on the possibility of attack from the north. Again, however, the same emphasis on personal life and moral sensitivity appears: "many a prophet has learned to read the tragedy of man and God's verdict upon sin in his experience of human life ... Micah is no longer a book, or an oration, but flesh and blood upon a home and a countryside of his own".[82] Smith also highlights Micah's concern for the poor, and the fact that "social wrongs are always felt most acutely, not in the town, but in the country",[83] where power easily falls into the hands of the few over the many. In such a situation, he argues, history has indicated that revolutions generally give way to the anticipation of, and longing for, a deliverer – a personal figure who will right the wrong. To Micah, Smith gives the honour of being the first "who thus focussed the hopes of Israel upon a great Redeemer",[84] a Hero, whose advent would be at Bethlehem. The image of the redeemer as shepherd (Micah 5:4) would have appealed to a rustic people.

---

[77] *The Book of the Twelve*, Vol 1, p231.
[78] Ibid., p377.
[79] Ibid., p378.
[80] Ibid., p379.
[81] Ibid., p382.
[82] Ibid.
[83] Ibid., p386. At this point in the Commentary, Smith refers to current problems in rural parts of Ireland and the Scottish Highlands.
[84] Ibid., p410.

Smith treats the remainder of the corpus in Volume 2, which he prefaces by a contextual history of the seventh century before Christ. Social stability, urban prosperity and rural simplicity have gone; the Assyrian has invaded and religion is defiled. Israel and Judah are still under threat from foreign powers, and leadership is compromised and sterile. The prophets of the seventh century – Zephaniah, Nahum, Habakkuk and Jeremiah – like their predecessors, have a moral insight and a clear ability to read and discern the signs of the times. Again, "the assurance of the prophet in Israel arose from the coincidence of his conscience with his political observation".[85] The fate of Nineveh becomes the focus of Nahum and Habakkuk's interest, the former exulting in its downfall, the latter seeing the hand of God in the extraordinary success of the Chaldean forces. Josiah's reforms in 621 are unable to halt the general moral and spiritual decline in Israel, in spite of Zephaniah's warning voice, and Jeremiah is left to herald the exile on the eve of the fall of Jerusalem.

Smith deals first with Zephaniah. He describes this book as "one of the most difficult in the prophetic canon",[86] on account of an extremely corrupted text and the high number of *hapax legomena*. Smith argues that the language of Zephaniah shows affinities with later writings, separating it from that of the older prophets.[87]

Smith believes that Zephaniah's prophecies grew out of his intimate acquaintance with the events of his day, most notably the reforms of King Josiah. But he then makes an extraordinary hermeneutical leap in insisting that the prophet, "though he found his material in the events of his own day, tears himself loose from history altogether",[88] and introduces an apocalyptic note which earlier prophets did not have. How else can we account, Smith reasons, for the absence of the mention of Josiah's reforms, given that the prophets would have welcomed such measures?   Part of the text of Nahum (1:1-2:4) Smith says "has been badly mauled and is clamant for reconstruction of some kind";[89] but although Smith surveys the status of contemporary criticism, he does not offer a closure of the textual question himself. This need not affect the message of the prophet, however, since Smith is still willing to aver that the first chapter "is theological, affirming those general principles of divine

---

[85] *The Book of the Twelve*, Volume 2, p17.

[86] Ibid., p35.

[87] Ibid., p36, although modern commentators, such as O.Palmer Robertson in *The Books of Nahum, Habakkuk and Zephaniah*, New International Commentary on the Old Testament (Grand Rapids, Michigan, 1990), are more ready to argue a correspondence between Zephaniah and the Deuteronomic writings (see Robertson, p27, where he argues that "Zephaniah's style is dictated in part by his extensive dependence on the phraseology of the Book of Deuteronomy"). Contrary to Smith's view of the corrupt state of the text of Zephaniah, R.K. Harrison argues that it is, in fact, well preserved (see his *Introduction to the Old Testament* [Grand Rapids, Michigan, 1969] p943).

[88] *The Book of the Twelve*, Volume 2, p49.

[89] Ibid., p82.

Providence, by which the overthrow of the tyrant is certain and God's own people are assured of deliverance".[90] Smith sees significance in the absence of any concrete reference to Israel in this section; no national passions are stirred, simply "the outraged conscience of mankind ... another proof ... of the large, human heart of prophecy".[91]

In Habakkuk, Smith discerns "a new school of religion in Israel".[92] He distinguishes between the style of the classical prophets and that of Habakkuk by suggesting that while "they address the nation Israel, on behalf of God, he rather speaks to God on behalf of Israel".[93] For Habakkuk, the prophetic revelation has been codified in the Deuteronomic law; the concern of the prophet is to expostulate with God and to seek reasons why the law is not working to regulate the lives of the people. This, Smith suggests, "is the beginning of speculation in Israel".[94] Smith reflects on the similarity between Habakkuk's age and his own at the close of the nineteenth century.

The problems encountered in a critical study of Obadiah are, according to Smith, out of all proportion to the size of the book. Yet only "the reasonable methods of Old Testament criticism"[95] can lead towards certainty. Smith himself concludes that the work is exilic, and that the spirit of the prophecy against Edom testifies to this. The ethical questions raised by the relationship between Israel (=Jacob) and Edom (=Esau) are raised and discussed by Smith. He acknowledges that while the book of Obadiah "brings no spiritual message",[96] and while the dark notes of its contents seem to stain the stream of revelation, nonetheless the instinct of prophecy is heard even in the dark chords of Obadiah's lament, with his vengeful cries acting as a foil to the revelation of Israel's Messiah.

The second section of the second volume deals with the prophets of the Persian period (539-331), and covers Haggai, Zechariah, Malachi and Joel. Smith gives an introduction to this period, in which he describes Israel as "no longer a kingdom but a colony",[97] dominated by an Aryan race for the first time in its history. Prophecy, he says, has to descend to a new level. The tendency to move into apocalyptic thought dominates, and the prophetic office becomes

---

[90] Ibid., p91.
[91] Ibid., p103.
[92] Ibid., p130.
[93] Ibid., p130.
[94] Ibid., p131. Cf. O. Palmer Robertson, who highlights the distinctiveness of Habakkuk's style under the rubric of a "dialogue of protest". Although aware of this unique and personal style, Robertson is not willing to drive as large a wedge as Smith does between Habakkuk and the former prophets (see Robertson, pp27-8).
[95] Ibid., p164.
[96] Ibid., p178.
[97] Ibid., p189.

dominated by the cultus. The dating of these events is notoriously difficult, as Smith concedes.[98]

To those who detect in Haggai a complete collapse of the classical prophetic style, and who argued that a call to build an edifice of wood and stone was much removed from the high work of the prophets of old, Smith asks: "the man felt what the moment needed, and that is the supreme mark of the prophet. Set a prophet there, and what else could a prophet have done?"[99] Far from minimising Haggai's role, we ought to see in it "the sanity and the spiritual essence of prophecy in Israel".[100] Again, it is Haggai's keen moral insight and spiritual sensitivity that characterise him as a true prophet.

The visions and oracles of Zechariah 1-8 belong, according to Smith, to the time of Haggai, and assist the work of consolidating the religion of Israel and building the Temple both "by historical retrospect and by glowing hopes of the Messianic effects of its completion".[101] Smith concludes that the first eight chapters of the prophecy are genuine prophecies of Zechariah. He has greater difficulty in demonstrating a correspondence between the plain language of Zechariah and the intricate and artistic style of the visionary material. There is on the one hand a simple appeal to the older prophetic material of the Old Testament, and on the other "a carefully constructed symbolism of the divine truths with which the prophet was entrusted by his God".[102] Smith traces the influence of these artificial images to the fact that the exile divorced the Israelites from the realities of civic and political life. They had more time to brood, dream and imagine. "The exiles," he says, were not responsible citizens or statesmen, but dreamers".[103] Out of the fertile imagination of the exiles, according to Smith, there grew an apocalyptic view of reality, a belief in angels and the development of ritual. Historical events are hidden in the visionary material; although Zechariah predicts deliverance and hope, he cannot, unlike his predecessors, see the political channels by which this can be effected. The result is that

> a people such as that poor colony of exiles, with no issue upon history, is forced to take refuge in Apocalypse, and carries with it even those of its

---

[98] Ibid., p195. Although Smith argues that the dating of Ezra has little bearing on his study, nonetheless not even he can avoid the implications of his chosen date of 458 for Ezra's arrival (204ff). For further discussion see J. Stafford Wright, *The Date of Ezra's coming to Jerusalem* (London, 1947) and J.A. Emerton, "Did Ezra to go Jerusalem in 428BC?", *Journal of Theological Studies*, 17 (1966), pp1-15.
[99] Ibid., p236.
[100] Ibid., p237.
[101] Ibid., p257.
[102] Ibid., p274.
[103] Ibid., p275.

prophets whose conscience, like Zechariah's, is most strongly bent upon the practical present.[104]

Although Smith attempts to place the visionary material of Zechariah firmly within the prophetic line of the Old Testament, he is forced into a radical subjectivism in his treatment of these visions. Did the exile really reduce the thinkers of Israel to mere dreamers, whose imaginations ran riot in the absence of civil life? At the same time, Smith interprets the visionary material with reference to contemporary events, and even uses the third vision (of 2:1-5) to give a lesson in interpreting prophecy. In particular, he suggests that the visions warn against hiding behind inadequate religious bulwarks:

> Whether these ancient and sacred defences be dogmas or institutions, we have no right, God tells us, to cramp behind them his powers for the future.[105]

Although Smith finds in Malachi points both of comparison and divergence from the Deuteronomic code, his concerns focus more on the state of the text. Smith perceives in Malachi the turning of prophecy "into the scholasticism of the rabbis",[106] in which the prophets turn more to exposition and discussion of law rather than application of its ethical principles.

Smith sees this further developed in Joel, a book which, he suggests, "carries the student further into the problems of Old Testament criticism".[107] While the simplicity of the language and the apparent unity of the nation seem to suggest an early date for Joel, Smith sides with the critics who ascribe to him a post-exilic date. An interesting feature of the commentary at this point is in chapter 28, which deals with Joel's vision of the plague of locusts. Smith dismisses allegorical interpretations of this plague, suggesting that Joel has in fact seen such a plague, and applies it to the imminent judgement of God. Smith, however, has also seen a plague of locusts, and his description on pages 398-9 is characterised by his evocative prose style.

The final section of the commentary deals with Zechariah 9-14 and the Book of Jonah, both of which Smith assigns to the Greek period from 331BC onwards. The former of these is, according to Smith, the nadir in prophetic utterance, with an insatiable thirst for the blood of the enemies of Israel. The latter, although undated, he is willing to place last, as a work which caps the Book of the Twelve by giving prophecy a lofty role.

Smith assigns deutero-Zechariah a late date on the basis of the historical and geographical references in Zechariah 9-14. The history of criticism on the point

---

[104] Ibid., p281.
[105] Ibid., p290.
[106] Ibid., p346.
[107] Ibid., p375.

of authorship is discussed at length. Smith is willing to believe in the unity of the section, but bemoans the "terrible grimness" with which the destruction of the heathen is anticipated and longed for.[108] The Book of Jonah, on the other hand – which Smith takes as a parable – has as its purpose "to illustrate the mission of prophecy to the Gentiles, God's care for them, and their susceptibility to His word".[109] By using a parable, laced with Semitic mythology, in which the reluctant prophet represents Israel, the point is made that

> out there, beyond the Covenant, in the great world lying in darkness, there live, not beings created for ignorance and hostility to God, elect for destruction, but men with consciences and hearts, able to turn at His Word and to hope in His Mercy.[110]

Literary criticism of the Old Testament now tends to move beyond Smith, seeing in the book of Jonah a complex form of Hebrew satire, with a historical basis,[111] whose purpose, as Smith stated, was to vindicate God's love "to the jealousy of those who thought that it was theirs alone".[112]

Smith's former teacher, A.B. Davidson, was one of the first to congratulate him on his work on the *Twelve*. He wrote to him: "You have the art of making even a catalogue of names interesting and much more the thought of the prophets".[113] In particular, Davidson drew attention to Smith's handling of Nahum and Habakkuk, which were, he said, "notoriously difficult" books, but of which he said that Smith's commentary would do much "to rescue these small and difficult prophets from the neglect into which they have fallen largely from their obscurity".[114] A review in *The Times* suggested that "each separate prophecy calls out an appropriate literary and historical commentary written with a true sense for life and reality, and with that effort to get at the psychological and historical background which characterises all that is best in modern critical work", and said that it was the work of "an interesting writer, [and] an excellent theologian".[115]

A.S. Peake later recalled that Smith's contributions on the prophets to the Expositor's Bible Commentary Series "were by common consent among the

---

[108] Ibid., p486.
[109] Ibid., p501.
[110] Ibid., pp533-4.
[111] Cf. Branson L. Woodward, "Jonah" in L. Ryken and T.Longman III (eds), *A Complete Literary Guide to the Bible* (Grand Rapids, Michigan, 1993) Chapter 25.
[112] *The Book of the Twelve*, Vol 2, p541.
[113] A.B. Davidson to GAS, 3 February 1898, NLS Acc 9446 No 25.
[114] Ibid.
[115] Quoted in the endpiece of *Four Psalms*.

most striking in that very unequal series".[116] The contributors to the series were chosen to represent "several evangelical churches and various schools of criticism".[117] The series as a whole was a significant marker in the combining of critical biblical studies and evangelical Christian faith.

Later, Adam Welch, who was to become Professor of Old Testament at New College from 1913-1934, expressed the view that, in addition to their exegetical insights, these volumes – particularly the volumes contributed by Free Churchmen – helped to stay the fears of those who had been rocked by the Robertson Smith affair. The Church, having been moved by the events which led to Robertson Smith's deposition, had to make an adjustment to critical thinking, and in Welch's view,

> the great value of G.A. Smith's work was that it helped to steady the minds of at least more thoughtful men. Applying the same critical method to the Old Testament, he set himself to show the positive results of such a study ... It is no exaggeration to say that Smith rediscovered for his own generation the place and the meaning of Old Testament prophecy.[118]

There is no doubt that at an academic level, Smith's work represented the intellectual dynamism of the Free Church in the latter half of the nineteenth century. If the commentaries demonstrated anything, they showed that the deposing of Robertson Smith had not, in fact, closed the door to critical enquiry. But they also demonstrated that the Church could not accommodate the higher criticism without a restructuring of her confessional commitment. The Declaratory Act, as we have seen, clearly relaxed the terms by which ministers of the Free Church of Scotland could relate to the Westminster Confession, and therefore to the Bible itself. This gave room for wide divergence of approaches to, and interpretations of, the biblical text, and paved the way for the domesticating of the New Evangelicalism. However, it remains difficult to counter the argument of the post-1900 Free Church that in order to accommodate the higher criticism, the church itself had been required to make a huge constitutional shift.[119]

---

[116] A.S. Peake, *Recollections and Appreciations* (London, 1938) p92.
[117] W.H. Bennett, "General Introduction to the Expositors' Bible: Old Testament" in S.G. Ayres, *Complete Index to the Expositor's Bible* (London, 1905) p15.
[118] A.C. Welch, "The Spirit of Prophecy", *The British Weekly*, 24 October 1935, p71.
[119] The difference of viewpoint between the Free Presbyterians, who left the Free Church over the Declaratory Act, and the conservative Free Churchmen who remained within the Church, was over the extent to which the Act altered the constitution of the Church. The post-1900 Free Church of Scotland, to the present day, has argued that there was no change of constitution, and that the Act remained a piece of uncompleted legislation until it was incorporated into the Questions put to ministers, and the Formula to which they subscribed. Both seceding and non-seceding opponents of the Act agreed that it allowed mental reservation over statements in the Church's Confession; the Act

Social Work in Glasgow

We have already noted (in chapter 2) the extent of Smith's interest in social problems while in his Aberdeen pastorate. His involvement in social concerns in Glasgow was one of the prophetic elements of his own contribution to Scottish church life there.

Smith moved to Glasgow at a time when the city was undergoing vast social changes and facing widespread social problems. Indeed, in his study of nineteenth-century Scotland, historian John F. McCaffrey states that in comparison with other cities, "Glasgow, with its swollen population, contained the greatest problems". [120] In a sermon delivered in 1907, Smith makes explicit reference to the need for the Church in Glasgow to act as a catalyst in bridging the gulf between the poor and the more affluent areas of the city:

> There are surely a certain proportion of our west-end families who would not find it a great sacrifice to connect themselves with east-end churches. Besides contributing to the moral and financial support of these they would remove from us the reproach that the rich and the poor no longer worship under the same roof.[121]

In addition to his academic work, Smith took care of the Broomielaw Church, which was set in an extremely poor and disadvantaged area of the city. Although some distance from their home, the Smiths quickly became fully involved in the lives and problems of the members of the congregation.

Smith was engaged by various societies which were concerned with improving the lot of the city's poor and disadvantaged. *The Largs and Millport Weekly* for 23 August 1894 reported that he addressed the Scottish Girls' Friendly Society, commending them for developing the "Fresh Air Fortnight's Scheme for the poor children of the city", and arguing that "no one ... was at all likely to succeed in life or to reach any high point of character or inflence who was not ready for what might be called extra work".[122] Similarly, as Honorary Vice-president of the Glasgow Association of the YMCA, Smith was reported as "a man of varied gifts and interests", who, in addition to his duties as Professor, "superintends the operations of the Students' Missions in Carrick Street. There his personal influence does much to sustain that spirit of faith and

---

was also an important step to domesticating the higher criticism within the Free Church of the period.

[120] John F. McCaffrey, *Scotland in the Nineteenth Century* (London, 1998) p88.

[121] GAS, *The Home Missions of the Churches*, Sermon preached in Park Parish Church, Glasgow, on St Patrick's Day, 1907, p11.

[122] *The Largs and Milport Weekly News*, 23 August 1894, NLS Acc 9446 No 23.

enthusiasm which is the soul of all successful mission effort".[123] A glimpse at Smith's diaries further confirms the number of meetings he attended and addressed relating to social issues: a social meeting at the Broomielaw on 15 March 1905,[124] a meeting with the Sweating Committee of the Community Council at 3pm on 19 December 1906,[125] a presidential address to the Sweated Industries Conference on 11 October 1907,[126] and an appointment on 11 September 1908 to "preside at the opening – Conference of ministers and others in the City Chambers at 3pm; Subject: 'The attitude of the Church to the Social Question'".[127]

Donald C. Smith relates such recovery of a social conscience in the Church to what he describes as "the gradual weakening of Calvinistic orthodoxy".[128] However, it must be remembered that some of the most notable efforts at addressing social problems earlier in the century had come from first-rank Calvinists, from Thomas Chalmers to James Begg.[129] Donald Smith is much nearer the mark when he cites the "rediscovery of the Old Testament prophets"[130] as a major factor in the contribution of scholarship to the church's social conscience. Indeed, Smith's work on the Twelve is replete with references to the practical interest of the Old Testament prophets in the social questions of their day.

Undergirding Smith's social concerns, therefore, is a worldview, derived from study of the prophetic material, which saw the whole of life as a framework for service to God. Coupled with this was the fact that the late 1880s and early 1890s witnessed a growing understanding of the relationship between social conditions and individual development (which led to the formation of the Scottish Labour Party in 1888). On a formal level, the need for increased intervention by the state for the good of the individual was one explanation for the rise of the Scottish Labour movement.[131] Increasingly, socialism, bolstered by the new social theology of the Churchmen, was seen as

---

[123] *The Young Men's Christian Magazine*, Vol xvi, No. 1 (October 1894), in a series entitled "Some of our office-bearers" – no. XII. George Adam Smith DD, NLS Acc 9446 No 23.

[124] Diary of GAS 1905, NLS Acc 9446 No 272.

[125] Diary of GAS 1906, NLS Acc 9446 No 273.

[126] Diary of GAS 1907, NLS Acc 9446 No 274.

[127] Diary of GAS 1908, NLS Acc 9446 No 275.

[128] Donald C. Smith, *Passive Obedience and Prophetic Protest: Social Criticism in the Scottish Church 1830-1945* (New York, 1981) p254.

[129] Cf. for example, Callum Brown's statement about James Begg, whom he describes as "severe Calvinist and scourge of worship reformers in the Free Church" yet whom he acknowledges as "the leading Scottish advocate, lay or clerical, of municipal and philanthropic housing improvement" (*The Social History of Religion in Scotland* [London, 1987] p172).

[130] Ibid.

[131] T.M. Devine, *The Scottish Nation 1700-2000* (London, 1999) p381.

a major contributory factor to the establishing of the Kingdom of God in Scottish society.[132]

This has to be balanced with the assessment of social historian Callum Brown, who argues that the development of higher criticism undercut the traditional evangelical basis for social philanthropy and amelioration, and that as the social gospel movement gained support and impetus, there was a converse downgrading of specifically evangelistic work in the Church. While there was a marked increase in the attention given to social improvement, Brown suggests that "the numbers started falling in the Free Church from 1890"[133], and that this in turn affected the whole position of the Church in its relation to society. After the 1880s, for example, Brown argues that "with poor promotional prospects in the context of suburbanization and rationalization of congregations, careers were made out of evangelizing city slums"[134]. The disappearance of the old evangelical certainties did have a secularising effect on the church; and the emphasis on a new centre of Old Testament (prophetic) theology, focussing on issues of practical concern, gave impetus to work among the poor and destitute of Scotland's cities. Yet the irony in all of this – and in Smith's approach also – is that the Scottish Church was never able to communicate the message of the Bible as effectively as she had done in the days of evangelical ascendancy and Calvinistic certainty.

The United Free Church and Controversy

The great Union of the Free Church of Scotland and the United Presbyterian Church of Scotland took place in October 1900. Smith attended the Union Assembly in Waverley Market, Edinburgh, and was a powerful advocate of the United Free position. The Free Church Case – the claim of the minority of Free Churchmen who had refused to enter the Union to be the legitimate successors of the original Free Church of Scotland and inheritors of the properties of the denomination – culminated in the landmark decision of the House of Lords in 1904 to award the properties of the Church to the minority. This decision required refinement through a Commission of Parliament which was charged with allocating properties more equitably.

Smith was one of the main speakers at a large meeting on 6 July 1905 in the Queen's Hall, London, at which 2,000 people gathered to hear views on the practical implications of the House of Lords Decision. He addressed the subject of the charges made against the United Free Church, to the effect that they had acted despotically towards the minority, that they had never made proportionate funds available to the minority, that they had evicted anti-Unionist men from their manses and churches, and had deprived them of their retirement

---

[132] cf. Brown, *Social History*, p190: "The principle of the new social theology was that the objective of all social effort is the realisation of the Kingdom of God on earth".
[133] Ibid., p181.
[134] Ibid.

allowances. Smith demonstrated cogently that the United Free Church had been magnanimous in respecting the position of the minority, to the extent of allowing them use of their buildings. More fundamental is Smith's statement as to why the Judgement of the House of Lords was given:

> The Judgement of the House of Lords was given against us, not upon any doctrinal grounds – only one Judge, one out of seven, based his judgement against us upon that ground. No, we lost the Judgement, we were condemned to lose our property, and were adjudged to have lost our identity, not because we have been decreed to be unfaithful to the great fundamentals of the Christian faith, but for a very different reason indeed; because we declined to abstain from profiting by the practical experience of our history since 1843, which led us to see that that which never was a fundamental of Christianity from the beginning of time to the present day, the so-called Establishment Principle, was an indifferent thing, and might be held among us without damage to the essentials as an open question.[135]

The minority, for their part, argued their position strongly on doctrinal and constitutional grounds; and it can scarcely be denied, as Kenneth Ross argues, that "the events of the Free Church 'Crisis' cannot be understood without reference to the immense bearing which the theological conflict had upon them".[136]

Even if Smith himself wished to downplay the theological issues involved in the Free Church Case, it was precisely on such grounds that his own orthodoxy was challenged in1902, following the publication of Smith's *Modern Criticism and the Preaching of the Old Testament*. In 1899 Smith was invited to Yale, to deliver the Lyman Beecher lectures. His extensive correspondence during the journey has been preserved.[137] Smith set sail from Liverpool on 25 March 1899, and kept a daily record of his trip. With his reputation as a biblical scholar established, and invitations to teach and lecture throughout Britain and America growing, Smith's 1899 trip to the United States was to lead to his most famous involvement with the Courts of the Church. What is less well-known is the fact that the famous lectures were almost lost at sea, as Smith writes in a letter dated Monday 27 March 1899:

> I woke at 5 this morning to the sound of water swishing about the cabin. I turned on the light and found two to three inches of water sweeping across the floor at every lurch of the ship ... I moved to an empty cabin, and spent

---

[135] Taken from a speech of GAS 6 July 1905, and printed in a pamphlet entitled *The Scottish Churches Bill*, New College Special Collections, MSS.SMI 1.9.
[136] K.R. Ross, *Church and Creed,* p218.
[137] NLS Acc 9446 No 91.

the next hour or two laying out my stained books and papers to dry. The kit bag, containing these, had suffered most...[138]

Richard Riesen may be right in suggesting that Smith's case "has been all but forgotten now",[139] but the incident ought to give us pause!

The lectures were published in 1901. They represent an expansion of the principles enunciated in his *The Preaching of the Old Testament to the Age*. The first lecture deals with the authority – or charter – for Old Testament criticism. For Smith it was axiomatic that the supreme sanction of the Old Testament was that which it received from Christ; but, he adds, "we must never forget that He was also its first Critic".[140] Thus, Smith insists that

> the New Testament treatment of the Old not only bequeaths to the Church the liberty of Criticism, but along many lines the need and obligation of Criticism; not only delivers us once for all from bondage to the doctrine of the literal inspiration and equal divinity of all parts of the Old Testament, but prompts every line of research and discussion along which the modern criticism of the Old Testament has been conducted.[141]

The second lecture charts the "course and character of modern criticism" and highlights the main movements in the rise and progress of critical thought. It is Smith's contention that criticism has affected mainly historical questions, and that the main findings of criticism have been confirmed by extrabiblical evidence. Smith ended the lecture by stating confidently: "Modern Criticism has won its war against the Traditional Theories. It only remains to fix the amount of the indemnity".[142] While one correspondent assured Smith that this was "an innocent enough statement",[143] Principal Rainy was furious. "I know nothing of indemnity," he said, scathingly; "when I see evidence for facts, they are God's facts".[144] Rainy, who was eager to secure the place of critical scholarship within the Church, nonetheless found Smith's assertion unnecessarily triumphalistic.

In his assessment of Smith's words, Old Testament scholar Robert Davidson suggests that Smith's optimism "might have been tempered somewhat had he known that eighty years later 'Traditional Theories' had refused to accept defeat and were displaying vigorous recuperative powers. Part of the reason for

---

[138] Ibid., 27 March 1899.

[139] Riesen, *Faith and Criticism*, p7.

[140] GAS, *Modern Criticism and the Preaching of the Old Testament*, (hereinafter MCPOT) London, 1901, p11.

[141] Ibid., p22.

[142] Ibid., p72.

[143] D. [?] to GAS 15 April 1902, on reading the College Report, NLS Acc 9446 No 29.

[144] P. Carnegie Simpson, *The Life of Principal Rainy*, Vol 2 (London 1909), p273.

this may lie in the fact that this indemnity was to prove much greater than Smith envisaged".[145] It was certainly true that at the turn of the century, Smith reckoned that the case was closed: traditional views of the Old Testament were on the way out. His assertions were the sign of a confidence that within the Church, the new biblical criticism had triumphed.

The third lecture is concerned with the historical basis of the Old Testament; when criticism has done its work, what is left to us? Smith argues that much of the historical allusions of the Old Testament are "practically of no importance to the Christian preacher";[146] the service of criticism has been to highlight what is of supreme importance: issues of ethics and character, confidence and hope, the application of Jehovah's word to everyday life. Criticism has enabled us, according to Smith, to extract the ethical teaching of the Old Testament and view it untrammelled by the accretion of dubious historical reference and allusion. Thus, according to Smith,

> if criticism, with the help of archaeology, has failed to establish the literal truth of these stories as personal biographies, it has on the other hand displayed their utter fidelity to the characters of the peoples developed. The power of the patriarchal narratives on the heart, the imagination, the faith of men can never die: it is immortal with truthfulness to the realities of human nature and of God's education of mankind.[147]

In his lecture on the spirit of Christ in the Old Testament, Smith wishes to move away from traditional and arbitrary methods of interpretation and

> to place the whole subject of the prophecy of Christ in the Old Testament and the presence of His Spirit in the history of Israel upon historical and ethical lines ...[148]

Citing episodes in the history of Israel, and highlighting some of the characters and personalities who made up that history, Smith argues that "accepting the results of modern criticism, we shall yet be sure of finding across that whole stretch of the Old Testament ... the presence of Divine Grace, of the Spirit of Christ, and of the virtues of forgivingness and self-sacrifice which these call forth in men".[149] For Smith, the presence of the Spirit of Christ in the Old Testament is not to be found in vague allusions, but in the development of an ethical character which allowed men and women to do exploits for their people.

---

[145] R. Davidson "Biblical Classics: V. George Adam Smith: Modern Criticism and the Preaching of the Old Testament", *The Expository Times*, 90 (1978-9), p101.
[146] MCPOT, p84.
[147] Ibid., p109.
[148] Ibid., p148.
[149] Ibid., p157.

Smith sees the spirit of Christ in them, because they prefigure the example of Christ Himself; in treating the Song of Deborah, for example (Judges 4), Smith makes reference to Zebulun and Naphtali's having hazarded their lives, and says that it was in doing so that "the Spirit of Christ which was in Israel from the beginning won its earliest triumphs".[150] It is in Jeremiah in particular, "beyond every other in the old dispensation" that Smith sees a "forerunner of Jesus Christ".[151] In Jeremiah's personal alienation from the community of Israel, as well as in his proclamation of a new Covenant, there are clear traces of the presence of Christ.

The remaining lectures, on the hope of immortality in the Old Testament (Lecture VI), on the influence of the prophets on social ethics (Lecture VII) and on preaching from the Wisdom literature (Lecture VIII), contain much that is of interest, but little that expands on the central thesis of the book as a whole. Smith gives some useful pointers as to how the Old Testament should be handled by the Christian preacher. His main point in Lecture VI is that the preaching of the Gospel should follow the example of the Old Testament by making the hope of immortality "one of the secondary and inferential elements of religious experience".[152] The emphasis of the preacher, Smith implies, ought to be upon the presence of God with us here, rather than our presence with him in the hereafter.

Smith's lectures were well received within his own scholarly and critical circle. Following their publication, President Gilman of Johns Hopkins University wrote to him lamenting "why were you not born and bred in America, where men, critics, scholars, preachers like you are so much needed!"[153] A former student of A.B. Davidson, James Campbell, wrote to Smith saying that since his College days

> I have ever since found the Old Testament a living book and preaching on it a continual delight. But there has been no book known to me which has so fully, frankly, lucidly and satisfactorily stated the present position and possibilities. You have cleared away many stumbling blocks and opened up mines of inexhaustible wealth for today's use of the Old Book.[154]

Another colleague, Robert Primrose, wrote in May 1902 to tell Smith that

> I have just read your book *Modern Criticism and the Preaching of the Old Testament* for the second time and wish to thank you. It has been a virtual

---

[150] Ibid., p154. Other examples are drawn upon to illustrate the same point, such as Gideon, Samuel and David.
[151] Ibid., p163.
[152] Ibid., p214.
[153] President Dwight to GAS, 1 March 1901, NLS Acc 9446 No 26.
[154] James A. Campbell to GAS, 26 July 1901, NLS Acc 9446 No 26.

revelation to me, and I hope to be a better man and a more helpful preacher from my study of your book.[155]

Others gave it a warm welcome, while taking issue on several points. William Robertson Nicoll, for example, described it in private correspondence as "as good as anything you have done", but expressed his inclination to give more room for an allegorical approach than Smith had allowed.[156] One concern among proponents of the critical approach was that the lectures would cause "uneasiness". Having brought the Scottish Church thus far, they thought that the lectures might be unnecessarily provocative. Thus from South Uist, the Rev Donald J. Nicolson wrote to Smith saying "I cannot but admire the ability shown in the book, while I question the wisdom of having it published in this crisis of our church's history".[157]

Although the lectures are stimulating to read and study, they still have the power to be provocative. In particular, Smith's justification of the critical method on the grounds of Christ's use of the Old Testament must be challenged. It is true that Jesus' use of Scripture surprised many in his day, as he drew forth conclusions and applications which the most avid students of the text – notably the scribes and Pharisees – had failed to see. Yet Christ claimed only to be extracting a meaning intrinsic to the text of the Old Testament itself, without the kind of restructuring demanded by the nineteenth century critics. Jesus found the true meaning of the text as he assumed the Mosaic authorship of the Pentateuch, the authorial unity of Isaiah and the early dating of Deuteronomy. To justify the critical task, as Smith defines it, on the grounds of Christ's handling of the Old Testament text is entirely unwarranted. As Donald Macleod puts it: "the most serious problem remains: the sheer scale of the difference between the historical Jewish view of the Scriptures (endorsed by Jesus) and the modern critical view ... If the prevailing consensus is correct, Jesus was completely mistaken as to the fundamental nature of Israel's religion".[158]

To some, therefore, the lectures proved that Smith was acting in *dis*loyalty to the Christian faith. James Johnston, one of Smith's fellow-Presbyters, published a lengthy reply to Smith, entitled *Destructive Results of the Higher Criticism, as Disclosed in 'Modern Criticism and the Preaching of the Old Testament'*. Johnston wields his pen scathingly. His main argument is that Smith's evangelicalism and his scholarship

---

[155] Robert Primrose to GAS, 19 May 1902, ibid.
[156] William R. Nicoll to GAS, 29 January 1901, ibid.
[157] D.J. Nicolson to GAS, 18 January 1902, ibid.
[158] D. Macleod, "Jesus and Scripture" in P. Helm and C.R. Trueman (eds), *The Trustworthiness of God* (Grand Rapids, 2002), p91.

meet, but do not combine ... the holy oil of the nursery will not mix with the secular water of the German schools. The one is from above, the other is of the earth, and tastes of the earth.[159]

Given the changed and more relaxed atmosphere in the Scottish Church following the Free Presbyterian secession, the adoption of the Declaratory Act and the Union of 1900, the intensity of the storm that was gathering is a surprise. But Johnston was not alone. The year 1901 also saw the publication of *The Old Bible and the New: Being a Review of Prof. G.A. Smith's 'Modern Criticism and the Preaching of the Old Testament'*. The title-page simply stated that this work was "prepared by a committee of ministers and elders", who took issue with Smith's views on the revelation of God's nature in the Old Testament, his view of inspiration and his concessions to biblical criticism in general. "Confidence in Wellhausen or German critics generally," they opined, "is not conducive to the discovery of sacred truth. Sometimes at least it leads to serious error. But the spirit of overweening confidence in its own statements, that pervades the book, alarms a reader for what follows".[160]

This negative reaction to Smith's work was the prelude to an attempt to raise an ecclesiastical charge against Smith for his "unorthodox" views. On 30 September 1901, a meeting of ministers and elders of the United Free Church of Scotland was held in Edinburgh, and a Memorial was drawn up, which had as its aim to draw the attention of the College Committee to the "revolutionary opinions" set forth in *Modern Criticism*.[161] Although Richard Riesen is strictly correct to say that it was with the Memorial that the case began,[162] it had a long pedigree. The Memorial drew the attention of the Committee to Smith's affirmation of the polytheistic character of Israelite religion, the "absence of history" from the first nine chapters of Genesis, the "fanciful ... character of the patriarchal narratives" in Smith's treatment, the "naturalistic treatment of Messianic prophecies" and "his far-reaching doctrine with respect to the Old Testament sacrificial system".

The College Committee met with Smith on 9 January 1902. At that meeting, Smith counter-charged the Memorialists with giving "a false perspective" on

---

[159] J. Johnston, *Destructive Results of the Higher Criticism as Disclosed in* Modern Criticism and the Preaching of the Old Testament (London, 1901) p7.

[160] *The Old Bible and the New: Being a Review of Prof G.A. Smith's* 'Modern Criticism and the Preaching of the Old Testament', Prepared by a Committee of Ministers and Elders (London, 1901) p28.

[161] The Memorial was published as an appendix to the *Special Report by the College Committee to the General Assembly of 1902*, in Reports to the General Assembly of the United Free Church of Scotland, 1902.

[162] Riesen, *Faith and Criticism*, p7. For a full and fair summary of the case, together with the report of the Committee, the reply of Smith and that counter-reponse of the Memorialists, as well as the passage of the Report during the Assembly, see Riesen, pp7-15.

his book, since they "carefully ignore the general purpose of the book, and in particular its detailed argument for the Old Testament as containing the authentic revelation of God".[163]

On the character of Israel's religion, Smith appealed to the biblical evidence behind his view of a primitive polytheism, and urged his detractors to do the same:

> Until the Memorialists offer a more rational explanation of all these phenomena, I must continue to regard the latter as proving that early Israel, while obliged to worship Jehovah alone (as the First Commandment enjoins), continued to believe in the reality of other gods, and in the legitimacy of their worship by their respective peoples, to whom, according to the Deuteronomist, Jehovah himself had assigned them.[164]

Similarly, on the charge of having questioned the historicity of Genesis, Smith reiterated his position that "Revelation was not confined to actual history",[165] but that the revelation of God in the Old Testament employed forms with which primitive man was familiar, but which criticism has shown to be scientifically untenable. Smith wrote that he could not understand why this should be deemed heretical, and said

> I am ashamed to have to repeat ideas, so generally accepted by believing scholars among us. But they are the proof that the fact that the earlier chapters of Genesis are woven of "the raw material" of the primitive conceptions of the universe, is a fact compatible with belief in these chapters as the vehicle of Divine revelation.[166]

The Report of the Committee was highly favourable to Smith; it acknowledged that in places Smith might have expressed himself unfortunately, but was prepared to respect his deference to the evangelical faith. Nor was the Committee persuaded that Church doctrine had been contravened. Therefore, the Committee decided "that it is not the duty of the College Committee or of the Church to institute any process against Dr Smith in connection with these Lectures".[167]

Dr James Kidd of Glasgow, the Convener of the College Committee, presented the Report to the General Assembly of 1902 (meeting in Glasgow,

---

[163] *Statement to the Sub-Committee of the College Committee of the United Free Church of Scotland, anent a Memorial against the volume* Modern Criticism and the Preaching of the Old Testament, published as Appendix II of the *Special Report*, p9.
[164] Ibid., p11.
[165] Ibid., p12.
[166] Ibid., p13.
[167] Ibid., p7.

while the Assembly Hall in Edinburgh was being refurbished to accommodate the needs of the new denomination). Dr Kidd reminded the Assembly that the case dealt not simply with one book or one individual, but with

> a great movement – a movement that was widespread, a movement that touched and embraced within it questions of literary analysis, questions needing detailed examination; and it would have been on that movement as a whole that the church would have been called to give a decision, had the College Committee itself originated, or advised the origination, of a process.[168]

He also clarified the point that while the Committee were not recommending that a process against Smith be initiated, it was not because they accepted all his conclusions, but that in their opinion, discussion on the issues raised should be allowed. This Report was set against an overture from the Synod of Glenelg (representing the Highland and Island Presbyteries of the Church) which drew attention to the unease in the Church at the spread and progress of critical views. Principal Rainy moved that

> The Assembly receive the Report and adopt the recommendation with which it closes, that it is not the duty of the Church to institute any process against Professor G.A. Smith, in connection with his lectures recently published.
>
> At the same time, the Assembly declare that they are not to be held as accepting or authorising the critical theories therein set forth. In dealing with the subject of this Report, the Assembly desire to give expression to the unabated reverence cherished in this Church for the written word, as the lively oracles through which the voice of God reaches His children for teaching, for comfort, and for admonition; and they declare their unwavering acceptance of it as the supreme rule of faith and life.
>
> And while they do not feel called upon to interfere with serious discussion of questions now raised, unless the interests of Christian truth should plainly seem to require it, the Assembly call upon ministers and professors who may take part in such discussion, to take care that reverence for Holy Scripture should be conspicuously manifest in their writings, and to treat, with the consideration that is so plainly due, views hitherto associated in the minds of our people with the believing use of the Bible.
>
> Finally, the Assembly recognise that the discussions in regard to the origin and history of Biblical books, which for a number of years have exercised the minds of learned men, have tended to create perplexity and anxiety for many Christian people; yet, recalling the results of former

---

[168] PDGAUFCS, 1902, p88. Riesen *Faith and Criticism*, is incorrect to state (p12 n.19) that these proceedings are to be found only in the Mitchell Library, Glasgow, since New College Library also houses a set.

discussions, the Assembly earnestly exhort their people not to be soon shaken in mind by what they hear of statements regarding the Bible, or regarding some parts of its contents. These will, in due time, be weighed, adjusted, and put in their proper place. Above all the fluctuations of human opinion the Lord rules and overrules; and His Word abides. The grass withereth, the flower thereof fadeth away, but the Word of the Lord endureth for ever.[169]

The speech that followed, was, in Carnegie Simpson's view, the best that Rainy ever made on the question of the critical movement within the Church.[170] In it, Rainy pointed out that were the Church to initiate proceedings against people every time new or even apparently contradictory views appeared, the Church would never be free from litigation. Opinions were constantly being revised in the light of new scientific discoveries, he said, and it was incumbent upon the Church to urge their people to believe in the Bible. The Bible, he said, would live triumphantly through all facts and their consequences.

A counter-motion urged the Assembly not to accept the Committee's recommendation, with John Smith arguing that the welfare of the Church depended on how the Assembly would declare itself as standing in relation to the Bible. He also refused to believe that any minister could define the essentials of the creed, which Smith had stated that he had not broken. In John Smith's view, only "when the United Free Church exercised its powers under the Declaratory Act, and defined what it meant by these essentials",[171] would the Assembly have a meaningful standard by which to judge claims and counter-claims as to whether new views accorded with the creeds of the Scottish Church.

One significant aspect of the debate was the appearance of Smith himself on the platform. While he wished to add nothing to his earlier written testimony, he said that it was the misrepresentation of his critical views, rather than these views themselves, which had occasioned unease throughout the Church.[172] In drawing attention to both the Old Testament attitude to Christ, and Christ's attitude to the Old Testament, Smith urged consideration of his evangelical approach to the Old Testament. According to George Reith, "while Professor Smith was speaking, the sun broke through the gloom and lit up his face – an omen of good hope and cheer to his friends".[173]

---

[169] PDGAUFCS, pp90-91.

[170] Simpson, *Life of Rainy*, Vol 2, p272.

[171] PDGAUFCS, p107.

[172] Ibid., p115.

[173] G.M. Reith, *Reminiscences of the United Free Church General Assembly* (London, 1933) p31. This fact is confirmed in LAS's account; she writes: "I shall never forget his standing on the platform of the great hall, a ray of sunshine striking upon him ..." (LAS, p83).

The portent was realised when the vote was taken, and Rainy's motion carried by 534 votes to 263, a majority of 271. The Moderator, in his closing address, reminded the Church that while it had decided not to initiate any process against Smith, neither had it sanctioned the critical movement or any of its conclusions. It would be, he said,

> a misrepresentation of the Church's attitude to say that by its decision it has either altered its relation to Holy Scripture, or given to its professors or ministers a general license to say whatever they please regarding the Holy Scripture.[174]

While the finding of the Assembly vindicated Smith's position as a scholar and a Churchman, it was far from being an outright acquittal. It said more about the place afforded to critical scholarship within the fledgling denomination than about the orthodoxy – or otherwise – of its Old Testament Professor; arguably, what Rainy won was a victory for both dogmatics *and* criticism. In many ways, therefore, the near trial of Smith was a defining moment in the history of the newborn United Free Church of Scotland.

What ought to give us pause, however, was not the size of the majority in Smith's favour, but the size of the opposition. The United Free Church of Scotland had come into being purged on at least two occasions of a narrow and conservative viewpoint, and with its credal commitment loosened under cover of a Declaratory Act. That a third of the Assembly should be of the opinion that Smith's views warranted action against him showed that the new criticism could not be accommodated in the new Church as readily either as Rainy or as Smith himself thought. Smith's acquittal does little to disguise the clear signal within the Assembly that he was essentially wrong: the new criticism had not, in fact, won the war over traditional theories.

And John Smith did have a point. The essentials of the Church's creed were not anywhere defined. Rainy's motion sought to find some middle ground between the Church's tradition and its new learning, and in doing so cut the gordian knot on the issue of how progress in learning and scholarship could relate to the Church's confession. There was probably much truth in the assessment of "A Scottish Presbyter" writing an account of the Assembly's decision for an American publication that "The Assembly's action virtually resolved itself into unbounded adulation of the *man* instead of a quiet, judicial sifting of the statements and tendencies of the *book*".[175]

For many of Smith's contemporaries, however, the outcome was hailed as a victory for critical thinking and scholarship. John Kelman, Smith's former assistant, wrote to him claiming that

---

[174] PDGAUFCS, p323.

[175] A Scottish Presbyter, "The Case of Prof George Adam Smith" in *The Presbyterian and Reformed Review*, Vol XVI (1902), p597.

the victory you have won for us all is almost incredible. It will do more for Christ's cause in the bit of Scotland I know best than anything that could have happened.[176]

Many similar messages of congratulation, must have been an inspiration to Smith, who managed to get on with his work; following the conclusion of his case, for example, he addressed a special meeting for working men on the Saturday evening of the Assembly week in Glasgow. But there is probably no small measure of truth in his wife's memoir, which claims that Smith's health was affected by the case, as well as by his amazement that the Church "which he had served so faithfully ... should have so misunderstood him".[177] On the other hand, had Smith himself understood his Church, he might have been more cautious in his lectures when he declared victory over the traditionalists.

Personal

Whether the strain of the trial was a contributory factor or not, the following year, while on a third visit to America, Smith succumbed to typhoid fever, which resulted in prolonged incapacitation. Smith was unable to resume his academic duties for several months. On 22 October 1903 the Senate of the United Free Church College received a letter from Thomas Buzzard MD "in which he expressed the opinion that Dr Smith should not resume his duties during the course of this Session and also that he should go abroad in order to recuperate".[178] This was a great blow to Smith's colleagues in the College. In a letter to William Robertson Nicoll, James Denney wrote that

> Smith, as you will know, has sailed for India: his work is divided by Eaton and Welch. He had been dreadfully ill, and though he was up to his old weight before he left he seemed strangely pithless – for *him*. I sincerely hope the year off may do him all the good he needs: we miss him dreadfully at the hall.[179]

The visit to India was made possible through the generosity of some of the Smiths' Glasgow friends. This was the first time Smith had returned to the country of his birth since leaving as a young boy of two years old. Smith's widowed brother Dunlop, now Political Agent for the Native States, following a successful army career, was resident in the Punjab, while his sister Minnie

---

[176] John Kelman to GAS, 23 May 1902, NLS Acc 9446 No 29.
[177] LAS, p84.
[178] Minutes of the Senatus of the United Free Church College, Glasgow, 22 October 1903, Glasgow University Archives, DC84 1/1.
[179] *Letters of Principal James Denney to W. Robertson Nicoll 1893-1917* (London, 1920) pp33-4.

lived with him as housekeeper. The reunion was a highlight of the travels in the Orient. Another sister, Ann, was married to the Assistant Commissioner for the Attock District, Montagu Butler. New Year's Day, 1904 was spent in Calcutta, the city of Smith's birth, and a visit there was followed by extensive travels throughout the Indian continent.[180] The journey home was made via Jerusalem, where Smith was engaged in some explorations with a view to his forthcoming book on Jerusalem.

Smith's contacts with America represented an important development in his academic career. His first visit as Professor was to Baltimore in 1896 to deliver his Lectures on the Poetry of Israel. This visit enabled the Smiths to visit Canada. The second was to Yale, where he delivered the Lyman Beecher lectures, and also to Chicago. His lectures drew large audiences – up to 5,000 according to Lilian's own diaries.[181] Smith spent six weeks at the University of Chicago, after which he visited D.L. Moody at Northfield. The Summer School at Chautauqua, New York, an institution for popular education, gave him an opportunity to popularise the critical method of approaching the Old Testament. At the end of his lectures he wrote with an air of contentment and confidence that

> the students at least are pleased, and pleased for a reason which pleases me more than any other possibly could do. They say that they have secured their bearings in the Old Testament, which had been put by criticism, and have new faith in it as the Word of God, and material for themselves as preachers...[182]

The third visit, as we have seen, was cut short by illness. Smith had been invited to Cleveland, Ohio, to lecture at the Western Reserve University for the summer of 1903. The illness struck almost immediately, however, and led to an unscheduled visit to India, and to a year away from the College.

The fourth visit was in 1909, when Smith was invited to be "Convocation Orator"[183] at the University of Chicago, and Visiting Professor for the Summer. He stopped for three days in Washington, where James Bryce, the British ambassador, an old Aberdonian friend (who was also an important Liberal historian), entertained him and presented him to President Taft in the White House. After a gruelling schedule at Chicago, Smith explored the Western

---

[180] See LAS, pp86-90 for an extensive account of the visit to India.
[181] LAS Diary for 20 August 1899, where she writes that George "preached in the amphitheatre [in Chautauqua] ... full 5,000 people". Both GAS and LAS kept parallel accounts of the trip, LAS basing her accounts on GAS's letters. NLS Acc 9446 No 221.
[182] GAS to LAS from Newhaven, Friday 21 April 1899, NLS Acc 9446 No 91.
[183] The phrase is borrowed from LAS, p124, and probably meant that he gave the commencement address.

coastline and visited Los Angeles, Berkeley and Seattle before entering Canada and returning home.

At one level these contacts are a signal of Smith's growing popularity and a recognition of his own academic prowess. But at another level they are a sign of the far-reaching influence of the work being done in the Free (now United Free) Church Colleges, as seed-beds of the burgeoning critical movement. Already indebted to Scotland for its Presbyterian structures and for settlements in many districts and cities during the course of the nineteenth century, America also followed Britain in its acceptance of the critical movement. Mark Noll states that "Britons began to pay serious attention to modern biblical criticism only a short time before their American colleagues",[184] and the American schools felt indebted to the Scottish Colleges as champions of the critical view of Scripture. The fusion between evangelicalism and criticism also appealed to the American theologians: by speaking on issues of biblical criticism in an evangelical context of commitment to the Reformed Faith, the Scottish teachers were regarded as particularly authoritative within the evangelical tradition.

As far back as 1896, however, Smith had been conscious of the differences between the American and Scottish theological systems. Whereas wealthy Christians in America took seriously the need for rigorous training of ministers and were willing to endow schools and Colleges to this end, things in Scotland were very different. Smith argued that

> in Scotland, if the Presbyterian Church were not to be left behind with the training of their ministry, this work with its new demands and opportunities must be felt to be not merely the duty of the professors and the college committee but the interest, the responsibility and the burden of the whole Church.[185]

It is clear from Smith's writings that he wished to see critical theories advanced because he believed that a critical view of the Bible was in the best interests of preaching, and therefore of the Church. It is also arguable, conversely, that Smith expected the Church in Scotland to be as magnanimous in supporting critical scholarship as he found the American churches to be. While he was more or less successful in realising the first of these ambitions, the second was to elude him, as the trial before the 1902 Assembly made abundantly clear. The Scottish Church never did give unanimous assent to the school of enquiry

---

[184] Mark Noll, *Between Faith and Criticism: Evangelicals, Scholarship and the Bible* (Leicester, 1991) p62.
[185] *The Glasgow Herald* 22 October 1896, in NLS Acc 9446 No 412.

which Smith represented, and the suspicions which were raised early and which culminated in 1902 cast a long shadow.[186]

Smith's time in Glasgow was punctuated by several honours, including the conferring of a Doctor of Laws upon him by Aberdeen University in 1895 and a Doctor of Divinity by Dublin University in 1908. In 1909 the Society for Biblical Study made him the first recipient of its Silver Medal for Biblical Research, which was presented to him at a ceremony in London. In addition, he was invited to consider a Call from Marylebone Presbyterian Church, London, as well as the Chairs of History and Hebrew in the University of Glasgow. In January 1907, Smith's name was being considered for the Principalship of Glasgow University, with his popularity with students placing him high on the list of possible candidates.[187] In the event Sir Donald MacAlister was appointed, and Smith remained in the College, wishing to serve not only the academic world, but also the Church in which he had been reared and whose ethos he was so influential in fashioning.

However, following his return from America in 1909, Smith was offered the Principalship of Aberdeen University, and felt that he could not decline this prestigious honour. At a farewell dinner in his honour in Glasgow on 1 March 1910, Smith reminisced on his involvement in the life of the city, and praised the Provost of Glasgow for "the wonderful amount of time and ability devoted gratuitously by your wealthier citizens to civic affairs, and to the management of the philanthropic institutions and movements of Glasgow".[188] In response to the lavish praise heaped upon him as a scholar of the Old Testament, Smith said

> I have no gifts of philosophy nor powers of original speculation. Beyond the Christian faith and love of hard work which I owe to my father and mother, I have little except perhaps some ability to interpret to the present age the messages of the ancient prophets.[189]

In this, he acknowledged, he was not alone; Scotland had bred many fine scholars. But Smith acknowledged that he owed a debt to Glasgow, whose views and sounds would long remain in his mind and memory. And evidently, as those who gathered to bid him farewell acknowledged, Glasgow owed no small debt to him.

---

[186] Cf. D. Macleod, "The Free Church College 1900-1970" in *Disruption to Diversity*, p222, writing on the Robertson Smith case: "His case left the Free Church with an endemic reluctance to appoint young men to College chairs ... It also bequeathed a persistent attitude of mistrust between the College and the Church as a whole".

[187] So *Letters of Principal Denney*, p78.

[188] GAS, Speech in Glasgow on removal to Aberdeen, 1910, p7.

[189] Ibid., p8.

Conclusion

This chapter has concentrated on the ecclesiastical, social and academic aspects of Smith's work, and the contributions he made to Old Testament scholarship. These were not only happy years, but also Smith's most influential and most productive years. His concern from the commencement of his professoriate was to make scholarship the servant of the Church, and he raised issues that were seminal for twentieth-century biblical scholarship.

Smith's primary concern as a biblical scholar continued to be the *preaching* of the Old Testament. By emphasising the ethical concerns of the Bible, Smith believed that it was possible to wed the ancient revelation of Jehovah to the real, practical needs of people. But his own experience amply demonstrated what happens when new wine is put into old wineskins. The Church he sought to serve found it difficult to accommodate his critical views; they represented an immigrant which could not easily be naturalised within Scottish Church life.

Smith's scholarship may be characterised in various ways. He was certainly erudite; the work on the Prophets shows the breadth of his reading and the extent of his research. He leans heavily on Continental work and shows deference to his teacher, A.B. Davidson, and his forerunner, William Robertson Smith.[190] He moves around the standard contemporary works with consummate ease, and gleans much from them.

Despite that, or perhaps because of it, it cannot be said that his work was original. While the works on historical geography had been ground-breaking, the result of painstaking field-work and original research, the expositions of the prophetic works do not show the same kind of originality. The citations from the Continental scholars are often uncritical, and his engagement with them leaves one feeling that Smith is content simply to facilitate German scholarship. Of the fact that these are views which he himself has espoused there can be no doubt, yet there is a dearth of original thought.

This, in turn, leads to his work being open to the charge of superficiality; while Smith is aware of who the principal players in the field are, engagement with them is slow. Throughout, there is simply the assumption that his views are correct, bolstered as they are by the insights of Wellhausen, Delitzsch, Ewald and others. This also leaves his scholarship rather arrogant; why, for example, is it necessary to accept that there are in Hosea "verses which cannot well be authentic"[191] or that the title "Malachi" was "a purely artificial one borrowed from 3:1"[192]? These insights may well be correct, but it is the simple and self-confident assumption of them, rather than the clear demonstration of them, that opens Smith to the charge of intellectual imperiousness.

There is no doubt, however, that Smith's superb style gave his academic works a wide appeal, and led to his scholarship being popular. Ironically,

---

[190] For example, in *The Book of the Twelve Prophets*, Vol II, p43, note 1.
[191] *The Book of the Twelve Prophets*, Vol I, p212.
[192] *The Book of the Twelve Prophets*, Vol II, p332.

however, perhaps his lack of critical engagement and his attempt to popularise actually contributed to a downgrading of the Scottish pulpit, fostering a spirit and sense of dependence upon the higher critics, instead of a sense of dependence upon the text of Scripture itself. For Smith the Old Testament can be read only through the lens of criticism – this is his core commitment, and it is a position he argues well; but it is arguable that the net result is a distancing of the message of the Bible from the people. For all Smith's insistence on suiting preaching to the needs of people, his exegetical work often requires a massive re-evaluating of the text before anyone can have access to it.

Although the Principalship of Aberdeen University was a great honour, and Smith was the last ordained clergyman to hold the post in the twentieth century, it is arguable that both Smith himself and the Church needed the change. In terms of biblical scholarship, Smith had made a distinctive contribution. Had he continued in his post, perhaps other commentaries might have come from his hand; but as a popular figure and able administrator, the time had come for him to make a more general contribution to Scottish higher education as a University Principal, even if *The British Weekly* lamented that his loss both to the College and the city of Glasgow was "very serious".[193]

Smith's work as Principal and Vice-Chancellor of Aberdeen University will be explored in Chapter 6. The following chapter will be concerned more specifically with his contribution to Church and State during the first World War, which broke just four years after Smith returned to Aberdeen.

---

[193] *British Weekly*, 28 October 1909.

CHAPTER 5

Representative of Church and State: The War Years

Smith was inaugurated as Principal and Vice-Chancellor of the University of Aberdeen on 9 November 1909. According to his wife's memoir, the appointment of another ordained clergyman as Principal, in succession to the Very Rev Dr Marshall Lang, led to "criticism in some quarters".[1] Nonetheless, she hastened to defend the appointment on the grounds that it was "as a scholar rather than as a Churchman" that Smith received the position.[2]

The following year the new Vice-Chancellor moved into Chanonry Lodge, the official residence of the Principal of the University of Aberdeen.[3] Shortly thereafter another child was born – Margaret Elphinstone, who shared her middle name with the fifteenth century founder of the University, Bishop William Elphinstone. According to Lilian Smith, the name symbolised the fact that, within living memory, no child had been born to a Principal of Aberdeen during tenure of that office, although Margaret herself in later years considered the choice "arrogant".[4] She was the seventh and last child of George and Lilian.

Chanonry Lodge was a large house, which, after some renovation, accommodated the large family comfortably. In her biography of John Buchan, Janet Adam Smith, who was five years old when her father moved to Aberdeen, recalls that

> in my Aberdeen childhood we used to condemn as "English" any stuffiness of manner, any undue deference to "good form", any lack of interest outside a restricted social circle, any sense of people being measured and judged by accent or schooling, which we associated with the South, and which made us cross and uncomfortable.[5]

---

[1] LAS, p136.
[2] Ibid. Cf. the statement in A.L. Drummond and J. Bulloch *The Church in Late Victorian Scotland 1874-1900* (Edinburgh, 1978) p134 that Smith "owed his appointment entirely to his scholarship and personal qualifications".
[3] The offices of Principal and Vice-Chancellor have traditionally been occupied by the same individual in Scottish Universities. The former is administrative, while the latter is primarily ceremonial.
[4] "They christened me, rather arrogantly I think, Margaret Elphinstone" *Transcript of interview with Mrs Margaret Clarke*, 20 March 1998.
[5] Janet Adam Smith, *John Buchan* (London, 1965) p226.

By implication, the Smith home bred a different atmosphere: where "stuffiness" was absent and wide interests were entertained and encouraged, and people were accepted for what they were.

The following chapter will look more generally at Smith's administrative work in the University, as well as some of the personal and domestic aspects of the years of Smith's Principalship. This chapter will focus more specifically on Smith's role as a leader and representative, both in Church and State, during the War years.

Effects of the War

The First World War broke in August 1914, and, as Lilian Smith puts it, "From that time, for four years, the war dominated our thoughts and lives".[6] Smith's interest in the war was both professional and personal. As Principal of the University, he took an interest in the students and alumni who had enlisted, and in the University's wider engagement in war activity. In an address at the Spring graduation in March 1916, Smith said

> Altogether I reckon that about 380 students have entered on service with the colours since the war began; of whom over 350 offered themselves while the voluntary system of enlistment still prevailed. The total of graduates alumni, students, staff, and servants of the University on active service is therefore about 1730 as compared with 1200 a year ago.[7]

In addition to those on active service, others were involved in Red Cross service and at naval sick quarters. Smith himself encouraged the training of officers, and, in the words of Eric Linklater, "got authority to establish an Officers' Training Corps"[8] which was linked to the University. The OTC in Aberdeen University was a medical unit; Smith was unsuccessful in establishing an infantry OTC in the University, the War Office considering that this would be of limited value. In addition, the local links with the Gordon Highlanders meant that there was a preference within the University that its own "U Company" – a student Volunteer military company formed in 1898 – should support the Gordon Highlanders.[9] When war broke out, U Company

---

[6] LAS, p155.

[7] GAS, "Two Years of War: The Record of the University", *Aberdeen University Review*, Vol 3 No 9, (June 1916) p215.

[8] Linklater, E., *Fanfare for a Tin Hat* (London, 1970) p82.

[9] See R. Anderson, *The Student Community at Aberdeen 1860-1939* (Aberdeen, 1988) p76. Cf. also J.J. Carter and C.A. McLaren *Crown and Gown: An Illustrated History of the University of Aberdeen*, (Aberdeen, 1994) p99: "The First World War hit Aberdeen hard ... its students formed U Company in the Territorial Army Reserve of the local regiment, the Gordon Highlanders". For a history of U Company, see John McConachie, *The Student Soldiers* (Elgin, 1995).

was mobilised immediately,[10] bringing the University into the war from the outset.

During the war years Smith encouraged voluntary enlistment, took an active interest in training[11], and kept a careful record of the University's contribution to the war. Smith visited the student soldiers in their training for military service, and in 1915 reached Bedford, where some of the students were engaged in preparations for war, *en route* to the front. One student described the descent of the troops on the English town as "a peaceful penetration" but one which "shattered the calm of 700 years".[12] One private, John Knowles, who kept a diary of his war experiences in the Aberdeen University contingent, recalls a visit from the Principal in January and February of 1915. Knowles said that the Principal "was very short and seemed rather at a loss for words ... The speech he made was not very pointed. He wished us God-speed and a safe return if we went to the front".[13] A service by the Principal on Sunday 7 February at the training Camp "dealt with the causes of the war and bid us ever remember in the heat of battle the righteousness of the cause for which we fight."[14] Knowles had to confess, however, that "It was not quite what I expected and I was rather disappointed".[15] As late as 1927, Smith was still visiting the students who were engaged at camps for military training,[16] and he made this a priority, not least because Smith believed that the Universities in the Allied countries were ideally poised for contributing to the war effort:

> They have contributed, among the Allies, to the understanding of the great issues; they have swelled, more than most institutions and I believe in a degree equal to the churches, the volume of that national conscience which is our chief and our lasting power in fighting for a cause so just and so sacred. Above all, they have sent lavishly of their men, both teachers and taught, both students and graduates, to the forces of the Allies; and they have contributed, in full proportion to their number, to the colossal sacrifices which the manhood of their nations has made to the most sacred cause ever fought for in the whole range of human history.[17]

---

[10] Linklater, *Fanfare*, p83.
[11] Letters to Smith in July 1916, for example, were addressed c/o Captain Kinloch, Aberdeen University OTC, Kings Meadows, Peebles (see NLS Acc 9446 No 58).
[12] Alexander Rule, *Students Under Arms: Being the War Adventures of the Aberdeen University Company of the Gordon Highlanders* (Aberdeen, 1934).
[13] McConachie, *Student Soldiers*, p37.
[14] Ibid., p52.
[15] Ibid.
[16] See R.B. Strathdee, *Aberdeen University Contingent: Officers Training Corps, Senior Training Corps* (Aberdeen, 1947).
[17] GAS, *Our Common Conscience: Addresses delivered in America during the Great War* (London, 1918) pp154-5. This was part of an address delivered to the University of

Smith's two eldest sons enlisted in the War, and their deaths during different campaigns led to Smith publishing their memoirs privately. George Buchanan Smith (1890-1915) had been born in Aberdeen, and received his education in Glasgow High School and the University of Glasgow. He trained with the Glasgow University OTC, and, on the day War was declared on 4 August 1914, was granted a commission as 2nd Lieutenant with the Gordon Highlanders. In his father's emotive (and naturally biased) assessment,

> He had long wished ... to be a soldier; and had shown gifts suitable to the profession – coolness and courage, patience under the heaviest fatigue, thoughtfulness ... for the men under him, familiarity with the tactics of great commanders and the course of their campaigns, and an uncommon eye, whether by day or night, for 'the lie and the lift' of a landscape. It was that conscience of his country's cause, with these gifts ... that inspired, as with thousands of others, his quiet devotion to the service of his country, and nursed his growing keenness to get out to the Front.[18]

George was seriously wounded in his first engagement in the War, at Kemmel, in Flanders. He took a bullet in the back of his neck, which rendered him unconscious. When he regained strength he continued firing at the enemy, until another bullet shattered his left hand. Seventy years later, his sister recalls the grim fascination she had for the wounded hand.[19] Remaining on the battlefield all day, under fire, he was able eventually to lead the survivors to safety.[20] George was subsequently hospitalised in London and was able to join the family in Aberdeen for a short while. In August 1915 he was in action again in France, and his battalion was engaged at the Battle of Loos the following month. Leading his men in the battle, he was killed instantly when a shell exploded beside him. A popular student, George Buchanan Smith's death was felt within the University circle, with the student magazine, *Alma Mater*, recalling him with affection, saying that "his was a straight life, a brave death, with a host of friends to salute his memory".[21]

Chicago, and was reprinted in their magazine, *The University Record*, Vol IV, No 3 (July 1918). The quotation is on page 122.

[18] GAS, *George Buchanan Smith 1890-1915* (Glasgow, 1916) pp57-8.

[19] "George I remember ... he was wounded in the war – he lost a finger – it sort of fascinated me in a horrid way, when you're very small", *Transcript of interview with Margaret Clarke*, 20 March 1998.

[20] See the *University of Aberdeen Book of Remembrance* (Aberdeen, 1952), entry under "George Buchanan Smith".

[21] *Alma Mater Memorial Number* (Aberdeen ,1916). Smith wrote the foreword for this special edition of *Alma Mater*, in the following terms: "No praise from us can add to the glory of their conscience, their courage and their devotion unto death. Our duty is to see

The War Years 149

The Smith household was now experiencing intense pain and loss, in common with many other Scottish (and, indeed, manse) families. In compiling the commemorative volume on his son, Smith wrote

> it is six months since he gave his life for us. The days do not lessen the pain of our loss, but for him all is well. Such a death in such a cause can only have been the entrance upon a higher service.[22]

For Smith, the personal pain yielded to the greater consideration of the vicariousness of such losses. The life of his son was given *for* Smith, *for* the country, *for* the cause. In the words of C.H. Myers, a former student of Smith's in Glasgow, and now minister of Pilgrim Congregational Church in Tennessee, such deaths could only properly be regarded as vicarious: "They," he wrote to Smith in November 1917, "the dear lads, have saved us, who, alas, have been so unworthy of their sacrifice and so insensible to the real issues of the struggle".[23] By thus integrating the war losses into the Christian concept of vicariousness and substitution, a rationale could be found for them. Perhaps this goes some way to explaining how Smith, in spite of personal tragedy, was able to continue his work, with its various demands, and enter into correspondence so soon over such issues as the Moderatorship, a fairly arduous role given the recent loss of a member of his family.

George's brother Robert Dunlop Smith (1892-1917), nicknamed "Beppo", was another casualty of the war.[24] Robert attended the University of Aberdeen for the session 1910-11; like his brother he also trained with the Glasgow Officers' Training Corps. He received a commission with the Rifle Brigade of the Indian Army, rising to the rank of Captain with the 33rd Punjabis. Smith and his son George had travelled to Southampton to bid farewell to Robert, who left for India in February 1913 on a five-year term of commission. Smith notes that it was 60 years since his own father, George Smith, had been brought to Southampton by *his* father, Adam Smith, to sail for India.[25]

Smith never saw Robert again. When his patrol was ambushed by a German force near Kilwa, East Africa, in June 1917, Robert was killed by a bomb. Robert was buried there, under cover of the Union Jack. Smith saw in his interment a potent symbol of the unity of the British Empire; "do they not man the outposts of our Empire," he asks, "and testify to its unity, the young British

---

that we prove worthy of them, and to keep pure and strenuous the lives, individual and national, for which they have so freely given theirs..."

[22] *George Buchanan Smith*, p88.
[23] C.H. Myers to GAS, 6 November 1917, NLS Acc 9446 No 86.
[24] There is also an entry on Robert in the University of Aberdeen's *Book of Remembrance*, and the names of the two sons appear on the wall of King's College Chapel, University of Aberdeen.
[25] LAS and GAS, *Robert Dunlop Smith 1892-1917* (Aberdeen, 1921) p27.

Officer and his Indian soldiers, whose bodies lie together in the jungle of East Africa?"[26] Especially poignant was a treasured letter, written from Robert to his father in December 1915:

> If I do go, I hope I'll keep up the honour of my home and country and die worthy of my old school, and of the two regiments to which I have belonged. Don't sorrow for me. You know that I shall be with George and other friends who have gone in this War. I shall have died happily. One can't die better than in doing one's duty.[27]

The firm conviction that these deaths on the side of the Allies were for the benefit of others fortified both the soldiers in action as well as their families at home. For the survivors, the only way in which the reality could be assimilated and the grief contained was in believing that the deaths of their loved ones were not in vain, and were, in their own way, glorious. Visiting another bereaved mother, a Mrs Macneil, whose son, Lowe, had been a friend of George's, Lilian Smith said of her "I don't think I use a wrong word when I say her heart is broken – but she is quiet and brave and says how for Lowe she could have wished no finer end".[28] By thus viewing the deaths in terms of vicarious suffering and with shades of glory, Smith could read the Roll of Honour in King's College Chapel, Aberdeen, including the names of his own sons, with a steady voice, and with "even a note of triumph in it".[29]

From the outset, Smith had used his influential role as Principal, as well as his gifts as preacher, to aid the war effort. 1915 saw the publication of *War and Peace*, two sermons which Smith preached originally in King's College Chapel. The first, on Isaiah 30:15 ("In quietness and confidence shall be your strength"), was a call to exercise faith in God along with obedience and commitment to his will. In it, he set the Great War within the context of just wars of history: Cromwell, the Covenanters and Abraham Lincoln are invoked as men who fought "not in despite of their faith, but because of it, and in obedience to the conscience which God had kindled in them".[30] He describes war as a *sacrament*:

> a sacrament in the full sense of that name as we Scots have been brought up to understand it … war is not only the consecration of the soldiers themselves to the sacred cause for which it is waged, but it yields a more

---

[26] Ibid., p204.
[27] Robert Dunlop Smith to GAS, quoted in *Robert Dunlop Smith 1892-1917*, p216.
[28] LAS to GAS, 13 July 1916, NLS Acc 9446 No 58.
[29] LAS, p168.
[30] GAS, *War and Peace: Two Sermons delivered in King's College Chapel, Aberdeen* (London, 1915) p11.

vital, and sometimes it may even be a more articulate, expression of the truth involved in the cause than was possible in times of peace.[31]

This is more than a triumphalistic vindication of the War; this is an attempt to domesticate it within the contours of Christian theology. War becomes a means of commitment and an aid to faith. German arrogance, hatred and insensitivity combine, in Smith's view, to demonstrate that the War is one "for justice and freedom",[32] in which treason would be "to abate our hopes, to grow wearied or fearful, to lose faith in God",[33] no matter what casualties there may yet be.

In the second sermon, on "Peace" (based on John 14:27 and 16:33), Smith argues that Christ's promises of peace cannot be equated with pacifism, since Christ "never pledged us political peace".[34] Christ, he urges, never condemned war; and to the argument that it is written of the Messiah that he "did no violence", Smith appeals to the Christian emphasis on righteousness and on duty as the necessary precursor of peace. He argues that the War has amply demonstrated what John 16:33 promised: that the peace of Christ would be experienced within the tribulations of the world. This, he says, is what the commitment to the allied cause had already achieved since war began:

> A peace unprecedented at home and throughout our Empire – the stilling of party strife and of faction, a great decrease of class and race hatred, an imperial unity which is far above what we or any other Empire ever before experienced; but deeper still the tranquillity of heart and soul reserved for all who set their affection on spiritual things, and who have resolved, come what may, to do their duty by God and their fellow-men.[35]

Smith's sermons were typical of the way in which most Scottish Presbyterian ministers responded to the war. James Denney, for example, proclaimed that "the highest calling of faith at this moment, the final proof we can give that we are believing men, is to strike with all our might on the Lord's side in the Lord's battle".[36] W.L. Walker declared that the call to enter the war was "a Call of Duty ... a *moral* summons borne in on the conscience and the heart. Although all may not have recognized it, that Call of Duty was the Call

---

[31] Ibid., p13.
[32] Ibid., p28.
[33] Ibid., p31.
[34] Ibid., p37.
[35] Ibid., p49.
[36] J. Denney, *War and the Fear of God* (London, 1916) p95.

of God".[37] This is what D.S. Cairns described as God "drawing us all on into a new discipleship".[38]

Such war sermons were an attempt both to give a rationale for the War and to encourage and fortify people against its harsh realities. In his study of this theme, Peter Matheson concludes that while the sermons did comfort the bereaved and bring consolation to those on the Home Front, there is evidence to suggest that

> their main failing was a tendency to domesticate the war, to find meaning and dignity where there was none, to lard the bitter realities with a generous layer of idealism in order to make them bearable for themselves and others.[39]

This became the approach both of chaplains and of Christian officers on the field, as well as ministers at home. General Haig, for example, took consolation in the field from the Old Testament's words "the battle is not yours, but God's".[40] And while there were some dissenting voices among Scottish clergy, the general approach of the Church of Scotland and the United Free Church of Scotland was, in historian Stewart Brown's words, "to identify the cause of Christian morality with that of the British war effort".[41]

In addition, Smith used his expertise in Old Testament studies for promoting the war effort. In 1915-16 he delivered the Murtle Lecture, which was on the theme of "Jeremiah's Poems on War", and was published as an article under that title in the *Aberdeen University Review*. After some introductory comments on personal and literary aspects of Jeremiah's life, Smith enumerates the wars which the prophet's country suffered during his lifetime. These included "the Scythian raids which swept across Palestine to the borders of Egypt in 625BC, the Egyptian invasion in 612 when the King and the flower of the army fell at Megiddo, and the treble Babylonian invasion culminating in the siege, overthrow and sack of Jerusalem in 586".[42] Smith adds: "I think we shall find his reflections of these events not irrelevant to the circumstances of our allies

---

[37] W.L. Walker, *The War, God and our Duty* (London, 1917) p63.

[38] D.S. Cairns, "The Task Before the Church" in Matthews, B., (ed.) *Christ: and the World at War* (London, 1917) p52.

[39] P.C. Matheson, "Scottish War Sermons 1914-1919", *Records of the Scottish Church History Society*, Vol XVII (1972) p213.

[40] G.J. de Groot, "'We are safe whatever happens' – Douglas Haig, the Reverend George Duncan, and the Conduct of War 1916-1918", from N. Macdougal (ed), *Scotland at War AD79-1918* (London, 1990) p204.

[41] S.J. Brown, "'A Solemn Purification by Fire': Responses to the Great War in the Scottish Presbyterian Churches, 1914-19", *Journal of Ecclesiastical History*, Vol 45, No 1 (January 1994) p90.

[42] GAS, "Jeremiah's Poems on War", *Aberdeen University Review*, Vol 3 No 8 (February 1916) pp121-2.

and ourselves in the present war".[43] Smith highlights Jeremiah's artistry and realism, which combine to portray "raw Judean landscapes under the pitiless light".[44] The effect of the whole resonates in the experience of the Allies in the War, and leads to a further Christianising of the war effort:

> As we have need of our Heavenly Father's sympathy and grace in any warfare for righteousness to which He may call us, so He has need of such courage and initiative as, being His children and the brethren of Jesus Christ, He trusts us to be able to show.[45]

If it was true that "it was in the pulpit of King's College Chapel ... that George Adam Smith made manifest his real authority",[46] he had no difficulty in wedding that pulpit to the cause of the Allies. The Great War represented a cause every bit as righteous as the wars of God's people throughout the course of the Old Testament, and was therefore justly waged, justly fought, and would be justly won only if the Allies were the victors.

Honour and Preferment

The year 1916 – midway through the conflict – was to be of great significance for Smith, as a year of recognition and preferment. Four important honours were bestowed upon him that year. The first was his election as a Fellow of the British Academy. This prestigious institution was founded in 1901 as an independent fellowship of scholars to represent the interests of scholarship in the humanities both nationally and internationally. It was under the auspices of the Academy that Smith had already delivered the Schweich lectures on "The Early Poetry of Israel" in 1910.[47] The second was his membership of the Athenaeum Club, a society which was instituted

> for the association of individuals known for their scientific or literary attainments, artists of eminence in any class of the fine arts, and noblemen and gentlemen distinguished as liberal patrons of science, literature or the arts.[48]

No more than nine new members were elected in any one year, and Smith's name was proposed by the Archbishop of Canterbury. Lord Bryce, the British

---

[43] Ibid., p122.
[44] Ibid., p123.
[45] Ibid., p126.
[46] Linklater, *Fanfare*, p78.
[47] See next chapter for comment upon these lectures, which were not published until 1912.
[48] Handbook entitled *Athenaeum: Rules 1913*, p7, NLS Acc 9446 No 62.

Ambassador to the USA, wrote to him "you would have been greatly gratified if you could have heard what was said about you..."[49]

A further honour was his knighthood, conferred on him in the New Year's Honours List. As his wife pointed out, "clergymen are not usually honoured in this way",[50] and she offers no explanation for this outstanding distinction. From Russia, one alumnus of Aberdeen wrote that "the honour, well earned by your scholarly attainments, falls indirectly on our 'Alma Mater', the post of Principal of which you so worthily fill".[51]

Greater than these, however, was the news that Smith was to be nominated as Moderator of the 1916 General Assembly of the United Free Church of Scotland. As early as July of the previous year, Smith's former assistant, John Kelman, was urging the relevant Committee to consider Smith's candidature for the office. Citing not only Smith's unique and influential position as a University Principal, as well as his loyalty to the United Free Church of Scotland, he argued in defence of Smith's appointment

> the splendid service he has rendered to the country in connection with the War. His utterances on that subject have shown a wonderful grasp of historical fact and principle, a practical wisdom worthy alike of the statesman and the military leader, and a humane and devout spirit which have carried these far above the levels of mere politics or strategy, and made them an essentially religious contribution to the defence of the State, and the well-being of humanity.[52]

The United Free Church *Record* argued that Smith's position as Principal of the University could only be to his advantage in the office of Moderator. The Church, it urged, "needed a man who could interpret the Christian view and make it intelligible and commanding to the whole people of Scotland".[53] Behind the appointment, therefore, was a desire to retain for the Church an appeal and status within Scottish society during the War years. It is arguable that while the nomination did confer a great honour upon Smith himself, it was also designed to secure the greater loyalty of the people to the Church through the appointment of a Moderator who might have a wide and far-reaching appeal.

---

[49] Bryce to GAS, 11 April 1916, NLS Acc 9446 No 62.

[50] LAS, p159.

[51] W. Sharpe Wilson (Imperial University of Petrograd, Russia) to GAS, 14 January 1916, NLS Acc 9446 No 60.

[52] John Kelman to "My dear John" (? – possibly John Young, Secretary of the United Free Church of Scotland), July 1915, NLS Acc 9446 No 55.

[53] "The Moderator-Designate", *Record of the Home and Foreign Mission Work of the United Free Church of Scotland*, No 182, February 1916, p43, reporting on the speech by Dr Macgregor in favour of Smith's nomination.

So it was that Smith was installed as Moderator of the General Assembly on Tuesday, 23 May 1916, with the distinction of being the only United Free Church Moderator to serve as a University Principal, (and consequently the only University Principal to be appointed Moderator of the United Free Church General Assembly[54]). He also occupied the Chair as an elder rather than as a serving minister, and "had the unique privilege of seeing his father sitting in the House as a member".[55]

Smith's Moderatorial address, given midway through the Great War, is itself of significance and deserves consideration. Not only was the nation at war, but the Moderator, along with many of the commissioners to the General Assembly, had lost a son in the conflict. The mood was sombre, and the air heavy. An account of the Assembly proceedings appeared in the denominational magazine in the form of a letter to a soldier on the War front, in which the writer said that "many in the Assembly never ceased to hear the roar of the guns above the steady stream of debate".[56] Nonetheless, Smith turned his attention to the pressing and urgent needs which the Church, in his view, had to address; among these he listed

> the masses of our people beyond all the Churches, the conditions in which both Church and State suffer so many families to exist, without anything worthy of the name of home, the annual destruction of infant life, the waste of the natural riches of our land, the unchecked luxury and vice, with all the want of courage in social administration because of the want of conscience in public opinion.[57]

Invoking the witness of history, Smith urged the Assembly to seek the Lord and to be faithful to His Spirit, so that the Church will continue its work "through another year of abnormal difficulties".[58]

Turning to the specific subject of the war, Smith said it was necessary for the country to be reminded of "the quality of the cause for which the nation contends".[59] The war, Smith argues, was a matter of conscience, "though the

---

[54] Although to have University Principals as Assembly Moderators was not itself without precedent, with George Buchanan of St Andrews, Alexander Arbuthnott of Aberdeen and Andrew Melville of Glasgow having had that honour in the pre-Disruption Church of Scotland (see PDGAUFCS, 1916, p42).

[55] G.M. Reith, *Reminiscences of the United Free Church General Assembly 1900-1929* (Edinburgh, 1933) p171.

[56] *Record of the Home and Foreign Mission Work of the United Free Church of Scotland*, July 1916, p180. The writer continues: "A sense of the tragedy and sadness of the war came into all its deliberations, and the realities of the battlefield were forced again and again on its attention by men straight from the area of conflict".

[57] PDGAUFCS, 1916, p45.

[58] Ibid., p46.

[59] Ibid., p47.

mind reeled before the crisis and every other instinct recoiled from battle".[60] The reason for this, he says, has become "the great commonplace of the war ... Germany broke her word".[61] She violated the neutrality she had sworn to uphold, and broke faith, thus dissolving any hope for a brotherhood between nations. Smith takes issue with those who sought to vindicate Germany on the grounds that fear of Russia drove her to war. In the face of Germany's refusal to enter into arbitration, the allies, he says, had no alternative but to enter into the conflict. And against the arguments of Professor Ernst Troeltsch of Heidelberg, who accused the allies of violating the reciprocal duties which member countries of the European community have towards one another, Smith argues that Germany subverted these very principles of allegiance by insisting that her citizens retain German citizenship even when naturalised elsewhere. The rising power of Germany, Smith says, shows that she regarded herself as "superior to the moral law" and "reckless of humanity".[62] Subsequent action has shown, he argues, that while Germany remained free, her rulers remained blind.

Turning to the position and response of the Churches to this, Smith first defends the Bible from the cavil that the Old Testament was all for war, and the New all for peace.[63] On the contrary, he says; the Old Testament shows how Israel left her barbarity behind to develop a conscience sensitive to the claims of God, and the New Testament sets this faith before the Church as her duty and privilege. Repeating the message of *War and Peace*, Smith then reiterated his conviction that the peace Christ pledged "was not political, but the inward tranquillity of reconciliation to God, of faith in His Father's love, and of devotion to His will; which will is always righteousness before it is peace".[64] Non-resistance, Smith argued, was nowhere sanctioned in the Gospels.

Smith used his Moderatorial position to address the issue of the Military Service Act, by which Asquith's coalition government had introduced conscription. The story of the Act, and the consequent effects of its passage, has been told in John Rae's *Conscience and Politics*, in which Rae says that

> the Military Service Bill did not, as some politicians had forecast, automatically provide the army with sufficient men; in terms of the numbers involved, the most important aspect of conscription was not that it made service compulsory, but that it made exemption legal.[65]

---

[60] Ibid.
[61] Ibid.
[62] Ibid., p50.
[63] Ibid., pp51-2.
[64] Ibid., p52.
[65] J. Rae, *Conscience and Politics: The British Government and the Conscientious Objector to Military Service 1916-1919* (London, 1970) p66.

One consequence of the Act was that much time and effort – which might have been better spent in direct engagement with other war issues – was expended over the issue of the conscientious objector. While Smith recognised that the Bill was marked by an "irrelevant and unfortunate entanglement with party politics",[66] nonetheless democratic government possesses, in Smith's view a "moral authority equalled by no other form of rule".[67] This has been vindicated, Smith says, in the fact that "in a few months the system has produced some millions of as good soldiers as will be found in any people".[68]

However, in vindicating the moral right of government to conscript into service, Smith has some harsh words for the conscientious objectors. The taking up of arms he identifies with Christ's call to take up a cross and follow him.[69] By implication, those who object to military service are objecting to Christian duty and to Christian service. Smith does not seem prepared to admit the validity of any objection; indeed, he finds no common ground with the objectors – if their objection is conscientious, so too is his response.

Smith then distinguishes between the moral obligations of the war, and individual duty to the state. These are distinct but inseparable. For that reason, to descend into party political wranglings is to be distracted "from the spiritual principles of our conflict and our duty to God and humanity".[70] Smith praised the King and Queen, urged support for the Government, and acknowledged the positive role of the Scottish press for their coverage of the war. He concluded his address with a rallying-cry to the commissioners:

> Let us strengthen each other's faith in God, that He who never sends His servants to warfare on their own charges will at last, in spite of the weakness, the sins, and the errors of His unworthy instruments, vindicate by victory, not us, but the sacred and holy cause to which He has called us.[71]

The Assembly over which Smith then presided followed the normal pattern, hearing reports from Church Committees, and dealing with various aspects of Church administration. It was not a particularly historic or significant Assembly, but there were several points worth noting about it. First, because of night-time raids on Edinburgh by the Germans, lighting was restricted, and this curtailed the length of many evening debates. Second, the role of women in the Church also came before the Assembly, which heard a special report on this subject. At one level, this shows that important subjects relating to Church life could not be neglected, in spite of the war. At another, it registers the fact that

---

[66] PDGAUFCS, 1916, p53.
[67] Ibid.
[68] Ibid.
[69] Ibid., p54.
[70] Ibid.
[71] Ibid., p56.

women were contributing much to the war effort in ancillary services; it is not surprising that their contribution to church life should also come under review. At another level, still, it is important because of Smith's long-standing social interests in improving the lot of women in society. Nonetheless, the ordination of women to ecclesiastical office was a contentious issue, and the narrow victory in the Assembly for those in favour of women's ordination as deacons was not only a change from long-established male dominance in Church affairs, but also opened the way for women's ordination to ministry to be accepted in the united Church of Scotland after 1929. Thirdly, the Assembly appointed a Commission on the War which reported to the 1917 Assembly calling for radical change in society as a consequence of the War.

The subject of the war occupied Smith's closing Moderatorial address to the Assembly, in which he turned to focus upon the theme of Empire, turning, as he put it, "from our foes to ourselves".[72] Smith first drew attention to the fact of the imperial background to the Gospels and Acts, and drew an analogy between the Roman and the British Empires:

> Since these facts of earthly empire were the opportunities of our religion, the condition of its first expansion, it would be incredible if in the British Empire of our own days we failed to find something not only analogous to the blessings I have hastily recalled, but much of still firmer advantage to the gospel and of sympathy with its claims.[73]

Thus the gospel can be regarded not only as having claims on the individual, but, in Smith's view, also upon the conscience of nations within the fraternity of empire.

The moral aspects of empire, are, Smith says, what has given stability in times of crisis and now in time of War. The "temper of politics" which builds on justice and a desire for freedom he describes as "spiritual assets of incomparable value to mankind".[74] The fact that the British Empire was in Smith's day dispersed throughout the world, has, he says "taught us a patriotism which ends beyond itself and endued our politics with the ideals of sacrifice as well as of justice and freedom".[75]

Smith then turned to acknowledge the faults of empire. He warns against racial prejudice, pride and wastefulness. The latter charge he develops with regard to physical training and education, both of which, he says have been neglected since the outbreak of War, and with regard to temperance, a favourite

---

[72] Ibid., p403.
[73] Ibid., p404.
[74] Ibid., p405.
[75] Ibid.

theme among preachers during wartime.[76] Smith also turns on the government for their frugality in meeting social issues, given the wealth of the nation. The war, he suggests, had shown the country the financial resources in its possession: "the national wealth," Smith says, "and its mobility have been revealed by the war to a degree beyond the imagination of any of us".[77] Smith called on the government to apply some of these resources to the social needs and questions of the day.

He also applied the same criteria, however, to the Church, calling, first, on ministers to ensure "without any self-pity"[78] that they give themselves fully to their calling. Smith reckoned that the War was changing everything, and that if the Church was to be fit to receive back into its fold those who had gone off to fight on the front, ministers required to put even more thought into preaching and even more dedication into the pastoral work of the Church:

> We are told that, when [the War] is over, our men will be returning to their congregations with altered views of life and religion, with a more virile piety and more heroic ideals of sainthood. Well, at least in the war they will have come to themselves. They will have found their manhood and its possibilities of courage and self-sacrifice in the face of death. And the question for each of their ministers will be: "Have you, too, yet found yourself, and can you meet them with a manliness and a forsaking of all things that do not matter, equal to their own?[79]

These are highly idealistic words, and beg the question of whether Smith really appreciated the horrors of trench warfare. His approach was to see the Western Front as a purging and purifying experience; the reality of bloodshed, carnage and death was quite different.

In addition, Smith said, it was necessary for the Church to address the question of its own central administration, which constantly ran the risk of being wasteful in the extreme. Given, also, that a great deal of the Church's work was being duplicated in the Church of Scotland, Smith spoke in favour of union: "Our conferences have shown us how much in common we have with our brethren of the Church of Scotland, and what possibilities there are of the removal of the differences between us".[80] The closing note of the Assembly

---

[76] Cf, for example, James Denney's sermon on "Prohibition" in *War and the Fear of God*, pp137-151. In reporting on the Assembly proceedings, the UF *Record* said that "No subject occupied the minds of members more this year than that of Temperance" (*Record of the Home and Foreign Mission Work of the United Free Church of Scotland*, July 1916, p187).

[77] PDGAUFCS, 31 May 1916, p408.

[78] Ibid., p409.

[79] Ibid.

[80] Ibid., p410.

was a call to continued allegiance to Christ as "King of the Nation as well as of the Church".[81]

Smith's Moderatorial addresses were received to widespread acclaim. The opening address on the war was reported in the Church's *Record* as "not so much one to the Assembly as one to the nation".[82] The note struck by Smith was appreciated beyond Scotland. From London, Robert Younger wrote to him:

> It is not given to us here in London to have our true aims in this War set before us. For the most part we are left to choose between an enervating and cowardly pacifism and a repellant and offensive militarism and those of us who believe that our lads are giving their lives for a great ideal and who feel ourselves, in the safety of our homes, like deserters, really need – and as we need, so we welcome – such a trumpet call to duty and sacrifice as we find in those addresses for which I shall never cease to be grateful.[83]

However, it is difficult not to conclude that Smith went too far both in his sermons and in his Moderatorial address. While ready to analyse and criticise some aspects of the War effort, and while acknowledging that it was only with heavy hearts that the country went to war, Smith rarely distinguishes between the principle of war itself and the conduct of the Great War. While other United Free Church ministers were ready to aver that war in itself was an evil thing, something that "*cannot* be harmonized with God",[84] there is little of this in Smith. To him the War was a sacrament, and its conduct a matter of spirituality and a sanctifying and teleological process. While he paid a high price for his idealism, in the loss of his sons, he was personally well rewarded with honours and preferment. More seriously still, Smith's identifying of the war effort with the will of God and with the spirituality of the nation, cannot go unchallenged. For Smith, the call to arms was the call of God, and the duty to the State equally a duty to the Church. The explicit imperialism which runs through Smith's Assembly addresses is a sign that his attitudes to war owed more to politics than to religion, even if he made attitudes to War a test of attitudes to Christ Himself.

Related to this was the vexed question of conscientious objectors. To Smith they had broken faith and turned Christianity upside down. By appealing to the non-combative philosophy and example of Christ, Smith accused them of having misappropriated and misused the Lord's example. As Smith caricatures them in this way, with rising passion, his speech is interrupted by "Applause" and "Laughter".[85] "The things of Caesar and the things of God are the same

---

[81] Ibid.
[82] UF *Record*, p181.
[83] Robert Younger to GAS from London 30 December 1916, NLS Acc 9446 No 55.
[84] W.L. Walker, *The War, God and our Duty* (London, 1917) p8.
[85] See PDGAUFCS 23 May 1916, p52.

The War Years

things", Smith urges,[86] and to suggest that rendering to Caesar is applicable only in the matter of taxes and not in the matter of military service he regards as a nonsense.

Some United Free Church ministers, like James Barr, raised a contrary issue of principle. The church, Barr declared, is called "to the cause of the complete abolition of War".[87] For Barr, as Stewart Brown puts it, "the war was the bitter fruit of imperialism, the arms race and nationalist literature".[88] But Barr's was a lone voice in 1916. Not only was Smith reflecting the majority Church view on the subject, he was also legitimising the Government's position, reflected in the recent Military Service Bill. And for their part, local tribunals which were set up to evaluate and pronounce on applications for exemption, were quick to use the position of the Church against those who applied to them. Historian J.R. Fleming, for example, cites the case of one tribunal who tried to browbeat an applicant by quoting from Smith's Moderatorial address.[89] If it was true that between tribunals and applicants a "mutual suspicion" developed,[90] it was also true that conscientious objectors were alienated from the church also, although there were cases where United Free Church ministers did provide accompanying documents supporting requests for exemption.[91]

Smith's addresses also touch on another theme which occupied the Church during the War: that of the need for building a suitable post-War church to which the soldiers could return. On the one hand Smith believed that the War could only be used under God "to bring religious revival and to restore the moral authority of the Churches within Scottish society".[92] The reality, however, was expressed by A.H. Gray in his *As Tommy Sees Us: A Book for Church Folk* that "the average male Britisher of today has not much respect for the church".[93] For Smith it was necessary for ministers to look critically at the matter and manner of their preaching, as well as the styles of worship, in order to provide a Church suitable for the returning soldiers. These very points were crystallised for Smith in a letter he received from France in March 1918, from a soldier who claimed to have spent three hours drafting a long (9-page) letter with his personal and honest thoughts of the war. The serviceman spoke of the comradeship of the army, and of how he wished to see the same mutual reliance evident at home:

---

[86] Ibid.
[87] J. Barr, *The United Free Church of Scotland* (London, 1934) p291.
[88] Brown, "Solemn Purification", p90.
[89] Quoted in A.C. Cheyne, *The Transforming of the Kirk* (Edinburgh, 1983) p181.
[90] Rae, *Conscience and Politics*, p95.
[91] Example cited in E. Annesley, "The Response of the Church of Scotland and the United Free Church of Scotland to the First World War", MTh, University of Glasgow, 1991, p127.
[92] Brown, "Solemn Purification", p91.
[93] A.H. Gray, *As Tommy Sees Us: A Book for Church Folk* (London, 1917) p6.

> There is much that is really loveable in the raw human nature you meet in our primitive condition of life out here, and you want to feel you could do something to bring the same thing into life at home – see it go through all the nation – that sense of kinship and responsibility for the life of your fellowman. We learn it here till it becomes a reality.[94]

At the same time, he said, "You see the horror of war – the sheer uselessness and waste of it as you come off a fight".[95] As far as the church was concerned, Smith was told that "if the churches could rise up and give a solid lead, nothing could be better. If they don't do something they will be the first to go down as churches ... Christianity has not failed. Its practice is living in the army today as I never dreamt of it living in real life, but it is not the Christianity of the Respectable Church. It is only the Christianity of the publicans and sinners".[96]

The letter was a stark warning to the Church, and a signal that those who were engaged in the front lines of battle were become increasingly disillusioned by what they perceived as the "respectable" Churches at home. Smith's addresses to the Assembly show that there was a respect within the Church for the soldiers engaged in fighting; but the respect was not reciprocated.

As part of his Moderatorial duties, Smith made two significant visits: one to the Western and Northern Isles (of strategic importance for British defence), and another in the company of the Moderator of the Church of Scotland to the war Front in France. Preliminary enquiries regarding this visit had been made in early Summer. Although the Commander-in-Chief of the British Armies in France was willing that this should take place, it was initially postponed "in view ... of the conditions at present obtaining in France".[97] The visit took place in October, with Smith recording on the 10th of that month that he rushed home from a meeting of the University Court to don his Chaplain's Uniform and to set off for London.[98] The sight of young soldiers preparing for the war at Charing Cross Station humbled him; "these young fellows are carrying their lives to the front", Smith wrote, "we only our poor words".[99] One of his first visits was to the No. 7 Stationary Hospital for Officers in France, where his son had been hospitalised. The sights in the army hospitals moved him deeply; as did the realisation of how wounded German soldiers were being looked after:

---

[94] R. Soutter (?) to GAS, from "Somewhere in France, Midnight 8/9 March 1918", NLS Acc 9446 No 59, p1.
[95] Ibid., p4.
[96] Ibid., p7.
[97] A.C. Strange to GAS from War Office, London, 10 July 1916, NLS Acc 9446 No 57.
[98] GAS, Diary of my Visit to the British Army in France, Tuesday 10 October 1916 (New College Special Collections, MSS.SMI 1.2).
[99] *Diary*, Thursday 12 October 1916.

"in their own lines," he says, "they had been apparently crammed with lies about British cruelty".[100]

One of Smith's main duties on the Front was to conduct services for the troops. On Sunday 15 October he addressed a group of 650 soldiers from various Scottish regiments. He says: "I took the intercessory prayer and gave an address of 30 minutes on the three secrets of courage – clean heart, just cause, trust in God – after a few words of greeting from home for the men".[101] A second service followed almost immediately, for some 760 men of the Gordon Highlanders, a moving sight for Smith:

> There was the tartan George fought and fell in ... I never had a congregation like this. Many were mere boys and all were going up the line very soon – some tonight. It was awesome but my heart was opened.[102]

The following week was spent "on the tracks of GBS",[103] and although Smith saw the battlefield at Loos, he was not able to see the spot where his son was buried on account of the constant shelling. Instead, he was able to place flowers on the grave of Lowe Macneil, where he "prayed God that the sacrifice of themselves which these young men had made for our sacred Cause may not be in vain."[104]

Sunday 22 October found Smith addressing another congregation of Gordons, of which he gives the following moving account:

> I had the privilege of addressing them as they stood in a semi-circle under the fir-trees and giving them messages from home and the assurance of their people's confidence in them, and reminding them of the true source of courage in a clean heart, a just cause, and faith in God ... I shall never forget speaking into the faces of these boys from Deeside – from Aberdeen to Braemar – under the fir-trees of Picardy, while the guns were booming, and they, in an hour, would be on their march to the trenches ... They gave me three cheers when I had finished, but I turned away feeling like a deserter.[105]

The scene humbled him; as did also the commemoration of the Lord's Supper in a tent, surrounded by the noise of war:

> Every man present will remember this service as long as he lives. A very heavy bombardment was taking place at the time, our big guns speaking

---

[100] Ibid., Friday 13 October 1916.
[101] Ibid., Sunday 15 October 1916.
[102] Ibid.
[103] Ibid., Monday 16 October 1916.
[104] Ibid., Saturday 21 October 1916.
[105] Ibid., Sunday 22 October 1916.

their loudest, and the silence of the Feast of Love within the tent was wonderful. Surely it was the tabernacle of God.[106]

"It was," Smith records in his Diary, "the most solemn service I ever took part in".[107]

"A just cause, a devoted heart, and faith in God". This was the three-fold cord by which the Church sought to bind itself to the men on the Front, in the trenches. Behind such counsel was a philosophy which regarded the Great War as of a piece with the whole movement of Christianity, and devotion to it as on a parallel with devotion to God. By applying the language of faith to the role of the troops, the Church, however much she might be averse to war itself, could nonetheless use the fact of war for the furtherance of the Gospel, and the Gospel message for the interpretation of the war. In a sermon in King's College Chapel, Aberdeen in 1915, Smith had counselled as follows:

> Let us remember what war did for Israel. "By war", says God elsewhere to Israel, "by war I took you", and we may extend the meaning of these words beyond the mere fact that so He brought them to freedom, up to the moral assurance that by the call to fight He redeemed them from selfishness, from servitude to material aims, from schisms within themselves, and from disloyalty to His cause. The battlefield was the Golgotha of ancient Israel ... Our own system of voluntary service is for us Christians nothing less than the opportunity to show that we have the same Spirit, especially when, as now, an equally sacred cause requires all that system's still unexhausted resources.[108]

Smith's application of the Old Testament to the experience of war resulted in an interpretation of the war in terms of the Spirit of Christ. For many, however, the Christian vocabulary was inadequate fully to explain or interpret the situation created by the Great War. Part of the reason for this was the fact that although the message of Smith and others was dominant, it was not unanimous. Others were equally forcefully arguing that "the conditions of warfare are not an evangelistic agency. One sees there, side by side, the deterioration of character as well as the exaltation of character just as one sees in life everywhere, and the conviction grows in my mind that in this war the balance of influence for individuals and nationalities and for all Christian Europe leans strongly to the side of evil".[109] These words are all the more striking for they

---

[106] "The Moderator within Sound of the Guns", *Record of the Home and Foreign Mission Work of the United Free Church of Scotland* (December 1916) p308.

[107] *Diary*, Sunday 22 October 1916.

[108] GAS, "After Fifteen Months of War", *The British Weekly*, 28 October 1915.

[109] Letter of the Rev J.A. Tweedie, Arbroath, serving as a chaplain in Gallipoli, reported in "Notable Views of Chaplains at the Front: The War not an Evangelistic Agency",

The War Years 165

were written by a chaplain at the Front, face to face with the horrors of war and its effects on those who were participating in it.

The reality was that the Church did not know what to do, or what to say, about the War. The great conflagration had shattered the optimistic worldview of many ministers and members within the Church, and called for a particular application of Christian principles which the spokesmen of the Church found difficult to articulate. Men like Smith owed a great intellectual debt to Germany; now the treachery of Germany had turned the War into a Christian campaign. But to Christianise the conflict led to the alienating of the conscientious objectors, and bred a view that the war would lead to personal and national renewal. If the Church was not ready for the War in the first place, she was certainly not ready for the disillusionment which followed.

Smith's *Syria and the Holy Land* appeared in 1918. According to Lilian Smith, it was written at the request of the War Office,[110] and was essentially a summary of his *Historical Geography of the Holy Land*. In his treatment of the First World War, historian A.J.P. Taylor highlighted the need for the British forces to protect the Suez Canal, and, consequently, the need to extend their forces beyond it, into Syria:

> Clearly the Suez Canal had to be protected. Equally clearly this could be done only by advancing beyond it. But there lay the desert of Sinai. It, too, must be crossed. Thus the British pushed into Palestine, their need of men growing ever larger.[111]

The 56-page *Syria and the Holy Land* could be read as a condensed version of the *Historical Geography*, with phrases in the former familiar to readers of the latter. Smith describes the nomenclature of the Holy Land, its climate, the coastal regions, the mountain ranges and the geographical structures of the land. But two-thirds of the way through the booklet Smith turns to deal with "The Discredited Turk", and argues that Turkish domination has led to "the decay of large areas of fertility" and "the depression and embitterment of the rest of the peasantry".[112] It was necessary, Smith argued, to remove the Turk and recover the land for the settlement of the Jews in their native land. This Zionism Smith views as "only a part of what the civilised world owes to the Jew",[113] and the war, he says, has accelerated the need to liberate Palestine by

---

Record of the Home and Foreign Mission Work of the United Free Church of Scotland (January 1916) p7.

[110] LAS, p168.

[111] A.J.P. Taylor, *The First World War: An Illustrated History* (London, 1963) p106.

[112] GAS, *Syria and the Holy Land* (London, 1918) p33.

[113] Ibid., p41.

securing a lasting settlement for the Jews in their homeland.[114] The booklet ends with a reference to General Allenby's liberating of Jerusalem in 1917, which Smith calls a "wonderful beginning", and expresses the desire that it will be

> the earnest of the creation, for the first time on earth, of a government devoted wholly to peace, with no temptation to war in itself and no provocation to other States, because founded by the agreement and solemn guarantees of all people to whom the land is dear and holy.[115]

Thus what begins as a geographical description ends with a further theologico-biblical rationale and apologetic for the Allied war effort, full of an optimism grounded upon the identification of the British Empire with the Kingdom of God, and the extension of the Empire coterminous with the advent of a new Christendom. It may have been true that "[Smith] followed the campaign in Palestine with most eager interest";[116] but Taylor's assessment that the half million men engaged in Palestine by the end of the war had contributed nothing to the defeat of Germany[117] brings a shade of realism into what Smith saw as the War to end all wars.

Allied Ambassador to the United States

In 1918 Smith embarked on a mission to America, to speak at various venues on the war, and particularly on the moral aspects of the conflict. Lilian Smith's biography relates that the invitation to lecture in the United States came simultaneously – and coincidentally – from the Foreign Office and from the American National Committee on the Churches and the Moral Aims of the Allies.[118] Smith understood his own status to be that he was going "on the invitation of the National Committee on Churches and the Moral Aims of the War but with the sanction and full approval of the Foreign Office of Great Britain".[119] In addition, Smith secured the services of his daughter Lilian Mary

---

[114] Smith's views on the resettlement of Jews in Palestine led to the British Palestine Committee writing to him in the following terms: "There are many Jewish nationalists in England who look forward to the establishment of a Jewish state in Palestine under the British crown. There are also many Englishmen who hold it to be a very important British interest that Palestine should be part of the British Imperialist system in the East" (Israel M. Sieff to GAS, 1 November 1916, New College Special Collections, MSS.SMI 1.4.5). The letter went on to ask Smith to become a patron of the Committee, but there is no indication among his papers of his reply.
[115] Ibid., p56.
[116] LAS, p168.
[117] Taylor, *First World War*, pp106-7.
[118] LAS, p169.
[119] GAS to R.F. Roxburgh, 13 February 1918, Public Record Office, FO 395/214 File 41739.

(Maisie) as his companion; the Foreign Office informed him that "Miss Smith will be allowed to go with you to America in the capacity of your secretary".[120]

By any standard the visit, between April and June, was a remarkable and exhausting round of meetings and services.[121] Smith contributed a full account of his trip in three articles to the *Aberdeen University Review*.[122] In addition, *The British Weekly* kept its readers informed of Smith's progress and itinerary.

The visit took Smith to many different places, at which he "addressed 127 meetings, as well as delivering many sermons, and he travelled 22,000 miles by rail".[123] Smith's visit to America seems to have operated on three different levels. First, there was the church interest. On 19 May, for example, Smith preached at Rochester, New York, and subsequently addressed the General Assembly of the Presbyterian Church (USA), delivering a fraternal letter of greeting from the United Free Church of Scotland. Several churches invited him to preach; in this way he was able to foster a bond with the United Free Church of Scotland.

Secondly, there was a University interest. At a University Conference in New York, Smith represented the Scottish Universities. He regarded it as important to foster relations with America at an educational as well as an ecclesiastical level: "I shall be able to tell the Conference," he wrote, "how far the Scottish University Courts and Senates have considered the question of courses and degrees for postgraduate students and researchers from Universities beyond the seas, and what some of us have resolved..."[124] He also remarked that "In visiting so many of the Universities, I have been able to learn much that I hope will be of use to our own".[125] Many of Smith's meetings were hosted by the American Universities.

The third dimension of the visit was political. At a meeting in Philadelphia on 17 May, held under the auspices of the League to Enforce Peace, Smith shared a platform with the British and French Ambassadors; he notes "I was suddenly summoned to speak for Great Britain".[126] In Boston he was invited to speak to the House of Representatives of the Massachusetts Legislature in Boston, and was afterwards received by the State Governor. There was more than a little truth in a comment from Prof W. MacNeil Dixon of the Ministry of

---

[120] James Baird to GAS, 11 March 1918, NLS Acc 9446 No 64.

[121] A copy of his preliminary itinerary can be seen in the Public Record Office, FO 395/214 File 41739.

[122] In Vol 5 No 15 (June 1918) pp232-5, Vol 6 No 16 (November 1918) pp 36-9, and Ibid., pp130-6.

[123] LAS, p174.

[124] GAS to Stephen Gaselee, 14 March 1918, Public Records Office, FO 395/214, File 41739.

[125] "The Principal's Itinerary in the United States", *Aberdeen University Review*, 5.15 (June 1918) p235.

[126] Ibid., p233.

Information that Smith had made "a kind of royal progress through the country!"[127]

This reached a climax at the White House, where Smith had an audience with President Woodrow Wilson. Both Presbyterians, both historians, and both of Scottish ancestry, Smith and Wilson had much in common. Smith kept a full record of his interview with Wilson.[128] During it they discovered that they were contemporaries; but they also found common ground in their attitude to Germany. According to Smith's record, Wilson said to him: "I have been schooling myself in the incredible ... till it has become terribly familiar to me. Our men who were educated at German Universities like yourself ... have seen an enormous change in the German people in 35 years".[129] Although Wilson had initially pursued a policy of neutrality, keeping America out of the war and fostering the efforts of the League to Enforce Peace, events had brought him to change his mind by early 1917. Having broken off diplomatic relations with Germany in February, he was ready to bring America into the conflict by Spring-time. In his famous war message to Congress, he declared that "neutrality is no longer feasible or desirable" and that "the world must be made safe for democracy".[130] It was recognised that "When the United States entered World War I, the Allies stood in dire peril of failure – of losing the war".[131] Even within the United Free Church of Scotland it was recognised that the involvement of America had become a necessity, and George Reith expressed thankfulness that President Wilson had descended "from the clouds of his idealism to the solid earth of fact",[132] and had "drawn his sword" at last.

In his audience with the President, Smith informed him that America's delay in entering the war had resulted in two things:

> First, that they came in as a united people, and second, that by the deliberate way they exhausted every means of dealing with Germany short of war ... they provided a great moral vindication of our ... conscience.[133]

Smith also recalled Wilson's counsel that

> Our soldiers ... are fighting for humanity. You must go home and tell your people there that on the return of the soldiers we cannot face them if we do

---

[127] W.M. Dixon to GAS 25 September 1918, NLS Acc 9446 No 70.
[128] NLS Acc 9446 No 65. The account runs to six pages.
[129] Ibid., p2.
[130] President Woodrow Wilson's War Message, 2 April 1917, downloaded from the Internet at www.lib.byu.edu/~rdh/wwi/1917/wilswarm on 20 September 2000.
[131] R.H. Ferrell, *Woodrow Wilson and World War I 1917-1921* (New York, 1985) p13.
[132] Reith, *Reminiscences*, p179.
[133] GAS's account of meeting with President Wilson, NLS Acc 9446 No 65, p2.

The War Years 169

not carry out (in our negotiations for peace) after the war the same sacred ideals as we have taught them to fight for.[134]

Woodrow Wilson's correspondence reveals his pleasure at having met with Smith. Writing to Frederick Lynch of the Committee on the Churches he wrote:

I very much enjoyed my interview with Sir George Smith and am very happy that he did not get away without my seeing him, and I was deeply and truly interested in what you and he told me of what he had been doing and of the general work of extending an intelligent understanding of the moral aims of the war.[135]

Smith's visit to the White House clarifies the obvious political strand of his visit. Few, if any, Scottish Presbyterian ministers were entertained by an American President; at one level Smith's presence in the White House is a further sign of his connections in high places. One of the first to congratulate him on the tour and its success was John Buchan of the Ministry of Information: "Of all the visitors we have ever been responsible for I think the greatest volume of American appreciation has gone to you".[136]

Smith's unpublished account of his voyage home in August and September 1918 runs to over forty pages of closely written text, and reflects his feelings at the close of the itinerary. It also reveals that even on the boat, where he saw soldiers "fore and aft ... standing closely crowded",[137] Smith took the opportunity to press home the moral issues of the conflict. "I was asked if I would speak to the troops in the afternoon, and my heart jumped at the idea ... I spoke for twenty minutes on our Common Conscience and our Courage".[138] Addressing meetings of fellow-passengers, Smith says that "some of my figures amazed the audiences",[139] as he related Britain's role in the war. At one meeting he said that having delivered over 120 addresses in 39 places, and having read almost seventy leading articles in American newspapers, he was left with the distinct impression of "the practically complete unanimity of public opinion in America with regard to the justice of our cause and the duty of supporting it by arms".[140] He had, he said, found few exceptions to this, given the remarkable diversity of races within American society. Indeed, the loyalty of the majority of immigrant Germans to the Allied cause he took as a vindication of the Allied

---

[134] Ibid., p6.
[135] Woodrow Wilson to Frederick Lynch, 22 July 1918, NLS Acc 9446 No 64.
[136] John Buchan to GAS, 25 July 1918, NLS Acc 9446 No 70.
[137] GAS, Diary of Voyage Home from United States of America, p12 (Sunday 25 August 1918), New College Special Collections, MSS.SMI.1.3.
[138] Ibid.
[139] Ibid., p19.
[140] Ibid., p20.

position. Again he stressed that America's late entry was in itself an important justification of the Allied effort:

> Then I repeated what I have dwelt on in my addresses, the moral vindication of our original necessarily hastily formed conscience in going to war by the patient deliberate decision of America to join us after she had exhausted all means short of war in dealing with Germany and found them futile.[141]

While most of the diary is taken up with personal accounts of meetings and conversations on board ship, the unmistakable refrain of Smith's wartime message is heard throughout – the need for courage, based on a just cause, a clean heart, and faith in God.

A selection of Smith's addresses and sermons in America was published in 1919 under the title *Our Common Conscience*. In the preface, Smith sets his mission in context. It began, he said, "with the close of America's first year at war"[142], when the Allied cause seemed at its lowest. The fortunes of the Allies were turned around with America's entry into the war. Smith regards their belated entry as a moral vindication of the Allied position, and, although the publication of the lectures may seem anachronistic, it is his expressed hope that they will nonetheless help readers to understand

> why we Allies went to war, what were the sources of our courage under our unparalleled sufferings and despite our sense of our unfitness, what was the faith which sustained us and the grounds on which we pled before God, to our own and each other's hearts, the justice of our Cause".[143]

The argument at the heart of the book is found in the first lecture on "The Moral Aims of the Allies", in which Smith describes the Great War as "the most sacred cause to which nations were ever called".[144] In addressing the American people, Smith explains his commission as being "to relate as far as I can the efforts of Great Britain on the many fronts of the war... and to expound from the British point of view the moral aims common to the Allies in their warfare".[145] These aims, he says, represented nothing less than "justice, freedom, and peace for the whole world"[146]:

> Hating war, we Allies are at war for no other purpose than to end for ever such forms of war as Germany had forced upon the world, and to restore

---

[141] Ibid., p21.
[142] *Our Common Conscience*, px.
[143] Ibid., ppxi-xii.
[144] Ibid., p1.
[145] Ibid., p3.
[146] Ibid., p4.

those foundations of Christian civilisation which have been shaken and rent by the perfidy and cruelty of the people that boasted itself to be civilisation's supreme representative.[147]

Reflecting the point made in his Moderatorial address, Smith argues that the war has been occasioned by Germany's having broken her word.[148] By invading Belgium, Germany had broken faith with the rest of Europe. For Smith, Britain's call to arms was a heroic moment:

> I well remember that hot August night and day in which we restlessly waited for the decision of our leaders, and the sigh, or rather the roar, of relief that went up from all the borders of the United Kingdom when it was learned that our Government had not flinched from its duty, that we meant to keep our word to Belgium and Europe.[149]

This "original conscience"[150], Smith argues, commended itself to the British people. The War, far from diminishing it, has only maintained it: "our faith in the justice of our cause, our sense of our duty to fight for it, our determination to see it through to victory stand unshaken and unshakeable".[151] By citing German leaders and politicians, Smith strove to show that Germany's governors "were blinded by the criminal passion for war",[152] with the result that her arrogance and self-assertiveness, issuing in her aggression against Belgium have provided the materials which "have strengthened and articulated the conscience of my people".[153] In thanking the Americans for their involvement, Smith spoke of the sacrifices of his native Scots, which had only served to show in clear relief the sacredness of the cause in which they had been engaged.[154]

This point is made throughout the book, in lectures such as those on "Britain's part in the War", "The British Hope and its Grounds", "The Witness of France" and "Some Religious Effects of the War". And, in his oft-recurring words, Smith, in his sermon on Psalms 42 and 43, identifies as the three sources of courage "a just cause, a clean heart and faith in God".[155]

---

[147] Ibid., p5.
[148] Ibid., p6.
[149] Ibid., p8.
[150] Ibid., p10.
[151] Ibid., p11.
[152] Ibid., p23.
[153] Ibid., p27.
[154] Ibid., p34.
[155] Ibid., p237.

In a letter from Arthur E. Bestor of the Committee on Public Information, Washington, to H.E. Atkinson of the National Committee on the Churches and the Moral Aims of the War, Bestor opined:

> If you had done nothing else than bring to this country Sir George Adam Smith, and arranged for his 120 meetings across the continent, you would have performed a noteworthy service. There has been no Britisher who has had so influential a hearing in America since the beginning of the war, but this is only one of your speakers and only one of the activities...[156]

The tour, in Buchan's words, was "far beyond praise".[157]

But in spite of the voluminous records of his tour,[158] two problems remain. The first was that for the most part, Smith seems to have had only one sermon to preach: the three-point excursus on "a just cause, a clean heart, and faith in God". That refrain is incessant, and provides him with material for addressing meetings in Scotland, in France and in America. With it he rounds on the conscientious objectors, legitimises the role of the Churches and domesticates the war within a Christian imperialistic worldview. But he has little else to say; and, as we have noticed, at times even this is not enough. One is conscious that behind the figure of Smith, striding like a colossus across America in defence of the Allied cause, there is a struggle to say something meaningful and relevant.

Secondly, there is a notable absence of any concrete vision, any clear view of what lasting peace will require. Perhaps no-one knew, of course, but if Smith struggles with words in addressing the war itself, he struggles the more to assess what the future will require in order to achieve a lasting peace. It may be true, in historian Andrew Monaghan's words, that Smith emerged as "something of a 'sabre-rattler', an eloquent propagandist for the justice of the cause of the Allies against Germany",[159] and while it was true that he was willing to support the campaign for a League of Nations, it was also the case that Smith lacked the politician's eye for what the future peace of the world required. His visit to America cast him in the role of a statesman, which he fulfilled well; but he was a Churchman first, whose view of a Christian Empire was shattered by the realities of the Great War. While the war against traditional theories of inspiration found him pulling down strongholds and

---

[156] Bestor to Atkinson, 3 August 1918, NLS Acc 9446 No 64.

[157] John Buchan to GAS, 25 September 1918, NLS Acc 9446 No 64.

[158] It is perhaps worth pointing out that there was only one trip to America specifically to aid the war effort, contra the assertion of I.G.C. Hutchison that Smith made "several transatlantic trips to raise support in the United States" (in C.M.M.Macdonald and E.W. McFarland (eds) *Scotland and the Great War*, [London, 1999] p47).

[159] A. Monaghan, *God's People? One Hundred and Ten Characters in the Story of Scottish Religion* (Edinburgh, 1991) p232.

mapping out the future of the discipline, the war against Germany found him thrust into a role for which he was quite unprepared.

Conclusion

In his recent work on Scottish history, Professor Tom Devine suggests that the Great War had two effects. The first is that it "accelerated unbelief",[160] because the stark horror of the War gave the lie to the imperialistic, anti-pacifist, self-righteous worldview of the Presbyterian Churches. Not that it eradicated faith; in some cases faith was strengthened during the war years.[161] But in its attempt to wed the Gospel to the situation that obtained during the War years, the Church struggled to keep faith alive. Historian Anthony Wood, who sees the War as marking the end of an era and the beginning of the twentieth century proper, says that "the effect of that experience seared the minds of a whole generation".[162] If that was true within secular society, it was also true within the Church. If unbelief was not hastened by the war, faith was certainly not helped. The jingoism of the Churches sounded hollow in the extreme against the backdrop of the guns of war.

But the War also led to "an acceleration of the movement towards Presbyterian unity".[163] That is hardly surprising: the war had witnessed a remarkable co-operation of effort and of energy. Men and women, whose roles in nineteenth-century society had been distinctive and separate, now worked together. Within the churches, too, this had its own effect. The War had brought ministers and Moderators side by side in an attempt to bolster Allied interest. It was not surprising that the decade following the war should see the Scottish Churches working strenuously in co-operation.

George Adam Smith was an ecclesiastical leader, highly regarded outside his own Church circles during the war years. His personal losses bolstered his testimony to the justice of the great cause. But even his message of a just cause, a clean heart and faith in God did little to stem the disillusionment that crept in when the Great War failed to produce the religious revival the Churches had been expecting.

---

[160] Tom Devine, *The Scottish Nation 1700-2000* (London, 1999) p385.
[161] See S.J. Brown, "Reform, Reconstruction, Reaction: The Social Vision of Scottish Presbyterianism c.1830-c.1930", *Scottish Journal of Theology*, 44 (1991), pp489-517, especially 504-7.
[162] A. Wood, *Nineteenth Century Britain 1815-1914* (London, 1982) p426.
[163] Devine, *Scottish Nation*, p385

CHAPTER 6

The Principal: The Later Aberdeen Years (1910-1935)

The University over which George Adam Smith presided from 1910 to 1935 was the result of a "Fusion" of two collegiate Universities in Aberdeen: King's College in the Old Town, and Marischal College in the New. The former of these had been established by a Papal Bull on the instigation of Bishop William Elphinstone in 1494[1] and had four Faculties of Theology, Law, Medicine and Arts. A century later, in 1593, George Keith, the fifth Earl Marischal, founded a second University in the New Town with the same Faculties. William Douglas Simpson, for long the Clerk and Registrar of the General Council of the University of Aberdeen, says in his history of the University that

> while it cannot be maintained that Marischal College was set up deliberately as a Protestant rival to her elder sister in the Aulton, nevertheless it is certain that much crypto-Catholicism hung around King's, and that Marischal College was founded strictly and expressly, as an organ of the Reformed Church.[2]

The union of the two Universities took place in 1858. One of the practical results of the amalgamation was that the Faculties of Arts and Divinity were situated at King's, while Law, Medicine and Science would be taught at Marischal. A new coat of Arms was designed for the united University.

Professor James Stalker says that when Smith became Principal and Vice-Chancellor, the prospects for the University were "as bright as they have ever been; and the sentiment may be breathed with confidence that under a head so wise and sympathetic the University may flourish".[3] One of the inducements which the Secretary for Scotland – Lord Pentland – used to persuade Smith to

---

[1] The Pope was Alexander VI (Rodrigo Borgia), and Elphinstone's name is commemorated by one of the buildings of Aberdeen University being named after him.

[2] W. Douglas Simpson, "The University of Aberdeen 1860-1960" in Simpson, W.D, (ed.), *The Fusion of 1860: A Record of the Centenary Celebration and a History of the United University of Aberdeen 1860-1960* (London, 1963) p8. *The Fusion* is an indispensable guide to the history of the University.

[3] James Stalker, "Our Vice-Chancellor and Principal", *Aberdeen University Review*, Vol 1 No 2 (February 1914) p122.

allow his name to go forward was the prospect of a rise in the Principal's salary[4] (from £800 to £1500[5]). Notwithstanding this, Smith had two main misgivings. The first was a personal doubt about his own ability as an administrator; the second about whether the University staff would welcome him.[6] Smith's fears were groundless, however. After his death the University librarian recalled "the breath of new vigour he brought with him" when he became Principal,[7] and his successor, W. Hamilton Fyfe, wrote that he had never heard even a whisper of criticism about Smith's running of the University.[8] And whatever the staff thought of him when he came, by the time he left Aberdeen University the Professor of Medicine, Ashley Mackintosh, could write: "I wonder if you realise how much you mean to your – sometimes unruly but always devoted – team?"[9]

The Royal Commission appointing Smith as Principal was dated 29 October 1909, although news of the appointment had broken earlier. On 24 October Smith could write to his father "We have already over 450 letters and telegrams of congratulations".[10] It was particularly pleasing to Smith that he could tell his father "I have almost as many greetings from Established Church ministers as United Free".[11] Ministers of his own denomination were particularly delighted with the appointment. Alexander Lee, Secretary to the Highlands and Islands Committee, said that "Your appointment is a compliment to our whole Church".[12]

In a more perceptive comment, however, W. Leslie Mackenzie, a former Aberdeen student and a member of the Local Government Board in Edinburgh, wrote to Smith and congratulated him that "you have now got the Church without the Creed".[13] Mackenzie says he had already asked John Kelman, Smith's former assistant, "are you to give us a church without a creed that all serious men can work with?"[14] The question registers the increasing anti-confessionalism and anti-credalism growing within the Scottish Church at the turn of the century, and is a penetrating insight into why the Principalship, for all Smith's misgivings, was attractive. Less than a decade after his near-trial

---

[4] Lord Pentland to GAS, 2 October 1909, NLS Acc 9446 No 218.
[5] This figure appears in the *British Weekly* of 28 October 1909.
[6] These appear in a small document headed "Notes of conversation with Pentland"; Smith had written down his impressions and misgivings following a discussion with the Secretary for Scotland, and this conversation had included the level at which the Principal's salary would be set. The notes are filed at NLS Acc 9446 No 218.
[7] Maud S. Best to LAS, n.d. 1942, NLS Acc 9446 No 75.
[8] Principal Fyfe to LAS, 4 March 1942, NLS Acc 9446 No 75.
[9] Mackintosh to GAS, 4 January 1930, NLS Acc 9446 No 217.
[10] GAS to George Smith, postcard dated 24 October 1909, NLS Acc 9446 No 43.
[11] Ibid.
[12] Alexander Lee to GAS from Edinburgh, 21 October 1909, NLS Acc 9446 No 52.
[13] W.L. Mackenzie to GAS from Edinburgh, n.d. NLS Acc 9446 No 45.
[14] Ibid.

within the Church, Smith found himself in a pastoral role which allowed him to engage with scholars in a wide variety of fields, and at the same time be free from the strict parameters of credal commitment. Mackenzie's congratulations came with, perhaps, no small measure of envy; and, pleased though he may have been with Smith's appointment, he wished the situation in the University could be replicated within the Church.

In this chapter we shall set Smith's Principalship in context by looking first at some areas of development within the University during the period 1910-1935. Some of these developments were the result of Government initiative and were not all the result of his proactive work as Principal. This was a transitional period for the Universities in Scotland. In the words of Sydney Wood in a recent history of Aberdeen, "the casual approach to studies that had characterised student behaviour for much of the nineteenth century began to decline. In the 1860s and 1870s no less than 53 per cent of students failed to graduate, but by the 1890s a course of at least three years before graduation was taken by most students."[15] The growth of numbers studying in Universities was coupled with the development of formal programmes of higher education. It will be important therefore to look at Smith's own work against this background. We shall then look, secondly at some of Smith's more directly personal contributions to the life and work of the University, and finally at some of the significant works of scholarship which he produced during this period.

The University of Aberdeen 1910-1935

In 1925 the University hosted a jubilee gathering for students who had been in the Arts Class between 1875 and 1879. Smith gave an address to the jubilee reunion, which touched "on the leading changes and developments within the University in the past fifty years".[16] This review will serve as a convenient basis for summarising the University's growth during the years of Smith's Principalship.

First, Smith draws attention to "the entrance of women to the Scottish Universities, which has been in course since 1890".[17] W. Douglas Simpson says that July 1892 saw the first admission of women to graduation in the University.[18] Historian R.D. Anderson, in his study of the student community at Aberdeen during the period, describes the admission of women as "the most significant result of the Universities (Scotland) Act of 1889".[19] In her study of

---

[15] S. Wood, "Education" in W.H. Fraser and C.H. Lee *Aberdeen 1800-2000: A New History* (Edinburgh, 2000) p344.
[16] "A Fifty Years' Review", *Aberdeen University Review*, Vol 13 No 38 (March 1926).
[17] Ibid., p38.
[18] Simpson, *The Fusion*, p13.
[19] R.D. Anderson, *The Student Community at Aberdeen 1860-1939*, Quincentennial Studies in the History of the University of Aberdeen (Aberdeen, 1988) p56.

this subject, Lindy Moore argues that while the provision of education for women at Aberdeen University was "too little, too late, enabling the other Scottish universities to gain the advantage",[20] nonetheless it was significant that by 1895, Aberdeen was "the only Scottish university to have admitted women to both degrees and instruction in all its faculties".[21]

Smith favoured and encouraged this growth of female participation, even when it led to unforeseen complications. When, for example, the first female President of the Students' Representative Council, Mary Esslemont, was elected in 1922, two men dissented from the election of a woman as President.[22] Esslemont was an outstanding student who had graduated in Science in 1914, and Arts in 1915; after the war she became a student of Medicine. On the occasion of the "kirking" of the SRC, the Convener of the Chapel Committee objected to a woman reading the lesson, a duty which would normally fall to the President of the SRC. Esslemont writes: "So then I rang up the principal, G.A. Smith, and he said, 'Of course the President reads the lesson'".[23]

The increasing number of women students, therefore, was a marked feature of Smith's term as Principal. Dr L.A.O. Macdonald, in her study of women in Presbyterian Scotland, is right to point out, however, that "it was one thing to open academic doors, but quite another to consider that women might want to make use of such opportunities to develop professional, remunerated careers".[24] In addition, Professor Tom Devine points out that "the progress of women in the academic community was slow. No Scottish woman professor was appointed before the Second World War, although some women did become lecturers or assistants".[25] Given these limitations, however, progress was beginning, and Smith encouraged it.

In his address to the jubilee gathering, Smith went on to highlight, secondly, the growth of the University over the period in terms of the appointments of

---

[20] L. Moore, *Bajanellas and Semilinas: Aberdeen University and the Education of Women 1860-1920* (Aberdeen, 1991) p134.

[21] Ibid.

[22] Moore's record contains the following: "a disapproving Eric Linklater later told her [Mary Esslemont] that her appointment had 'split student opinion'" (p91). This, however, does not accord with the statement in Linklater's autobiography, *Fanfare for a Tin Hat* (London, 1970), p85, where he describes himself as "one of a clique ... that engineered the election of a woman as President of the Students' Representative Council ... Our campaign roused bitter feeling and angry opposition, but Mary Esslemont, our candidate, was a young woman of uncommon ability, of great strength of character, and her elevation was only a prelude to the lifetime of service she has since given to Aberdeen".

[23] Moore, *Bajanellas and Semilinas*, p91. See also the potted biography of Esslemont in *Aberdeen 1800-2000*, p57.

[24] L.A.O. Macdonald, *A Unique and Glorious Mission: Women and Presbyterianism in Scotland 1830-1930* (Edinburgh, 2000) p279.

[25] T.M. Devine, *The Scottish Nation 1700-2000* (London, 1999) p408.

Professors and the growing number of Chairs. From twenty-one Professors in 1875, he said, there were now twenty-eight, with the prospect of a further three by the end of that year. Within the thirteen years from around 1913 to 1925, he said that seven new Chairs had been founded, six of these in the most recent academic session. While these changes may seem minor in the light of modern advances in higher education, Smith could justifiably conclude:

> All this proves that your old University, ancient as she is, has not ceased growing and rising to the increasing requirements of the times. Indeed, there has never been a period in her history of such rapid expansion as that which began after the Universities' Commission of 1889, and still continues.[26]

In particular, the Faculties of Medicine, Law and Divinity grew remarkably during this period.

One significant step which was taken shortly after Smith had become Principal – and which shows his active involvement in University life – was the commencement of the publication of the *Aberdeen University Review*, an annual chronicle of events in the life of the University. Smith contributed much to its pages, and also penned the foreword to the first edition. Amid the aims of the *Review*, Smith listed the following:

> Recent years have brought to the University of Aberdeen, as to her Scottish sisters, a great increase of resources, and this not too soon to meet the rapidly multiplying needs and opportunities of the intellectual life of our time ... New questions of academic policy have arisen ... efforts will be made to state with justice and intelligence the complex problems of policy which it raises ...

> We hope to give from time to time reports of all these and other changes and expansions in the equipment, the teaching and the discipline of the University, as well as of their educational and financial results.[27]

In 1910 the number of students was 1007, peaking at 1655 in 1920, and 1288 by the time Smith retired in 1935.[28] The total number of students enrolled in Scottish Universities in the period is given by Professor T.M. Devine as 6,000 in 1900 and 10,000 in 1938,[29] which shows the small proportion attending Aberdeen itself. Thus while the institution over which Smith presided may have seen phenomenal growth in the period, and been characterised by

---

[26] "A Fifty Years' Review", p38.
[27] GAS, Foreword to the *Aberdeen University Review*, Vol 1 No 1 (October 1913) pp2-3.
[28] Statistics taken from Anderson, Appendix I, Tables 2 and 3, pp133-4.
[29] Devine, *Scottish Nation*, p410.

change and reform, it was not a large institution. In the case of Aberdeen, the comparison with a Presbyterian congregation was reasonable and apt. As Principal, Smith entered into a pastoral role with considerable ease.

A further point made by Smith in his speech to the jubilee gathering was the significant contribution made to the expansion and development of the University by the Carnegie Trust. Andrew Carnegie, though born into poverty in Dunfermline in 1835, had emigrated to America in 1848, and became, by 1901, one of the world's richest men.[30] While his financial success was the fruit of "a sharp brain and a fair measure of ruthlessness",[31] the Carnegie Trust was able to provide crucial grants and bursaries for Scottish students. The capital sum of £2,000,000 had been given by Carnegie both for the "improvement and expansion of the Universities of Scotland" and the payment of fees of Scottish students.[32] By 1910, according to Devine, it was "covering part of the fees of about half of all university students in Scotland".[33] In an address delivered in 1936 on the centenary of Andrew Carnegie's birth, Smith described the donation as "an overpowering gift from one who himself never enjoyed the opportunities of a University education", and went on to point out that "but for the Carnegie grants the Universities could hardly have weathered the years of the Great War, when their incomes from student fees were so greatly diminished".[34] There is an irony here when one recalls the social gospel position adopted by Smith in the 1880s and 1890s; his endorsement of Carnegie, a flamboyant and (some would argue) ruthless business-man, hardly accords with Smith's earlier views. Nonetheless, Smith did acknowledge the need for such a Trust if Scottish higher education was to become accessible to all, and his personal acquaintance with Carnegie was an important factor in his support for the Trust.[35]

Smith did his utmost to assist others in benefiting from the terms of the Trust. In an article in 1935 the recently formed student newspaper at Aberdeen, the *Gaudie,* could say that "few know the time and care which Sir George has expended on the presentation of cases for consideration by the trustees of this and other trusts".[36] Corroboration of this can be found in a letter from Dr Camilla Hay of University College, Hull to Lilian Smith after the Principal's death:

---

[30] A recent article in *The Herald* described Carnegie as "The Bill Gates of his Generation" (Melanie Reid, "A Man with money to give away", *The Herald*, 13 March 2001, p12).

[31] Ibid., p12

[32] L. Donald "The History of the General Council of the University of Aberdeen 1860-1960" in Simpson, *The Fusion*, p92.

[33] Devine, *Scottish Nation*, p410.

[34] GAS, *The British Benefactions of Andrew Carnegie* (New York, 1936) p4.

[35] LAS, pp147-8

[36] "Sir George Adam Smith – an Appreciation", *Gaudie*, Vol II.1 15 (October 1935) p4.

I personally owe him a tremendous debt of gratitude for the interest he took in my University career, not only while I was a student at Aberdeen, but afterwards too. It was through him, you remember, that I was awarded the Carnegie Research Scholarship which sent me to Poitiers and made it possible for me to study for my Doctorate.[37]

Smith's Principalship from 1910 to 1935 therefore witnessed the growth and consolidation of the institution over which he presided. It also marked a period of change in attitudes to higher education at the beginning of the twentieth century, which led to widening research and greater opportunity. We shall now turn to look at Smith's personal role in the evolving life of the University.

Smith's Contribution to University Life

In an interview made with him in a magazine for young people, Smith offers the following statement of his new position:

> A modern Principal has to listen to and learn from those who know about horses, cattle and poultry, research into the nature of soils, woods and timber, as well as about Homer and Virgil![38]

It was one which

> required a scholar with an outlook far beyond his own range of subjects; a business man with a close grasp of detail; an organiser with shrewdness and foresight, and an administrator to take and distribute responsibility, to cope with difficulties, and to create an atmosphere of trust and friendliness in which unnecessary friction might be avoided.[39]

In her memoir, from which these words are taken, Lilian Adam Smith admits that while "with some of these qualities George was already well equipped, others had to be painstakingly developed".[40] His transition from teacher to administrator did require the learning of new skills and the grasp of new structures.

It helped that Smith was an efficient manager of people. Alexander Gray, who was Professor of Political Economy at Aberdeen from 1921-34, recalls being interviewed by the University Court for the newly founded Chair. He acknowledges his reticence in applying for the post, and reminisced that "a

---

[37] Camilla Hay to LAS from University College, Hull 5 March 1942, NLS Acc 9446 No 75.
[38] "Ten Talks with Useful People: IX. Sir George Adam Smith", *Greatheart: The Scottish Churches Magazine for Boys and Girls* (September 1929) p206.
[39] LAS, p151.
[40] Ibid.

characteristically gracious letter from the Principal persuaded me that I ought to go north for a general talk with the Court about things at large".[41] His interview showed not only "the Principal's skill in managing the Court", but also, Professor Gray says, "how skilfully the Principal had managed *me*!"[42] Similarly, Professor F.F. Bruce recalls Smith's skill in dealing with a heckler when E.W. Barnes, Bishop of Birmingham, was presenting the Gifford Lectures in 1926-8.[43] When the man was about to interrupt a second time, Bruce says that

> Principal Sir George Adam Smith, who was in the chair and who knew his Aberdonians, rose and quieted him with a soothing gesture: "Write to the paper about it tomorrow".[44]

This was an important quality, and it goes some way to explaining Smith's popularity. He had a genial and warm nature: his successor could say of him that what impressed him "was not so much the widespread admiration for the scholar, preacher and administrator, but the even more widespread affection for the man".[45] Similarly, while John Kelman believed that "the work of the Principalship will suit his genius", he also believed that Smith's "rich and glorious human spirit will be of priceless worth to the University life".[46]

Smith also contributed to the life of the University a determination to see the University develop as an independent and self-contained centre of higher education. Though it was small enough to have a sense of homeliness and intimacy, Smith nonetheless wished to see the University at the forefront of academic enquiry. It was with a fair measure of contentment, therefore, that Smith could say in 1925 that the University had become famous "for an intellectual character and distinctive habits of industry all her own", and that her alumni could look back on her with loyalty and pride.[47]

When the University presented Smith with his portrait in 1928, Lord Alness, in making the presentation, spoke of Smith's having "piloted" the University "from a position of comparative obscurity to the proud eminence which it has

---

[41] Simpson, *The Fusion*, p152.
[42] Ibid.
[43] These lectures, established under the provisions of the will of Lord Gifford of Scotland (d. 1885), were intended to explore topics in Natural Theology, and quickly became the foremost intellectual event in religion in the four ancient Universities of Scotland: Edinburgh, St. Andrews, Glasgow and Aberdeen. Ernest W. Barnes, appointed Bishop of Birmingham in 1924 was a controversial choice, not least because of his pacifist views during the war. It would be interesting to know the role of the Principal in the selection of these lecturers.
[44] F.F Bruce, *In Retrospect: Remembrance of Things Past* (London, 1980) p47.
[45] Principal Fyfe to LAS, 4 March 1942, NLS Acc 9446 No 75.
[46] John Kelman to George Smith, 23 October 1909, NLS Acc 9446 No 43.
[47] GAS, "A Fifty Years' Review", p39.

attained in the academic life of today".[48] The granting of the freedom of the city of Aberdeen to Smith, in October 1931, was also a recognition of the central and important place of the University in city life.[49] The progress in education was one which Smith had been at pains to encourage.

At the same time, Smith was less than happy with the trend towards departmentalisation. In a sermon preached by Smith in Glasgow University Chapel, he argued against *over*-specialisation. In Smith's opinion,

> Over-specialization ... ever tended to selfishness and narrow views, even to ignorance and injustice, even to envy and quarrelsome tempers. Another peril in the increasing specialization of modern study was that it tempted to a narrow regard for the merely economic and utilitarian profits which it promised to secure to them as individuals. To yield to that was to miss the chief object of a University.[50]

Smith had approached University learning with a different philosophy. To Smith, "the chief object of a University was to give ... a liberal education, both of mind and heart, and an understanding and sympathy with their fellows".[51]

Smith's own academic record demonstrated the need for diversity and comprehensiveness. The subjects of his academic research, as we have seen, embraced the disciplines of Hebrew, Greek, history, geography, historical geography, theology and biblical studies. As he piloted the University, while encouraging new fields of study and establishing new research Chairs and institutions, Smith was concerned to move away from the departmentalisation that only led to the compartmentalising of truth. However, in this regard Aberdeen, like other Universities, suffered as a consequence of its own growth, and by the end of his term as Principal, departmental specialisation was well advanced, though not, one surmises, entirely to his liking.

Smith was determined to encourage the development of agriculture at the University. In an early volume of the *Scottish Journal of Agriculture*, Smith said of his experience in Aberdeen that "there has been a diminution of the prejudice against academic instruction for farmers, land-agents and land-owners which used to prevail".[52] The University had gained by opening up courses of instruction for farmers in the north-east of Scotland. Science

---

[48] "The Principal's Portrait", *Aberdeen University Review*, Vol 15 No 45 (July 1928) p229.

[49] "Honouring the Principal", *Aberdeen University Review*, Vol 19 No 55 (November 1931) p35. See also Dr. I.G.C. Hutchison's interesting discussion of "The University Elite" in *Aberdeen: A New History*, pp392-3.

[50] "Dangers of Over-Specialization", *Aberdeen University Review*, Vol 19 No 57 (July 1932) p261.

[51] Ibid.

[52] GAS, "Agricultural Education and its Needs", *The Scottish Journal of Agriculture*, Vol III.2 (April 1920) p157.

departments had, he said, provided material and personal resources, and there had been the kind of interdependence and co-operation between departments which he sought to encourage:

> After all, the physiology and pathology, the problems of nutrition and disease of animals and of men respectively, are inseparably connected: the closer the association and reaction between the University and the College departments, which treat of them, the greater is the advantage to both.[53]

For Smith, fieldwork and practical experience were vital if a city University were to offer courses in agriculture. His own experience in the plains, deserts and towns of Palestine had amply illustrated the need for fieldwork, and his article encourages farm residency as well as scientific education in topics related to agriculture.[54] The article also shows the dexterity with which Smith was able to turn from biblical scholarship to issues of practical management and administration, and reveals a determination to encourage scholarship outwith his own particular field of interest.

Smith was keen to encourage Aberdeen University's contribution to other institutions of learning and research. For example, when the British Museum wished to purchase the Codex Sinaiticus from the Russian Government, Smith encouraged Aberdeen University to make a donation to this end. Smith wrote to the Director of the British Museum, George Hill, in January 1934, intimating that "the Senatus Academicus of the University of Aberdeen has voted the sum of £50 towards the purchase of the Greek manuscript of the Bible from Mount Sinai".[55] In his reply, Hill noted that Aberdeen's was the first contribution to the attempt to obtain the Codex. This, he said, was especially gratifying in view of the fact that

> there has been so much apathy displayed in quarters where one would have least expected it, so much ignorance of the real significance of the Codex, that the action of your University is all the more welcome.[56]

---

[53] Ibid. The College to which he refers is the Northern College of Agriculture, set up in 1904 with a formalised connection with the University in place since 1911.

[54] Ibid., p158.

[55] GAS to George Hill, 31 January 1934, British Library Manuscripts, ADD 68923, folio 316.

[56] George Hill to GAS, 3 February 1934, British Library Manuscripts, ADD 68923, folio 329. For a discussion of the importance of the Codex Sinaiticus, discovered by Tischendorf in a monastery on Mt Sinai, see M. Black and R. Davidson *Constantin von Tischendorf and the Greek New Testament* (Glasgow, 1981).

It was Smith's concern not only to bring into Aberdeen and into the University a wide range of academic interests and endeavours, but also to make the University itself a means of enrichment for British cultural life.

Despite this, Smith came in for criticism in the area of finance administration. In the opinion of the University Grants Committee (set up by the Government in 1919), Smith's administration pursued a fiscal policy which was too cautious, unimaginative and sterile. Iain Hutchison notes that

> in its quinquennial submissions in the 1920s the University had repeatedly stated that it was pursuing a policy of fiscal prudence by not overspending and by committing itself only to projects which it could afford. The UGC seems to have felt that this caution had hardened in the next decade to negativism.[57]

Aberdeen's failure to stake a claim for UGC funding seems to give credence to these criticisms. During the latter period of Smith's principalship, the University received minimal external support, and the resources of the University were pretty much expended on the science and medical buildings. Although there had been some savings made overall, the net result was that the University in the mid-1930s was not at a point of financial security and stability.

However, the University did make its contribution to the world of ideas, and distinguished itself intellectually. Among the appointments made during Smith's Principalship was that of George Paget Thomson as Professor of Natural Philosophy, a post which he occupied from 1922 to 1930. His work in Aberdeen was later to lead to his sharing the Nobel Prize in physics in 1937. Thomson also married Smith's daughter, Kathleen, in 1924. Another close friend of Smith's was Sir Herbert Grierson, whose tenure at Aberdeen saw the publication of a seminal edition of John Donne's poetry in 1912. Thus the growing University under Smith's Principalship distinguished itself in many branches of learning.

During his Principalship Smith was a frequent guest of the Royal Families both at Balmoral, the royal Highland retreat purchased by Prince Albert for Queen Victoria in 1852, and at Holyrood Palace, Edinburgh, the King's official residence in Scotland.[58] In 1920 George and Lilian were guests of King George

---

[57] I.G.C. Hutchison, *The University and the State: The Case of Aberdeen 1860-1963*, Quincentennial Studies in the history of the University of Aberdeen (Aberdeen, 1997) p57.

[58] NLS Acc 9446 No 151 contains a selection of invitations to the Smiths to Holyrood Palace in 1920, 1931, 1934 and 1937. Further invitations to Holyrood came from the Lord High Commissioner, the monarch's representative at the General Assembly of the Church of Scotland. John Buchan was Lord High Commissioner in 1934, and the Duke of Kent in 1935. On both occasions Smith was invited to Holyrood.

V and Queen Mary in Edinburgh. Later that year, while Lilian was visiting her daughter Maisie in America, George and their daughter Kathleen entertained Queen Mary and Princess Mary at Chanonry Lodge, for which they were profoundly thanked by their majesties.[59] In 1933, Smith was appointed as a Chaplain-in-Ordinary to the King in Scotland, an honour which drew many expressions of congratulations. The appointment required ecclesiastical induction, which took place in St Giles Cathedral, Edinburgh, on 20 May 1934. His daughters treated it in cavalier fashion, Kathleen writing "We all send you lots of congratulations. And how nice for the king!",[60] and Janet enquiring "What duties does it involve? Nothing too arduous, I hope!".[61] One duty it did involve in 1934 was a sermon by Smith in Crathie Church, Deeside, which had been attended by the Royal Family when in residence in Balmoral since the days of Victoria. Smith preached on Matthew 14:15-16[62], on the need to tackle impossible tasks with courage. As in the case of Jesus, he said, "the strain was the strength",[63] so we too need to tackle the impossible. The war, he said, had brought an end to carelessness and mental indolence; the nation had learned that new questions, however disturbing, needed to be addressed.

These royal connections not only add colour to the personal biography; they also remind us of the weight of statesmanship which Smith added to the life of the University. They are a comment upon his high social standing, which in turn gave added stature to his University position. Not a small part of the contribution he made to University life was the fact that he could walk with kings, and still not lose the common touch. But his prowess lay in his scholarship, and in spite of the demands of the Principalship, Smith made several important contributions during these years.

Smith's Scholarship 1910-1935

The Schweich Lectures

In 1910 Smith was invited by the British Academy to deliver the Schweich Lectures on Biblical Archaeology. These lectures were delivered in London, on

---

[59] Lady Joan Vermey, Lady-in-waiting to Queen Mary, wrote GAS from Balmoral "to express to you Her Majesty's thanks for all the trouble you took to make Her Majesty's visit to Aberdeen a success, and for your most hospitable entertainment" (Lady Joan Vermey to GAS, 11 September 1920, NLS Acc 9446 No 149). Accompanying the letter were gifts of a photograph of the Queen and a blue pottery vase.

[60] Kathleen Buchanan Smith to GAS, 6 October 1933, NLS Acc 9446 No 150.

[61] Janet Adam Smith to GAS, 5 October 1933, NLS Acc 9446 No 150.

[62] Matthew 14:15-16: 'And when it was evening, his disciples came to him saying, This is a desert place and the time is now past: send the multitude away that they may go into the villages, and buy themselves victuals. But Jesus said unto them, They need not depart; give ye them to eat.'

[63] GAS, Handwritten draft of sermon preached at Crathie Kirk before King George V and Queen Mary, 16 September 1934. The Smiths resided at Balmoral Castle from the Saturday to the Monday on this occasion.

2, 5 and 7 December 1910, on the subject of *The Early Poetry of Israel in its Physical and Social Origins*, and were published under that title two years later. By that time Sir Israel Gollancz, the Secretary of the British Academy, could say that their publication "has been eagerly looked forward to by many"[64]. The three lectures, one on the subject of "Language, Structure and Rhythm", and two on the subject of "Substance and Spirit", show Smith at his most technical. They are a study of the impact of Israel's social setting on the early poetry of the Jewish people, by which Smith means the poetic material which has been incorporated into the patriarchal narratives, the historical sections, and some of the prophetic sections of the Old Testament, poetry written prior to the eighth century. The subject-area is thus extremely narrow. In the preface to the published work, Smith makes it clear that he intended to publish a larger work on the subject[65], but he never did. The importance of the subject is underlined by the view of scholars such as D.N. Freedman, who says that "the early poetry of Israel constitutes a prime source for the reconstruction of Israel's history".[66]

The first lecture deals with the distinctive features of the Hebrew language. Its sonorous, guttural sounds Smith explains with the hypothesis that "the dry climate and large leisure of the East bestow on the lower chords of the voice a greater depth and suppleness".[67] This adds its own music to the cadence of the poetry; Smith describes the natural speaking style of the Jew, and says that, like other Orientals, the typical Jew "made a strenuous use of the doubled consonant".[68] Smith cites Judges 5:22, the Song of Deborah, and other passages to illustrate "the musical value of the doubled consonant in Hebrew".[69] In this way, the very speaking style of the Jew is taken as an explanation for the distinctive poetry of the Hebrews. But also important, in their own ways, are what Smith identifies as the two elements which Hebrew lacks: terms of abstraction and compound words.[70] Smith concludes that the Hebrew language has not progressed beyond the simplicity of the root stage, and in the absence of case endings, this lends a simplicity to the poetry also. There is, Smith reckons, an absence of metaphor,[71] as well as an absence of the metaphysical. Hebrew poetry "tells" rather than "describes", which is fitting for a nomadic race.[72]

---

[64] Gollancz to GAS 2 December 1912, NLS Acc 9446 No 143.
[65] "I reserve the right to use the contents of these Lectures in a larger work on Hebrew poetry which I hope some day to publish", *The Early Poetry of Israel in its Physical and Social Origins* (London, 1912) pviii.
[66] D.N. Freedman, *Pottery, Poetry and Prophecy: Studies in Early Hebrew Poetry* (Winona Lake, Indiana, 1980) p167.
[67] *The Early Poetry of Israel*, p2.
[68] Ibid., p5.
[69] Ibid.
[70] Ibid., p7.
[71] Ibid., p8.
[72] Ibid., p9.

According to Smith, the dominant characteristic of the poetry is its distinctive parallelism, with lines formed into couplets (or, in some cases, triplets). The parallelism Smith further distinguishes as being exact (where the second line repeats the thought of the first), or it may be progressive (where the second line advances on the first), or antithetic (where the second is adversative of the first), or the phenomenon may be a modified parallelism, which Smith terms "spiralism".[73] This occurs, he suggests, where subsequent lines pick up on words or expressions already stated, taking them a stage further.[74] "The fact is," says Smith, "poetry was primitively the art of saying the same beautiful things over and over again in similarly charming ways".[75] And if it is true that the Hebrew gutturals modify the lines, then the parallelism modifies the words, since the parallelism will require each line to be more or less self-contained. But this does not mean that Hebrew poetry is made up of lines of equal length; in fact, says Smith, the Hebrew poets suffered from a clear "Symmetrophobia" - an abhorrence of absolute symmetry in the structure of the poems. Consequently Smith reckons "unscientific" any attempt in modern translation to reconstruct the Hebrew verse in terms of strict and absolute symmetry. Another corollary of this is that differences in rhythm need not suggest differences of authorship, but may be due to thematic changes in the poem itself.[76]

In the second and third lectures, Smith is concerned to show how the physical condition of the Hebrews had a direct bearing on the subject of the early poetry. Israel's poetry requires, Smith argues, to be compared with that of other Semitic peoples, and also requires that attention be paid to the social origins of the Jewish people. They were originally nomads, living a pastoral life, with little agriculture or industry. Life is cursed by famine and war, and, Smith says, "in such a society, the strongest moral motive is shame - shame before one's parents or before one's fellow-tribesmen".[77] The idea of shame shapes the poetry: it leads to the praising of the brave and the heaping of opprobrium on the cowardly. For such a race, born and nursed in the desert until eventually drawn into the fertile plains of Canaan, the poetry was centred on several distinctive themes: the return of victorious warriors, rhythms of horse and camel-travel, and desert scenery. The fact that there is little on trade in the poetry is also an indicator of the compositional context. The desert scenery, especially, was a powerful motivator, leading to the Hebrew poets being taken up with the phenomena of desert life, rather than metaphysical

---

[73] Ibid., p13.
[74] A recent article by D.J.A. Clines on "The Parallelism of Greater Precision" in E.R. Follis (ed.) *Directions in Biblical Hebrew Poetry* (Sheffield, 1987) echoes much of Smith, although without reference to his work.
[75] *The Early Poetry of Israel*, p16.
[76] Ibid., p21.
[77] Ibid., p27.

speculation on death and the after-life. Indeed, says Smith, "the Hebrew mind is not speculative".[78] Only the distinct influences of Hebrew religion open the way for a theology of ultimate destiny. This, coupled with the personal temperament of the Hebrew (Smith cites a combination of "strong sensual grossness" with "equally strong tempers of reverence and worship"), leads to a subjectivism which means that objective analysis or description is lacking. Only with more mature reflection on the events shaping the history could the Hebrew mind stretch out to contemplate the future. For Smith, such a study emphasises for the student of the Old Testament "the historical value of the poetry"[79]. Just as the prophets were to be interpreted solely in terms of their historical circumstances, so the poetry of Israel must also be interpreted historically. And only when the Hebrews are finally settled in their own land, do they begin, in Smith's view, to think beyond their own immediate historical Sitz-im-Leben.

The third lecture is taken up for the most part with citations to illustrate the principles enunciated in the second. Here, Smith's strictly historical approach influences his exegesis of certain poetic passages. For example, of Genesis 9:26-7, which speaks of Japheth dwelling in Shem's tents, Smith wants to confine his exegesis to strict historical circumstances. The poem may refer, he suggests, to "either a friendly or a hostile invasion"[80], and Smith conjectures which it may be. He does not allow for an analogical or metaphoric use of the terminology. He has already stated that early Hebrew poets were not – and could not be – abstract in their thinking. But his position does justice neither to the imaginative talent of the writers, nor to the metaphoric use of language. Similarly, theophanic passages, such as Psalm 18:7-12 (=2 Samuel 22:8-13), Smith takes as evidence of a primitive mythology having been cast off, rather than as evidence of an already existing objective theology.[81] Smith's insistence that the Hebrews passed through a phrase of concrete thinking to a stage of abstract thinking prevents him from entertaining the idea that the metaphysical element may have actually been present from an extremely early stage.

Smith's work gives many useful insights into the relation between temperament and poetry, language and poetry, and physical setting and poetry. The work was seminal, and it is a great pity that Smith found no time to develop it. On the other hand, without severe modification, the usefulness of such a large-scale work would have been limited. Unlike his earlier, more popular works, the lectures on early Hebrew poetry were technical and

---

[78] Ibid., p34.
[79] Ibid., p35.
[80] Ibid., p46.
[81] The rhetorical question which Smith asks is: 'Do the Psalms and other poems in the Old Testament which chant of similar theophanies likewise belong to our period, before Israel had cast off the influences of the mythology characteristic of the desert ...? (Ibid., p57).

academic. The *Expository Times* described them as 'popular' because there are no Hebrew characters on the pages, and therefore the original could be read in transliteration[82]; in reality, however, they make for taxing reading. They certainly struck a note of authority at the commencement of his Principalship, perhaps as much to demonstrate the academic prowess of the new Principal in the face of possible objections to his having been appointed. As the *Princeton Theological Review* said of his work, "With all that may be fanciful in his tracing of analogies, his service to scholarship is unquestionable".[83]

Deuteronomy
Smith's contribution on *Deuteronomy* to the *Cambridge Bible for Schools and Colleges* series was published in 1918, the fruit of protracted and often interrupted research. He had been working on it while on holiday in the Lake District as early as 1913.[84] Determined to finish it before his departure for America in 1918, his wife says that "he slaved at it, literally to the last moment, and the day before he left we went together to the little post office in Old Aberdeen and sent off the final manuscript and corrections".[85]

The series was intended to popularise the critical approach to the Old Testament, and to facilitate its use in the education system. Smith's volume contains some 120 pages of introduction, followed by the Revised Version translation of Deuteronomy with extensive annotation. In his introduction, Smith states that the elevated prose of Deuteronomy has as its purpose "to expound" the law, with impulses of "religious fervour and the passion to instruct".[86] The result is a piece of writing which Smith regards as powerful, almost oratorical, and which he describes "like a flowing tide on a long beach, the long parallel waves dashing, withdrawing, then dashing again".[87] After comparing the style of Deuteronomy to the constituent documents of the Pentateuch, Smith concludes that Deuteronomy has a style of its own, with characteristic formulae, such as "Jehovah our/your/thy God" appearing over 300 times. And although the deuteronomic writer has leaned heavily on pentateuchal documents, in Smith's view the publication was intended to promulgate the law in Israel, against the background of "a more mature and

---

[82] "Notes on Literature", *The Expository Times* Vol XXIV, No 7 (April 1913) p313.
[83] J. Oscar Boyd, Review of GAS, *The Early Poetry of Israel in its Physical and Social Origins*, *Princeton Theological Review*, Vol XII (January 1914) p137.
[84] LAS, p150: "We were then at the farmhouse of Manisty on Derwentwater; and while the Dickens readings were the joy of the evenings, the days were spent by my husband in work upon the *Atlas of the Holy Land* and *Deuteronomy*."
[85] Ibid., p169. Lilian Smith continues: "Then he came home and made his will".
[86] GAS, *Deuteronomy* (London, 1918) pxiii.
[87] Ibid.

complex form of society than that for which the codes of JE ... are designed".[88] But Deuteronomy, Smith suggests, not only reveals a more complex society, but also shows varying degrees of relationship with earlier writings regarding the religious character of the people. Smith contends that the P document distinguishes between priests and Levites, while in Deuteronomy the terms are synonymous. At the same time, Deuteronomy is distinguished by a central doctrine: that of the "One Altar and Sanctuary".[89] Smith concludes that while the religious conditions in Deuteronomy are "more developed than those reflected in JE", the book "exhibits an organisation of religion far less developed than that in P".[90]

Smith sees another dominant feature in the theology of Deuteronomy: the love of God to man and the love of man to God are "everywhere".[91] Deuteronomy, he says, "has a heart of its own – a bigger, richer heart than any of its fellows in the Pentateuch".[92] With the settlement of Israel in Canaan, the threat from the local tribal deities in the shrines of Canaan was such that a central Altar was "the only practical safeguard of the creed of the One God".[93] Deuteronomy's ruthless denunciation of the worship of other gods, the "fanatical zeal" of its "monotheistic creed"[94] lies side by side with its warm, devotional emphasis on love between God and men.

Smith goes on to discuss the ethics and social laws of Deuteronomy, which search deep into motives and personal morality. He also discusses the relationship between the canonical Deuteronomy and the law-book which was discovered in the Temple by King Josiah, as well as the relationship between the divisions and subdivisions of the book itself. After a thorough examination of the various law passages, Smith concludes that Deuteronomy "is the result of growth and compilation from various sources – new laws, expansions and modifications of old ones, while some probably are the reduction to writing for the first time of unwritten practices".[95] Smith wishes neither to side with the more conservative critics, who, while acknowledging editorial influences in the writing of Deuteronomy, "do not sufficiently appreciate the amount of them",[96] nor with those who "on arbitrary grounds and often in the interests of particular schemes of analysis exaggerate the quantity of editorial matter".[97] Smith is

---

[88] Ibid., pxxii. Smith is here using the standard form of referring to the Pentateuchal writings or sources (the so-called documentary hypothesis), in which J refers to a Yahweh source, E an Elohim (=God) source, and P a Priestly source.
[89] Ibid., pxxiv.
[90] Ibid., pxxv.
[91] Ibid., pxxvi.
[92] Ibid., pxxviii.
[93] Ibid., pxxxi.
[94] Ibid., pxxxii.
[95] Ibid., plxxi.
[96] Ibid., plxxxix.
[97] Ibid.

confident in his assertion, however, both that editorial influence is clear, and that there is unity of purpose in Deuteronomy. The unity reflects the uniqueness of Israel's role:

> The whole Israel is here, as in no other book in the Old Testament – the whole Israel in its limitations as in its potentiality, in its sins as in its aspirations, in its narrow fanatic tempers as in its vision and passion for the Highest.[98]

On the dating of Deuteronomy, Smith says that the only certain date in the deuteronomical history is the discovery of the Book of the Law during the reign of Josiah in 621BC, but since the canonical form is different to that which Josiah discovered, this date is of limited value. Given the subsequent reforms of Josiah's reign, Smith argues that the redaction of Deuteronomy is to be placed *no later than* Josiah's death in 608; and that any point in the previous hundred years might have yielded a suitable starting-point. Smith, drawing on what he considers to be archaisms in the language of Deuteronomy, and its affinities with the constitutive documents of the Pentateuch, wishes to drive the earliest forms of the Book back to the reign of Hezekiah, as early as the commencement of his reign in 725. The use of Moses as speaker throughout, Smith argues, is a stylistic form, comparable with other Near Eastern literature. He also argues that this style betrays a deficiency in the Oriental mind, an inability to "conceive of authority except as personal and immediate",[99] and an ignoring of secondary causes. Smith's Orientalism at this point is of the kind criticised by Edward Said in his study of the subject, one which tried "to reduce the Orient to a kind of human flatness, which exposed its characteristics easily to scrutiny and removed from it its complicating humanity".[100] It may well be, of course, that the use of Moses serves as an editorial and structural tool; but that assertion requires to be demonstrated on grounds other than a subjective assessment of the limitations of Oriental thinking. Indeed, Smith concedes that the doctrines of Deuteronomy were originally and substantially taught by Moses,[101] although he wishes to move beyond Moses and to say that Deuteronomy is a *development* of Mosaic thought.

Smith's conclusion that Deuteronomy is a work of reformation is based on his premise that it is a work which has developed over a period of time. This in turn is premised on the documentary hypothesis regarding the compilation of the Pentateuch itself; Smith's acceptance of this hypothesis shows his dependence on William Robertson Smith, whose *The Old Testament in the Jewish Church* (1881) had introduced Wellhausen's documentary scheme to

---

[98] Ibid., pxciv.
[99] Ibid., pcxii.
[100] Edward W. Said, *Orientalism* (London, 1995) p150.
[101] *Deuteronomy*, pcxv.

Scottish scholarship. The hypothesis has been subjected to intense scrutiny in recent times, with modern scholarship struggling between the extremes of regarding the Pentateuch as a kind of ideological fiction, and others wishing to preserve the historical element by emphasising oral patterning, which may go some way to resolving the difficulties over repetitious passages, and divergent names for God.[102] Smith's reliance on documentary sources for the Pentateuch shows him to be a child of his times, but the assumptions of his times are now being challenged. In addition, recent scholarship has drawn attention to the covenant form of the Book of Deuteronomy as a whole, and the correspondence of its style to the Ancient Near Eastern vassal treaty,[103] which Smith does not consider in his work. The view of Smith and other contemporary expositors that Deuteronomy shows a late and highly developed emphasis on the One Altar of Jehovah is also problematic. E.J. Young's point that "the unity of the altar was apparently the law of Israel's life from the beginning"[104] is difficult to refute.

Smith's approach to Deuteronomy reflects his own situation in 1918. The proofs were posted to the printer on the eve of his departure to America to encourage the war effort, during a time, as we have seen, which required the church to re-adapt, to consider its traditions and to question whether these were adequate to the needs of the time. Whatever the War did, it forced the churches in Scotland to question whether they were best serving the interests of a nation going through a period of cataclysmic change. It was time for Scotland, like Josiah in 621BC, to recover the Book of the Law, use what was best from the past, and reformulate and re-apply that Law for a new time and a new age.

The commentary ends with an appendix on clean and unclean animals. Smith is still cited in modern commentaries[105] as well as in studies of

---

[102] See the discussion by Gordon J. Wenham "Pondering the Pentateuch: The Search for a New Paradigm" in D.W. Baker and B.T. Arnold (eds.) *The Face of Old Testament Studies* (Leicester, 1999) Chapter 5.

[103] See, for example, Meredith G. Kline *Treaty of the Great King: The Covenant Structure of Deuteronomy* (Grand Rapids, Michigan, 1963) applied more recently to Deuteronomy by Paul R. House, *Old Testament Theology*, Downers Grove, Illinois, 1998, Chapter 6, especially pages 171-2. As Tremper Longman III has observed, "It is significant to discover that Deuteronomy is in the form of a treaty, that the narrator shapes the reader's responses to the characters of a text in different ways, and that repetition is not necessarily a sign of multiple sources but a literary device" (in "Literary Approaches to Biblical Interpretation", *Foundations of Contemporary Interpretation*, M. Silva (ed.) [Leicester, 1997] p132).

[104] E.J. Young, *Introduction to the Old Testament* (Grand Rapids, Michigan, 1964) p140.

[105] Such as Peter Craigie, *The Book of Deuteronomy* (Grand Rapids, Michigan, 1976) in the New International Commentary on the Old Testament Series, who refers the reader to Smith several times, as at the discussion on the "Anakim" (p102, n.7), and the nature of acacia wood (p199 n.3). Clearly on the physical and geographical features, quite apart from the theological, Smith's research has proved invaluable.

Deuteronomy within Israelite tradition.[106] His stature as a critical Old Testament scholar was enhanced with the publication, even if his approach can be questioned on modern historiographical grounds. It is still a valid approach, *contra* Smith, to assert that Deuteronomy "had been written *before* the awful litany of events that ensued, rather than as a theological apologetic for what happened as a retrospective analysis".[107] Smith's approach, while typical of his times, and while continuing to advance and popularise the Higher Critical approach, nonetheless depends on a treatment of the text of the Pentateuch which is still being debated.

Jeremiah
Although Smith's major work on the prophet Jeremiah did not appear until 1923, he had shown considerable interest in this subject on previous occasions. According to his wife, a sermon on Jeremiah preached in Oxford in the mid 1890s kindled an interest which later bore fruit in the appearance of the Jeremiah volume[108]; in addition, further lectures on Jeremiah had been given in Bristol and Manchester in 1902, and in 1905 to the clergy of the diocese of Ripon.[109] But the Baird Lectureship in Glasgow – under the trusteeship of prominent Church of Scotland clergymen – afforded him the opportunity of extended treatment of this theme in 1922, and the lectures were published the following year. From the outset the reader is made aware of a kindred spirit in both Jeremiah and Smith: both had lived through years of war, both had been passionate for peace, but both had the conviction that the divine will did not lie in that direction. Smith states at the outset that "The Great War invested the experience of the Prophet, who is the subject of this Lecture, with a fresh and poignant relevance to our own problems and duties".[110] The Book consists of eight lectures, on the subjects of "The Man and the Book", "The Poet", "The Prophet", "The Prophet in the Reign of Josiah (627-608)", "Under Jehoiakim (608-597)", "To the End and After", "The Story of his Soul", and "God, Man and the New Covenant". The whole is an attractive and warmly written - to the point of being devotional - guide through the Book of the Prophet Jeremiah. That Smith is still cited by modern commentators on Jeremiah is testimony to the freshness and power of his exposition.[111]

---

[106] Such as E.W. Nicholson *Deuteronomy and Tradition* (Oxford, 1967) who refers the reader to Smith on various issues in footnotes on consecutive pages from page 20-24.
[107] W. Kaiser, *A History of Israel from the Bronze Age through the Jewish Wars* (New York, 1998) p132.
[108] LAS, p72.
[109] Ibid., p95.
[110] GAS, *Jeremiah* (London, 1923) pi.
[111] See, for example, William L. Holladay, *Jeremiah 2: A Commentary on the Book of the Prophet Jeremiah Chapters 26-52*, Hermeneia Commentary Series (Minneapolis, 1989) whose exposition of Jeremiah 31:20 is clearly, and explicitly, influenced by Smith's comparison of the passage to Jesus' parable of the prodigal son. Given his high

Smith's professed aim is to get inside the prophet - to recover not only Jeremiah's historical situation, and its effect on his ministry, but also to have an understanding of his temperament and personality. It is true of every prophet, Smith says, that personality influences ministry, but in Smith's view "no prophet started so deeply from himself as Jeremiah did".[112] Passing through some defining moments in the spiritual history of Israel – such as the codification of the Deuteronomic law, its ultimate collapse, the failure of national religion and the dispersion of the nation – "what was henceforth finest in the religion of Israel had, however ancient its sources, been recast in the furnace of his spirit".[113] Jeremiah's ministry consequently was characterised by its stress upon the individual, emphasising personal responsibility before God.

The sources for the work are collections of genuine oracles and discourses, narratives of Jeremiah's life, and exilic and post-exilic additions.[114] The Lecture on "Jeremiah the Poet" echoes much of what appeared in Smith's Schweich lectures. Taking issue with scholars who argued that Jeremiah always used the elegiac style, Smith concludes rather that "this rural prophet, brought up in a country village and addressing a people of peasants, used the same license with his metres that we have observed in other poetries of his own race".[115] And while it was probable, says Smith, that Jeremiah used prose, although most of what remains of his public statements is in verse form, it is natural to suppose that he used the medium of folklore common and familiar to his people:

> the stunted desert-shrub in contrast to the riverside oaks, the incomparable olive, the dropped sheaf and even the dung upon the fields; the vulture, stork, crane and swift; the lion, wolf and spotted leopard coming up from the desert or the jungles of Jordan; the hinnying stallions and the heifer in her heat; the black Ethiopian, already familiar in the streets of Jerusalem, the potter and his wheel, the shepherd, plowman and vinedresser, the driver with his ox's yoke upon his shoulders; the harlot by the wayside; the light in the home and sound of the hand-mill – all everyday objects of his people's sight and hearing as they herded, ploughed, sowed, reaped or went to market in

---

praise of Smith elsewhere, it is strange that Robert Carroll's commentary on the prophet (London, 1986) does not even cite Smith in the bibliography. Other commentators have argued against Smith's view - H.H. Rowley, in "The Early Prophecies of Jeremiah" in L.G. Perdue and B.W. Kovacks *A Prophet to the Nations: Essays in Jeremiah Studies* (Indiana, 1984) pp33-61, for example, says that at one point Smith is given to idle speculation, but the reference nonetheless betrays the far-reaching influence of Smith's exposition.

[112] GAS, *Jeremiah*, p5.
[113] Ibid., p5.
[114] Ibid., p29.
[115] Ibid., p39.

the city – he brings them in simply and with natural ease as figures of the truth he is enforcing.[116]

But if his *method* was dictated by what he saw in everyday life, Jeremiah's *message* was dictated by his moral vehemence. Both his name and that of his father, Hilkiah, Smith takes to be a token of the family's loyalty to Yahweh. This also explains, according to Smith, references in Jeremiah to Israel's earlier history, which, in all probability he learned from his father. Aware as he was of the cross-currents of politics which influenced Palestine – invasions from the north and Greek threats from the south – Jeremiah's one concern was "What had God to say?".[117] While ignorant worshippers still deferred to local deities, Jeremiah's great concern was the result of "a thought of God".[118] And it was a thought of God for the nations: he had received a Word from God, "which no Hebrew prophet received without an instinct of its world-wide range and its powers of both destruction and creation".[119]

During the reign of Josiah (627-608 BC), Jeremiah had a three-fold ministry: one to the nation prior to the discovery of the lawbook in the Temple (which Smith dates at 621-620BC), another in connection with the Scythian invasions, and a third during the period after which the enforcement of the lawcode had begun. There are moving passages in Smith's treatment of these, such as his comment that "human nature even at its worst has tracts other than those on which there has been careless sowing among thorns, moral possibilities below those of its abused or neglected surfaces",[120] or his comment on the Deuteronomical code with what Smith describes as its "three cardinal doctrines: the One God, the One altar, and the One people".[121] The deuteronomic code, Smith says, enforces a personal morality but has no personal hope beyond death, stresses the dubious dogma that personal righteousness will always lead to prosperity and breeds an unhealthy, superstitious confidence in the religious institutions of Israel. Smith quotes approvingly the words of A.B. Davidson that "Pharisaism and Deuteronomy came into the world on the same day".[122]

Nonetheless, it is impossible to imagine, says Smith, that Jeremiah could have remained unmoved by the discovery of Deuteronomy in the Temple. Deuteronomy deals both with ethics and with ritual, and both emphases are present in Jeremiah's message. Only the prophet is ready to condemn what the popular mind commends: formality in religion grows not out of a spiritual, but

---

[116] Ibid., pp54-5.
[117] Ibid., p77.
[118] Ibid., p78.
[119] Ibid., p84.
[120] Ibid., p109.
[121] Ibid., p136.
[122] Ibid., p139.

a carnal impulse, and Jeremiah's message to his people is that a bare trust in the Temple is as bad as their trust in Egypt or Assyria. The ritualistic and the political are no substitute for a complete trust in Jehovah. The emergent conflict between Jeremiah's personal experience of God and the dogmatic assertions of Israel concerning the inviolability of the Temple and its worship, form the source of his prophetic message:

> it was the System and the Dogma that were defective, and the Man and his Experience of life that started, if not for himself yet for a later generation pondering his experience, the solution of these problems, which against the deuteronomic teaching he raised in brave agony to God's own face.[123]

This echoes the same tensions of Smith's own thought, between dogma and experience. It is easy to see why his wife could say of Smith that "Jeremiah was the companion of his later years".[124]

The beginning of the reign of Jehoiakim (608-597/8BC) marked a period of disillusionment in Judah. Despite their trust in the Temple, the people had not been delivered from the Egyptian invasion. In Smith's words, "the hopes falsely kindled upon the letter of Deuteronomy lay quenched on Megiddo",[125] the scene of Pharaoh-Necoh's victory over Josiah. Liberty from Assyria had only led to captivity to a new tyrant, to Egypt. Jeremiah's faithful denunciation of his people's false confidence led to their conspiring to kill him. Smith is at pains to stress that this popular enmity is occasioned not because the people believe Jeremiah to be speaking lies, but because they recognise the authentic voice of the true "Speaker-for-God". Both priests and people turn against him, and he is contrasted not only with them, but with other pretended prophets (such as Urijah, 26: 20-24). Jeremiah's word is authenticated by symbolic actions and parables, recounted in chapters 13, 17-20 and 35. The parable of the potter (chapter 18) Smith takes as illustrative of Jeremiah's ultimate confidence in divine predestination,[126] and shows that in the breach of the relationship between Israel and her God, it is Israel, and not God, who has strayed. The so-called Oracles of Doom (chapters 7-18, 22, 45) Smith sees as particularly relevant to a nation which has just come through the experience of war - the prophet and his contemporaries are, says Smith, brought "very near".[127] Yet in spite of evident judgement and divine displeasure, the people have remained unmoved.

The years of exile, though hard, were for Jeremiah the beginnings of hope, although the delineation of that hope escapes him. Nonetheless, the purifying

---

[123] Ibid., p160.
[124] LAS, p204.
[125] *Jeremiah*, p165.
[126] Ibid., pp186-7.
[127] Ibid., p230.

effects of Exile were for Jeremiah the seed-bed of hope that Israel and Judah might emerge "re-born".[128] For this to be the case, however, Jeremiah had to maintain a moral certainty in his preaching:

> Jeremiah was compelled by his faith in the holiness and absolute justice of God to proclaim that, however close and dear His age-long relations to Israel had been and however high his designs for them, He was by His nature bound to break from a generation which had spurned his love and his law and proved unworthy of his designs.[129]

And, while other prophets were blinded by patriotism, Jeremiah continued to use the events of history to address the fact of God's deep ethical workings in human history.

As Smith lectures on the story of Jeremiah's soul, he argues that the prophet's faithfulness was born out of sympathy with his people and the high ideals of their religion, and yet out of scepticism as they rejected God, fell back on formalism, and gave ear to false prophets. This has stirred up passion in Jeremiah, which Smith suggests is expressed in his poetry. And what gives his prophecies such colour and effect is his own temper, which, uncontrolled, requires to be rebuked by God (as at 12:5). In Smith's words, "His strength as a poet may have been his weakness as a man".[130] His faith in predestination was not in God's choosing Israel to eternal life, but to service, shaping character for particular ends. God is not a sheer, absolute, unbending will, but a God who works through his people. The fact is that the people have forsaken God, and the prophet is thrown back upon the strength of his own individual moral character, having to distance himself from his people in order to be of help to them. In this way, Smith can talk of the "vicarious agony" of Jeremiah's soul, his "real substitution, his vicarious offering for his people".[131] Jeremiah's highest and greatest glory as a prophet is that in this vicariousness he foreshadows Christ himself, and his sense of the heart of God brings Jeremiah into the very fellowship of Christ's sufferings.[132] For Smith, Jeremiah's is "a prophecy of Christianity which has hardly its equal in the Old Testament".[133]

While the *Expository Times* could say of Smith's *Jeremiah* that "In the best sense of the word this is a conservative book",[134] on the grounds that it was not as extreme in its rejection of portions of the prophets as Duhm, for example, had asserted, others saw it as yet another sign of liberal reductionism. Old

---

[128] Ibid., p 241.
[129] Ibid., p260.
[130] Ibid., p 333.
[131] Ibid., p347.
[132] Ibid., p364.
[133] Ibid., p380, quoting Giesebrecht.
[134] Notes on Literature, *The Expository Times*, Vol XXXV (1923) p196.

Testament scholar Oswald T. Allis, for example, who was no obscurantist, devoted almost fifty pages in *The Princeton Theological Review* to a review of Smith's work, entitled "A Modernistic View of Jeremiah".[135] In it he conceded that Smith's scholarship showed his "artistic temperament, human insight and sympathy, passion for social righteousness, religious ardor and homiletic instinct",[136] but argued that Smith's treatment of the text of Jeremiah betrayed "a confidence in his own ability to distinguish the genuine from the spurious"[137] which introduces a subjective element into his exposition.

Thus while some applauded the work on Jeremiah as conservative, others considered that it yielded too much to speculation and an arbitrary treatment of the Old Testament text. The work certainly bore the hallmarks of Smith's scholarship: a confidence in the critical approach to biblical literature, which blossoms into an assertion that Smith's is the only legitimate approach. But no less important in the work is Smith's attempt to ground a Messianic strain in Old Testament prophecy in a historical and ethical reading of the text.

The Kirk in Scotland

One of the most significant ecclesiastical events which took place during Smith's tenure as Principal of Aberdeen was the reunion of the Scottish Churches in 1929. Its significance lies not only in the fact that the majority of the United Free Church of Scotland united with the Church of Scotland to form the present-day Church of Scotland, but also in the fact that Smith co-authored a volume with John Buchan to mark the event. Interestingly, it was "To the Union of the Scottish Churches" that Smith's *Jeremiah* was dedicated.

The move toward further union was hastened following the House of Lords decision concerning the Free Church Case in 1904. Following the ruling that the properties of the denomination belonged to the minority Free Church of Scotland who had refused to enter the Union of 1900, the United Free Church of Scotland found herself open to approaches from the Church of Scotland towards closer co-operation and eventual union: approaches which were driven by a wide ecumenical impulse. In his biography of John White, a leading Church of Scotland minister and the principal architect of the 1929 re-union, Augustus Muir suggests that these moves had their origins in the Church of Scotland's practical support for the United Free Church of Scotland, when they were disenfranchised as a result of the House of Lords decision:

> Such sympathy, shown at all levels, evoked a quick response among United Free ministers, elders and members, and caused many to wonder whether the

---

[135] O.T. Allis, "A Modernistic View of Jeremiah: The Baird Lecture for 1922", *Princeton Theological Review*, Volume XXIII (1925) 82-132.
[136] Ibid., p83.
[137] Ibid., p85.

two Churches could not come closer together, in one way or another, in spite of constitutional differences.[138]

But the constitutional issues were not inconsequential. Since the Church of Scotland was established by law, any such union between the Church of Scotland and the United Free Church of Scotland required careful planning, and subsequently entailed lengthy and interminable discussion. Parliamentary sanction was required, for, as Professor Duncan Forrester has pointed out, "The reunion of Presbyterian Scotland would only be possible if the Church of Scotland were able to assert its spiritual independence and demonstrate its allegiance to the complementary relationship of Church and State which had been dominant since the Reformation".[139] Disestablishment had been an important plank in the formation of the United Free Church of Scotland, and much discussion in the union negotiations centred around the differing views of the two bodies on this question. The voluntary position of the United Free Church of Scotland would be a barrier to union unless parliamentary legislation could guarantee the spiritual independence of the Church of Scotland.

Union negotiations began in 1909, with each denomination appointing a committee of one hundred. They held their first conference in November 1909, which marked the beginning of two decades of talks. The *Articles Declaratory of the Church of Scotland in Matters Spiritual* were subsequently drafted in 1913, and received the approval of Presbyteries under the Barrier Act in 1919. The way was open then for the Parliamentary settlement of 1921, which recognised the spiritual independence of the Church of Scotland in the Declaratory Articles[140], and the Church of Scotland (Property and Endowments) Act of 1925, which gave financial stability to the National Church.

George Adam Smith himself was heavily involved with University work and was not a key player in the union negotiations. But there is evidence that he found the whole debate over establishment unnecessary after 1900. He writes, for example, in a notebook for 1914-18 under the heading "Church Union" the following notes on the positions of the two Churches:

Sons of the same mother – holding together not only the fundamentals of our religion but the same forms of Church Government and of worship...
No man will say that either establishment by the State or independence of the State is a fundamental principle of his religion ... he would not affirm

---

[138] A. Muir, *John White* (London, 1958) p104.
[139] D. Forrester, *"Ecclesia Scoticana* – Established, Free or National?", *Theology*, Vol CII No 806 (March/April 1999) p84.
[140] Which, in an amusing misprint in Devine, *The Scottish Nation*, p385 are named as the *Declamatory* Articles, a nomenclature which some of the more extreme voluntarys in the United Free Church may have preferred!

that either principle was the mark of the true church as distinct from the false.[141]

It is difficult to contextualise these notes. They may have been Smith's own thoughts – perhaps notes written down in preparation for a speech somewhere – or they may have been written down as he listened to someone else speaking. They might be quotations from a newspaper or some other printed document. But that he wrote them down at all shows that Smith regarded the two Churches as being one in worship, doctrine and government, and that the question of establishment need be no barrier to union. This view is corroborated in Smith's address to elders from both denominations in Aberdeen on 8 February 1926, subsequently published as *The Re-Union of the Two Great Scottish Churches*. In it he states his conviction that

> our two Churches have the same creed, the same standards of doctrine supreme and subordinate, the same orders and system of government, with (I say advisedly) no fundamental distinction between their ideals of national religion and conceptions of the mutual duties of Church and State.[142]

It was not without reason that Smith inserted the *caveat* that he was speaking advisedly in saying that the two denominations made "no fundamental distinction" in their views on establishment. This ought not to be taken to mean that no such distinction existed, for, however much Smith wished to play it down, the establishment question was precisely the issue. And, in spite of Smith's pleadings, it is difficult to agree with him. It was not enough to highlight areas of similarity between the two Churches, when the question of the relation between Church and State was so central and fundamental. Smith, however, argued that since the 1921 Act recognised the spiritual freedom of the Church, and the 1925 Act both cleared the Church of Scotland of the charge of "clinging to the temporalities"[143] and showed State recognition of her legitimate properties, then

> we cannot but recognise, with all respect to those who may differ from us, that it is our bounden duty to press forward to the consummation of that Re-Union in the faith that this is the Will of God...[144]

---

[141] GAS Notebook 1914-1918, notes on "Church Union", NLS Acc 9446 No 61.
[142] GAS, *The Reunion of the Two Great Scottish Churches: An Address to the Aberdeen Elders' Union of the Church of Scotland and the Aberdeen United Free Church Elders' Association 8th February 1926* (London, 1926) p6.
[143] Ibid., p18.
[144] Ibid., p19.

Smith also argued the point on the floor of the United Free Church General Assembly. In seconding the deliverance of the Committee on Conference with the Church of Scotland at the Assembly of 1926, Smith spoke after Principal Martin of New College. Smith said that

> It was certain that all people in that House, of whatever degrees of opinion and of feeling they might be, would acknowledge mutually the sincerity of the convictions differing from their own, and that they were equally in earnest to secure what was best not only for the just interests of their own Church, but for the fulfilment of their fathers' ideals, prayers and struggles, which had been both for religious unity and religious freedom – best, too, for the spiritual needs of the Scottish people in the vastly altered conditions of their distribution throughout the country."[145]

Pressing both the desire for Church Union, the State's recognition of the Church of Scotland's spiritual independence and the great opportunity which now existed for realising a great dream, Smith urged the anti-Unionists within the Assembly to bring "the rich fruitfulness of their common voluntaryism into the life of the united, the free and the national church".[146] For Smith the question of union was supreme, and the common ground between the Churches ought to be emphasised, rather than the differences between them. As a member of Lord Haldane's Special Commission to discuss the spiritual and temporal questions involved in the Union, Smith was aware of the issues. But he seems too ready to bury the past, and to make establishment or disestablishment an open question.

In *The Kirk in Scotland*, Smith's pen is employed to paint a picture of the first Union Assembly in his distinctive felicitous prose. Smith describes the last separate Assemblies held on 24 May 1929, the Church of Scotland Assembly under the Moderatorship of Dr Joseph Mitchell, and that of the United Free Church under the Moderatorship of Principal Martin. On 2 October 1929, both Assemblies were constituted, and then walked in procession to the High Kirk of Edinburgh, where a service was held in the presence of the Duke and Duchess of York; the Duke of York would later act as Lord High Commissioner to the united Assembly. The choice of Moderator of the new Assembly was the principal architect of the Union, the Rev John White, who "received a full-hearted ovation as he took his place in the Moderator's Chair".[147] Smith summarises White's address to the Assembly, during which White emphasised that the foremost task of the new Church was "the moral, social and religious well-being of the Scottish people".[148] There follows a description of the

---

[145] PDGAUFCS, Friday 4 June 1926, p203.
[146] Ibid., p205.
[147] Muir, *White*, p265.
[148] GAS, *The Kirk in Scotland* (London, 1930) p158.

delegates present from other churches, and the main items of business transacted. Smith lays emphasis on a speech by Professor Paterson, which referred to the bodies who still lay outwith the pale of the national Church of Scotland: the Free Presbyterian Church, the Free Church of Scotland and, now, a minority of the United Free Church of Scotland who had not entered the union. The latter group proved a great disappointment both to the architects of the Union, and to the majority United Free Church. But they refused to concede their voluntary principles, and in a rallying speech as Moderator of the continuing United Free Church Assembly in Glasgow in October 1929, as the marriage of the two large denominations was taking place in Edinburgh, James Barr said that "that old Voluntary banner of ours, the symbol as John Locke described it of 'equal and impartial liberty' ... we once again as a Church fling proudly to the breeze ...".[149] This position was arguably more faithful to that of the United Free Church in 1900, although much removed from the position of the Disruption Free Church in 1843.[150] Once again, however, Scottish Presbyterianism had shown its penchant for fracturing.

Smith closes his account of the Union Assembly with a record of what he describes as "three great addresses": one by Dr Henry Sloan Coffin of New York, Joseph Oldham, who had served for long on the foreign mission field, and Randall Davidson, Archbishop of Canterbury from 1903 to 1928. The choice of speakers was clearly an attempt to foster a spirit of ecumenism and co-operation, as all three had been involved in ecumenical work at some level. Smith concludes:

> Amid all the sacred joys of these great days – their precious memories and richer hopes and visions, our gratitude to our leaders, and the uplifting of our fellowship in faith and prayer – the strongest impression upon us as we left was that of the deeply searching power of the addresses we had heard. We came back to the world with a new conscience of our shortcomings in the past, and of the tasks awaiting our faith in the days to come.[151]

Conclusion

Smith concluded his term as Principal as a minister in the reunited Church of Scotland. In 1931, as we have noted, the City of Aberdeen honoured Smith by

---

[149] Quoted in James Barr *The United Free Church of Scotland* (London 1934) p184.

[150] This fact was not lost on the island of Scalpay, in the Western Isles, where almost to a man the people returned to the Free Church of Scotland after 1929. They had entered the Union of 1900 "on the assurance that the Free Church Unionists would be taking the full testimony of the Free Church of Scotland with them" (G.N.M. Collins *The Heritage of our Fathers* [Edinburgh, 1974] p155), but they altered their opinion on this after the re-union was accomplished.

[151] *The Kirk in Scotland*, pp211-2.

conferring on him the Freedom of the City. The Speech of Lord Provost Rust summarised Smith's stature:

> The Principal is not only a man of wide humanity and great personal gifts; he is an erudite scholar of international reputation. In his great classic on Isaiah and in his monumental work on the geography of the Holy Land, the Principal has opened up the Old Testament and made it a living book. As an interpreter of the greatest of the Hebrew prophets he stands in splendid isolation ... [152]

Nor was this an exaggeration. By the time Smith retired from the Principalship of Aberdeen University in 1935, he had secured a place of world-wide repute as a biblical scholar and as an accomplished statesman. He had received honorary degrees from the Universities of Edinburgh, Aberdeen, Cambridge, Oxford, Sheffield and Durham. His work on the prophets of the Old Testament laid a foundation on which biblical scholars are building, even if from the dizzy ramparts of modern scholarship the foundation seems very far away.

Other honours and duties came his way in the closing years of Smith's Principalship. The presentation of his portrait was in itself a glowing tribute to his work. Painted by Sir Willam Orpen, it was presented to the University in March 1928. And although his wife confessed to not liking the expression on his face,[153] there was no denying the honour. "If you ask me," said Lord Alness in making the presentation, "why it was decided to present his portrait to Sir George, I should be disposed to reply – because of what he has done, and because of what he is".[154] A subsequent portrait was painted by J.B. Souter, a brother of Alexander Souter, Professor of Humanity at Aberdeen, and a close colleague of Smith's. The portrait was presented to Smith from the Aberdeen Incorporated Trades, of which he had been a patron since 1924.

Smith counted it a particular honour to be chosen President of the Sir Walter Scott Club in 1930, particularly because of a Royal High School connection between Walter Scott and Alexander Adam (Smith's great grand-uncle).

A more poignant duty fell to Smith that same year, when he was asked to unveil the Memorial erected at Loos by the Imperial War Graves Commission. Loos being the scene of his son, George's, death, the ceremony must have had its own peculiar difficulties. But Smith dedicated the memorial

---

[152] Speech of Lord Provost Rust in conferring the Freedom of the City of Aberdeen on George Adam Smith, 7 October 1931, NLS Acc 9446 No 219.

[153] LAS, p210: "We valued most deeply the kindness and generosity of our friends, but the portrait itself disappointed us. It is a wonderful piece of painting – a study in black and silver of the Vice-Chancellor's robe and cap – but the expression on the face is hard and stern, and not one that is familiar".

[154] "The Principal's Portrait", *Aberdeen University Review*, Vol 15 No 45 (July 1928) p228.

> To the glory of God and in grateful memory of 20,598 soldiers who gave their lives in the Battles of Loos and Bethune ... praying that, inspired by the example of these our brothers, we who remain may give our lives in service and sacrifice for the progress of humanity, so that we may not be ashamed when we meet with them beyond the grave.[155]

One of Smith's final, and significant, duties as Principal was to host a meeting of the British Association for the Advancement of Science in Aberdeen on 5-12 September 1934. The occasion was widely reported in the media, and served as an occasion for Smith to make a final *apologia* for his approach to biblical scholarship. The sermon Smith preached before the British Association, on 9 September 1934 in the West Church of St Nicholas on Psalm 121:1-2, was significant for two reasons: first, because it was broadcast over the radio, and second, because of what it reveals concerning Smith's philosophy of biblical criticism. Outlining the disservice done by theologians who have baulked at the theory of Darwinian evolution, Smith asserted that

> from first to last the Old Testament is the tale of the gradual development, not only intellectual but moral, of the conception of God from being that of a mere national deity to that of the Father and Creator of all mankind, from being that of a God of wrath irreconcilable, to that of One of infinite pity and grace ... there is no just reason for supposing that evolution means the denial of a personal God, or need lead to any new opposition between science and religion. On the contrary, religion is here, as elsewhere, deeply indebted to science.[156]

According to his wife's memoir, "several people said or wrote that they thought George had reached his best in that sermon".[157] That, of course, is a matter of taste; but what is indisputable is the fact that the sentiments of the sermon reveal Smith's mature reflection on the relationship between biblical scholarship and progress being made in other departments of learning and science. Rounding on those who said that evolutionary theory was the enemy of religion, Smith laid emphasis on the view which he regarded to be at the heart of biblical criticism: that evolutionary theory is the very essence of a critical appreciation of the biblical narrative. The development of religion, which he claims to be fundamental in the Old Testament, does not stand in antipathy to science, but is of the nature of science, and learns from science. Smith's swan-

---

[155] LAS, p231; *Aberdeen University Review*, Vol 18 No 52 (November 1930) p83.

[156] Presscutting from *The Glasgow Herald*, 10 September 1934, in NLS Acc 9446 No 219.

[157] LAS, p241.

song was as much an encouragement for the future of the discipline as it was an apologetic for a lifetime of devotion to the cause of biblical criticism.

Yet, once again, this is both the strength and the weakness of Smith's scholarship. To the British Association, Smith's argument was a concession to science; biblical criticism stood in its debt, and deferred to its conclusions. At that level, he can legitimately claim a place for biblical criticism on the stage of contemporary academic advance. Yet at another level it is arguable that the converse is true: that the fact that his is a *scientific* approach limits its usefulness to all but the devotees of the new learning. It requires an acceptance of Smith's presuppositions, and a similar mastery of the theological terrain, to make the Old Testament of use to the modern mind, which was the professed aim of his scholarship from the beginning. But at last, one cannot help wondering whether lesser mortals could move with such ease around the field. While Smith's own academic status is unquestioned – it is true that he stands "in splendid isolation" – that very fact marks both the beginning and the end of his scholarship. Master craftsman though he was, he had few apprentices of similar calibre.

But Alexander Gray recalled that back of all Smith's scholarship, learning and erudition lay one simple fact: "in the end we get as near as possible to the core of things if we fall back on the simple, and yet majestic language of one of his own prophets, and say of him that he was a man who walked humbly with his God. For therein lies the essence of all that George Adam Smith was and did".[158]

---

[158] Alexander Gray, "George Adam Smith", *The Fusion*, p155.

CHAPTER 7

George Adam Smith: Retirement and Retrospect

After an association of some twenty-six years, it was easy neither for the University of Aberdeen nor for George Adam Smith himself to sever the link between them. He was anxious, however, to pass his twenty-fifth year as Principal and intended to retire in 1934 (although his wife states that she had wanted him to retire earlier[1]). In the event, the fact that Aberdeen University was to host the 1934 meeting of the British Association persuaded him to postpone his retirement until after that prestigious event, by which time Smith was almost eighty years of age. The University Court of 9 July 1935 minuted the following:

> Throughout all these years – years which included the crisis and strain and bereavements of a terrible war – the Principal has guided the affairs of the University with a loyalty, with an unsurpassed devotion, with a prudence, with a receptiveness to new conditions and new demands, and with a width of human sympathy which have been of inestimable value to the University itself and will have earned the deep and abiding gratitude of all its members ...
> In regretfully accepting the termination of an association which has been so fruitful in its results for the University and so uniformly happy in its personal relations, the Court desires to assure the Principal of its high regard and esteem, of its warm acknowledgement of the part which Lady Adam Smith has taken in the social life of the University, and of its sincere wishes for their happiness in the years of retirement which lie before them.[2]

In addition to paying its tribute to Smith, the Senate also marked the occasion by awarding an honorary Doctor of Laws degree to Lilian Smith, as a token of appreciation for the work she had performed during the long term of the Principalship. "My husband," she writes, "was more delighted about this than any of the honours that had come to him, and, needless to say, I was very pleased and so were all the family".[3]

---

[1] LAS, p241.
[2] Quoted in *Aberdeen University Review*, Vol 23 No 67 (November 1935) p53.
[3] LAS, p245.

And so the long Principalship – the longest in the University's modern history – came to a close. It was a significant term of office, described by Lord Provost Alexander at a meeting of Aberdeen University Court in the following manner:

> It had witnessed changes and expansions in many directions. It had seen the number of students rise from 1007 in 1909 to 1272 in 1935, it had seen the teaching staff of the University grow from 24 professors and 19 lecturers in 1909 to 33 professors, 3 readers and 66 lecturers in 1935. It had seen the erection of new buildings and the renovation and improvement of existing buildings. It had seen the foundation and rise of new sister, or rather daughter, institutions, which had brought fresh strength to the University. It had seen many changes in the curriculum and in the internal economy of the University. And it had witnessed the crisis and strain of a terrible war.[4]

By the time of Lilian's graduation, in December 1935, the Smiths had moved from Aberdeen to Balerno, a small village South-West of Edinburgh. There is a reference to Balerno, and to the Smiths, in the memoirs of English Professor John Dover Wilson, who moved to the same village when he retired from King's College, London in 1936. Of Balerno he says

> It is an ugly village, as many Scottish villages are, lying just across the Water of Leith, and communicating with Edinburgh, when I first knew it, by a village road branching off the main route to Lanark along which our house lay. Many of the villagers' houses were most insanitary; and indeed the slums of Balerno were worse than some of the slums of London of that date. Yet how genial – merry, indeed – were the dwellers in those slum houses; and how kindhearted and ready to help in any emergency![5]

Lilian paints no such negative picture of her new residence. While admitting that her new home was "a modern house with no particular beauty",[6] she says that this was compensated for by a view of "the long, undulating line of the Pentland Hills".[7] Their son, Alick, who would later be given a life peerage and assume the title Lord Balerno,[8] was of great help to his aged parents in securing this residence for them near his own. Lilian's acknowledgement that "Alick

---

[4] "The Principal's Retirement", *Aberdeen University Review*, Vol 22 No 66 (July 1935) p263.
[5] J. Dover Wilson, *Milestones on the Dover Road* (London, 1969) p145.
[6] LAS, p246.
[7] Ibid.
[8] The Baronetcy of Balerno became extinct with his death in 1984. Alick was the father of the Scots MP Alick Laidlaw Buchanan-Smith, who died in 1991.

was my right hand in preparing Sweethillocks"[9] may be a tacit indication of Smith's failing health. The home in Balerno was refitted to house Smith's books and memorabilia, and he and Lilian settled into a tranquil routine there: "in the morning a walk to the village of Balerno, making friends in the little shops and chatting with the housewives he met or the children coming from school; another walk in the afternoon along the country roads with Micky, his unfailing companion".[10] Micky, the pet dog, was named after Micah the prophet, as a previous canine companion had been named Jerry, for Jeremiah!

In his memoirs Wilson goes on to recall seeing the Smiths attend church in Currie, a neighbouring village. Occupying the same gallery in the church, Wilson says that the Smiths had arrived "a couple of years before we did and became great friends of ours".[11] In her memoir of these days, Lilian quotes from a letter subsequently received from Wilson, in which he spoke of his thrill of being introduced to Smith, of whom he recalls:

The distinguished scholar, the world-famous preacher, the writer as well known among soldiers as among theologians, the Vice-Chancellor of an ancient University, was as direct and simple-minded as a child; he was, in fact, as I have found with the few really great men it has been my fortune to know, without complexes. I doubt whether it ever occurred to him to think about himself.[12]

Such an assessment could probably not have been made forty years earlier, when Smith had been at the peak of his intellectual strength. The reality was that he was now spent, and if a child-like simplicity characterised him, it was in no small part due to his increasing senility. Although his wife says that his lack of energy was because he was "too tired"[13] to do further work, her biography furnishes evidence that he was beginning to lose his grasp of events. Given his advanced age, as well as the lack of intellectual activity and literary output following his retirement, it may be that Smith was suffering from some form of senile dementia which became more acute in the last two years of his life.

Lilian says that she nursed a hope that Smith would write his memoirs during his retirement years, but this was not realised. The loss is, no doubt, considerable, and may itself be an indicator of increasing incapacity. One small work that did see the light of day after his retirement was a collection of poems which had been written at various points during his life. A copy of this collection, published by Aberdeen University Press in 1936 under the title

---

[9] LAS, p245. Sweethillocks was the name of the home to which the Smiths retired, and was called after a farm in Moray which Lilian knew as a child.
[10] LAS, p246. .
[11] Wilson, p147.
[12] LAS, p250.
[13] Ibid., p248.

Verses Grave and Gay, was donated to Aberdeen University Library by Lilian Smith, with the following hand-written note inside the front cover:

> ...knowing that whoever reads them will understand that they were gathered together in a haphazard way by the writer just as an amusement in his old age – and for the interest and amusement of his children and grandchildren.[14]

The earliest poems in the collection date to 1876, with a composition entitled "Where is our Hebrew?", reflecting on the William Robertson Smith controversy. Other poems were personal in nature, and written for purposes of entertainment rather than edification. Apart from these, however, no further literary material was published by Smith during his retirement years.

Smith did, however, conduct some services during retirement, and represented the Church of Scotland at major functions, such as the funeral of King George V in 1936. He also conducted a Jubilee service of Thanksgiving that year in connection with the Edinburgh battalion of the Boys' Brigade. Lilian states: "his very last public appearance was at the Annual Service of the Boys' Brigade in the Usher Hall on 27th March 1938".[15] That year saw him pay a return visit to King's College for the dedication of stained-glass windows.

Lilian Smith notes that a decline in Smith's health was noticeable following the celebration of their Golden Wedding Anniversary in 1939. Although he retained an interest in family activities – he had been thrilled, for example, that his daughters had shared his love for mountaineering[16] - and although the Smiths enjoyed some leisurely holidays with their children and grandchildren, his mind began to lose its sharpness. 1939 marked the outbreak of the Second World War, of which Lilian says that "George did not fully realise the present war; it puzzled and perplexed him as he tried to understand what it was all about".[17] Given the prominent role Smith played during the course of the first conflict, his failure to grasp the issues involved in the second is a sign of deterioration. Even when news came of the death of their daughter, Kathleen, in New York, in 1941, Lilian writes, rather sadly, that "he scarcely seemed to

---

[14] Handwritten note by LAS, in frontispiece of the edition of GAS *Verses Grave and Gay* (Aberdeen, 1936) presented to the University of Aberdeen. Now housed in the Special Collections Department of Aberdeen University.
[15] LAS, p249.
[16] One of his poems from 1929 was dedicated to his youngest daughters, and entitled "To JBAS and MEAS", and contained the lines:
> These peaks I scaled these [five and] forty years ago
> Their rocks, moraines, their glaciers, fields of snow...
> I leave them all unto my daughters twain,
> To conquer for their father once again...

(*Verses Grave and Gay*, p34).
[17] LAS, p257.

grieve".[18] "Small things," she says, "pleased him so much, while the bigger ones passed him by".[19]

In 1941, Percy Hodder Williams, of Hodder and Stoughton, wrote Smith to inform him that since its first appearance in 1894, Smith's *Historical Geography of the Holy Land* had sold 35,237 copies.[20] He responded by letter, saying "It is a great satisfaction to me to know that my work has been useful and appreciated".[21] At the same time, Smith was wrestling with a sense of utter uselessness, which was accelerated by his senility and gradual detachment. "I'm no use any more," he said to his wife on one occasion in 1941.[22] The depressive nature of his thinking at this point was lifted momentarily by letters such as that from his publishers.

His last illness, however, over the winter of 1941/2, left him extremely weakened. Lilian was his constant companion and nurse. Smith passed away peacefully on Tuesday 3 March 1942. Lilian quotes the comment of Dr David Stewart, their minister at the time: "It was a gracious ending ... one in which his good genius did not fail him, or, as he himself would rather have put it, in this as in much else God had been good to him".[23]

Smith's death was reported in the national press, and obituaries appeared in a plethora of journals. Letters of condolence poured in to Lilian Adam Smith following her husband's death, and show the extraordinarily wide influence of his life. There were letters, for example, from the Royal High School Club, the Rowett Research Institute, the Royal Incorporation of Architects in Scotland, the Edinburgh Medical Missionary Society, the Glasgow University Oriental Society, the Scottish Mountaineering Club, the Boys' Brigade and the Aberdeen Savings Bank.[24] The range of these letters shows that Smith's influence was by no means confined to the narrow circles of his ecclesiastical commitment.

For many preachers trained under his tutelage, Smith's death marked the end of an era. James Black, the minister of St George's West, Edinburgh, for example, wrote that

> George Adam (as we familiarly called him) was himself always young, and he even imparted his perennial enthusiasm in his own subject to careless students ... I can picture him round that raised contour map, where he so often gathered us, enthusiastically explaining why such-and-such an

---

[18] Ibid.
[19] Ibid.
[20] P. Hodder Williams to GAS, 30 July 1941, NLS Acc 9446 No 144.
[21] GAS to P. Hodder Williams, 5 September 1941, NLS Acc 9446 No 144.
[22] Quoted in LAS, p258.
[23] LAS, p259.
[24] These, and others, are collected with the George Adam Smith papers at NLS Acc 9446 numbers 75 and 76.

expedition went this way and not that. It was all so infectious and so natural. And it made preachers.[25]

Perhaps that was the greatest tribute that could be paid to him. While some recalled the power of the early Queen's Cross ministry, and others the training they received in the Free Church College, Glasgow, and still others remarked on the administrative genius of the Principal of Aberdeen, Smith had certainly inspired would-be preachers. His abiding influence was realised in the perpetuation of the liberal evangelical pulpit in Scotland. In a surprisingly short obituary in the Church of Scotland's denominational magazine, *Life and Work*, the writer, "G.C.", surmised:

> Many tributes have been paid to the fine ministries of his earlier years, to his distinguished service as Principal of the University of Aberdeen, and to the books which he has left; but, perhaps more than in any of these ways, it was as the inspirer of successions of young men studying for the ministry that his greatest service to the Church was rendered.[26]

Smith was buried in Currie Churchyard on 6 March 1942. A memorial service was held in St Giles' Cathedral the following day, at which New Testament scholar Professor William Manson of New College gave a tribute to Smith's work. Manson said that while Smith's work would be eulogised and praised, "what rises before us in this hour and commands our reverence and gratitude is the man himself, as his spirit impressed itself on us ... In George Adam Smith the work has been in a peculiar sense the objectification of the man".[27] Another service was held at King's College Chapel, Aberdeen, on Sunday 8 March. Professor George Henderson, then Professor of Church History at the University of Aberdeen, spoke at this service, describing Smith in the words of Job 33:23 as "an interpreter, one among a thousand". Describing the practical results of Smith's biblical criticism, Henderson said that as a result of it

> people got more out of their Bible; they found in it more richly the power of God unto salvation, and so Biblical Criticism came to be recognised as in fact an aid to devotion as well as an instrument of scientific enquiry.[28]

---

[25] James Black to LAS, 5 March 1942, NLS Acc 9446 No 74.
[26] "Sir George Adam Smith, DD, LLD, DLitt,", *Life and Work*, Vol XIII (April 1942) p56.
[27] "Sir George Adam Smith: Tribute by Professor Manson", *The Scotsman*, 9 March 1942.
[28] "George Adam Smith: Scholar, Teacher and Christian Humanist", *Aberdeen Bon-Accord and Northern Pictorial*, 12 March 1942, NLS Acc 9446 No 73, also quoted in *Aberdeen University Review* Vol 29 No 86, p97.

It was from this point of view that Professor Norman Porteous mourned Smith's passing in an obituary in the *Palestine Exploration Quarterly*. The science of biblical archaeology had, he said, "lost one of its most distinguished representatives and biblical scholarship an expositor of renown".[29] This note was also struck in the most thorough of the obituaries to appear in 1942, that by Professor S.A. Cook in the *Proceedings of the British Academy*. Cook said that in topographical research, Smith "stood above all others of his time",[30] and that what was "of the greatest importance to biblical students was his first-hand knowledge of Oriental life and conditions, coupled with critical insight".[31] Cook is ready to acknowledge that Smith's scholarship was not exhaustive, and that even within the scope of his lifetime certain lines of enquiry had advanced beyond Smith, but the academic world mourned the passing of an outstanding scientist in the field of biblical studies.

Others had a more personal story to write. Adam Philip was a friend of long standing, whose letter to Lilian recalled that Smith was "full of vitality, keenness", and highlighted "the enthusiasm which he brought into everything he did, climbing mountains, teaching Hebrew, studying Palestine, lecturing, preaching".[32] Archibald Main of the Department of Ecclesiastical History at the University of Glasgow simply said that Smith "came into my life many years ago, and I've never forgotten him ... He was a great man".[33]

In Retrospect

Smith cut a large figure in a movement of change within the late nineteenth- and early twentieth-century Scottish church. Along with other scholars, such as A.B. Davidson, W.R. Smith, Marcus Dods and James Denney, George Adam Smith represented a generation for whom evangelical scholarship in Scotland had to respond both to scientific advance (notably the Darwinian challenge to biblical faith) and to the burgeoning critical scholarship on the continent of Europe. Smith also, however, belonged to a Church which was committed to the Westminster Confession of Faith, with its clearly defined statements regarding the inspiration and inerrancy of the Bible, along with clear Calvinistic emphases in its doctrine of the atonement. The primary difficulty before these scholars was a harmonisation of their academic research with their ecclesiastical credalism. For one wing of the Church, the Confessional position was clear, and anything that deviated from it was heresy. And while the heresy-hunters of late nineteenth-century Scottish Presbyterianism have tended to

---

[29] N.W. Porteous, "Sir George Adam Smith", *Palestine Exploration Quarterly,* Jan-Apr 1943, p68.
[30] S.A. Cook, "George Adam Smith", *Proceedings of the British Academy*, 1942, p340.
[31] Ibid.
[32] Adam Philip to LAS, 5 March 1942, NLS Acc 9446 No74.
[33] Archibald Main to LAS, 5 March 1942, NLS Acc 9446 No 74.

receive a bad press,[34] they were, at the very least, acting in accordance with the letter of their credal position. For a more liberal wing, however, the Church had to accommodate the scholarship by some form of revision; it is no surprise, therefore, to find a move for credal revision (centering around the Declaratory Act) going hand in hand with the advances in scholarship. If the Church was to retain its commitment both to its creed *and* its scholarship, harmonisation was well-nigh impossible. Something had to give.

Few students of the period share the extreme view of Alistair Hunter that it was a mistake from the outset to imagine that the Scottish church could accommodate the scholarship it was producing. According to Hunter

> historical criticism and traditional doctrine are not in ready harmony. Until the churches recognise this uncomfortable fact, they will be condemned to an involuntary support of those Free Church doctrines of inspiration and authority which William Robertson Smith and George Adam Smith endorsed wholeheartedly ... The church today loses out to the conservatives because of its evident pusillanimity, its craven refusal to ask serious questions.[35]

For Hunter, therefore, there can be no accommodation. George Adam Smith operates on two different levels simultaneously: as an evangelical (via his churchmanship) and as a scholar (via his critical approach to Scripture). But on this thesis, there is no point at which these merge: Smith's evangelical conservatism and his academic liberalism run like parallel lines which never meet. The significance of this is to be found in Hunter's view that only by jettisoning its traditional doctrines can the church today accept the insights of biblical criticism. Alistair Hunter at least recognises that our view of Smith's scholarship is a matter not only for historical research, but has a bearing on the nature of confessional scholarship still.

Nonetheless, it is difficult to imagine George Adam Smith agreeing with Hunter on this point. While his detractors were arguing that because of his espousal of higher criticism, Smith had compromised his evangelicalism, Smith himself was remonstrating that only by accepting the insights of criticism could a meaningful evangelicalism emerge. It was *criticism* which had, he argued, made the Old Testament accessible. The Declaratory Act provided the latitude

---

[34] In his lecture on William Robertson Smith's *The Prophets of Israel*, for example, Robert Carroll speaks of "the reactionary conservatism which drives the philistinism of current Presbyterian politics", and continues: "so my sympathies are all with Smith in his crucifixion last century. 'Twas ever thus!" (R.P. Carroll, "The Biblical Prophets as Apologists for the Christian Religion" in W. Johnstone (ed.) *William Robertson Smith: Essays in Reassessment* [Sheffield, 1995] p148, n.1).

[35] A.G. Hunter, "The Indemnity: William Robertson Smith and George Adam Smith", in Johnstone, *Willliam Robertson Smith*, p65.

necessary for the domestication of higher criticism within the Church, and in Smith's view, old barriers of verbal inspiration and biblical inerrancy could be torn down.

Scholars have laboured over how to characterise this change, and how to assess Smith's role in it. A variety of epithets appears in modern studies: the *Dictionary of Scottish Church History and Theology*, for example, describes the work of Smith and others as "believing criticism" in an article of that title.[36] Kenneth R. Ross, in his work on the changing relationship between church and creed in this period, prefers to speak of the "New Evangelism",[37] while David Bebbington cites Smith as an example of "liberal Evangelicalism".[38] Various other terms are used to describe the same phenomenon: "the new criticism" (Drummond and Bulloch[39]), "evangelical criticism" (Mark Noll[40]), "devout criticism" (N.M. de S. Cameron[41]), "the new scholarship" (A.C. Cheyne[42]), "believing criticism" (James Macleod[43]).

To be sure, it is difficult to find adequate terminology, if only because the scholarship of men like Smith covered so wide a field. Indeed, in Smith's case the learning, as we have seen, straddled an amazing variety of themes and academic disciplines. It is important to look, therefore, at Smith's commitments, all of which informed his work and contribution to Scottish intellectual life.

He was committed, first, to the Scottish church. It is impossible – and therefore quite wrong – to assess Smith's work apart from his churchmanship. He was, both literally and metaphorically, a child of the Disruption Free Church, born into a missionary family, a child whose birth symbolised the evangelistic commitment of the Free Church of Scotland in the middle of the nineteenth century. In later life, Smith's letters to his father were, as we have seen, frequent and passionate. His close relationship with his father, who returned to Scotland to become Secretary of the Foreign Missions Board of the

---

[36] See the article "Believing Criticism" in Cameron, N.M. de S. (ed.), *Dictionary of Scottish Church History and Theology* (Edinburgh, 1993) p69.

[37] K.R. Ross, *Church and Creed in Scotland: the Free Church Case 1900-1904 and its origins* (Edinburgh, 1988) p169.

[38] D.W. Bebbington, *Evangelicalism in Modern Britain: A History from the 1730s to the 1980s* (Edinburgh, 1994) pp184-5.

[39] A.L. Drummond, and J. Bulloch, *The Church in Late Victorian Scotland 1874-1900* (Edinburgh, 1978) p259.

[40] M. Noll, *Between Faith and Criticism: Evangelicals, Scholarship and the Bible* (Leicester, 1991) p67.

[41] N.M. de S. Cameron, *Biblical Higher Criticism and the Defense of Infallibilism in 19th century Britain* (New York, 1987) p266.

[42] A.C. Cheyne, *Studies in Scottish Church History* (Edinburgh, 1999) p133.

[43] J.L. Macleod, *The Second Disruption: The Free Church in Victorian Scotland and the Origins of the Free Presbyterian Church* (Edinburgh, 2000) p72.

Free and United Free Church of Scotland, was a major factor in Smith's denominational affiliation and commitment.

Throughout his career (and particularly at the point of the near trial for heresy in 1902), Smith made it clear that he had no interest in academic work for its own sake. His inaugural address as Old Testament Professor, as well as the Lyman Beecher lectures at Yale, made it clear that his main interest was in scholarship for the sake of the pulpit. A master of the craft of preaching himself, Smith was concerned that his prowess in learning, and his propagation of the critical view of Scripture, should be harnessed to the pulpit. Further, it was his persuasion that only a critical view of Scripture could make the Gospel appealing to the mind of his generation, awash as it was with the scientific principles of evolutionary development. This was an age of new ideas and new philosophies. For the church to stay in the race, it was necessary that the Gospel be made relevant and appealing; and it was Smith's conviction that the study of the Scriptures by methods of scientific criticism could uncover a word from God for contemporary man.

But Smith's ecclesiastical commitment spanned three denominations: the Free Church of Scotland (from 1880-1900), the United Free Church of Scotland (from 1900-1929) and the Church of Scotland (from 1929 until his death). Smith believed that the reunited national Church which emerged in 1929 represented the principles of the Free Church of 1843, although it is difficult to agree with this assessment. The Disruption Church had an unqualified commitment to the Westminster Confession of Faith, and was formed on the basis of the Establishment Principle. By the end of the century, Smith's was one voice among many calling for disestablishment and for creed revision, which came in the form of the Declaratory Act of 1892, and the Declaratory Articles of 1921. It is difficult, if not impossible, to argue that the denomination in which Smith ended his days was the same as the one in which he had begun them.

Nonetheless, Smith believed in the church as an institution, and was a tireless ambassador for his denomination(s). He believed that the church had something to offer society, both in times of peace and in times of war. A passionate defender of the social gospel in the late nineteenth century, he constantly urged the Church to remember the poor, and his relationship with Andrew Carnegie and the Carnegie Trust casts an interesting light on these principles. There appears to be a tension in Smith's thinking on the relationship between church and scholarship. He contrasts, for example, the liberality of the American churches in their support of theological colleges with the frugality of the Scottish church in this connection. But there is a change of emphasis: while his earlier concern is for academic support of the church as an institution, his later commitment is to church support of the theological academy. While Smith, therefore, was the consummate ecclesiastic, his desire was for the church to support its scholars, and theological scholarship to serve the church's ministry. So while Chalmers and other Disruption leaders had campaigned in the mid-nineteenth century for Establishment on the basis of the mutual support of church and state, by the end of the century Smith was arguing for disestablishment and the mutual support of church and academy. This explains some of the tensions which run throughout his career, as the church found it difficult to accommodate the new learning which he represented, and the scholarship in which he was engaged did not command the universal approbation of his denomination. Smith was correct to identify in his Yale lectures that a war had been going on between new insights and old theories, but he was too hasty when he concluded that the war had been fought and won. As far as the ideological war was concerned, Smith in actual fact saw no cessation of hostilities in his lifetime. What he saw was a widening of the field of conflict – a re-constituted and re-united Church in Scotland whose theological commitment to Calvinism was hedged around by articles declaratory. What emerges at the end of Smith's career is a church broad enough to accommodate a variety of opinions, but, arguably, one which was not sure of what she believed.

There is something else. It is possible to trace an evolution within Smith's churchmanship itself. A defender of the principles of the social gospel, Smith's early church career was very much concerned with the needs of the poor. As a student he had been involved in the home mission movement, and both in Aberdeen and Glasgow he expended time and energy in the social cause of the church. Yet his career was always a middle-class one, and it is arguable that the new church at Queen's Cross, which Smith pastored early in his career, was erected on the wealth of an emerging middle-class suburban society. And while Smith's preaching, no doubt, was instrumental in attracting a large congregation, the church was, in the 1880s, a fashionable middle-class institution. In evaluating Scotland's subsequent religious history, Callum Brown suggests that the Victorian and Edwardian periods saw "the unchallenged hegemony of evangelicalism ... confronted by secular progress in the form of the labour movement and state welfarism"[44], as a result of which "the mainstream Protestant churches were fairly sharply separated from the working classes"[45]. This is exemplified in Smith's own career, by the end of which he has become one of society's elite himself. In his study of "Elite Society" in Aberdeen, Dr I.G.C. Hutchison cites Smith as an example of a University figure whose early career was largely divorced from civic life. One result, Hutchison argues, of the growth of the University was that many professors resided outwith Old Aberdeen, thus breaking down barriers between the academy and the city.[46] By the time Smith was granted the Freedom of the

---

[44] C.J. Brown, *The Social History of Religion in Scotland since 1730* (London, 1987) p250.
[45] Ibid.
[46] See I.G.C. Hutchison "Elite Society" in *Aberdeen 1800-2000: A New History* (Aberdeen, 2001) especially the section "The University Elite", pages 392-3.

City of Aberdeen in 1931, a marked change had taken place between the early and the later days of Smith's career. He had moved away from the ideals of the social gospel to full participation in the higher echelons of civic and social life. It is arguable that this paralleled the evolution of the Scottish church during the period, which became less concerned with the amelioration of society and more involved in matters of state and civic life. Smith's churchmanship over the course of his career is unquestioned; what requires further analysis is the extent to which his career represented a change in the social position and status of the Scottish church, not to speak of the changes in what the church perceived her priority to be.

Secondly, Smith was committed to evangelicalism. Indeed, it was his contention that "in this country at the present day nearly every leader in Old Testament criticism ... is a believer in evangelical Christianity".[47] The content, however, of Smith's evangelical beliefs, is difficult to ascertain. Apart from a late collection of his Queen's Cross sermons, published in 1904, Smith's writings were the products of his academic, specialist interests. However, it is possible to glean from some of these writings what Smith regarded as the essential elements of a truly evangelical faith.

It is clear that the revivalistic and evangelistic campaigns of Moody and Sankey had a profound effect on George Adam Smith. As has been noted in Chapter 1, Smith devotes several pages of his biography of Henry Drummond to these campaigns and their influence. In assessing the overall effects of the Mission on the life of Scotland, Smith argued that both the preaching of the evangelists and that of Drummond helped to recover a contemporary evangelicalism which was rooted in the Bible and was suited to modern life:

> This Mission lifted thousands and tens of thousands of persons already trained in relation to a more clear and decided consciousness of their Christianity. It baptized crowds in the Spirit of Jesus, and opened the eyes of innumerable men and women to the reality of the great facts of repentance and conversion, to the possibility of self-control and of peace by God's Spirit ... today one can point to ministers in many churches, and to laymen in charge of the municipial and social interests of almost every town, who were first roused to faith, and first enlisted in the cause of God and of their fellowmen by the evangelists of 1873-75.[48]

This is not simply the reporting of an event; it is a statement of Smith's own evangelical commitment. So too is his observation that "the Great Mission of 1873-75 had quickened ... the practical use of the Bible"[49]; for Smith this emphasis on the Bible was also fundamental. In a letter to his father, in which

---

[47] GAS, *The Preaching of the Old Testament to the Age* (London, 1893) p33.
[48] GAS, *The Life of Henry Drummond* (London, 1899), pp92-3
[49] Ibid., p129.

he recounts the story of his meeting William Robertson Smith in Cairo, he refers to "Smith's aggressive Evangelicalism," which he illustrates by saying "I wish everybody could know the missionary work he did in Arabia distributing Bibles".[50]

A further emphasis in Smith is on the centrality of Jesus Christ:

> In the Christianity which [Drummond] presents as the crown of the life of the universe, the spring and cause is Jesus Christ. He is the Source of all life and light; the assurance of the forgiveness of sins; the daily nourishment of the soul; the one power sufficient for a noble life; the solution of all problems; the motive and example of all service.[51]

This Christocentricism is also crucial to Smith's evangelicalism. Forgiveness, as he puts it in his sermon on "The Forgiveness of Sins" in the collection of that title, is assured to us "Through the perfect sacrifice offered once for all in the life and death of Jesus Christ, the Son of God".[52] Coupled with this is an emphasis on the love of God, of which Smith says that "we must feel what our pardon cost the Love of God, and how much that Love in Christ endured for us".[53] Only by personal experience of this love and atonement can any good follow, either for the individual or society: "What remedy have we," Smith asks, "against all that waste of the soul except by receiving God and his daily gift of life in Jesus Christ?"[54] Then, with our hearts attuned to the life and love of God in Christ, Smith argues that society itself will be transformed: "there is no doubt", he says, "by the God we believe in, by the conscience he has set in us, by the life and death of Jesus Christ, his son, that a perfect righteousness is the ultimate future of human experience".[55] So, even although Smith has to acknowledge the poverty of some of Moody's addresses,[56] nonetheless he redeems both Moody and Sankey by stating that "the evangelists were practical",[57] and goes on to highlight that "one of the most striking features of the movement was the social and philanthropic work which it stimulated".[58]

So for Smith the study of the Bible became a paramount feature of his evangelicalism, modified, of course, by his view that modern criticism alone could give adequate insight into biblical truth. But, in addition, his evangelicalism is also marked by a clear objectivising of the faith. While there

---

[50] GAS to George Smith from Cairo, 7 April 1880, NLS Acc 9446 No 16.
[51] *Life of Drummond*, p326.
[52] GAS, *The Forgiveness of Sins and Other Sermons* (New York, 1904) p1.
[53] Ibid., p114-5.
[54] Ibid., p239.
[55] Ibid., p136.
[56] *Life of Drummond*, p56.
[57] Ibid., p57.
[58] Ibid., p61.

is an element of subjectivity in Smith's preaching – he states, for example, that "we must come into contact with Christ"[59] – there is little guidance in Smith as to how such contact may be secured, or how "conversion" might come about. Smith prefers to emphasise the ethical aspect of Christianity, rather than its dogmatic content; consequently he views "conversion" as an objective element in personal experience, yielding to the example of Jesus Christ:

> Have you ever understand what [Christ] desires of you? It is not the taking of an arbitrary bond. It is not trust in a bare transaction. It is not assent to a creed. It is the giving of the heart and will to a living love and victorious example which have never failed any who have put their trust in Him.[60]

This is also the burden of a sermon Smith preached in King's College Chapel in 1912 on "The Experience of Balaam as Symbolic of the Origins of Prophecy". In the Old Testament Balaam was summoned by Barak, king of Moab, to pronounce a curse upon Israel (Numbers 22ff). However, he refused to do so, preferring to wait for a word from God. Smith argues that Balaam bases his conviction "on the fact that God has already blessed Israel. There is no use in him, Balaam, fighting against a Divine Fact".[61] As Balaam rehearses in poetic form the history and past experiences of Israel, Smith says that "It is in these facts, obvious to the plain man but rhythmic and eloquent to the poet, that Balaam finds the Presence and the Will of God",[62] and that "it is historical and obvious facts on which he insists".[63] In the experience of Balaam, Smith sees an allegory of the development of prophecy in Israel, and concludes that the strength of the message of the classical prophets was that God educated them "to see and to be true to facts".[64] Thus as Smith approaches the Old Testament writings, his concern is to uncover the historical, factual basis upon which the faith of the people of God came to rest.

To put it otherwise, in the second volume of the Isaiah commentary, Smith says that "it makes all the difference to a man how he conceives his religion – whether as something that he has to carry, or as something that will carry him".[65] This form of expression represents an objectification of the evangelical faith; although the cardinal elements of that faith are present, they are present not as a religion to be carried in a dogmatic fashion, but as a religion which can carry man, and which will give an impetus and zeal to man to live for the good

---

[59] *The Forgiveness of Sins*, p253.
[60] Ibid., p190
[61] GAS, "The Experience of Balaam as Symbolic of the Origins of Prophecy", *Expositor*, 8th Series, No. 5, 1913, p5.
[62] Ibid., p7.
[63] Ibid.
[64] Ibid., p9.
[65] GAS, *The Book of Isaiah,* Vol 2 (London, 1892) p181.

of others. There is a clear correlation here between what Smith conceives evangelicalism to be, and what he sees as the nature of the Old Testament itself:

> The Old Testament is not a set of dogmas, nor a philosophy, nor a vision; but a history, the record of a providence, the testimony of experience, the utterances called forth by historical occasions from a life conscious of the purpose for which God has called it and set it apart through the ages.[66]

Similarly, on Smith's understanding of the nature of the Gospel, it is the consciousness of the purpose of God through Jesus Christ that enables us to experience his grace, and live the life to which God has set us apart.

In assessing Smith's commitment to evangelicalism, therefore, we must recognise that the kind of evangelicalism to which Smith was committed represented less of a subjectivising tendency in the proclamation of the gospel, and more of a declaration of the facts of the biblical revelation, as seen through the eyes of higher criticism. This objectification of the doctrines of the Christian religion led, arguably, to a weakening of evangelical commitment, since it implies that to experience the love of God it is sufficient to assent to facts. It is doubtful whether the traditional orthodoxy could be content with such a presentation, and any divide between the Highland church, with a strong subjective and experiential emphasis, and the Lowland church, with a more liberal and objective evangelicalism, could well be explained in these terms.

Thirdly, Smith was committed to a critical approach to the study of the Bible. Old Testament scholar Carl Armerding opens his work on *The Old Testament and Criticism* with the words:

> From the days of such men of piety as George Adam Smith and James Orr in Scotland, or C.F. Keil and Franz Delitzsch in Germany, evangelical students of the Old Testament have struggled with the question of biblical criticism. There is no avoiding the fact that in the years since Julius Wellhausen of Greifswald published his *Prolegomena zur Geschichte Israels*, commitment to some form of a critically reconstructed Old Testament has become a new scholarly orthodoxy.[67]

Leaving aside for the moment the question of Smith's piety and its relation to his scholarly commitment, it is important to define the nature of Smith's approach to the critical study of the Old Testament.

We have already noted that according to Smith one of the benefits of the Moody and Sankey campaigns was that they led to increased study of the Bible in the churches. As people responded to the proclamation and preaching of

---

[66] Ibid., p325.
[67] C.E. Armerding, *The Old Testament and Criticism* (Grand Rapids, Michigan, 1983) p1.

Christ, they turned to the Bible. For Smith the complement of this was the critical study of the Bible; "the revival of the experimental study of the Scriptures in Scotland", he says, "preceded that of the critical".[68] The application of the Bible to life, which was one of the legacies of the new preaching, also led to a realisation that the meaning of the biblical text could only be found through a critical reading and reconstruction of it. For Smith and his contemporaries, that meant that

> the promise of the Holy Spirit for the education of His Church was being fulfilled not less in the critical than in the experimental use of the Bible; they defended criticism on the highest grounds of faith in God and loyalty to Christ.[69]

In the same volume, Smith writes in defence of William Robertson Smith, stating that "in his own practical use of the Bible he exercised a new discrimination, and he often said that the critical movement had removed very many difficulties in the Old Testament which puzzled him".[70] But what was George Adam Smith's own view of the critical movement?

One answer to this is given in a lecture delivered by Smith to a conference of University and Schoolteachers in Cambridge in 1923, significant not least because it reflects Smith's mature thought on the critical movement. He acknowledges at the outset his debt to, among others, Heinrich Ewald, A.B. Davidson and Robertson Smith, claiming that their critical reading of the Old Testament was characterised not only by a "freedom from tradition, dogma and ritual", but also a "faith in a living God and the vision of His ceaseless working in history both past and present".[71] He claims that a critical reading of the Hebrew text helps to illuminate and clarify: "it has helped us to separate dead tradition from living truth".[72] Smith continues:

> The critical movement not only gives us firmer and clearer ground for the belief that the Old Testament contains the record of a Divine revelation, but exhibits that Revelation proceeding, as do all the works of God, by gradual development – a development in which the influence of Nature has its place, to which historical experiences contribute, but of which the highest factors are started by the communion of individual souls with the Spirit of God. I speak now upon over forty-five years' experience of the influence of modern criticism on my faith, and I say that this movement, whatever individual

---

[68] *Life of Henry Drummond*, p129.
[69] Ibid.
[70] Ibid., p131.
[71] GAS, *The Teaching of the Old Testament in Schools*, An Address to the Conference of University Tutors and Schoolmasters at Cambridge, January 1923, p3.
[72] Ibid., p4.

aberrations within it may have been, has only confirmed and cleared up my belief that the Old Testament contains a genuine Revelation of God and of His will for mankind.[73]

As in *Modern Criticism and the Preaching of the Old Testament*, Smith appeals to Christ as exemplar in the area of a critical reading of the Old Testament. There is a duality, Smith argues, in the portrayal of Christ in the Gospels; on the one hand the Hebrew Scriptures were "the Bible of His education and of His ministry";[74] on the other, Smith says that Christ acted with liberty to reverse, ignore or act against the letter of the Old Testament.[75] To follow Christ's example is to see, Smith says, that his spirit is evident among the Old Testament prophets themselves. Amos and Jeremiah, for example, he says, contradict the ritualistic and legalistic elements of the deuteronomic and levitical codes.[76]

Smith makes two points about the use of criticism which are worth emphasising here. First, he suggests that the discussion, debate and differences of opinion which are the necessary corollary of a critical approach to the Old Testament, are indispensable for discovery of the truth. As the classical prophets of the Old Testament re-read and re-interpreted the value of earlier ritualistic and religious practice in Israel, so the evangelical spirit was breathed out of the Hebrew Bible:

> Such differences between the legal and prophetic Scriptures remind us that as in all other ages and nations controversy between opposite opinions has been a means of reaching the truth, this played a similar part in the history of Israel by leading to and elucidating Revelation from God.[77]

The significance of this statement is not only that the true meaning of the Old Testament is to be discerned by an assessment and weighing up of opinions and counter-opinions regarding the literary and textual questions raised in the text. Its significance is deeper, implying that such discussion, controversy and debate was found within Judaism itself. In other words, when we read Jeremiah, for example, through the eyes of biblical criticism, we find that he was a bible critic! The same is true of the prophets from Isaiah onwards: a critical understanding of them shows us that they too were critics both of the law and the cultus. The supreme example of such an approach, according to Smith, is Jesus himself. Both the prophets and Jesus are to be found at the end of the critical process, and their ministries are regarded as validators of that

---

[73] Ibid.
[74] Ibid., p5.
[75] Ibid.
[76] Ibid., p4.
[77] Ibid.

process. The Bible, therefore, both requires and vindicates the critical task. For Smith, the revelation from God which the Bible contains is discernible by means of a critical analysis of the text; and the text bears witness to the critical task.

Implicit in this approach is the idea of development within the Old Testament itself (for how can the later revelation evaluate the former critically unless it has progressed from it?). Indeed, Smith says so explicitly, describing the biblical record as "the record of a long and a gradual struggle under Divine guidance of the mind of Israel from poor beginnings towards ultimate and undeniable truth".[78] The prophets, therefore, become "great souls struggling towards a purer faith through debates with God and themselves and conflicts with priestly and legal tradition".[79]

Smith regards this evolution as an ethical development, "an advance to higher conceptions of the character of the Deity".[80] The primitive form of Old Testament religion Smith regards as of a piece with other tribal forms in the Semitic world; the development of that religion, however, is what has provided an authentic revelation of God in the Old Testament. In the steady progress towards a higher ethical conception of God, the prophets played a critical role, and Smith regards the ministries of Jeremiah and Amos as pivotal in this connection:

> According to Jeremiah the duty of a prophet was "to bring forth the precious from the vile". These words might well stand as a motto for the bent of the Hebrew ethical genius till at least the end of the prophetic period.[81]

The corollary of this is, as Smith puts it so eloquently in a sermon on 'The Word of God', "Do not let us, therefore, do the Bible the childish injustice of estimating it by things which its spirit finally outgrew; the defeat and outdistancing of which represent its divine victory and triumph."[82] If it is true that the Old Testament leaves behind a "defective morality" in order that it might reveal more clearly "the ethical service of God",[83] then criticism is vital to a proper understanding of the meaning, message and relevance of the Old Testament Scriptures. Again, however, the appropriation of Old Testament teaching is contingent upon a particular understanding and application of certain critical principles. This immediately places the benefits of Old Testament study out of the reach of readers unfamiliar with these principles.

---

[78] Ibid., p6.
[79] Ibid., pp10-11.
[80] GAS, "The Hebrew Genius as Exhibited in the Old Testament" in E.R. Bevan and C. Singer (eds.) *The Legacy of Israel* (Oxford, 1927) p8.
[81] Ibid.
[82] *The Forgiveness of Sins*, p35.
[83] Ibid.

But, secondly, Smith himself supplies an appellation for his approach: he says "it is because the methods of modern criticism guide and enlighten us in the use of that liberty, that I have called the critical discipline **constructive** and not destructive".[84] While some of his more conservative colleagues were claiming that criticism destroyed belief in the prophetic Scriptures and that the critics of the prophets left "their writings cut to pieces",[85] it was Smith's own conviction that a critical approach was *constructive*, and led to a more thorough appreciation of the meaning of the Old Testament text. If any epithet is to be applied to him, therefore, it ought to be, on his own admission, that he was a "constructive critic" of the Old Testament. And in approaching the Hebrew Scriptures in this way, Smith claimed that he was following the prophets themselves, but, supremely, that he was following the example of Jesus Christ.

It is a strong argument indeed for the validity of the critical approach to the Hebrew Bible that it was 'criticised' by Christ himself. But the difficulty of Smith's position is that the nature of 'criticism' is rarely defined. In the second chapter of *Modern Criticism and the Preaching of the Old Testament*, Smith speaks of criticism in terms of literary and historical reconstruction of the Old Testament text. Arguments against a critical approach, he describes as 'baseless'; and his approach may well be summarised in the following statement:

> criticism does not depend mainly on linguistic analysis, but still more on historical evidence furnished by the Old Testament itself: the conclusions are not refuted, but to a remarkable extent corroborated, by the evidence of archaeology and geography.[86]

However, Smith's critique of critical scholarship, such as in his 1907 article reviewing recent work on Isaiah and Jeremiah, shows that his standards for the evaluation of the ancient text differed from that of other scholars. "The tendency of criticism," he writes in reviewing the work of Herrmann Guthe on Isaiah, "to confine each of the prophets to one line of thought or temper, is also on this point astray and misleading".[87] He continues: "we must judge the criticism which denies to them more than a single role of thought as both psychologically and historically inaccurate".[88] The problem, as others have already noted, lies in the definition of criticism. Nigel de S. Cameron, for

---

[84] *Teaching of the Old Testament in Schools*, p5. Emphasis mine.
[85] D.K. Paton writing on the views of Prof. G. A. Smith in *The Higher Criticism: the Greatest Apostasy of the Age* (London, 1898) p197.
[86] GAS, *Modern Criticism and the Preaching of the Old Testament* (London, 1901) pp70-71.
[87] GAS, "A Survey of Recent Criticism of the Books of Isaiah and Jeremiah", *Review of Theology and Philosophy*, Vol III, 1907-1908, p10.
[88] Ibid.

example, in his study of 'biblical infallibilism' in nineteenth-century Britain, asks "what, precisely, was the Critical method? It is not easy to say. Everyone spoke of it, scholars increasingly argued for it and, in diminishing numbers, denounced it".[89] The literature of the evangelical scholars was, he says, "singularly lacking in extended methodological discussions of how the tools of secular critical history may be made to apply to the Christian revelation."[90] Mark Noll, in his survey of evangelical scholarship in Great Britain from 1860-1937 also observes that "In Britain during these years a certain ambiguity clung to terms like 'criticism'".[91] So although Smith commends the critical method, he rarely defines it, and the weakness of his position is in the lack of a comprehensive methodological statement.

That criticism – however defined – was necessary is evident also from the information Smith supplies in his Drummond biography, when he says that he collaborated with Drummond in the publication of a tract aimed at popularising the critical approach. Although the tract has been lost, Smith gives us a hint as to what was in it:

> Drummond once asked me to help in the preparation of a popular tract on the Higher Criticism. A rhetorical Bishop, a defender of the Mosaic origin of the Pentateuch, had asked what the critics would answer when in the next world Moses met them with the challenge, "How dared you say that I did *not* write the Pentateuch?" I pointed out that, considering the absence of all claims of Mosaic authorship in the Pentateuch itself, it was equally reasonable to put the question in the very opposite way; and Drummond's proposal was to write the tract in the form of a dream by the same Bishop, as though, being conveyed to heaven and meeting Moses, Moses should ask him, "How dared you say that I *did* write the Pentateuch!"[92]

Implicit in this approach is Smith's confident assertion in the conclusions of criticism, without any treatment of methodology. As an Old Testament scholar, set on popularising a critical approach to the Bible, Smith marches triumphantly in his assault on the citadel of conservative orthodoxy. He is, to use his own metaphor, waging a war.[93] But there is little consensus over battle tactics; only the confident note that victory will be with the critics.

Evangelical Critic?

Smith, therefore, has a threefold commitment: to the church, to the evangel, and to critical scholarship. Any study of his life will show that this trinity did not sit

---

[89] Cameron, *Biblical Higher Criticism*, pp266-7.
[90] Ibid., p267.
[91] Noll, *Between Faith and Criticism*, p71.
[92] *The Life of Drummond*, p132.
[93] See *Modern Criticism*, p72.

easily together. For all his confidence in his scholarship, it was not easy for that scholarship to be domesticated within the church. Arguably the Aberdeen Principalship freed him from what he regarded as the fetters of confessional orthodoxy to pursue critical scholarship in a liberal academic environment. Smith's insistence that only a critical reading of the Scriptures uncovers the evangel appears, on the surface at least, to place the Gospel outwith the reach of those who could not appreciate, or would not accept, such an approach to the Bible. Yet insist he did, and perhaps that was Smith's greatest failing. For, while regarding himself as a propagator and populariser of the critical movement, he failed to win conservative support. Nigel Cameron is correct to state that Robertson Smith and his colleagues "leave the relation of critical, historical study and the unique, supernatural, revelatory nature of Scripture unresolved".[94] Cameron then goes on to say of (G.A.) Smith that "in place of developing an integrated conception of critical study in the context of faith, [he is] satisfied to practise a dualistic compromise".[95]

Smith fully believed that his ecclesiology, his gospel and his scholarship could be integrated. But history proved him wrong. It is arguable that if his life and work demonstrate anything, they demonstrate that at least one element of that trinity required modification. In Smith's case it was his Church that had to change if his gospel was to be preached and his scholarship naturalised. Ultimately, while he himself was intellectually satisfied that he had synthesised his evangelicalism and his scholarship, his position did not command universal assent and consequently failed to unite the Church. His move from church to university was the natural transition of a scholar whose dogmatic conclusions regarding criticism could only clash dramatically with the dogmatics of his Church's creed.

Perhaps, however, the problem lies more with Smith's legacy than with his own achievements. That Smith believed he was able to integrate faith and criticism is beyond question, and that he was able to apply his scholarship to pulpit ministry is also undeniable. That he inspired and "made" preachers is probably also true. But it is questionable whether his successors in the pastorates of the emergent Scottish church were able to move as easily as Smith himself around the same field. In his own day Smith's views were divisive; for a future day, therefore, they laid the groundwork for a diversification of evangelical commitment and critical scholarship. While Smith grounded his critique of the Westminster Confession of Faith, for example, in the conclusions of Higher Criticism, later Scottish evangelicalism would fire from a different gun. Scholars such as T.F. Torrance, would accuse the Westminster Confession of Faith of having a legalistic form of federalism "authoritatively

---

[94] Cameron, *Biblical Higher Criticism*, p269.
[95] Ibid.

grafted on to the more evangelical Calvinism of the older Scottish tradition"[96], thus grounding his critique of the Church's confessional position in a Barthian approach rather than in a higher critical one. At the same time, critical scholarship of the biblical text tended to move away from its courtship with evangelicalism (could it be said today, for example that "nearly every leader in Old Testament criticism is a believer in evangelical Christianity"?).[97] For the greater part of the twentieth century, therefore, evangelical scholarship in Scotland tended to be informed by the neo-orthodoxy of Karl Barth, while critical approaches to the Old Testament tended to become even more radical than the nineteenth-century conservatives could envisage.[98] Thus, while on one reading George Adam Smith may be viewed as one of the first to synthesise a conservative evangelical faith with critical biblical scholarship, on another he may be regarded as one of the last.

On leaving Glasgow, Smith said, rather modestly, of his ability that "I have little, except perhaps some ability to interpret to the present age the messages of the ancient prophets."[99] That his preaching was able to bridge the gulf between ancient text and contemporary audience is beyond doubt. He could not have filled Queen's Cross or commanded international respect were it not for his contemporising expositions of the Old Testament, and his ability to extract from the ancient text something of relevance for a modern age. What is open to scrutiny is the method he employed in the construction of this bridge; and what is debatable is the ability of preachers (as opposed to scholars) who could see to its maintenance and preservation after him. And, ultimately, what is questionable is Smith's view that the proclamation of the Gospel was dependent on a critical approach to the Bible. To the extent that Smith demonstrates the integrity of scholarship and faith, he leaves a good example; but to the extent that he argues for an evangelicalism based on a re-evaluation of the biblical text, his example is inimical to the very task of reaching a lost world with the message of God's salvation.

---

[96] T.F. Torrance, *Scottish Theology from John Knox to John McLeod Campbell* (Edinburgh, 1996) p127.
[97] See the discussion of Bebbington, *Evangelicalism*, Chapter 6, which looks at the gradual fragmentation of evangelicalism in Britain in the interwar years and concludes that "By the Second World War, Evangelicalism had become much more fragmented than it had been a century before" (p228).
[98] Witness, for example, the statement of Hunter above that critical study and conservatism are utterly disharmonious (p213).
[99] *Speech on leaving Glasgow*, 1 March 1910, p8

BIBLIOGRAPHY

Archives
The George Adam Smith Papers (National Library of Scotland)
The British Library Manuscripts
Trinity College Archives (University of Glasgow)
Aberdeen University Archives (University of Aberdeen)
Foreign Office Papers (Public Record Office)
New College Special Collections
Presbytery Records of the Free Presbytery of Aberdeen (Scottish Records Office)

Papers and Periodicals
Aberdeen University Review
Alma Mater
Biblical Archaeological Review
British Weekly
Bulletin of the John Rylands Library
Calcutta Review
Commonwealth
Evangelical Quarterly
Expositor
Expository Times
Gaudie
Greatheart: The Scottish Churches Magazine for Boys and Girls
Journal of Ecclesiastical History
Journal of Historical Geography
Largs and Milport Weekly News
Life and Work
Mayfair: A Tuesday Journal of Politics, Literature and Society
Monthly Record of the Free Church of Scotland
Palestine Exploration Fund Quarterly Statement
Presbyterian and Reformed Review
Proceedings of the British Academy
Record of the Home and Foreign Mission Work of the United Free Church of Scotland
Records of the Scottish Church History Society
Review of Theology and Philosophy
Scotsman
Union Magazine
University Record (University of Aberdeen)
Young Men's Christian Magazine

Works by George Adam Smith

1884

A Few Plain words to the Younger members of my Congregation on the Differences Between Presbyterianism and Episcopacy and the Alleged Possibility of a Union, Aberdeen

1886 (?)

"The Messiah in Isaiah i-xxxix", *The Theological Review and Free Church Quarterly,* Vol 1, pp322-38

1888

The Book of Isaiah, Vol 1, London

The Children More Sinned Against than Sinning: A Sermon on the Manners and Morals of Young Aberdeen, Aberdeen

1889

"Recent Literature on the Old Testament", *The Expositor,* 3rd series, No.10, pp386-400

1890

"The Ethiopian and the Old Testament - Acts viii:26-40", *The Expository Times ,* Vol 1 No. 10, July 1890, pp233-238

1891

Review of The New Edition of Baedeker's Palestine, *The Expositor,* 4th series, Vol IV, pp467-468

"The Longsuffering of God": A sermon on Romans 2:4, *The British Weekly,* 19 November 1891, p49

1892

The Book of Isaiah, Vol 2, London

"Duhm's Isaiah and the New Commentary to the Old Testament", *The Expositor,* 4th Series, No.6, pp312-318

1893

The Preaching of the Old Testament to the Age, London

"Recent German Literature on the Old Testament", *The Expositor,* 4th series, No.10, pp150-160

1894

The Historical Geography of the Holy Land, London

"An Action Sermon: 'He took Bread', Luke 22:19", in The Free Church Pulpit, *The Monthly Record of the Free Church of Scotland,* October 1894, pp227-228

1895

"On Aphek in Sharon", *Palestine Exploration Fund Quarterly Statement,* pp252-253

"The Twenty-Third Psalm", *The Expositor,* 5th series, No.1, pp33-44

1896

Four Psalms: XXIII, XXXVI, LII, CXXI: Interpreted for Practical Use, London

The Book of the Twelve Prophets commonly called the Minor, Volume 1, London

"Buhl's New Geography of Palestine, and certain geographical problems", *The Expositor*, 5th series, No.4, pp401-413

"Professor Cheyne on my Criticism of Micah iv-vii", *The Expositor*, Vol II, No 1, October 1896, p48

1898
The Book of the Twelve Prophets commonly called the Minor, Volume 2, London

1899
The Life of Henry Drummond, London

1901
Modern Criticism and the Preaching of the Old Testament: Eight Lectures on the Lyman Beecher Foundation, Yale University, London

"A Century of Scottish History by Sir Henry Craik, KCB", *The Union Magazine*, April 1901, pp148-151

"Notes of a Journey through Hauran, with inscriptions found by the way", *Palestine Exploration Fund Quarterly Statement*, pp340-361

1902
"Further Notes on the Inscriptions found at Tell El-ashari", *Palestine Exploration Fund Quarterly Statement*, pp27-29

"The Messages of the Prophets", *The Union Magazine*, January 1902, pp15-17

"Professor A.B. Davidson", Part 1,*The Union Magazine*, March 1902, pp107-112

"Professor A.B. Davidson", Part 2,*The Union Magazine*, April 1902, pp160-163

"Professor A.B. Davidson", Part 3,*The Union Magazine*, May 1902, pp203-205

1903
"The Christian Social Movement in Scotland", *The Commonwealth*, Vol iii, pp44-46

"Trade and Commerce", *Encyclopedia Biblica*, Eds: T.K. Cheyne, J.S. Black, Vol IV, pp5145-5199

1904
The Forgiveness of Sins and Other Sermons, London

"The Roman Road between Kerak and Madeba", *Palestine Exploration Fund Quarterly Statement*, pp367-377

"Notices of Foreign Publications", *Palestine Exploration Fund Quarterly Statement*, pp397-400

"Isaiah" in J. Hastings (ed.), *A Dictionary of the Bible*, Volume 2, Edinburgh, pp485-499

1905
"The Roman Road between Kerak and Madeba", *Palestine Exploration Fund Quarterly Statement*, pp39-48

"Notes on "The Roman Road between Kerak and Madeba", *Palestine Exploration Fund Quarterly Statement*, pp148-149

"Callirrhoe; Machaerus; Ataroth", *Palestine Exploration Fund Quarterly*

Statement, p170

"Callirrhoe and Machaerus", *Palestine Exploration Fund Quarterly Statement,* pp219-230

"From Machaerus to Ataroth", *Palestine Exploration Fund Quarterly Statement,* pp357-363

"Notices of Foreign Publications", *Palestine Exploration Fund Quarterly Statement,* pp70-76

1906

"Jeremiah's Jerusalem", *The Expositor,* 7th series, No.1, pp61-77, 97-114

"The Desolate City", *The Expositor,* 7th series, No.1, pp320-336

"The Ideal City and the Real", *The Expositor,* 7th series, No.1, pp435-452

"The Second Temple, from Zechariah to Ezra", *The Expositor,* 7th series, No.1, pp510-523

"Ezra and Nehemiah", *The Expositor,* 7th series, No.2, pp1-18

"Nehemiah's Jerusalem", *The Expositor,* 7th series, No.2, pp121-134

"The Jewish Constitution from Nehemiah to the Maccabees", *The Expositor,* 7th series, No.2, pp193-209

"The Jewish Constitution from the Maccabees to the End", *The Expositor,* 7th series, No.2, pp348-364

Tribute to Principal Rainy, *The Sunday Review,* 27 December 1906

1907

Jerusalem: The Topography, Economics and History from the earliest times to AD70, Vol 1, London

The Home Mission of the Churches, preached Park Parish Church, Glasgow, St. Patrick's Day

1908

Jerusalem: The Topography, Economics and History from the earliest times to AD70, Vol 2, London

"Herr Alois Musil on the Land of Moab", *The Expositor,* 7th series, No.6, pp1-16; 131-150

"Have the Hebrews been Nomads? A Reply to Professor Eerdmans", *The Expositor,* 7th series, No.6, pp254-272

"The Land of Edom", *The Expositor,* 7th series, No.6, pp325-336; 506-517

"A Survey of Recent Criticism of the Books of Isaiah and Jeremiah", *Review of Theology and Philosophy,* Vol III (July 1907-June 1908), pp1-12, 65-77

Mohammedanism and Christianity: A Sermon preached on 30 September 1908 at the Autumn Session of the Baptist Missionary Society, held in Bradford, London, 1908

1910

Speech in Glasgow on removal to Aberdeen, 1 March

Speech to the Aberdeen University Club on the occasion of the 54th Half-yearly dinner 16 November 1910, The Aberdeen University Club, London.

1912

The Early Poetry of Israel in its Physical and Social Origins, The Schweich

Lectures 1910, London

"The Natural Strength of the Psalms", *The Expositor*, 8th series, No.3, pp1-15

1913

"The Experience of Balaam as Symbolic of the origins of Prophecy", *The Expositor*, 8th series, No.5, pp1-11

Foreword to Vol 1 No 1 of *The Aberdeen University Review*, October 1913

1915

War and Peace: Two Sermons delivered in King's College Chapel, University of Aberdeen, London

Atlas of the Historical Geography of the Holy Land, London

"After Fifteen Months of War", *The British Weekly*, 25 October 1915

1916

George Buchanan Smith 1890-1915, Glasgow

"Jeremiah's Poems on War", *The Aberdeen University Review*, Vol 3 No 8, February pp120-127

"Two Years of War: the Record of the University", *The Aberdeen University Review*, Vol 3 No 9, June 1916, pp214-233

"The Moderator's Tour: Some Impressions of Church Life in the North", in *The Record of the Home and Foreign Mission Work of the United Free Church of Scotland*, November 1916, p286

Diary of My Visit to the British Army in France on the Invitation of the Commander-in-Chief October 12th-24th 1916 (unpublished), New College Library Special Collections

1917

Review of J. Strahan, *Andrew Bruce Davidson, DD, LLD, DLitt*, in *The Aberdeen University Review*, Vol 4 No 12, June 1917, pp237-241

1918

Our Common Conscience: Addresses delivered in America during the Great War, London

Syria and the Holy Land, London

The Book of Deuteronomy in the Revised Version, with Introduction and Notes (Cambridge Bible for Schools and Colleges), Cambridge

"The Principal's Itinerary in the United States", *The Aberdeen University Review*, Vol 5 No 15, June 1918, pp232-235

"The Universities and the War", *The University Record*, Vol IV, No. 3, July 1918, Chicago, Vol IV, No. 3, pp119-128

"The Principal's Itinerary in the United States – II", *The Aberdeen University Review*, Vol 6 No 16, November 1918, pp36-39

"The Principal's Itinerary in the United States – III", *The Aberdeen University Review,* Vol 6 No 16, November 1918, pp130-136

Diary of Voyage Home from the United States of America, 20th August-5th September (unpublished), New College Library Special Collections

1919

"Sir David Steward, LL.D., of Banchory and Leggart", *The Aberdeen*

University Review, Vol 7 No 19, November 1919, pp134-137
"Donaldson Rose Thom, Late Secretary of the University", *The Aberdeen University Review*, Vol 7 No 19, November 1919, pp138-144
1920
"Agricultural Education and its Needs", *The Scottish Journal of Agriculture*, Vol.III, No.2 (April 1920), pp155-160
1921
Robert Dunlop Smith 1892-1917, Aberdeen University Press, 1921
1923
Jeremiah: the Baird Lecture for 1922, London
The Teaching of the Old Testament in Schools: An Address to the Conference of University Tutors and Schoolmasters, Cambridge
1924
"Bishop Elphinstone and the Earl Marishcal", *The Aberdeen University Review*, Vol 11 No 32, November 1924, pp115-118
1926
The Re-Union of the Two Great Scottish Churches, London
"A Fifty Years' Review", *The Aberdeen University Review*, Vol 13 No 38, March 1926, pp38-39
1927
"The Meaning of the Memorial", introductory essay to *The Deliverance of Palestine*, published by the Committee for the Scottish Churches Memorial in Jerusalem, Edinburgh
"The Hebrew Genius as Exhibited in the Old Testament", in E.R. Bevan and C. Singer (eds.), *The Legacy of Israel*, Oxford, pp1-28
1930
(with John Buchan) *The Kirk in Scotland 1560-1929*, London
"Lord Birkenhead and Aberdeen University", *The Aberdeen University Review*, Vol 18 No 52, November 1930, pp1-2
1932
"Professor James Gilroy", *The Aberdeen University Review*, Vol 19 No 56, March 1932, pp97-99
"In Memoriam – Frederick Sidney Shears", *The Aberdeen University Review*, Vol 19 No 57, July 1932, pp193-194
1934
"Recent Additions to the History of the Holy Land", *The Aberdeen University Review*, Vol 21 No 63, pp193-202
1935
"The Universities of Aberdeen", *The Aberdeen University Review*, Vol 22 No 65, March 1935, pp97-108
1936
The British Benefactions of Andrew Carnegie, New York
Verses Grave and Gay, Aberdeen
Undated

"The Hebrew and the Hellene: Some Contrasts with Modifications", Speech as President of the Scottish Classical Association

Theses

Annesley, E., "The Response of the Church of Scotland and the United Free Church of Scotland to the First World War", M.Th. thesis, University of Glasgow, 1991

Basu, R. "Urban Society in Bengal, 1850-72, with special reference to Calcutta", unpublished Ph.D. thesis, University of London, School of Oriental and African Studies, 1974

Brown, J.H., "The Contribution of William Robertson Smith to Old Testament Scholarship, with special emphasis on Higher Criticism", Ph.D. thesis, Duke University, 1964

Enright, W.G., "Preaching and Theology in Scotland in the Nineteenth Century: A Study of the Context and the Content of the Evangelical Sermon", Ph.D. thesis, University of Edinburgh, 1968

Holmes, J.E., "Religious Revivalism and Popular Evangelicalism in Britain and Ireland 1859-1905", PhD Thesis, Queen's University, Belfast, 1995

Macdonald, L.A.O., "Women and Presbyterianism in Scotland c.1830-c.1930", Ph.D Thesis, University of Edinburgh, 1995

MacHaffie, B.J.Z., "The People and the Book: A Study of the Popularizing of Biblical Criticism in Britain, 1860-1914", 2 vols., Ph.D. thesis, University of Edinburgh 1977

Macleod, D., "Prophet with Honour: George Adam Smith", B.D. dissertation, University of Edinburgh, 1992

Macleod, J.L., "The Origins of the Free Presbyterian Church of Scotland", Ph.D. thesis, University of Edinburgh, 1993

Nelson, R.R., "The Life and Thought of William Robertson Smith 1846-1894", Ph.D., University of Michigan, 1969

Riesen, R.A., "Faith and Criticism in Post-Disruption Scotland, with particular reference to A.B. Davidson, W.R. Smith and G.A. Smith", Ph.D. thesis, University of Edinburgh, 1981

Toone, M.J., "Evangelicalism in Transition: A comparative analysis of the work and theology of D.L. Moody and his proteges, Henry Drummond and R.A. Torrey," PhD. Thesis, University of St Andrews, 1988

Books and Articles

Primary Sources

Aalders, G.C., "The Turn of the Tide in Penteteuchal Criticism", *The Evangelical Quarterly,* Vol.2., No.1., January 1930, pp3-13

Allis, O.T., "A Modernistic View of Jeremiah", *Princeton Theological Review*, Volume XXIII (1925), pp82-132

A Scottish Presbyter, "The Case of Prof. George Adam Smith", *Presbyterian and Reformed Review*, Vol. XVI (1902), pp588-609

Ayres, S.G., *Complete Index to the Expositor's Bible*, London, 1905

Barr, J., *The United Free Church of Scotland*, London, 1934

Bennett, W.H., "General Introduction to the Expositor's Bible: Old Testament", in S.G. Ayres, *Complete Index to the Expositor's Bible*, London, 1905, pp15-36

Black, J.S. and Chrystal, G.W, *The Life of William Robertson Smith*, London, 1912

__ *Lectures and Essays of William Robertson Smith*, London, 1912

Boyd, J. Oscar, Review of GAS *The Early Poetry of Israel in its Physical and Social Origins*, *Princeton Theological Review*, XII (January 1914), pp136-137

Brown, D., *Life of the Late John Duncan*, Edinburgh, 1872

Brown, T., *Annals of the Disruption*, Edinburgh, 1884

Bruce, A.B., "The Rev George Adam Smith DD, LLD", *The British Weekly*, 30 July 1896, p226

Buchan, J. *A History of the Great War*, Vol II, London 1922

__ and Smith, G.A., *The Kirk in Scotland, 1560-1929,* London, 1930

Cairns, D.S., "The Overruling God" in "The Church, the Nation and the War", *The Record of the Home and Foreign Mission Work of the United Free Church of Scotland*, July 1915, pp288-289

__ "Sir George Adam Smith", *Religion in Life*, Vol XI No. 4, Autumn 1942, pp529-538

Carswell, D., *Brother Scots*, London, 1927

Chalmers, T., *Sermons preached in St John's Church, Glasgow*, Glasgow, 1823

Cheyne, T.K. and J.S. Black (eds), *Encyclopaedia Biblica*, London, 1903

Clow, W.M., *George Reith: A Scottish Ministry*, London, 1928

Cook, S.A., "George Adam Smith 1856-1942", *The Proceedings of the British Academy*, Vol XXVIII (1942), pp324-346

— "George Adam Smith", *The Expository Times*, Vol. LIV (1942-43), pp33-37

Darlow, T.H., *William Robertson Nicoll: Life and Letters*, London, 1925

Davidson, A.B., Review of *The Book of Isaiah* by Rev. George Adam Smith, *The Theological Review and Free Church College Quarterly*, Vol III, pp151-152

Denney, J., "The War, and the Voice of God to the Church", in "The Church, the Nation and the War", *The Record of the Home and Foreign Mission Work of the United Free Church of Scotland*, July 1915, pp285-286

__ *War and the Fear of God*, London, 1916

__ *Letters of Principal James Denney to W. Robertson Nicoll 1893-1917*, London, 1920

Drummond, H., *Dwight L. Moody: Impressions and Facts*, New York, 1900

Drummond, H., *The Greatest Thing in the World and other essays* (edited by P. Boobyer, Guildfod, Surrey, 1997; 1st edition 1891)

__ *The Changed Life* (edited by P. Boobyer, Guildford, Surrey, 2000; 1st

edition 1892)
"East Indian Education and the 'Doveton Colleges'", *The Calcutta Review*, Vol XXIV, 1855, pp288-330
Ewing, W., *Annals of the Free Church of Scotland*, 2 volumes, Edinburgh, 1914
Gammie, A., *The Churches of Aberdeen: Historical and Descriptive*, Aberdeen, 1909
G.C., "Sir George Adam Smith, D.D., LL.D., D.Litt", *Life and Work*, Vol XXIII, April 1942, p56
Gilroy, J., Review of George Adam Smith *Atlas of the Historical Geography of the Holy Land*, *The Aberdeen University Review*, Vol 3 No 9, June 1916, pp254-259
Gray, A.H., *As Tommy Sees us: A Book for Church Folk*, London, 1917
Highland News, No. 1718 (2 September 1916), "Sir George Adam Smith in Stornoway"
Highland News, No. 1719 (9 September 1916), "Sir George Adam Smith on Education"
Hunter, S.A., "The Water of the Nile Flows into Palestine!", *The United Presbyterian*, 26 December 1918
Innes, A.T., *The Law of Creeds in Scotland*, Edinburgh, 1867
Johnston, J., *Destructive Results of the Higher Criticism as Disclosed in "Modern Criticism and the Preaching of the Old Testament"*, London, 1901
Lamb, J.A. (ed.), *The Fasti of the United Free Church of Scotland 1900-1929*, Edinburgh, 1915
Leitch, M., Review of *Modern Criticism and the Preaching of the Old Testament*, *The Presbyterian and Reformed Review*, Vol. XIII (1902), pp132-143
Lendrum, R.A., et.al., *The Church College in Aberdeen: Free Church College 1843-1900 ; United Free Church College 1900-1929*, Aberdeen, 1936
Macgregor, W.M., *A Souvenir of the Union in 1929 with an historical sketch of the United Free Church College, Glasgow*, Glasgow, 1930
__ *The Convocation of 1904: A Record and Report*, with introduction by W.M. Macgregor, Edinburgh, 1905
Mann, H., Review of George Adam Smith *Jerusalem*, *The Daily News*, 25 May 1908
Manson, W., "Sir George Adam Smith", L.G.W Legg and E.T. Williams (eds) *The Dictionary of National Biography* (1941-1950) Oxford, 1959, pp792-794
Margoliouth, D.S., "Dr G.A. Smith on Jerusalem", *The Expositor*, 7th series, No.6, 1908, pp518-527
Mathews, B., (ed.), *Christ and the World at War*, London, 1917
Memorial to the College Committee of the United Free Church of Scotland, in *Reports to the General Assembly of the United free Church of Scotland*, 1902

Muir, W., "Far West and Far North: The Moderator's Visit to the Outposts" in *The Record of the Home and Foreign Mission Work of the United Free Church of Scotland*, October 1916, pp256-257

Nicoll, W.R., *Prayer in War-Time*, London, 1916

Nicoll, W.R., (ed.), *Letters of Principal James Denney to W. Robertson Nicoll, 1893-1917*, London, 1920

Orr, J., "The General Assembly of the United Free Church of Scotland", *Presbyterian and Reformed Review*, Vol XVI (1902), pp615-619

Paton, D.K., *The Higher Criticism: the Greatest Apostasy of the Age*, London, 1898

Paterson, W.P., *In the Day of Muster: Sermons in Time of War*, London, 1914

Peake, A.S., *Recent Developments in Old Testament Criticism*, London, 1928

__ *Recollections and Appreciations*, London, 1938

__ "The History of Theology" in A.S. Peake, B. Bosanquet and F. Bonaria (eds.), *Germany in the Nineteenth Century*, Manchester, 1915, pp129-184

Pocket Edition of the Manual of Practice and Procedure in the United Free Church of Scotland, Edinburgh, 1916

Proceedings and Debates of the General Assembly of the United Free Church of Scotland, 1902

Proceedings and Debates of the General Assembly of the United Free Church of Scotland, 1916

Rainy, R., and Mackenzie, J., *The Life of William Cunningham*, London, 1871

Ramsay, W.M., "Professor G.A. Smith's *Historical Geography of the Holy Land*", *The Expositor*, 5th series, Volume 1 (1895), pp55-66

Reith, G.M., *Reminiscences of the United Free Church General Assembly (1900-1929)*, Edinburgh, 1933

"Reports on Colleges and Schools in India", *The Calcutta Review*, Vol XLII, 1866, pp57-93

Reynolds, J.B. et al (eds) *Two Centuries of Christian Activity at Yale*, New York, 1901

Robinson, G.L., Review of *The Book of the Twelve Prophets, Vol 1*, in *The Presbyterian and Reformed Review*, Vol VIII No 29 (January 1897), pp111-113

__ Review of *The Book of the Twelve Prophets, Vol 2*, in *The Presbyterian and Reformed Review*, Vol X No 39 (July 1899), pp547-549

Robinson, H.W., "National Contributions to Biblical Science: II. The Contribution of Britain to Old Testament Study", *The Expository Times*, Vol 41, (1929-30), pp246-250

Rule, A., *Students Under Arms: Being the War Adventures of the Aberdeen University Company of the Gordon Highlanders*, Aberdeen, 1934

Selbie, J.A., Review of George Adam Smith *Jeremiah: The Baird Lectures for 1922*, *The Aberdeen University Review*, Vol 11 No 32, March 1924, pp142-145

__ "Sir George Adam Smith's *Twelve Prophets*, *The Aberdeen University*

Review, Vol 16 No 48, July 1929, pp235-238

Simpson, A.R., "The Enemy", in "The Church, the Nation and the War", *The Record of the Home and Foreign Mission Work of the United Free Church of Scotland*, July 1915, pp286-288

Simpson, P. Carnegie, *The Life of Principal Rainy*, Edinburgh, 1904

Smith, George, *The Conversion of India from Pantaenus to the present time AD 193-1893*, London, 1893

__ *The Life of Alexander Duff, DD, LLD*, London, 1881

__ "Half a Century's Growth of Protestant Missions in India", *The Missionary Record of the United Free Church of Scotland*, No.25, January 1903, p8

"Smith, George Adam (Very Rev, Sir)", *Scottish Biographies 1938*, London, 1938, p694

Smith, J., *The Integrity of Scripture: Plain Reasons for Rejecting the Critical Hypothesis*, London, 1902

Smith, Lilian Adam, *George Adam Smith: A Personal Memoir and Family Chronicle*, London, 1943

__ [with George Adam Smith], *George Buchanan Smith 1890-1915*, Glasgow, 1916

__ [with George Adam Smith], *Robert Dunlop Smith 1892-1917*, Aberdeen, 1921

__ *East of the Jordan*, n.d.

__ Letters to Principal McGregor of Trinity College, Glasgow, dated 29 December 1931 and 9 February [1932], in the archives of the University of Glasgow, filed with various items of correspondence, listed under DC84/3/4

Special Report by the College Committee Anent Memorial on Professor George Adam Smith's Work, entitled "Modern Criticism and the Preaching of the Old Testament", Reports to the General Assembly of the United Free Church of Scotland, 1902

Stalker, J., "Our Vice-Chancellor and Principal – Dr. George Adam Smith", *The Aberdeen University Review*, Vol 1 No 2, February 1914, pp117-122

Statement to the Sub-Committee of the College Committee of the United Free Church of Scotland, anent a Memorial against the volume 'Modern Criticism and the Preaching of the Old Testament, in *Reports to the General Assembly of the United Free Church of Scotland,* 1902

Stewart, A and Cameron, J.K., *The Free Church of Scotland 1843-1910*, Edinburgh, 1910

Strahan, J., *Andrew Bruce Davidson*, London, 1917

The Glasgow Hebrew Chair: Testimonials in Favour of the Rev George Adam Smith MA, Aberdeen, 1892

The Old Bible and the New: being a review of Prof. G.A. Smith's "Modern Criticism and the Preaching of the Old Testament", Prepared by a Committee of Ministers and Elders, London, 1901

Trinity College, Glasgow, Senate Meeting minutes, held in the archives of Glasgow University, listed DC84/1/1

__ Scroll Senate Minutes, listed DC84/1/2/2

Unmack, E.C., "Modern Criticism of the Old Testament", *The Evangelical Quarterly*, Vol 7., No. 1, January 1935 pp82-86

Walker, N., *Chapters from the History of the Free Church of Scotland*, London 1895

Walker, W.L., *The War, God and our Duty*, London 1917

Watson, C.M., *Palestine Exploration Fund: Fifty Years' Work in the Holy Land: a Record and Summary 1865-1915*, London, 1915

Watts, R., *The Newer Criticism and the Analogy of the Faith*, Edinburgh, 1881

Welch, A.C., "The Spirit of Prophecy", *The British Weekly*, 24 October 1935, pp71-72

Witton Davies, J., *Heinrich Ewald: Orientalist and Theologian, 1803-1903, A Centenary Appreciation*, London, 1903

Secondary Sources

Aharoni, Y., *The Land of the Bible* (tr. A.F. Rainey), Philadelphia, 1967

Anderson, F.I. and D.N. Freedman, *Amos: A New Translation with Introduction and Commentary*, The Anchor Bible, New York, 1989

Anderson, R.D., *The Student Community at Aberdeen 1860-1939*, Quincentennial Studies in the history of the University of Aberdeen, Aberdeen, 1988

Ansdell, D., *The People of the Great Faith: The Highland Church 1680-1900*, Stornoway, 1998

Annan, N.G., "The Intellectual Aristocracy" in Plumb, John H., *Studies in Social History: a Tribute to G.M. Trevelyan*, London, 1955, pp241-287

Armerding, C.E., *The Old Testament and Criticism*, Grand Rapids, Michigan, 1983

Auld, A.G., and Steiner, M., *Jerusalem I: From the Bronze Age to the Maccabees (Cities of the Biblical World)*, Cambridge, 1996

Baker, A.R.H. and Gregory, D. (eds.), *Explorations in Historical Geography: Interpretative Essays*, Cambridge, 1984

Barbour, G.F., "The Very Reverend Sir George Adam Smith", *The Aberdeen University Review*, Vol 29 No 86, pp93-95

Barr, J., *Lang Syne: Memoirs of Rev James Barr DD*, Glasgow, 1948

Barr, J., "Professor John Duncan (1796-1870)", *Records of the Scottish Church History Society*, Vol XXVIII 1998, pp93-100

Bartlett, J.R. (ed.), *Archaeology and Biblical Interpretation*, London, 1997

Bebbington, D.W., *Evangelicalism in Modern Britain: A History from the 1730s to the 1980s*, London, 1994

__ "Henry Drummond, Evangelicalism and Science", in T. Corts (ed.), *Henry Drummond: A Perpetual Benediction*, Edinburgh, 1999, pp19-38

__ "Mission in Scotland 1846-1946" in D. Searle (ed.), *Death or Glory: The Church's Mission in Scotland's Changing Society*, Edinburgh, 2001, pp32-53

Bell, C. (ed.), *Scotland's Century: An Autobiography of the Nation*, Glasgow, 1999
Ben-Arieh, J., *The Rediscovery of the Holy Land in the Nineteenth Century*, Jerusalem, 1983
Black, M., and Davidson, R., *Constantin von Tischendorf and the Greek New Testament*, Glasgow, 1981
Blakey, R.S., *The Man in the Manse*, Edinburgh, 1978
Bowler, P.J., *The Fontana History of the Environmental Sciences*, London, 1992
Bray, G., *Biblical Interpretation: Past and Present*, Leicester, 1996
Brown, C.G., *The Social History of Religion in Scotland since 1730*, London, 1987
__ "Did Urbanization Secularize Britain?" in *Urban History Yearbook*, 1988, pp1-14
__ *Religion and Society in Scotland since 1707*, Edinburgh, 1997
Brown, E.H. (ed.), *Geography Yesterday and Tomorrow*, Oxford, 1980
Brown, S.J., "Reform, Reconstruction, Reaction: the Social Vision of Scottish Presbyterianism c.1830-c.1930", *Scottish Journal of Theology*, Vol 44 (1991) pp489-517
__ "The Social Vision of Scottish Presbyterianism and the Union of 1929", *Records of the Scottish Church History Society*, Vol XXIV (1992), pp77-96
__ "'A Solemn Purification by Fire' - Responses to the Great War in the Scottish Presbyterian Churches 1914-1919", *The Journal of Ecclesiastical History*, Vol 45, No1, January 1994, pp82-104
__ "The Disruption and the Dream: The Making of New College 1843-1861" in D.F. Wright and G.D. Badcock (eds.), *Disruption to Diversity: Edinburgh Divinity 1846-1996*, Edinburgh, 1996, pp29-50
Brown, S.J. and Newlands, G. (eds), *Scottish Christianity in the Modern World*, Edinburgh, 2000
Bruce, F.F., *In Retrospect: Remembrance of Things Past*, London, 1980
__ *The Canon of Scripture*, London, 1988
Busenitz, I.A., "Must Expository Preaching always be Book Studies? Some Alternatives", *Master's Seminary Journal*, Vol 2 No 2, Fall 1991, pp139-156
Butlin, R., "George Adam Smith and the historical geography of the holy land: contents, contexts and connections", *Journal of Historical Geography*, Vol 14, No. 4 (1988), pp381-404
__ *Historical Geography: Through the Gates of Space and Time*, London, 1993
Butt, J., "Working-class housing in Glasgow 1851-1914" in S.D. Chapman (ed.), *The History of Working Class Housing: A Symposium*, London, 1971, pp55-92
Cairns, D.S., Review of Lilian Adam Smith: *George Adam Smith, A Personal Review and Family Chronicle*, in *Aberdeen University Review*, No. 90 (1944), pp243-249

Cameron, N.M. de S., *Biblical Higher Criticism and the Defense of Infallibilism in 19th century Britain*, New York, 1987
__ (ed.) *Dictionary of Scottish Church History and Theology*, Edinburgh, 1993
Campbell, I.D., "Fact not Dogma: George Adam Smith, Evangelicalism and Biblical Criticism," *Scottish Bulletin of Evangelical Theology*, Vol 18 No. 1, Spring 2000, pp3-20
Carter, J.J., and C.A. McLaren, *Crown and Gown: An Illustrated History of the University of Aberdeen 1495-1995*, Aberdeen, 1994
Checkland, S.G., *The Upas Tree: Glasgow 1875-95 – a study in growth and contraction*, Glasgow, 1976
Cheyne, A.C., *The Transforming of the Kirk: Victorian Scotland's Religious Revolution*, Edinburgh, 1983
__ *Studies in Scottish Church History*, Edinburgh, 1999
__ Introductory Essay to Tulloch, J., *Movements of Religious Thought in Britain during the Nineteenth Century* (1st published 1885), Leicester, 1971, pp7-34
Clements, R.E., *A Century of Old Testament Study*, London, 1976
Clements, K.A., *The Presidency of Woodrow Wilson*, Lawrence, Kansas, 1992
Cline, E.H., "In Pharaoh's Footsteps: History Repeats itself in General Allenby's 1918 march on Megiddo", *Archaeology Odyssey* (website of the Biblical Archaeology Society), Spring 1998, downloaded from the Internet at http://scholar.cc.emory.edu./scripts/BAS/cline.html on 23 September 1998
Collins, G.N.M., *The Heritage of our Fathers*, Edinburgh, 1974
Corts, T (ed), *Henry Drummond: A Perpetual Benediction*, Edinburgh, 1999
Craigie, P., *The Book of Deuteronomy*, Grand Rapids, Michigan, 1976
Davidson, R., "Biblical Classics V. George Adam smith: Modern Criticism and the Preaching of the Old Testament", *The Expository Times*, Vol 90 (1978-79), pp 100-104
Davies, P.R., *In Search of 'Ancient' Israel*, Sheffield, 1992
Devine, T., *The Scottish Nation 1700-2000*, London, 1999
Drummond, A.L., and Bulloch, J., *The Church in Late Victorian Scotland 1874-1900*, Edinburgh, 1978
Ellison, H.L., "The Importance of Ezra", *The Evangelical Quarterly*, Vol 53.1 (1981), pp48-53
Emerton, J.A., "Did Ezra go to Jerusalem in 428BC?", *Journal of Theological Studies*, 17 (1966), pp1-15
Fairbairn, P., *The Interpretation of Prophecy*, Edinburgh, 1964
Ferrell, R.H., *Woodrow Wilson and World War I, 1971-1921*, New York, 1985
Findlay, James F., *Dwight L. Moody: American Evangelist 1837-1899*, Chicago, 1969
Follis, E.R, (ed.), *Directions in Biblical Hebrew Poetry*, Sheffield, 1987
Forrester, Duncan B., "*Ecclesia Scoticana:* - Established, Free or National?", *Theology*, Vol CII, No 806, March/April 1999, pp80-89

Fraser, W.H., and C.H. Lee, *Aberdeen 1800-2000: A New History*, Edinburgh, 2000

Freedman, D.N., *Pottery, Poetry and Prophecy: Studies in Early Hebrew Poetry*, Winona Lake, Indiana, 1980

Fry, M., *The Scottish Empire*, Edinburgh, 2001

Gardiner, L. *Bartholomew: 150 Years*, Edinburgh, 1976

Gardner, B., *Allenby*, London, 1965

Gilbert, M., *Servant of India: A Study of Imperial Rule from 1905 to 1910 as told through the correspondence and diaries of Sir James Dunlop Smith*, London, 1966

Goldingay, J., "What are the Characteristics of Evangelical Study of the Old Testament?", *Evangelical Quarterly*, LXXIII (2), April 2001, pp99-117

Grogan, G.W., "Heilsgeographie: Geography as a Theological Concept", *The Scottish Bulletin of Evangelical Theology*, Vol 6 No 2, Autumn 1988, pp81-94

Hahn, H.F., *The Old Testament in Modern Research*, London, 1956

Hamilton, V.P., *The Book of Genesis Chapters 1-17*, Grand Rapids, Michigan, 1990

Hargreaves, John D., *Academe and Empire: Some Overseas Connections of Aberdeen University 1860-1990*, Quincentennial Studies in the History of the University of Aberdeen, Aberdeen, 1994

Harrison, R.K., *Introduction to the Old Testament*, Leicester, 1969

Harvey, C., *No Gods and Precious Few Heroes*, Edinburgh, 1998

Hazlett, P., (ed.), *Traditions of Theology in Glasgow 1450-1990: A Miscellany*, Edinburgh, 1993

Helm, P. and Trueman, C.r., (eds), *The Trustworthiness of God* Grand Rapids, 2002

Holladay, W.L., *Jeremiah 2: A Commentary on the Book of the Prophet Jeremiah Chapters 26-52*, Hermeneia Commentary Series, Minneapolis, 1989

House, P.R., *The Unity of the Twelve*, Sheffield, 1990

__ *Old Testament Theology*, Downers Grove, Illinois, 1998

Hunter, A.G., "The Indemnity: William Robertson Smith and George Adam Smith" in W. Johnstone (ed.), *William Robertson Smith: Essays in Reassessment*, Sheffield, 1995, pp 60-66

Hutchinson, I.G.C., *The University and the State: The Case of Aberdeen 1860-1963*, Quincentennial Studies in the History of the University of Aberdeen, Aberdeen, 1997

James, L, *Raj: The Making and unMaking of British India*, London, 1997

Johnstone, W., "They set us new paths: vi. Six Commentaries on the Hebrew Bible, 1888-1988", *The Expository Times*, Vol. 100 (1988-1989), pp164-169

__ (ed.) *William Robertson Smith: Essays in Reassessment*, Sheffield, 1995

Kaiser, W.C., *A History of Israel from the Bronze Age to the Jewish Wars*, New York, 1998

Kernohan, R.D., *John Buchan in a Nutshell*, Nutshell Series No. 7, Aberdeen, 2000

Kline, M.G., *Treaty of the Great King: The Covenant Structure of Deuteronomy*, Grand Rapids, Michigan, 1963

Laney, J.C., "The Prophets and Social Concern", *Bibliotheca Sacra*, Vol 147, No. 585 (January-March 1990), pp32-43

LaSor, W.S., Hubbard, D.A., and Bush, F.W., *Old Testament Survey*, Grand Rapids, Michigan, 1994

Lawson, P., *The East India Company: A History*, London, 1993

Lee, C.H., and Fraser, W.H. (eds.), *Aberdeen 1800-2000: A New History*, Edinburgh, 2000

Link, A.S. (ed.), *Woodrow Wilson: A Profile*, New York, 1968

Linklater, E., *Fanfare for a Tin Hat*, London, 1970

Lochhead, E.N., "Scotland as the Cradle of Modern Academic Geography in Britain", *Scottish Geographical Magazine*, 97 (1981), pp98-109

Lownie, A., *John Buchan: The Presbyterian Cavalier*, London, 1995

Lyall, H.F.C., *Vanishing Aberdeen*, Aberdeen, 1988

MacDonald, Ian R., *Aberdeen and the Highland Church 1785-1900*, Edinburgh, 2000

Macdonald, Lesley A.O., *A Unique and Glorious Mission: Women and Presbyterianism in Scotland 1830-1930*, Edinburgh, 2000

Macdougal, N. (ed.), *Scotland at War AD 79-1918*, London, 1990

Mackay, John L., "Cyrus, My shepherd and Messiah", *The Monthly Record of the Free Church of Scotland*, February 1991, pp30-33

__ *Haggai, Zechariah and Malachi: God's Restored People*, Fearn, 1994

MacLaren, A.A., *Religion and Social Class: the Disruption Years in Aberdeen*, London, 1947

Macleod, D., "The Free Church College 1900-1970" in Wright, D.F., and Badcock, G.D., *Disruption to Diversity: Edinburgh Divinity 1846-1996*, Edinburgh, 1996, pp221-237

Macleod, J.L., "The Influence of the Highland-Lowland Divide on the Free Presbyterian Disruption of 1893", *Records of the Scottish Church History Society,*, Vol XXV (1995), pp400-425

__ *The Second Disruption: The Free Church in Victorian Scotland and the Origins of the Free Presbyterian Church*, Scottish Historical Review Monograph No. 8, Edinburgh, 2000

Matheson, P.C., "Scottish War Sermons 1914-1919", *Records of the Scottish Church History Society*, Vol XII (1972), pp203-213

McCaffrey, J.F., *Scotland in the Nineteenth Century*, London, 1998

McConachie, J., *The Student Soldiers*, Elgin, 1995

McKim, D.K. (ed.) *Historical Handbook of Major Biblical Interpreters*, Leicester, 1998

McKnight, W., Review of Corts, T (ed), *Henry Drummond: A Perpetual Benediction*, *Reformed Theological Journal*, Volume 16 (November 2000),

pp97-99
Mechie, S., *Trinity College Glasgow 1856-1956*, Glasgow, 1956
Miller, M., "Old Testament History and Archaeology", *Biblical Archaeologist*, 50/1, March 1987, pp55-63
Milne, D.J., *A Century of History: The Establishment and First Century of the Department of History in the University of Aberdeen,* Aberdeen, 1998
Monaghan, A., *God's People? One Hundred and Ten Characters in the Story of Scottish Religion*, Edinburgh, 1991
Morris, J., *Heaven's Command: an Imperial Progress*, London, 1973
Moore, L., *Bajanellas and Semilinas: Aberdeen University and the Education of Women 1860-1920*, Aberdeen, 1991
Moorey, R., *A Century of Biblical Archaeology*, Cambridge, 1991
Moorhouse, G, *Calcutta: the City Revealed*, London, 1986
Muir, A., *John White*, London, 1958
Murray, I.H., *Revival and Revivalism: The Making and Marring of American Evangelicalism 1750-1858*, Edinburgh, 1994
Needham, N.R., *The Doctrine of Holy Scripture in the Free Church Fathers*, Edinburgh, 1991
Nicholson, E.W, *Deuteronomy and Tradition*, Oxford, 1967
Noll, M., *Between Faith and Criticism: Evangelicals, Scholarship and the Bible*, Leicester, 1991
One Hundred Years 1881-1981: To God be the Glory..., Centenary Publication ofQueen's Cross Church, Aberdeen, 1981
O'Neill, J.C., *The Bible's Authority*, Edinburgh, 1991
Owen, G.F., *Abraham to Allenby*, Grand Rapids, Michigan, 1939
Paxton, G.L., *Eretz Israel*, Faith Brethren Publishing, n.d., downloaded from the Internet at http://www.htcomp.net/fbp/ on 29 October 1998
Perdue, L.G., and Kovacks, B.W., *A Prophet to the Nations: Essays in Jeremiah Studies*, Winona Lake, Indiana, 1984
Porteous, N.W., "Sir George Adam Smith", *Palestine Exploration Quarterly*, Jan-Apr 1943, pp68-70
Rae, J., *Conscience and Politics: The British Government and the Conscientious Objector to Military Service 1916-1919*, Oxford, 1970
Reid, J.M. *Kirk and Nation: The Story of the Reformed Church of Scotland*, London, 1960
Renshaw, P., *The Longman Companion to America in the Era of the Two World Wars 1910-1945*, London, 1996
Robertson, O.P., *The Books of Nahum, Habbakuk and Zephaniah*, Grand Rapids, Michigan, 1990
__ *Understanding the Land of the Bible: A Biblical-Theological Guide*, Phillipsburg, New Jersey, 1996
Rogerson, J.W., *Old Testament Criticism in the Nineteenth Century: England and Germany* , London, 1984
__ *The Bible and Criticism in Victorian Britain: Profiles of F.D. Maurice and*

William Robertson Smith, Sheffield, 1995

Ross, Kenneth R., *Church and Creed in Scotland: the Free Church Case 1900-1904 and its Origins*, Edinburgh, 1988

Ryken, L., and Longman III, T., *A Complete Literary Guide to the Bible*, Grand Rapids, Michigan, 1993

Said, E., *Orientalism: Western Conceptions of the Orient*, London, 1995

Schwartz, J.M., "The Geography Lesson: photographs and the construction of imaginative geographies", *Journal of Historical Geography*, 22.1. (1996), pp16-45

Sell, A.P.F., *Declaring and Defending the Faith: Some Scottish Examples 1860-1920*, Exeter, 1987

Shepherd, N., *The Zealous Intruders*, London, 1987

Silva, M. (ed.), *Foundations of Contemporary Interpretation*, Leicester, 1997

Simpson, W.D., *The Fusion of 1860: A Record of the Centenary Celebration and a History of the United University of Aberdeen 1860-1960*, London, 1963

Smith, Donald C., *Passive Obedience and Prophetic Protest*, New York, 1981

Smith, Dunlop, *Servant of India: A Study of Imperial Rule from 1905-1910 as told through the correspondence and diaries of Sir James Dunlop Smith, Private Secretary to the Viceroy*, London, 1966

Smith, Graeme, "A Future Carved from the Past", *The Herald*, 16 December 2000, p30

Smith, Janet Adam, *John Buchan: A Biography*, London, 1965

__ *Mountain Holidays*, London, 1996

__ "A Family Century in the Alpine Club", *Alpine Journal*, 1982, pp142-158

Smout, T.C., *A Century of the Scottish People, 1830-1950*, London, 1986

Strathdee, R.B., *Aberdeen University Contingent: Officers Training Corps and Senior Training Corps*, Aberdeen, 1947

Sutherland, D., "The Interface between Theology and Historical Geography", *The Scottish Bulletin of Evangelical Theology*, Vol 11 No 1, Summer 1993, pp 17-30

Taylor, A.J.P., *The First World War*, London, 1963.

"Ten-Minute Talks with Useful People: IX. Sir George Adam Smith", *Greatheart: The Scottish Churches Magazine for Boys and Girls*, September 1929, pp205-208

Torrance, T.F., *Scottish Theology from John Knox to John McLeod Campbell*, Edinburgh, 1996

VanGemeren, W.A. (ed.), *New International Dictionary of Old Testament Theology and Exegesis*, 5 Volumes, Carlisle, 1997

Verhoef, P.A., *The Books of Haggai and Malachi*, Grand Rapids, Michigan, 1987

Watts, J.W., and House, P.R. (eds.), *Forming Prophetic Literature: Essays on Isaiah and the Twelve in Honor of John D.W. Watts*, Sheffield, 1996

Whitelam, K.W., *The Invention of Ancient Israel: the silencing of Palestinian*

History, London, 1996

Wilson, John D., *Milestones on the Dover Road*, London, 1969

Withrington, D.J., "The Churches in Scotland, c.1870-c.1900: Towards a New Social Conscience?", *Records of the Scottish Church History Society*, Vol XIX (1977), pp155-168

Wood, A., *Nineteenth Century Britain 1815-1914*, London, 1982

Worsdall, F., *The Tenement: A Way of Life. A Social, Historical and Architectural study of housing in Glasgow*, London, 1979

Wright, D.F., "Soundings in the Doctrine of Scripture in British Evangelicalism in the First Half of the Twentieth Century", *Tyndale Bulletin*, No 31 (1980), pp87-106

__ (ed.) *The Bible in Scottish Life and Literature*, Edinburgh, 1988

Wright, D.F. and Badcock, G.D. (eds.) *Disruption to Diversity: Edinburgh Divinity 1846-1996*, Edinburgh, 1996

Wright, J.S., *The Date of Ezra's coming to Jerusalem*, London, 1947

Wright, R.S., *Fathers of the Kirk*, London, 1960

Yamauchi, E.M., "The reverse order of Ezra/Nehemiah considered", *Themelios*, Vol 5, No. 3 (1980), pp7-13

Young, E.J., *Introduction to the Old Testament*, Grand Rapids, Michigan, 1983

Person Index

Adam, J.C. (mother) 11, 12, 13, 15, 18, 31
Allenby, E. 90, 91
Allis, O.T. 69, 198
Anderson, G. 16
Anderson, H. 13, 16, 17
Anderson, R.D. 146, 176
Ansdell, D. 2, 110
Anthony, H. 109
Annesley, E. 161
Arbuthnott, A. 155
Armerding, C. 220
Arnold, B.T. 192
Atkinson, H.E. 172
Auld, A.G. 97
Ayres, S.G. 125

Badcock, G.D. 26, 106
Bahn, P.G. 81
Baillie, J. 49
Baker, A.R.H. 80
Baker, D.W. 192
Balfour, R.G. 34, 48
Barbour, R., 25, 42, 73
Barnes, E.W. 181
Barr, J. 161, 202
Barth, K. 227
Bartholomew, J.G. 99, 100, 101
Bartlett, J. 78, 79
Basu, R. 14
Bebbington, D.W. 22, 115, 214, 227
Begg, J. 7, 57, 58, 127
Ben-Arieh, Y. 85, 102
Bennett, W.H. 125
Bestor, A.E. 172
Black, H. 51
Black, J.S. 36, 42, 44, 94, 98
Black, J. 210
Black, M. 183
Bloch, M. 80
Bowler, P.J. 82
Boyd, J.O. 189
Bray, G. 33

Bresinger, T.L. 88
Brown, C. 45, 46, 127, 128, 216
Brown, S.J. 26, 106, 152, 161, 173
Bruce, A.B. 51, 58, 86, 87, 101, 107
Bruce, F.F. 181
Bryant, S. 33
Bryce, J. 140
Buchan, J. 145, 169, 172, 184, 198
Buchanan, G. 71, 112
Buchanan, G. 155
Bulloch, J. 8, 20, 36, 145, 214
Bush, F.W. 83
Butlin, R. 79, 86, 93, 97, 100, 101
Buzzard, T. 139

Cairns, D.S. 111, 152
Cameron, G. 44
Cameron, J.K. 21
Cameron, N.M.de S. 28, 214, 224-226
Campbell, J. 132
Campbell, J.M. 5
Candlish, J.S. 107
Candlish, R. 27, 106
Carleton, J. see Smith, J.A.
Carlyle, T. 59, 60
Carnegie, A. 179, 215
Carroll, R.P. 37, 98, 194, 213
Chalmers, T. 7, 26, 58, 112, 127, 215
Charteris, A.H. 20, 56
Cheyne, A.C. 5, 21, 37, 49, 52, 105, 106, 161, 214
Cheyne, T.K. 94
Chrystal, G. 36, 42, 44, 98
Clarke, M.E. (daughter) 9, 18, 145, 148
Clements, R.E. 115
Cline, E.H. 91
Clines, D.J.A. 187
Coffin, H.S. 202
Collins, G.N.M. 6
Cook, S.A. 1, 11, 19, 30, 41, 91, 101, 108, 109, 212
Corts, T.E. 2, 115

Person Index

Craigie, P.C. 192
Cromwell, O. 150
Cunningham, W. 106

Darlow, T.H. 67
Davidson, A.B. 2, 27-30, 32, 35, 36, 41, 44, 51, 53, 67, 114, 115, 124, 132, 143, 195, 212, 221
Davidson, Randall, 202
Davidson, Robert 3, 130, 131, 183
Davies, P.R. 103
Davies, T.W. 27
Dearman, J.A. 36
De Groote, G.J. 152
De Wette, W.M.L. 27
Delitszch, F. 32, 143, 220
Denney, J. 51, 97, 139, 142, 151, 159, 212
Devine, T.M. 127, 173, 177-179, 199
Diestel, L. 31
Dixon, W.M. 167, 168
Dods, M. 67, 212
Donald, L. 179
Doveton, J. 11
Drummond, A.L. 8, 20, 36, 145, 214
Drummond, H. 2, 18-25, 44, 51, 55, 56, 73, 74, 107, 110, 113-115, 217, 221, 225
Drummond, R.J. 57
Duff, A. 27
Duff, A. (Mrs) 12
Duhm, B. 115
Duns, J. 40, 41

Elphinstone, W. 145, 174
Emerton, J.A. 122
Enright, W.G. 2, 76
Esslemont, M. 177
Ewald, H.G.A. 27, 29, 115, 143, 221
Ewing, W. 54

Fairbairn, P. 106
Farrar, F.W. 28
Febvre, L. 80
Ferrell, R.H. 168
Findlay, J.F. 20
Fisher, S.H. 26
Fleming, J.R. 161
Follis, E.R. 187

Forrester, D. 199
Fraser, J. 41
Fraser, W.H. 176
Freedman, D.N. 186
Freeman, T.W. 83
Fry, M. 37
Fyfe, W.H. 175

Gammie, A. 45-47
Gardiner, J. 60
Gardiner, L. 100, 101
Gardner, B. 91
Gentrup, W. 69
Gilbert, M. 15
Gladstone, W. 58
Gollancz, I. 186
Gray, A. 180, 181, 205
Gray, A.H. 161
Gregory, D. 80
Greidanus, S. 88
Grierson, H. 184
Grogan, G.W. 85
Guthe, H. 224

Hamilton, I. 105
Hamilton, V.P. 94
Harnack, A. 32
Harrison, R.K. 120
Hastings, J. 87
Hay, C. 179, 180
Heelis, W. 71
Henderson, G. 211
Henderson, J. 41
Hill, G. 183
Hodgson, W.B. 19
Holladay, W.L. 193
Holmes, J.E. 19, 22
House, P.R. 116, 192
Hubbard, D.A. 83
Humphries, R. 91
Hunter, A.G. 213, 227
Hutchison, I.G.C. 182, 216

Innes, A.T. 6, 105

James, L. 14
Johnston, J. 133
Jonhstone, W. 36, 64, 98, 213

Kaiser, W.C. 9, 10, 80, 193
Keil, C.F. 220
Kelman, J. 49, 51, 78, 103, 139, 154, 181
Knowles, J. 147
Kovacks, B.W. 194
Kidd, J. 135, 136
Kline, M.G. 192

Laidlaw, J. 46
Laird, J. 41
Lamont, S. 37
Lang, M. 145
Lasor, W.S. 83
Lawley, S. 90
Lee, A. 175
Lee, C.H. 176
Leslie, R. 91
Lincoln, A. 150
Lindsay, T.M. 107
Linklater, E. 146, 153, 177
Lloyd George, D. 90
Lochhead, E. 83, 100
Locke, J. 202
Long, V.P. 103
Longman, T. 88, 124
Lyall, H. 47
Lynch, F. 169

MacAlister, D. 142
Macaskill, M. 106
Macdonald, C.M.M. 172
Macdonald, I.R. 45
Macdonald, L.A.O. 177
Macdonald, P. 68
Macgregor, J. 27
MacHaffie, B. 2, 68
Mackenzie, W.L. 175, 176
Mackintosh, A. 175
MacLaren, A.A. 46
Macleod, D. 133, 142
Macleod, J.L. 2, 106, 109, 110, 214
Macleod, N. 57
Main, A. 212
Mann, H. 93
Manson, W. 86, 211
Margoliouth, D.S. 98, 99
Martin, A. 57, 201
Matheson, D. 31

Matheson, P. 152
Maurice, F.D. 36, 60
McCaffrey, J.F. 126
McConachie, J. 146, 147
McCrie, T. 7
McFarland, E.W. 172
McKim, D.K. 32, 36, 69
Mechie, S. 107
Melville, A. 155
Mildert, W.V. 28
Miller, M. 102
Mitchell, J. 201
Monson, J.M. 85
Moody, D.L. 1, 19-26, 50, 114, 140, 217, 218, 220
Moore, L. 177
Moorhouse, G. 13, 14
Moorey, R. 81
Monaghan, A. 172
Morgan, J. 47
Morgan, R.C. 20
Morison, J.L. 111
Morris, J. 13, 14
Morrison, P. 69
Muir, A. 57, 198, 199, 201
Myers, C.H. 149

Nicholson, E.W. 193
Nicoll, W.R. 62, 67, 72, 99, 113, 133, 139
Nicolson, D.J. 110, 133
Noll, M. 141, 214, 225

Oldham, J. 202
O'Neill, J.C. 27, 32, 33
Orpen, W. 203
Orr, J. 220
Owen G.F. 91

Paton, D.K. 224
Paul, M.J. 94
Paxton, G.L. 86
Peake, A.S. 89, 124, 125
Perdue, L.G. 194
Philip, A. 212
Philip, J. 51
Philip, R.G., 43
Pirie, J.B. 47
Porteous, N. 212

Person Index

Primrose, R. 132, 133

Rae, J. 156
Rainy, R. 6, 8, 26, 32, 36, 57, 74, 77, 105, 130, 136, 137
Ramsay, W.M. 86
Reid, M. 179
Reith, G.M. 137, 155, 168
Renan, E. 89
Reynolds, J.B. 26
Riesen, R.A. 2, 36, 53, 130
Robertson, O.P. 9, 102, 120, 121
Robinson, H.W. 68, 86, 90
Rogerson, J. 36
Ross, D.M. 25, 53-55, 57, 58, 60, 74
Ross, I. (sister) 12, 14, 17, 18
Ross, K.R. 25, 50, 105, 129, 214
Ross, W. 50
Roth, W. 31
Rowley, H.H. 194
Roxburgh, E. 49
Rule, A.147
Rumscheidt, H.M. 32
Ryken, L. 88, 124

Sachs, M. 42
Said, E.W. 191
Salmond, S.D.F. 41, 46, 47
Sankey, I.D. 19, 20, 23, 26, 50, 114, 217, 218, 220
Schwartz, J. 92, 93
Scott, C.A. 49, 77
Seaton, E. 71
Sefton, H.R. 42, 52
Shepherd, N. 81, 82
Sheppard, G.T. 69
Simpson, P.C. 6, 57, 77, 106, 130, 137
Simpson, W.D. 174, 176, 179
Smeaton, G. 6, 26
Smith, A. 2
Smith, A.L. Buchanan- (grandson) 207
Smith, A.D.B. (son) 112
Smith, D.C. 58, 60, 127
Smith, G. (father) 11-13, 15-18, 30, 31
Smith, G.B. (son) 13, 73, 148
Smith, H. (brother) 16, 18
Smith, I.M. (sister), see Ross, I.
Smith, I.K. (daughter) 112, 185

Smith, J. 137, 138
Smith, J.A. (daughter) 9, 71, 112, 145, 185
Smith, J.C. (sister) 16, 18
Smith, J.D. (brother) 13, 15, 16, 139
Smith, L.A. (wife) 1, 9, 16, 18, 23, 30, 33, 36, 43, 49, 50, 55, 70-73, 77, 84, 91, 92, 103, 111, 140, 145, 146, 149, 150, 154, 165, 179, 180, 189, 193, 196, 203, 204, 206-212
Smith, L.M.B. (daughter), 112, 166, 167
Smith, M. (aunt) 13, 17
Smith, M.M. (sister) 16, 18
Smith, R.D. (son) 73, 149, 150
Smith, W.R. 2, 8, 28, 29, 35, 37, 40-44, 53, 62, 98, 114, 115, 125, 143, 191, 209, 212, 213, 218, 221, 226
Smith, W.T. (brother) 16, 17
Smout, T.C. 4, 19, 34, 61
Spiro, S. 37
Sorley, W.R. 31, 36
Souter, A. 203
Soutter, R. 162
Stalker, J. 51, 174
Steiner, M. 97
Stewart, A. 21
Stewart, D. 210
Stoughton, T.W. 62
Strahan, J. 27, 28
Strange, A.C. 162
Strathdee, R.B. 147
Sutherland, D. 85
Sykes, H. 78

Taft, W.H. 140
Taylor, A.J.P. 91, 165, 166
Taylor, M. 16
Taylor, R. 106
Thomson, G.P. 184
Thorburn, D. 17
Toone, M.J. 19, 21, 26
Torrance, T.F. 226
Torrey, R.A. 19
Troeltsch, E. 156
Tweedie, J.A. 164

Walker, W.L. 151, 152, 160
Watson, C.M. 81

Watt, T. 50
Watts, J.W. 116
Welch, A. 125, 139
Wellhausen, J. 27, 69, 143
Wenborn, N. 60
Wenham, G.J. 192
White, J. 57, 198, 201
Whitelam, K. 102, 103
Whyte, A. 32, 51, 74
Williams, P.H. 210
Wilson, J.D. 207, 208
Wilson, J.H. 20
Wilson, W. 1, 168, 169
Wood, A. 173
Wood, S. 176
Woodward, B.L. 124
Wright, D.F. 26, 106, 107
Wright, J.S. 122
Wright, H.B. 26

Young, E.J. 69, 192
Younger, R. 160

Subject Index

Aberdeen, City of, 8, 45, 73, 182, 202
Aberdeen Free Church College, 8, 35, 40-43, 47, 75
Alps, 70-72
Amos, Book of, 117, 118, 222, 223
Apocalyptic literature, 122
Assyria, 117, 120, 196

Balerno, 207, 208
Bible, 5, 32, 35, 39, 50, 51, 54, 60, 61, 62, 65, 67, 68, 76, 80, 87, 91, 107, 125, 128, 136, 144, 156, 212, 217, 218, 220, 221, 222, 223, 224, 227
Biblical criticism, 87, 96, 99, 109, 113, 114, 115, 125, 131, 134, 135, 136, 138, 141, 198, 204, 211, 213, 220, 221, 223, 225, 226, 227
Book of the Twelve Prophets, 96, 115-125
Brechin, 40

Calvinism, 37, 42, 105, 127, 128, 212
Cambridge, 37
Carnegie Trust, 179, 215
Cartography, 99-101
Chicago, 140
Children More Sinned Against than Sinning, 61
Christianity and Social Life, 58-60
Church of Scotland, 4, 5, 6, 7, 20, 56, 57, 105, 152, 158, 159, 198, 199, 201, 202, 215
Conscientious objectors, 157, 160, 161
Credal subscription, 3, 105, 137, 138, 175, 176, 212, 213, 226
Cyrus, 63, 65, 66

Declaratory Act, 6, 105, 106, 125, 134, 137, 138, 213, 215
Declaratory Articles, 199, 215
Deuteronomy, Book of, 95, 121, 123, 189-193, 194, 195
Deuteronomy, 189-193

Disestablishment Campaign, 6, 55-58, 199, 216
Disruption, 2, 5-8, 10, 26, 28, 36, 45, 53, 56, 106, 112, 202, 214
Doveton College, 11, 12

Early Poetry of Israel, 186-189
Edinburgh, city of, 34
Egypt, 34, 37, 38, 40, 44, 77, 196
Enlightenment, 4
Episcopalianism, 52, 53
Establishment Principle, 6, 57, 129, 215, 216
Evangelicalism, 8, 19, 21, 53, 54, 56, 61, 69, 107, 108, 109, 118, 125, 137, 217, 218, 220, 226, 227
Evangelistic crusades, 19-24, 50, 217
Exile, 122, 123, 197
Expositor, The, 69
Expository Times, 3, 197

First World War, 3, 4, 9, 32, 73, 90, 101, 145-173, 206
Forgiveness of Sins and other Sermons, 109, 218
Four Psalms, 51, 88, 112, 113
Free Church of Scotland, 5, 6, 7, 8, 20, 21, 25, 26, 34, 36, 42-45, 49, 54, 56-58, 62, 78, 105, 110, 112, 113, 125, 126, 129, 141, 198, 202, 214, 215
Free Church College (post-1900), 142
Free Presbyterian Church of Scotland, 2, 7, 106, 109, 110, 125, 134, 202

Gaiety Club, 24
Genesis, Book of, 31, 134, 135
German hostility, 151, 156, 157, 166, 171
German theology, 8, 27, 30, 31, 32, 34, 35, 42, 143, 220
Gifford Lecutres, 181
Glasgow Free Church College, 3, 43, 74, 97, 104-144

Habakkuk, Book of, 120, 124
Haggai, Book of, 121, 122
Higher Criticism, 27, 28, 30, 126, 128, 144, 214, 220
Historical Atlas of the Holy Land, 100
Historical geography, 18, 64, 79, 82, 86, 101, 103, 203
Historical Geography of the Holy Land, 38, 64, 78, 79, 80, 85-91, 92, 102, 165
Hodder and Stoughton, 3, 9, 62, 100, 210
Hosea, Book of, 188, 143

India, 11-13, 17, 29, 31
Indian Mutiny, 13-15
Industrial Revolution, 4
Inspiration of Scripture, 25, 26, 76, 214
Instrumental music, 23
Isaiah, 61, 62-70, 90, 219
Isaiah, Book of, 3, 27, 32, 62-70, 87, 88, 95, 96, 98, 99, 219, 224
Israel, 66, 89, 103, 109, 116, 117, 122, 131, 135, 140, 186, 222

Jeremiah, Book of, 120, 132, 152, 193-198, 222, 223, 224
Jerusalem, 39, 77, 81, 82, 87, 88, 93, 95, 152, 166
Jerusalem: The Topography, Economics and History, 77, 90, 91-99
Job, Book of, 28

King's College, 174

Labour Party, 4, 59, 127
Liberalism, 4
Life of Henry Drummond, 19, 110, 113-115, 217, 218, 225

Malachi, Book of, 121, 123, 143
Marischal College, 47, 174
Melchizedek, 94, 95
Messiah, 62, 96, 98, 121, 122, 134, 151, 222, 224
Micah, Book of, 119
Mission work, 12
Moderator, 149, 154, 155-160, 162, 173, 201
Modern Criticism and the Preaching of the Old Testament, 33, 110, 129-134,

222, 224
Mountaineering, 70, 71

Nahum, Book of, 120, 124
Neo-orthodoxy, 227
New College 2, 6, 9, 25-28, 30, 35, 39, 42, 45, 111, 116, 125, 129
New Testament, 70

Obadiah, Book of, 121
Old Testament Criticism, 2, 7, 8, 32, 36, 69, 70, 76, 80, 89, 108, 114, 121, 123, 124, 130, 131, 193, 220, 221
Orientalism, 191, 212
Our Common Conscience, 32, 33, 147, 170-173

Palestine, 1, 9, 34, 38, 39, 40, 49, 71, 75, 76, 77, 78, 81, 82, 83, 84, 88, 89, 90, 92, 100, 101, 102, 103, 166, 183
Palestine Exploration Fund 1, 80, 81, 84, 87, 212
Patronage Act, 6, 56, 57
Pentateuch, 27, 190-193
Plain Words on the differences Between Presbyterianism and Episcopacy, 52
Poetry of Old Testament, 140, 153, 185-189
Preaching of the Old Testament to the Age, 51, 108, 130, 217
Princeton University, 49
Prophets, Old Testament, 59, 66, 89, 98, 115-125, 127, 142, 203, 205

Queen's Cross Free Church, 2, 43, 45-76, 103, 217, 227

Schweich Lectures, 185-189
Scottish Geographical Society, 71, 83
Scottish Journal of Agriculture, 1, 182
Second World War, 209
Social gospel, 22, 58, 61, 90, 126-128, 179
Spiritual Independence, 57, 200
Switzerland, 70, 71
Syria and the Holy Land, 85, 165

Teaching of Old Testament in Schools,

221, 224
Teinds, 57
Temperance, 22, 75, 158, 159
Temple, 96
Theological education, 106, 141
Trinity College, Glasgow, 18, 107, 110

United Free Church of Scotland 1, 7, 11, 107, 128, 129, 134, 137, 138, 141, 152, 155, 159, 160, 161, 168, 175, 198, 199, 201, 202, 215
United Presbyterian Church of Scotland, 6, 128
United States of America, 3, 139-142, 166-173
University of Aberdeen, 3, 27, 142, 144, 145-205, 206, 208
University of Edinburgh, 11, 19, 20, 26, 30, 112, 181
University of Glasgow, 110, 139, 142, 148, 181
University of St Andrews, 181
Urbanisation, 4, 34

War and Peace, 150, 151
Westminster Confession of Faith, 5, 6, 105, 109, 125, 212, 215, 226
Women in society, 158, 176, 177

Yale University, 26, 49, 129, 140, 215
Young Men's Christian Association, 22

Zechariah, Book of, 121, 122, 123
Zephaniah, Book of, 120

Paternoster Biblical Monographs

(All titles uniform with this volume)
Dates in bold are of projected publication

Joseph Abraham
Eve: Accused or Acquitted?
A Reconsideration of Feminist Readings of the Creation Narrative Texts in Genesis 1–3
Two contrary views dominate contemporary feminist biblical scholarship. One finds in the Bible an unequivocal equality between the sexes from the very creation of humanity, whilst the other sees the biblical text as irredeemably patriarchal and androcentric. Dr Abraham enters into dialogue with both camps as well as introducing his own method of approach. An invaluable tool for any one who is interested in this contemporary debate.
2002 / 0-85364-971-5 / xxiv + 272pp

Octavian D. Baban
Mimesis and Luke's On the Road Encounters in Luke-Acts
Luke's Theology of the Way and its Literary Representation
The book argues on theological and literary (mimetic) grounds that Luke's on-the-road encounters, especially those belonging to the post-Easter period, are part of his complex theology of the Way. Jesus' teaching and that of the apostles is presented by Luke as a challenging answer to the Hellenistic reader's thirst for adventure, good literature, and existential paradigms.
2005 / 1-84227253-5 / approx. 374pp

Paul Barker
The Triumph of Grace in Deuteronomy
This book is a textual and theological analysis of the interaction between the sin and faithlessness of Israel and the grace of Yahweh in response, looking especially at Deuteronomy chapters 1–3, 8–10 and 29–30. The author argues that the grace of Yahweh is determinative for the ongoing relationship between Yahweh and Israel and that Deuteronomy anticipates and fully expects Israel to be faithless.
2004 / 1-84227-226-8 / xxii + 270pp

Jonathan F. Bayes
The Weakness of the Law
God's Law and the Christian in New Testament Perspective
A study of the four New Testament books which refer to the law as weak (Acts, Romans, Galatians, Hebrews) leads to a defence of the third use in the Reformed debate about the law in the life of the believer.
2000 / 0-85364-957-X / xii + 244pp

Mark Bonnington
The Antioch Episode of Galatians 2:11-14 in Historical and Cultural Context
The Galatians 2 'incident' in Antioch over table-fellowship suggests significant disagreement between the leading apostles. This book analyses the background to the disagreement by locating the incident within the dynamics of social interaction between Jews and Gentiles. It proposes a new way of understanding the relationship between the individuals and issues involved.
2005 / 1-84227-050-8 / approx. 350pp

David Bostock
A Portrayal of Trust
The Theme of Faith in the Hezekiah Narratives
This study provides detailed and sensitive readings of the Hezekiah narratives (2 Kings 18–20 and Isaiah 36–39) from a theological perspective. It concentrates on the theme of faith, using narrative criticism as its methodology. Attention is paid especially to setting, plot, point of view and characterization within the narratives. A largely positive portrayal of Hezekiah emerges that underlines the importance and relevance of scripture.
2005 / 1-84227-314-0 / approx. 300pp

Mark Bredin
Jesus, Revolutionary of Peace
A Non-violent Christology in the Book of Revelation
This book aims to demonstrate that the figure of Jesus in the Book of Revelation can best be understood as an active non-violent revolutionary.
2003 / 1-84227-153-9 / xviii + 262pp

Robinson Butarbutar
Resolving a Dispute, Past and Present
An Exegetical Study of Paul's Apostolic Paradigm in 1 Corinthians 9
The author sees the apostolic paradigm in 1 Corinthians 9 as part of Paul's unified arguments in 1 Corinthians 8–10 in which he seeks to mediate in the dispute over the issue of food offered to idols. The book also sees its relevance for dispute-resolution today, taking the conflict within the author's church as an example.
2005 / 1-84227315-9 / approx. 280pp

Daniel J-S Chae
Paul as Apostle to the Gentiles
His Apostolic Self-awareness and its Influence on the Soteriological Argument in Romans
Opposing 'the post-Holocaust interpretation of Romans', Daniel Chae competently demonstrates that Paul argues for the equality of Jew and Gentile in Romans. Chae's fresh exegetical interpretation is academically outstanding and spiritually encouraging.
1997 / 0-85364-829-8 / xiv + 378pp

Luke L. Cheung
The Genre, Composition and Hermeneutics of the Epistle of James
The present work examines the employment of the wisdom genre with a certain compositional structure and the interpretation of the law through the Jesus tradition of the double love command by the author of the Epistle of James to serve his purpose in promoting perfection and warning against doubleness among the eschatologically renewed people of God in the Diaspora.
2003 / 1-84227-062-1 / xvi + 372pp

Youngmo Cho
Spirit and Kingdom in the Writings of Luke and Paul
The relationship between Spirit and Kingdom is a relatively unexplored area in Lukan and Pauline studies. This book offers a fresh perspective of two biblical writers on the subject. It explores the difference between Luke's and Paul's understanding of the Spirit by examining the specific question of the relationship of the concept of the Spirit to the concept of the Kingdom of God in each writer.
2005 / 1-84227-316-7 / approx. 270pp

Andrew C. Clark
Parallel Lives
The Relation of Paul to the Apostles in the Lucan Perspective
This study of the Peter-Paul parallels in Acts argues that their purpose was to emphasize the themes of continuity in salvation history and the unity of the Jewish and Gentile missions. New light is shed on Luke's literary techniques, partly through a comparison with Plutarch.
2001 / 1-84227-035-4 / xviii + 386pp

Andrew D. Clarke
Secular and Christian Leadership in Corinth
A Socio-Historical and Exegetical Study of 1 Corinthians 1–6
This volume is an investigation into the leadership structures and dynamics of first-century Roman Corinth. These are compared with the practice of leadership in the Corinthian Christian community which are reflected in 1 Corinthians 1–6, and contrasted with Paul's own principles of Christian leadership
2005 / 1-84227-229-2 / 200pp

Stephen Finamore
God, Order and Chaos
René Girard and the Apocalypse
Readers are often disturbed by the images of destruction in the book of Revelation and unsure why they are unleashed after the exaltation of Jesus. This book examines past approaches to these texts and uses René Girard's theories to revive some old ideas and propose some new ones.
2005 / 1-84227-197-0 / approx. 344pp

Scott J. Hafemann
Suffering and Ministry in the Spirit
Paul's Defence of His Ministry in II Corinthians 2:14–3:3
Shedding new light on the way Paul defended his apostleship, the author offers a careful, detailed study of 2 Corinthians 2:14–3:3 linked with other key passages throughout 1 and 2 Corinthians. Demonstrating the unity and coherence of Paul's argument in this passage, the author shows that Paul's suffering served as the vehicle for revealing God's power and glory through the Spirit.
2000 / 0-85364-967-7 / xiv + 262pp

Scott J. Hafemann
Paul, Moses and the History of Israel
The Letter/Spirit Contrast and the Argument from Scripture in 2 Corinthians 3
An exegetical study of the call of Moses, the second giving of the Law (Exodus 32–34), the new covenant, and the prophetic understanding of the history of Israel in 2 Corinthians 3. Hafemann's work demonstrates Paul's contextual use of the Old Testament and the essential unity between the Law and the Gospel within the context of the distinctive ministries of Moses and Paul.
2005 / 1-84227-317-5 / 498pp

Douglas S. McComiskey
Lukan Theology in the Light of the Gospel's Literary Structure
Luke's Gospel was purposefully written with theology embedded in its patterned literary structure. A critical analysis of this cyclical structure provides new windows into Luke's interpretation of the individual pericopes comprising the Gospel and illuminates several of his theological interests.
2004 / 1-84227-148-2 / approx. 400pp

Stephen Motyer
Your Father the Devil?
A New Approach to John and 'The Jews'
Who are 'the Jews' in John's Gospel? Defending John against the charge of antisemitism, Motyer argues that, far from demonising the Jews, the Gospel seeks to present Jesus as 'Good News for Jews' in a late first century setting.
1997 / 0-85364-832-8 / xiv + 260pp

Esther Ng
Reconstructing Christian Origins?
The Feminist Theology of Elizabeth Schüssler Fiorenza: An Evaluation
In a detailed evaluation, the author challenges Elizabeth Schüssler Fiorenza's reconstruction of early Christian origins and her underlying presuppositions. The author also presents her own views on women's roles both then and now.
2002 / 1-84227-055-9 / xxiv + 468pp

Robin Parry
Old Testament Story and Christian Ethics
The Rape of Dinah as a Case Study
What is the role of story in ethics and, more particularly, what is the role of Old Testament story in Christian ethics? This book, drawing on the work of contemporary philosophers, argues that narrative is crucial in the ethical shaping of people and, drawing on the work of contemporary Old Testament scholars, that story plays a key role in Old Testament ethics. Parry then argues that when situated in canonical context Old Testament stories can be reappropriated by Christian readers in their own ethical formation. The shocking story of the rape of Dinah and the massacre of the Shechemites provides a fascinating case study for exploring the parameters within which Christian ethical appropriations of Old Testament stories can live.
2004 / 1-84227-210-1 / xx + 350pp

Ian Paul
Power to See the World Anew
The Value of Paul Ricoeur's Hermeneutic of Metaphor in Interpreting the Symbolism of Revelation 12 and 13

This book is a study of the hermeneutics of metaphor of Paul Ricoeur, one of the most important writers on hermeneutics and metaphor of the last century. It sets out the key points of his theory, important criticisms of his work, and how his approach, modified in the light of these criticisms, offers a methodological framework for reading apocalyptic texts.

2005 / 1-84227-056-7 / approx. 350pp

Robert L. Plummer
Paul's Understanding of the Church's Mission
Did the Apostle Paul Expect the Early Christian Communities to Evangelize?

This book engages in a careful study of Paul's letters to determine if the apostle expected the communities to which he wrote to engage in missionary activity. It helpfully summarizes the discussion on this debated issue, judiciously handling contested texts, and provides a way forward in addressing this critical question. While admitting that Paul rarely explicitly commands the communities he founded to evangelize, Plummer amasses significant incidental data to provide a convincing case that Paul did indeed expect his churches to engage in mission activity. Throughout the study, Plummer progressively builds a theological basis for the church's mission that is both distinctively Pauline and compelling.

2005 / 0-85364-333-7 / approx. 324pp

David Powys
'Hell': A Hard Look at a Hard Question
The Fate of the Unrighteous in New Testament Thought

This comprehensive treatment seeks to unlock the original meaning of terms and phrases long thought to support the traditional doctrine of hell. It concludes that there is an alternative—one which is more biblical, and which can positively revive the rationale for Christian mission.

1997 / 0-85364-831-X / xxii + 478pp

Sorin Sabou
Between Horror and Hope
Paul's Metaphorical Language of Death in Romans 6.1-11

This book argues that Paul's metaphorical language of death in Romans 6.1-11 conveys two aspects: horror and hope. The 'horror' aspect is conveyed by the 'crucifixion' language, and the 'hope' aspect by 'burial' language. The life of the Christian believer is understood, as relationship with sin is concerned ('death to sin'), between these two realities: horror and hope.

2005 / 1-84227-322-1 / approx. 224pp

November 2004

Rosalind Selby
The Comical Doctrine
Mark and Hermeneutics
This book argues that the gospel breaks through postmodernity's critique of truth and the referential possibilities of textuality with its gift of grace. With a rigorous, philosophical challenge to modernist and postmodernist assumptions, Selby offers an alternative epistemology to all who would still read with faith *and* with academic credibility.
2005 / 1-84227-212-8 / approx. 350pp

Kevin Walton
Thou Traveller Unknown
The Presence and Absence of God in the Jacob Narrative
The author offers a fresh reading of the story of Jacob in the book of Genesis through the paradox of divine presence and absence. The work also seeks to make a contribution to Pentateuchal studies by bringing together a close reading of the final text with historical critical insights, doing justice to the text's historical depth, final form and canonical status.
2003 / 1-84227-059-1 / xvi + 238pp

George M. Wieland
The Significance of Salvation
A Study of Salvation Language in the Pastoral Epistles
The language and ideas of salvation pervade the three Pastoral Epistles. This study offers a close examination of their soteriological statements. In all three letters the idea of salvation is found to play a vital paraenetic role, but each also exhibits distinctive soteriological emphases. The results challenge common assumptions about the Pastoral Epistles as a corpus.
2005 / 1-84227257-8 / approx. 324pp

Alistair Wilson
When Will These Things Happen?
A Study of Jesus as Judge in Matthew 21–25
This study seeks to allow Matthew's carefully constructed presentation of Jesus to be given full weight in the modern evaluation of Jesus' eschatology. Careful analysis of the text of Matthew 21–25 reveals Jesus to be standing firmly in the Jewish prophetic and wisdom traditions as he proclaims and enacts imminent judgement on the Jewish authorities then boldly claims the central role in the final and universal judgement.
2004 / 1-84227-146-6 / xxii + 272pp

Lindsay Wilson
Joseph Wise and Otherwise
The Intersection of Covenant and Wisdom in Genesis 37–50
This book offers a careful literary reading of Genesis 37–50 that argues that the Joseph story contains both strong covenant themes and many wisdom-like elements. The connections between the two helps to explore how covenant and wisdom might intersect in an integrated biblical theology.
2004 / 1-84227-140-7 / xvi + 340pp

Stephen I. Wright
The Voice of Jesus
Studies in the Interpretation of Six Gospel Parables
This literary study considers how the 'voice' of Jesus has been heard in different periods of parable interpretation, and how the categories of figure and trope may help us towards a sensitive reading of the parables today.
2000 / 0-85364-975-8 / xiv + 280pp

Paternoster
9 Holdom Avenue
Bletchley
Milton Keynes MK1 1QR
United Kingdom

Web: www.authenticmedia.co.uk/paternoster

Paternoster Theological Monographs
(All titles uniform with this volume)
Dates in bold are of projected publication

Emil Bartos
Deification in Eastern Orthodox Theology
An Evaluation and Critique of the Theology of Dumitru Staniloae
Bartos studies a fundamental yet neglected aspect of Orthodox theology: deification. By examining the doctrines of anthropology, christology, soteriology and ecclesiology as they relate to deification, he provides an important contribution to contemporary dialogue between Eastern and Western theologians.
1999 / 0-85364-956-1 / xii + 370pp

Iain D. Campbell
Fixing the Indemnity
The Life and Work of George Adam Smith
When Old Testament scholar George Adam Smith (1856–1942) delivered the Lyman Beecher lectures at Yale University in 1899, he confidently declared that 'modern criticism has won its war against traditional theories. It only remains to fix the amount of the indemnity.' In this biography, Iain D. Campbell assesses Smith's critical approach to the Old Testament and evaluates its consequences, showing that Smith's life and work still raises questions about the relationship between biblical scholarship and evangelical faith.
2004 / 1-84227-228-4 / xx + 256pp

Tim Chester
Mission and the Coming of God
Eschatology, the Trinity and Mission in the Theology of Jürgen Moltmann
This book explores the theology and missiology of the influential contemporary theologian, Jürgen Moltmann. It highlights the important contribution Moltmann has made while offering a critique of his thought from an evangelical perspective. In so doing, it touches on pertinent issues for evangelical missiology. The conclusion takes Calvin as a starting point, proposing 'an eschatology of the cross' which offers a critique of the over-realised eschatologies in liberation theology and certain forms of evangelicalism.
2005 / 1-84227-320-5 / approx. 224pp

Sylvia Wilkey Collinson
Making Disciples
The Significance of Jesus' Educational Strategy for Today's Church
This study examines the biblical practice of discipling, formulates a definition, and makes comparisons with modern models of education. A recommendation is made for greater attention to its practice today.
2004 / 1-84227-116-4 / xiv + 278pp

Darrell Cosden
A Theology of Work
Work and the New Creation
Through dialogue with Moltmann, Pope John Paul II and others, this book develops a genitive 'theology of work', presenting a theological definition of work and a model for a theological ethics of work that shows work's nature, value and meaning now and eschatologically. Work is shown to be a transformative activity consisting of three dynamically inter-related dimensions: the instrumental, relational and ontological.
2004 / 1-84227-332-9 / xvi + 208pp

Stephen M. Dunning
The Crisis and the Quest
A Kierkegaardian Reading of Charles Williams
Employing Kierkegaardian categories and analysis, this study investigates both the central crisis in Charles Williams's authorship between hermetism and Christianity (Kierkegaard's Religions A and B), and the quest to resolve this crisis, a quest that ultimately presses the bounds of orthodoxy.
2000 / 0-85364-985-5 / xxiv + 254pp

Keith Ferdinando
The Triumph of Christ in African Perspective
A Study of Demonology and Redemption in the African Context
The book explores the implications of the gospel for traditional African fears of occult aggression. It analyses such traditional approaches to suffering and biblical responses to fears of demonic evil, concluding with an evaluation of African beliefs from the perspective of the gospel.
1999 / 0-85364-830-1 / xviii + 450pp

Andrew Goddard
Living the Word, Resisting the World
The Life and Thought of Jacques Ellul

This work offers a definitive study of both the life and thought of the French Reformed thinker Jacques Ellul (1912-1994). It will prove an indispensable resource for those interested in this influential theologian and sociologist and for Christian ethics and political thought generally.

2002 / 1-84227-053-2 / xxiv + 378pp

David Hilborn
The Words of our Lips
Language-Use in Free Church Worship

Studies of liturgical language have tended to focus on the written canons of Roman Catholic and Anglican communities. By contrast, David Hilborn analyses the more extemporary approach of English Nonconformity. Drawing on recent developments in linguistic pragmatics, he explores similarities and differences between 'fixed' and 'free' worship, and argues for the interdependence of each.

2005 / 0-85364-977-4

Roger Hitching
The Church and Deaf People
A Study of Identity, Communication and Relationships with Special Reference to the Ecclesiology of Jürgen Moltmann

In *The Church and Deaf People* Roger Hitching sensitively examines the history and present experience of deaf people and finds similarities between aspects of sign language and Moltmann's theological method that 'open up' new ways of understanding theological concepts.

2003 / 1-84227-222-5 / xxii + 236pp

John G. Kelly
One God, One People
The Differentiated Unity of the People of God in the Theology of Jürgen Moltmann

The author expounds and critiques Moltmann's doctrine of God and highlights the systematic connections between it and Moltmann's influential discussion of Israel. He then proposes a fresh approach to Jewish-Christian relations building on Moltmann's work using insights from Habermas and Rawls.

2005 / 0-85346-969-3 / approx. 350pp

Mark F.W. Lovatt
Confronting the Will-to-Power
A Reconsideration of the Theology of Reinhold Niebuhr
Confronting the Will-to-Power is an analysis of the theology of Reinhold Niebuhr, arguing that his work is an attempt to identify, and provide a practical theological answer to, the existence and nature of human evil.
2001 / 1-84227-054-0 / xviii + 216pp

Neil B. MacDonald
Karl Barth and the Strange New World within the Bible
Barth, Wittgenstein, and the Metadilemmas of the Enlightenment
Barth's discovery of the strange new world within the Bible is examined in the context of Kant, Hume, Overbeck, and, most importantly, Wittgenstein. MacDonald covers some fundamental issues in theology today: epistemology, the final form of the text and biblical truth-claims.
2000 / 0-85364-970-7 / xxvi + 374pp

Keith Mascord
No Challenge Unfaced
Alvin Plantinga's Contribution to Christian Apologetics
This book draws together the contributions of the philosopher, Alvin Plantinga, to the major contemporary challenges to Christian belief, highlighting in particular his ground-breaking work in epistemology and the problem of evil. Plantinga's theory that both theistic and Christian belief is warrantedly basic is explored and critiqued, and an assessment offered as to the significance of his work for apologetic theory and practice.
2005 / 1-84227-256-X / approx. 304pp

Gillian McCulloch
The Deconstruction of Dualism in Theology
With Reference to Ecofeminist Theology and New Age Spirituality
This book challenges eco-theological anti-dualism in Christian theology, arguing that dualism has a twofold function in Christian religious discourse. Firstly, it enables us to express the discontinuities and divisions that are part of the process of reality. Secondly, dualistic language allows us to express the mysteries of divine transcendence/immanence and the survival of the soul without collapsing into monism and materialism, both of which are problematic for Christian epistemology.
2002 / 1-84227-044-3 / xii + 282pp

November 2004

Leslie McCurdy
Attributes and Atonement
The Holy Love of God in the Theology of P.T. Forsyth
Attributes and Atonement is an intriguing full-length study of P.T. Forsyth's doctrine of the cross as it relates particularly to God's holy love. It includes an unparalleled bibliography of both primary and secondary material relating to Forsyth.
1999 / 0-85364-833-6 / xiv + 328pp

Nozomu Miyahira
Towards a Theology of the Concord of God
A Japanese Perspective on the Trinity
This book introduces a new Japanese theology and a unique Trinitarian formula based on the Japanese intellectual climate: three betweennesses and one concord. It also presents a new interpretation of the Trinity, a co-subordinationism, which is in line with orthodox Trinitarianism; each single person of the Trinity is eternally and equally subordinate (or serviceable) to the other persons, so that they retain the mutual dynamic equality.
2000 / 0-85364-863-8 / xiv + 256pp

Eddy José Muskus
The Origins and Early Development of Liberation Theology in Latin America
With Particular Reference to Gustavo Gutiérrez
This work challenges the fundamental premise of Liberation Theology, 'opting for the poor', and its claim that Christ is found in them. It also argues that Liberation Theology emerged as a direct result of the failure of the Roman Catholic Church in Latin America.
2002 / 0-85364-974-X / xiv + 296pp

Jim Purves
The Triune God and the Charismatic Movement
A Critical Appraisal from a Scottish Perspective
All emotion and no theology? Or a fundamental challenge to reappraise and realign our trinitarian theology in the light of Christian experience? This study of charismatic renewal as it found expression within Scotland at the end of the twentieth century evaluates the use of Patristic, Reformed and contemporary models of the Trinity in explaining the workings of the Holy Spirit.
2004 / 1-84227-321-3 / xxiv + 246pp

Anna Robbins
Methods in the Madness
Diversity in Twentieth-Century Christian Social Ethics
The author compares the ethical methods of Walter Rauschenbusch, Reinhold Niebuhr and others. She argues that unless Christians are clear about the ways that theology and philosophy are expressed practically they may lose the ability to discuss social ethics across contexts, let alone reach effective agreements.
2004 / 1-84227-211-X / xx + 294pp

Ed Rybarczyk
Beyond Salvation
Eastern Orthodoxy and Classical Pentecostalism on becoming like Christ
At first glance eastern Orthodoxy and classical Pentecostalism seem quite distinct. This ground-breaking study shows they share much in common, especially as it concerns the experiential elements of following Christ. Both traditions assert that authentic Christianity transcends the wooden categories of modernism.
2004 / 1-84227-144-X / xii + 356pp

Signe Sandsmark
Is World View Neutral Education Possible and Desirable?
A Christian Response to Liberal Arguments
(Published jointly with The Stapleford Centre)
This book discusses reasons for belief in world view neutrality, and argues that 'neutral' education will have a hidden, but strong world view influence. It discusses the place for Christian education in the common school.
2000 / 0-85364-973-1 / xiv + 182pp

Hazel Sherman
Reading Zechariah
The Allegorical Tradition of Biblical Interpretation through the Commentary of Didymus the Blind and Theodore of Mopsuestia
A close reading of the commentary on Zechariah by Didymus the Blind alongside that of Theodore of Mopsuestia suggests that popular categorising of Antiochene and Alexandrian biblical exegesis as 'historical' or 'allegorical' is inadequate and misleading.
2005 / 1-84227-213-6 / approx. 280pp

Andrew Sloane
On Being a Christian in the Academy
Nicholas Wolterstorff and the Practice of Christian Scholarship
An exposition and critical appraisal of Nicholas Wolterstorff's epistemology in the light of the philosophy of science, and an application of his thought to the practice of Christian scholarship.
2003 / 1-84227-058-3 / xvi + 274pp

Damon So
Jesus' Revelation of His Father
A Narrative-Conceptual Study of the Trinity with Special Reference to Karl Barth
This book explores the trinitarian dynamics in the context of Jesus' revelation of his Father in his earthly ministry with references to key passages in Matthew's Gospel. It develops from the exegeses of these passages a non-linear concept of revelation which links Jesus' communion with his Father to his revelatory words and actions through a nuanced understanding of the Holy Spirit, with references to K. Barth, G.W.H. Lampe, J.D.G. Dunn and E. Irving.
2005 / 1-84227-323-X / approx. 380pp

Daniel Strange
The Possibility of Salvation Among the Unevangelised
An Analysis of Inclusivism in Recent Evangelical Theology
For evangelical theologians the 'fate of the unevangelised' impinges upon fundamental tenets of evangelical identity. The position known as 'inclusivism', defined by the belief that the unevangelised can be ontologically saved by Christ whilst being epistemologically unaware of him, has been defended most vigorously by the Canadian evangelical Clark H. Pinnock. Through a detailed analysis and critique of Pinnock's work, this book examines a cluster of issues surrounding the unevangelised and its implications for christology, soteriology and the doctrine of revelation.
2002 / 1-84227-047-8 / xviii + 362pp

Scott Swain
God according to the Gospel
Biblical Narrative and the Identity of God in the Theology of Robert W. Jenson
Robert W. Jenson is one of the leading voices in contemporary Trinitarian theology. His boldest contribution in this area concerns his use of biblical narrative both to ground and explicate the Christian doctrine of God. *God according to the Gospel* critically examines Jenson's proposal and suggests an alternative way of reading the biblical portrayal of the triune God.
2006 / 1-84227-258-7 / approx. 180pp

Graham Tomlin
The Power of the Cross
Theology and the Death of Christ in Paul, Luther and Pascal
This book explores the theology of the cross in St Paul, Luther and Pascal. It offers new perspectives on the theology of each, and some implications for the nature of power, apologetics, theology and church life in a postmodern context.
1999 / 0-85364-984-7 / xiv + 344pp

Graham J. Watts
Revelation and the Spirit
A Comparative Study of the Relationship between the Doctrine of Revelation and Pneumatology in the Theology of Eberhard Jüngel and of Wolfhart Pannenberg
The relationship between Revelation and pneumatology is relatively unexplored. This approach offers a fresh angle on two important twentieth century theologians and raises pneumatological questions which are theologically crucial and relevant to mission in a postmodern culture.
2005 / 1-84227-104-0 / xxii + 232pp

Nigel G. Wright
Disavowing Constantine
Mission, Church and the Social Order in the Theologies of John Howard Yoder and Jürgen Moltmann
This book is a timely restatement of a radical theology of church and state in the Anabaptist and Baptist tradition. Dr Wright constructs his argument in dialogue and debate with Yoder and Moltmann, major contributors to a free church perspective.
2000 / 0-85364-978-2 / xvi + 252pp

Paternoster
9 Holdom Avenue
Bletchley
Milton Keynes MK1 1QR
United Kingdom

Web: www.authenticmedia.co.uk/paternoster

November 2004

www.ingramcontent.com/pod-product-compliance
Lightning Source LLC
Chambersburg PA
CBHW050339230426
43663CB00010B/1921